CREATIVITY: ITS EDUCATIONAL IMPLICATIONS

Second Edition

John Curtis Gowan
Professor Emeritus
California State University at Northridge

Joseph Khatena
Mississippi State University

E. Paul Torrance
University of Georgia

D0223483

KENDALL/HUNT PUBLISHING COMPANY
Dubuque, Iowa, USA • Toronto, Ontario, Canada

B   402467   01

Contents

Introduction

Of all the powers of man, that of creativity seems most unique. The generally accepted custom among the ancients was to ascribe divine origin, inspiration or direction to any great creative work. Even the aspects of initiation and selection which are universally found in creative function appear somewhat mysterious.

To create, the mind must withdraw upon itself for a time, to focus its forces, and then project an individualized image of itself onto an external medium. Psychologically this introspection and "focusing" takes the form of a heightened awareness of the peripheral asymmetries in a situation, and a subtle settling into consciousness of concepts at the boundaries of rationality or in the unconscious. It is understandable, then, that the time of creation is a "tender time" when man wishes to draw apart from his fellow men—whether up the mountain, into the desert, or away to his own source of solitude—but almost always into a silence. Creative withdrawal and return, as Toynbee has pointed out, is as characteristic of creative acts of groups as of individuals.

Considering the individual differences among one's fellows with regard to most aspects of physique or personality, one is immediately struck with the fact that (a) the variance is real and (b) its magnitude is ordinarily measured in percentages. Henry may be 20 percent taller than Edward, 30 percent heavier than Jack, and 25 percent brighter than Clyde; but he is unlikely to be twice as tall, as heavy, or as bright as anyone else.

Surprisingly enough this situation does not hold in regard to creativity. One of the most curious characteristics of creativity which generally appears to have escaped critical attention is the fact that the variability of it in different individuals far exceeds the limits of variability imposed upon other traits and abilities. Wechsler (1974:109), for example, has conclusively demonstrated that the interpersonal variability of such psychological and physiological measures as height, weight, cranial capacity, grip strength, blood pressure, respiration rate, reaction time, pitch, Snellen acuity, intelligence, mental age, and memory span has a limit of $e/1$, where $e = 2.718$, the basis of the natural logarithm system, and in most cases has a mean of 2.3 or less. Yet comparing the creative productions of a genius such as Einstein, Mozart, or Picasso with that of more ordinary mortals, one finds a ratio of $100/1$ or over. On any kind of creative scale used (and creative production of adults is as reliable as any), some individuals are found whose creative production exceeds that of their fellows, not by percentages, or even simple magnitudes; but it is more likely ten, fifty, or a hundred times as great. Obviously these fortunately creative persons are not that much different. Something has happened to turn them on. Creativity is a "threshold" variable. The nature of what that "something" is—the analysis of that threshold—is the task of this book.

Research indicates rather definitely that whereas intelligence and creativity are highly correlated below about 120 I.Q., above that figure they are nearly independent variables. If so, factors which produce creativity, must be different from factors which produce intelligence. It is our task in this introduction to examine the nature of these causes.

It may be appropriate at this point to make a statement about relationships between gift-edness and creativity. To do so, we must first distinguish between personal creativity and cultural creativity. Personal creativity refers to a creative style or process of living, which results in better ways of daily operation, welfare, and satisfaction. Examples might be a new cooking recipe, a more pleasing advertising campaign, an easier way to clean a bathroom, an improvement in a church service, a clever birthday rhyme, a more clear and useful answer on a test, etc. Cultural creativity refers to major discoveries, inventions, compositions, ideas, which are new to the culture, and of some lasting benefit to mankind. The personal belief of the senior editor is that anyone may be taught personal creativity, but that talent or giftedness in some aptitude is necessary for cultural creativity. Indeed, he would define giftedness as the potentiality for verbal creativity, and talent as the potential for non-verbal creativity.

In stating that verbal left-hemisphere ability is a necessary condition for cultural creativity to occur in the right hemisphere, we add that our interest in the gifted is precisely because in our view they alone possess this potential. A similar statement goes for the talented. The importance of the development of both kinds of talent so that a larger percentage of these uncommon individuals will become creative adults is, in our view a cultural priority of the first order. But it is to be emphasized that right hemisphere activity is the sufficient condition for any creativity to occur.

Before looking at theories about creativity, we should devote some space to characteristics of creative people. In order to summarize much diverse research into order, such materials can be grouped under three headings:

The creative person is able to tolerate conceptual ambiguity: he is not made anxious by configural disorder, but sees in it a clue to a higher synthesis.

From such considerations Barron (Taylor 1955:164) developed five hypotheses with regard to creative persons: (1) that they prefer complexity and some degree of apparent imbalance in phenomena, (2) that they are more complex psychodynamically and have greater personal scope, (3) that they are more independent in their judgment, (4) that they are more self-assertive and dominant, and (5) that they reject suppression as a mechanism for the control of impulse.

Creative people have a great fund of free energy. This free energy often seems to result from a high degree of psychological health.

One of the concomitants of creativity that has been mentioned by various authorities is the possession of much free energy. The source of this energy seems to come from within the person and is the effective release of his aptitudes as a result of good mental health. The ability to handle large amounts of anxiety without losing creative thrust or psychological health is an important consideration.

Creativity appears to be enhanced by the predisposing, focusing or constricting of interests and attention. This channeling occurs first in the child as a result of parental pressures and relationships: it is forwarded or retarded by the environmental stimulation of school, and it is finally refined and directed to its target by the self-motivation of early successes.

Attention may now be given to an extremely important group of researchers who have regarded creativity in the main as little else than problem solving. It is a form of rational thought which connects things, which combines parts into new wholes and which (like Sherlock Holmes) performs seeming miracles through observation, insight and meaningful analysis of semantic elements.

Hallman (1963) calls this condition *connectedness* and says that it imposes on man

> . . . the need to create by bringing already existing elements into a distinctive relation to each other. The essence of human creativeness is relational, and an analysis of its nature must refer to the connectedness of whatever elements enter into the creative relationship. The analysis must demonstrate that though man does not create the components, he can nevertheless produce new connections among them.

I: THE STRUCTURE OF INTELLECT THEORY

Guilford declares that creativity consists of a number of closely related factors of intellect in the divergent thinking slab of the structure of intellect model (see figure). Particularly important in this slab is the chimney formed by the intersection of semantic contents with divergent thinking production. This chimney of factors contains those we usually stereotype as "verbal creativity," including ideational fluency, spontaneous flexibility, associational fluency, and originality. Under this theory, creative gifted children are those with high endowments in these factors; whereas non-creative gifted children have their high endowments elsewhere.

As long as we believed that intelligence was fixed and unidimensional, the role of experience in facilitating its development was very limited. But if intelligence is multidimensional and partly environmental, then the role of experience becomes important indeed. The stimulation of potential factors of intellect may in some ways be regarded as similar to the refinement of athletic finesse through development and facilitation of aiming abilities and eye-hand coordination. To say so is not to resurrect the old ghost of formal discipline, but to infer that research has made us more sophisticated regarding the differing properties of the factors of intellect. The transfer capabilities of the cognition of semantic units (verbal comprehension) may be slight, whereas those of the evaluation of semantic implications (problem sensitivity) may be sizeable. If we reduce the structure of intellect cube to the two dimensions of operations and products (see figure), we find that ease of transfer is not the only variable that changes from "top left" (verbal comprehension) to "bottom right" (problem sensitivity). Other notable differences which also have important educational implications include the ease with which the factor ability is retained under stress, anxiety, or authoritarianism. There is also a developmental aspect in the young child's facility with factors at the "top left" as a necessary prelude toward his developing facility with those at the "bottom right."

II: CREATIVITY AS SOUND MENTAL HEALTH

This view of creativity, which owes much to Maslow, sees creativity in terms of complete character integration or lack of barriers between the conscious mind and its preconscious areas. The ability to "regress in the service of the ego," retrieve material from the preconscious, and return with it to the world of reality is a vital aspect of creative production, as Thurstone and others have noted. The result of such full-functioning is, of course, self actualization in the Maslovian sense.

The Semantic Contents Slab of the Guilford Structure of Intellect
(The three other slabs, are figural (F), symbolic (S), and behavioral (B).)

Operations 1st Letter 3rd Letter	Cognition O	Memory M	Convergent production N	Divergent production D	Evaluation E
U Units	CMU Verbal comprehension: To know meanings of words.	MMU Memory for ideas: To retrieve memorized ideas.	NMU Concept meaning: To discover an idea subsuming several given ideas.	DMU Ideational fluency: To produce many ideas.	EMU Idea selection: To judge which idea most meets a criterion.
C Classes	CMC Conceptual classes: To see common attributes of groups of ideas.		NMC Semantic classifying: To sort ideas into meaningful classes.	DMC Spontaneous flexibility: To generate many classes subsumed under an idea.	EMC Idea classification: To select ideas best subsuming several ideas.
R Relations	CMR Semantic relations: To see relations between ideas.	MMR Associational memory: To retrieve memorized associations.	NMR Semantic correlating: To produce an idea related to another in a specified way.	DMR Associational fluency: To produce manipulations having an idea in common.	EMR Semantic relation selection: To select best relationship.

	C	M	N	D	E
S Systems	CMS General reasoning: To see basic relationships in a problem.	MMS Memory for complex ideas: To recall the complex interrelations of ideas.	NMS Semantic patterning: To generate a system from several ideas.	DMS Expressional fluency: To produce many sets of ideas.	EMS Experimental evaluation: To judge which elements are congruent and consistent.
T Transformations	CMT Penetration: To see affects of a change of interpretation.		NMT Semantic redefining: To produce a change of interpretation or emphasis in ideas.	DMT Originality: To produce "effective surprise."	EMT Judgment: To choose best interpretation in terms of meaning.
I Implications	CMI Conceptual foresight: To foresee consequences or implications.		NMI Deduction: To deduce a statement of results from a set of ideas.	DMI Semantic elaborating: To produce many details elaborating an idea.	EMI Problem sensitivity: To explicate concern or uncertainty.

Such considerations suggest that the ability to handle the more complex factors of the structure of intellect model depend, not only on the result of a rich curriculum stimulation, but also on the improvement of emotional and ego strength on the part of the child. It takes longer to hold in tension a problem which has many answers (or none), than it does one which can be quickly solved convergently. The anxious child, however bright, may not be psychologically capable of the stress involved.

While it is incumbent upon the child to develop emergent synthesizing abilities at higher actualizing levels, it is incumbent upon society to see that his prior needs are satiated to the extent that he can devote his energies to intellectual tasks. The child who is hungry is too concerned with his hunger to learn. The child who is insecure about love and safety needs is too preoccupied to apply himself. The child whose social difficulties blunt his learning propensities is also operating at a lower hierarchial level.

Gifted children who have these problems are often able to "get by" while operating at a very low level of efficiency. But only when these primitive levels are satisfied can we expect bright children to perform at their cognitive best. Consequently a corollary of cognitive stimulation in the classroom is guidance which frees able children for the full-functioning in more complex intellectual areas. Ego strength and a healthy self-concept are part of the stock-in-trade which the child needs to operate in a world of reality. We can condition a psychotic, but to educate a child properly in the wide-spectrum of the structure of intellect model requires attention to his mental health as well as to his cognitive competence.

III: THE OPPOSITE OF AUTHORITARIANISM

Somewhat akin to the previous theory is the concept of creativity as the opposite of authoritarianism. The compartmentalization, stereotyping and anti-intraception of the authoritarian personality prevents creative functioning. Hence the degree to which we have been tarnished with authoritarian practice diminishes our creative potential, and narrows the possible avenues of creative endeavor. Investigations with the California Psychological Inventory, for example, show that flexibility (creativity) and tolerance (lack of authoritarianism) are well correlated. This view of creativity, like the previous, suggests that children can be helped to preserve their creativity by non-authoritarian attitudes on the part of parents and teachers, especially by not having negative evaluations put upon their initial efforts. The importance of the child's being first the recipient of, and later the producer of sound (rather than pejorative) evaluations is a most important adjunct to his becoming productively creative. For this kind of evaluation is the way in which creative fantasy becomes bonded to useful reality. Like sistole and diastole, they are the complementary components of "effective surprise." It may be worth a slight discussion to see why this is so.

In economics, the entrepreneur who has risk capital also has 1) a reasonably safe financial position from which to operate, 2) some excess capital which he values, but which he is willing to risk on a situation which he can partly control, and 3) some know-how or sophistication in the operation he proposes to prosecute, which, in his mind at least, increase his probability of gain over that of chance expectancy. He is encouraged by a) past success, b) ready-money and credit, and c) a climate which favors this kind of operation.

In education the "reasonable adventurer" has 1) a safe psychological base from which to venture, and to which to return, 2) some excess capital in the form of energy, prestige, ideas, which he is willing to risk, and 3) some sophistication in the "strategies" game. Like the entrepreneur, he is encouraged by a) past success, b) the availability of prestige and status (if you lose it on a bad guess, you get it back again), and c) a climate that encourages curiosity.

It is perfectly obvious that teachers have a great deal to do with a child's past successes, the availability of prestige, the control of authoritarianism, the type of evaluations, and the climate which encourages risk-taking in search of creativity. Oftentimes they subtly discourage children completely in such a search by leveling off the classroom, keeping a tight control on available prestige, and similar actions, so that the child may fear to make any guess, since it may lose him something which is irretrievable. The teacher can also discourage creativity through reasonable risk-taking by teaching toward convergent thinking exclusively, emphasizing memory processes, and by keeping the authoritarian level high. The only kind of risk taking which develops in such an atmosphere is the unrealistic risk-taking of the predelinquent, in which risk-taking is divorced from its probable consequences.

But the development of such attitudes of realistic risk-taking in search for ideas on the part of students does not depend alone on the avoidance of authoritarian tendencies on the part of the teacher. It also encompasses careful counseling efforts to parry the crushing effects of anxiety on creativity. It involves the education of curiosity as a respectable emotion. It requires the development of risk-capital in the form of ideas and strategies with which to experiment. If we are going to take responsibility for the impact of emotional and cultural factors on productive thinking (and we shall probably not get much creativity out of children unless we do), we must take a lot more responsibility for the guidance aspects of the child's emotional development than we have. We must come to see that even for the gifted child, a stimulating curriculum experience requires increased supportive guidance, since it increases the motivation of the child to deal at higher levels with the problems presented, and this higher level of operation requires better mental health for such full-functioning.

IV. THE OEDIPAL-INITIATIVE PERIOD THEORY

According to this theory, boys who were close to their mothers, and girls who were close to their fathers during the period from four to seven will become more creative than others. Such a theory, of course, would explain why there appear to be more creative men than women in the world. The child, at this time, enchanted by the warm affect of the opposite-sexed parent responds to this in the only way he can,—by the creative manipulation of his immediate environment, and by an enlargement of the bridge between his fantasy life and his real world. While this view of creativity has much more consequence for parents than for teachers, it is worth considering.

V. VARIGU'S "MAGNETIC" THEORY OF CREATIVITY

Varigu (197:23) visualizes the creative process as:

> A large number of simple mental elements, within the boundary of a creative energy field, which have such properties that (1) each mental element will respond to the influence of the creative field, and (2) all mental elements can interact with one another.

We can gain considerable understanding of the way in which mental elements respond to the influence of the creative field by using our previous example and examining in more detail the interaction between the magnetic field and the iron particles.

Now imagine that we place a magnet first far away, then gradually nearer a thin layer of iron filings. For a while nothing happens. Then, suddenly, the pattern springs together in almost complete form. Let us try to understand this startling event by observing it in slow motion. At first, the field is too weak to set the iron particles in motion. They are held in position by friction. As the intensity of the magnetic field increases, some of the iron particles overcome friction and begin to move, interacting with the nearby granules in a way that increases the overall magnetization. This in turn sets other particles in motion, accelerating the process and starting an "avalanche effect" or "chain reaction" which causes the pattern to suddenly form itself, independently of any further approach of the magnet.

VI. CREATIVITY AS RIGHT-HEMISPHERE IMAGERY

This theory states that right hemisphere imagery is the vehicle through which incubation produces creativity. In his famous paradigm of creative process, Graham Wallas (1926) identified four components: preparation, incubation, illumination, verification. By incubation, he meant any technique of relaxation of the conscious cognition (left cerebral hemisphere function), such as, but not confined to dreams, daydreams, fantasy, hypnosis, mediation, diversion, play, etc., which allows subliminal processes (right hemisphere functions) to operate. He saw preparation (academic discipline), as the necessary, and incubation (relaxation), as the sufficient condition for creative insights to emerge.

We shall assume the definition of mental imagery as essentially non-verbal (in the Guilford Structure-of-Intellect parlance—nonsymbolic) material occurring in consciousness not directly preceded by perceptual intake. By creativity, we shall mean the production of material or relationships new to the culture. To open up the discussion, we follow our initial statement with further elaboration: Whereas most functions of the left hemisphere are concerned with convergent production as described by Guilford, functions of the right hemisphere are principally concerned with divergent production. These functions involve imagery through which incubation produces creativity.

Growing awareness that right-hemisphere imagery is the source of creativity is an interdisciplinary phenomenon. Says prestigious M.I.T. Engineer, Professor Stanley West (1975:)

> With support from recent research in the neurosciences I speculate that minor scientific creativity is likely to be mainly left hemisphere cognitive excitation, while major scientific creativity is likely to involve the excitation and intercommunication of both cerebral hemispheres. . . . In other words, some kind of altered state of awareness . . . may be essential to creativity. . . . Creativity in many extraordinarily gifted individuals depends in part upon temporary dominance of the right cerebral hemisphere.

We have long thought of man's brain as a problem-solver; perhaps an even better model would be that of a radio receiver. When the set has been properly assembled through preparation and discipline, the static in the locality has been cleared through relaxation and incubation, and the power is on, then we may hear the faint calls of distant stations—signals which are always in the air, but are only received with the best equipment under the best and clearest operating conditions. Such a simile tells us why high giftedness enhances the creative range and why the easy production of verbal analogies (like the proportion between radio frequency and audio frequency) facilitates high-fidelity reception.

We are accustomed to think of imagery as something on the order of hallucination because of our implicit assumption that physical reality is "real" and "tangible." But this may be naive. Ferguson (1977) declares that Pribram of Stanford and Bohm of the University of London have proposed theories which, in a nutshell, state that "Our brains mathematically construct concrete reality by interpreting frequencies from another dimension, a realm of meaningful patterned primary reality that transcends time and space. The brain is a hologram interpreting a holographic universe."

If the physical universe has no more reality than the holographic (virtual) image we see in exhibitions, then the subordinate position of imaginative imagery to percepts of "reality" would be removed, and creative imagination would emerge as one of the central building blocks of consciousness. Hence its development, stimulation, control, and perfection would become the aim of both education and the life development of the individual. Such a view, which would elevate the controlled creative imagination to that of co-creator and would raise man from a reactive being to one with control over his future and destiny, would revolutionize both culture and education and enormously actualize the latent potential of mankind.

These ideas are so new that all we can do in turning from theory to practice is to sketch some ways in which such views may affect the classroom in the future. It would be a grave error to conclude that we should abandon all that has gone before and delve into divination and the occult; indeed, such a procedure would be disastrous. The Wallas paradigm still holds true and useful. Mental discipline and scholarship are still required for the preparation phase. What we are talking about is more conscious attention to the incubation phase.

1. We should study creativity directly in high school and university classes. Almost no schools at the present time have courses on this subject. The 21st century will find this lack incomprehensible.
2. We can help young children learn techniques of relaxation and incubation. This does not mean that we should teach them any particular form of meditation, but it might be useful for all children to know what meditation, relaxation, and other types of unstressing are.
3. We should help children practice imagination and imagery during such relaxed periods. The Torrance and Khatena records, *Thinking Creatively with Sounds and Words,* is only one of several devices on the market for this purpose. As a consequence of such periods we should encourage the production of poetry, art, music, etc.
4. As long as the child is in the concrete operations phase, the images will tend to be static and not particularly creative; but when he enters the formal operations phase one can expect and should push for more finished artistic creations, especially in poetic form. Children at this stage should be strongly encouraged to keep a journal and put their poetry and other thoughts into it. The development of the easy ability at this level helps the child to become truly creative in the next stage, and this is where (in upper high school and in lower division college) most gifted children do not make the transition to creative production. I think the most important facilitation which can take place at this time is a seminar-type home room where the adolescent can be with others of the same persuasion, for (because of the strong gregarious needs at this stage) nothing does more to inhibit creativity than group sanctions against it in other adolescents.

Now that psychology has centered creativity in human development rather than in divine afflatus, it is obvious that we shall have to increase our prospectus of man's reach and potential. Imagination as the precursor of this creativity and as its means of development seems destined to become far more important in the psychology and education of the future. As Huxley (1962:208) prophesied about that education of the child in his vision of Utopia:

> "How does he do his thinking, perceiving, and remembering? Is he a visualizer or a non-visualizer? Does his mind work with images or with words, with both at once or with neither? How close to the surface is his story-telling faculty? Does he see the world as Wordsworth and Traherne saw it when they were children? And if so, what can be done to prevent the glory and freshness from fading into the light of common day? Or in more general terms can we educate children on the conceptual level without killing their capacity for intense non-verbal experience? How can we reconcile analysis with vision?" (Huxley, 1962)

This revision, some fourteen years after the original edition, is fully representative of the very rapid development in the discipline during the interim. While we have preserved fifteen best of the original forty articles, particularly those of Professor Guilford, and others which have historical interest, we have very considerably modified both the content and the thrust of the revised volume with new writers, and newer ideas. There is more on measurement and testing for creativity, and a new chapter on imagery and the right hemisphere. Transpersonal and sociological views of creativity are also represented, especially in the last chapter.

The development of more creative talent in our country is not an education frill, but a central issue in the preservation of our culture. This is a task which educational institutions have thus far shirked in large measure, but it must be firmly addressed in future years if the United States is to retain its position in world affairs. May this book, and others like it inspire teachers and administrators at all levels of education toward more direct teaching and stimulation of creativity in the rising generation. We have the knowledge and capacity to produce this potential Renaissance; may we also possess the courage and determination to persevere in its actualization.

J. C. Gowan

References

Ferguson, M. "Editorial," *The Brain/Mind Bulletin,* June 4, 1977

Hallman, R. J. "The Necessary and Sufficient Conditions for Creativity," *J. Humanistic Psychology* 3:1, Spring, 1963

Huxley, A. *Island.* New York: Harper & Row, 1962

Varigu, J. "Creativity: The Purposeful Imagination" *Synthesis* 3–4, 17–53, 1977

Wallas, G. *The Art of Thought,* London: Watts, 1926

Wechsler, D. *The Collected Papers of David Wechsler,* New York: Academic Press, 1974

West, S. A. "Creativity, Altered States of Consciousness and Artificial Intelligence," *J. Altered States of Consciousness* 2:3:219–30, 1975

GENERAL

1. POTENTIALITY FOR CREATIVITY

J. P. Guilford

Members of this association are naturally and appropriately concerned about the identification of gifted children. If you were involved in public education in my home state of California, the task would be a very simple one. By state law, you would simply select as gifted those children with Stanford-Binet IQs of 130 and above.

In Southern California, where we have a relatively high density of recognized creative people—in architecture, painting, writing, musical composition, and drama, also in the sciences and the technologies—some of us, you may be sure, are not very happy about this situation. This is particularly true since it has been shown by Getzels and Jackson (1961) and by Torrance (1959), and others, that many potentially creative children are not as high in IQ as 130.

To this kind of information can be added some results from the Aptitudes Project at the University of Southern California, involving four samples of ninth-grade students of more than 200 each. Letting vocabulary-test scores and reading-comprehension-test scores represent measures of verbal intelligence, we correlated seven such scores with 14 different verbal divergent-production-test scores. The correlations ranged from $-.20$ to $+.52$, with a mean of $+.18$. From scattered information we can derive the hypothesis that the relationship between verbal IQ and creative-test scores is a non-linear one; that below an IQ of 120 in the population the correlation is higher and above an IQ of 120 it is lower. However this may be, selection on the basis of IQ alone will definitely miss many potentially gifted children. If we want to include all the potentially creative children in gifted groups, some very different selection procedures are needed.

SELECTION FOR CREATIVITY

There is sufficient experience with some of the tests of creative abilities to have some confidence in them for discriminating between those with higher and lower creative potential, in certain areas of creativity (Guilford, Merrifield, and Cox, 1961). The research of Getzels and Jackson and of Torrance indicates that high-scoring children in such tests are known for their superior imaginative and productive ways of thinking and writing. The tests used by these investigators, however, are limited in various ways.

In the research on creativity in the Aptitudes Project at USC, we have reached a general conclusion that the abilities in the structure of intellect that seem to have promise as direct contributors to successful creative thinking belong in two major categories. One is the category of divergent production, which includes abilities to generate varieties of information from given

Reprinted by permission of the author and *Gifted Child Quarterly*, Vol. 6, No. 3, 1962.

information; in other words, multiple responses, all of which are more or less appropriate, in response to a stimulus. In common terminology, the abilities represented are three different kinds of fluency, two kinds of flexibility, and an elaboration ability. The other category is composed of abilities dealing with transformations, that is, redefinitions, revisions, or other kinds of changes of information. This category represents a third kind of flexibility, a freedom from fixedness or from *Gestaltbindung*.

Let us see what all this implies, in comparison with the battery used by Getzels and Jackson for the selection of their highly creative group. In the structure-of-intellect model, there are 24 expected divergent-production abilities, of which 16 are now supported by factor-analytic information. There are 20 expected transformation abilities, of which eight are known. Since four factors are in common to the two categories, where they intersect in the model, the total expected is 40, and the number known is 22. How many of these abilities are represented in the Getzels and Jackson battery of five tests?

As nearly as one can tell from inspection of the tests, which the authors fortunately present in full in their recent book, I should say that four of the divergent-production abilities are represented and three of the transformation abilities, one being in common to the two operation categories. Four of the five tests involve verbal or semantic information or content and one involves figural content.

The aspect of creativity that dominates the battery, therefore, deals with verbal information. We should expect the composite score to predict best creative performances in writing, science, and planning; in other words, in school subjects and vocations in which verbal meanings are the dominant content of thinking. The score should not predict nearly so well, creative performance in the arts (except for writing), in invention of machines, in mathematics, or in interpersonal activity. Artists and inventors deal more with concrete information, such as lines, shapes, colors, and sounds. In mathematics, especially beyond arithmetic, creative thinking involves symbols and their interrelationships. Interpersonal activity is involved in dealing with the behavior of people. We should find it necessary to go beyond semantic tests in predicting success in creative interaction with others. Some of the vocations for which this kind of creativity should be especially important are teaching, psychotherapy, selling, police work, and politics.

IQ tests commonly emphasize abilities in the operation categories of cognition (which is defined in the structure of intellect in a narrower sense than is usual), memory, and convergent production, ignoring divergent production and slighting evaluation abilities, the latter being the basic aspects of critical thinking. As to categories of information, semantic content is very much emphasized, naturally, because verbal concepts are the "coin of the realm" in education. Words are the chief medium of teaching and examining. As to the kinds of *product* of information in the structure of intellect—units, classes, relations, systems, transformations, and implications—IQ tests devote most attention to units, as in vocabulary tests; to relations, as in analogies tests; and to systems, as in arithmetic-reasoning tests. Little attention is given to classes and none to transformations and implications. Transformation abilities were discussed in connection with creative abilities, implication abilities have to do with the everyday operations of prediction, foresight, and deduction, certainly very useful human qualities.

Conferences such as this one imply a recognition of the limitations of IQ tests in selecting gifted children, and a positive recognition of the importance of considering creative abilities in the same connection. But it should not be supposed that by adding a few tests of creative qualities to the few tests entering into IQ scales we have by any means exhausted the whole range of intellectual qualities. I am willing to grant that probably many of the other intellectual abilities may not be very significant in connection with ordinary academic performance, as curriculum and educational procedures are now constituted. It may well be questioned, however, whether the educational regime should not be giving attention to development of some of the intellectual qualities that it is now neglecting and whether those qualities should be involved in teaching and examining the student in some of the present courses of study.

In other words, I am urging that when we go beyond the IQ we go all the way and consider the relevance of all intellectual abilities, in selecting gifted children and in educational processes in general. I welcome the obvious enthusiasm of many educators for creativity. Creativity has become one of the "good" words, as "dynamic" and "reinforcement" have been to many psychologists in recent years. It is good to have enthusiasms, but it is also important to have enthusiasms wisely directed and to see that they are functional in bringing about desirable changes.

To me, the next steps in capitalizing upon the new knowledge concerning creativity and concerning intelligence in general is to re-examine educational objectives, both general and specific, in the light of the new knowledge. The new concepts appear to have natural applications to educational aims and procedures. It should be recognized, of course, that the operational steps of wisely applying those concepts imply a tremendous amount of developmental research. We need to know the relation of all possibly relevant primary abilities, as L. L. Thurstone called them, to all kinds of courses of instruction and to all teaching and learning methods. We need to know whether, as have suggested a number of times before, we may regard the basic abilities as being somewhat generalized skills that can be improved with the right kinds of practice. If we do so, what kinds of practice are needed?

As an example of one kind of developmental research, in the Aptitudes Project we have under way a study of the extent to which each of quite a number of intellectual factors is related to achievement in beginning algebra and in general mathematics at the ninth-grade level. In this study, we have emphasized tests of abilities to deal with symbolic information as well as a smaller number in the semantic area of information. We have started the early stages of a parallel study of basic aptitudes related to achievement in plane geometry at the tenth-grade level. In this connection, figural abilities will be emphasized, also convergent-production abilities and evaluative abilities, in view of the strong logical character of thinking in geometry.

CURRENT SELECTION PROCEDURES

My discussion has wandered a bit from the question of how to select creatively gifted children, but this was intentional in order to emphasize the much broader problem. Although present indications favor divergent-production, and transformation abilities, as the ones most directly involved in creative potential, it can well be said that almost any intellectual ability outside those categories may at some time be a heavy contributor to success in creative production. To be a good, imaginative writer, one must also have a vocabulary of substantial size, a condition that is strongly related to the verbal IQ. To be a good self critic, one must have good evaluative abilities. Viewed in this light, potential for creative production extends to almost all corners of the structure-of-intellect model. Potential for creative types of thinking, depends upon a more limited collection of abilities, but a by-no-means small number of basic abilities.

3

Although about 60 primary intellectual abilities have now been demonstrated, the number of these for which there are available tests is much smaller. More such tests will be forthcoming from our Project, but only as there is confidence in the test forms and in the basic knowledge underlying them.

In the meantime, there is much that teachers and others can do in sizing up children while "waiting for the doctor to come." Many children show unmistakable signs of creative potential in their everyday behavior. One child will make a collection of stones and will classify them for display in some novel way. The science fairs, that appear to be growing in popularity in some places, should be good sources of information, provided the work is the child's own contribution. The children's products, of course, must be interpreted and evaluated as to degree of creativity indicated. When allowed some freedom in art classes (and sometimes even when not), some children show potential for creative performance in that area. From what I have said about the differentiation of abilities as between areas of information, it would be risky to conclude that because a child shows signs of creativity in art he should also be creative in mathematics or in science, or vice versa.

Some of the qualities attributed to the more creative children as reported by Getzels and Jackson and by Torrance could be used as "symptoms," but I should say with some caution. A good number of them in combination should be confirming. The symptoms would more readily indicate the very highly creative child, but might miss others of less potential.

OVERACHIEVERS MAY BE CREATIVE

Some of the so-called overachievers may be in the creative category. When they achieve beyond the level predicted by the IQ, it may be that they are strong in other, non-IQ abilities, but these other abilities need not be in the divergent-production or transformation categories. Alas, some creative youngsters may also be *underachievers,* for lack of recognition and encouragement.

It is reported that the more creative children appreciate humor especially and have some facility in producing humor. As far as we know now, this may be true only of semantic types of creative abilities. A humorless child might still have creative potential in art or mathematics.

Evidently, the creative child is less bound by what we agree to as reality; he is ready to reinterpret it and to change it to suit his purposes. In this sense, he is closer to the brink of insanity than most other children, but not necessarily in any great danger of going over the brink. He does things that appear odd in the context of the behavior of other children. He takes liberties with what he observes and knows. He has a playful attitude toward his experiences. His thinking goes off in unusual directions. He is sometimes referred to as a rebel, but I am inclined to think that this does not apply to all creative children; more likely it applies to those who have felt frustrations because their creativity is not appreciated.

Many more signs could be added but there is not time to mention them; they may be found in the growing literature from continuing research such as that of Torrance. With you, I hope that it will not be too long before good tests have been produced for the various intellectual abilities, ready for experimental use in the educational context. Let us hope that the enthusiasm now generated in the name of creativity will last and that it can be channeled toward the necessary steps that are needed to achieve a full exploitation of our most precious resource—our human intellect.

References

Getzels, J. W. and Jackson, P. W. *Creativity and the Individual.* New York: John Wiley and Sons, 1961.

Guilford, J. P., Merrifield, P. R., and Cox, Anna B. Creative thinking in children at the junior high school levels. *Rep. psychol.* Lab., No. 26. Los Angeles: Univ. Southern California, 1961.

Torrance, E. P., Explorations in creative thinking in the early school years: a progress report. In C. W. Taylor, *The third (1959) University of Utah Research Conference on the identification of creative scientific talent.* Salt Lake City: Univ. of Utah Press, 1959.

2. TOWARD THE MORE HUMANE EDUCATION OF GIFTED CHILDREN

E. Paul Torrance

The treatment of the mentally ill and the education of the gifted are alike in many ways. Neither has ever been a popular cause. It has always been difficult to elicit either popular or legislative support for the improvement of either. Both have supplied outlets for some of man's needs to pity and to punish. Of the two, the need to punish has perhaps dominated. Both the mentally ill and the gifted have been regarded as being mysterious, beyond human understanding, evil and unrighteous. In our retribution, we have resorted to a primitive reaction—punishment. In recent years, realistic accounts of our inhumane treatment of the mentally ill have resulted in increased legislative support for their treatment and perhaps some small increase in public understanding. These gains have by no means ended the inhumane treatment of the mentally ill, but certainly we must admit that tremendous advances have been made.

Frequently, I hear the complaint that there is no emotional appeal involved in proposals to improve the education of the gifted. Having superior potential, gifted children will take care of themselves, I am informed. We are told that the gifted already have more than others, so why should society be concerned about giving them more. We hear such comments as this in spite of our great American dream of a kind of education which will give every child a better chance to become his potentialities. You would think sometimes that this dream must apply to the mentally retarded, but not to the gifted.

I wonder who can be so insensitive as to experience no emotional appeal in some of the stories which come to me of the inhumane treatment of gifted children by hard-working, well-meaning, conscientious parents and teachers. Let me share a few of these with you.

The mother of one gifted thirteen-year-old boy wrote me as follows:

"He is now 13 years old and has had a steadily declining academic record that ended in his being retained in the seventh grade this year. . . . He has a burning *main* interest in electronics and rocks and believe me, his knowledge and interest in these two subjects is great.

"His teachers, principals, and counselors have told me a confusing variety of things (confusing to me anyway). They all agree he is very bright, very bored (daydreams in class constantly), and very withdrawn though not rebellious. Two teachers have told me the school has destroyed his desire to learn. One teacher told me the school cannot help him because the only 'special class' they are informed enough to help are the 'slow' children. Another teacher said to me,'I'll make him work if I have to break his spirit to do it—and ridiculing and shaming him is the only way with children like him. . . .' Last spring the school counselor and principal decided that flunking him was the only way to make him 'buckle down and work or else.' . . . He can't join the different types of science clubs because he doesn't have a B average—to which the principal urged that he take up football.

"So many doors closed! Where is the spirit of educating and cultivating the child's natural desire to learn—some seed of it is always there, to some extent or another!

"Now, I will tell you of the boy I know, my son. . . . He is an irresponsible scatterbrain— he just can't harness his brain to such unimportant things as taking out the trash when he's hot

Reprinted by permission from *Gifted Child Quarterly,* Vol. 7, No. 4, 1963. Paper presented to Cincinnati Chapter, National Association for Gifted Children, November 15, 1963.

on the trail of discovering perpetual motion. He *never* daydreams, loves to learn, and is always getting books from the library. He is a hard worker; many times he almost collapses trying to work and experiment late in the night. He has energy enough for ten people. He has an outgoing bubbling personality and a terrific sense of humor. All this he is at home and in the rest of the world *until* he gets to school.

"He speaks of wanting to go to an 'electric college' but says he'll probably quit school when he's 16.

"I feel that he is in a steel box—I think he feels he is too and thinks the only way to be free is get out by quitting.

"How can doors be opened, can you tell me? Can you advise or suggest *anything* that could help?

"Please, don't be too busy to care or answer me. I just don't know where else to turn!"

Who is so callous as to be unmoved by the following poem written by a lonely, gifted nine-year-old girl?

"Loneliness is the stillness in the air,
Rain falling to the ground,
The cold wind whistling through the trees,
The darkness,
The damp, misty air chilling you,
The absence of love.
Loneliness is so many unsaid words."

Who would not be stirred emotionally by the account of the search by Graham's teachers and parents to find some punishment which will fit him. Ten-year-old Graham's mother describes their plight as follows:

"Let me try to list some of the things that are driving his teacher, my husband and me mad. . . .

"We have never found a punishment to fit Graham. If placed in a corner, he'd sing. If spanked, he'd howl like we were killing him, yet the minute we left the room the tears would snap off. If sent to his room, he'd simply lay down and go to sleep. Now that he is older, privileges are taken away. They too are taken with no hurt feeling on the surface.

"Graham shows a great capacity for school work when he wants to. He refused to finish addition and subtraction drills at school. It was thought he didn't know the answers. When multiplication was introduced, he surprised everyone by knowing the answers. . . . His teacher reports that he is always raising his hand, walking up to her desk, even trying to instruct the class (fourth grade).

". . . I want desperately to understand Graham. I'm sure his home life at the present time is not as happy as it could be. I'm anxious now because I know it will be more difficult as years progress. . . . Please let me know if and where I can get help. Believe me I'm shouting my plea."

The mother of a creatively gifted girl wrote in a similar vein, as follows:

". . . I gave her a hard time and spanked her often, figuring she was a very obstinate child. Consequently, she was very nervous and she and I had a pretty horrible relationship. . . ."

Why is it that such hard-working, conscientious, and well-meaning parents, teachers, counselors, and principals treat children in such inhumane ways and obtain such negative results? Why is it that we have today a growing attitude of greater harshness and punitiveness toward children in our society? Why are gifted children so often the special targets of such inhumane treatment?

It is my thesis that the inhumanities which prevail in the education of gifted children are primarily a result of our unwillingness to accept a realistically complex picture of the human mind and personality. In spite of his own complexity, man strives constantly for oversimplifications which lead him into error. I do not know whether this is basic to man's nature or the result of an education that has imbued him with a compulsion to determine the one "right" answer. From the very beginning of our research on giftedness, it has been our dream that we might develop a deeper and more complete understanding of the human mind and personality and their functioning. It is our hope that such understandings will give us the basis for developing a more human kind of education—the kind of education which will give all children (including gifted children) a better chance to become their potentialities.

I would like to try to show how this research is beginning to yield a deeper and more complete understanding of the human mind and personality, and how this understanding can be used in our struggle against the inhumanities caused by an oversimplified view of the functioning of the human mind and personality. It is my hope that in this way we can avoid some of the erroneous and misleading oversimplifications which some of my critics have placed upon our research and my interpretation of it.

I am always shocked to find that someone believes that I:

. . . favor creative learning *rather* than learning by authority;

. . . advocate the use of tests of creative talent in identifying the gifted *rather* than tests of intelligence;

. . . emphasize moral courage and honesty *rather* than personal and social maladjustment;

. . . advocate creative thinking and imagination *rather* than the acquisition of knowledge; original answers *rather* than correct ones;

. . . advocate that we reward divergent behavior *rather* than conforming behavior;

. . . believe in providing a responsive environment *rather* than a stimulating one;

. . . recommend that we treat boys and girls alike *rather* than differently; and

. . . encourage chaos and destructiveness *rather* than discipline and order.

In almost every instance, what I have tried to communicate is that the human mind and personality are wonderful and complex and that respect for human values demands that attention be given to both creative learning and learning by authority, to tests of creative thinking as *well* as to tests of intelligence, to moral courage as *well* as to personal and social adjustment, and so on. If you will try to be honest, I believe that you will find that this is possible and that one is not necessarily in conflict with the other, that both kinds of emphasis are not only possible but desirable. Quite briefly I would like to consider each of the dilemmas which critics have tried to construct from what I have reported.

CREATIVE LEARNING AND LEARNING BY AUTHORITY

Recently, a friend visiting in a city in New Jersey, sent me a newspaper clipping from a local newspaper interpreting my NEA pamphlet on "What Research Says to the Teacher about Creativity" (1963a). This newspaper article credited me with advocating the abolition of educational methods which involve teaching by authority. Let us see just what I said in this publication (pp. 12–13).

I did say that, in my opinion, the weight of present evidence indicates that man fundamentally prefers to learn in creative ways—by exploring, manipulating, questioning, experimenting, risking, testing and modifying ideas, and otherwise inquiring. I did not say that it was always good for man to learn creatively. In fact, I cautioned that although the needs underlying learning in creative ways is universal enough to make this way of learning valuable for all children, it should not be regarded as the exclusive method of education or even the exclusive method for any one child. I did insist that many things, though not all, can be learned more effectively and economically in creative ways rather than by authority. I also indicated that many children who have an especially strong preference for learning creatively, learn a great deal if permitted to use their creative thinking abilities, and make little educational progress if we insist that they learn exclusively by authority.

I tried to show how strong human needs are involved in each state of the process of thinking creatively. If we sense that something is missing or untrue, tension is aroused. We are uncomfortable and want to do something to relieve the tension. This makes us want to ask questions, make guesses, or otherwise inquire. Uncertain as to whether our guesses are correct, we continue to be uncomfortable. Thus, we are driven to test our guesses, correct our errors and modify our conclusions. Once we discover something, we want to tell someone about it. All of this is why it is so natural for man to want to learn creatively.

It is also true that man's nature requires that he have anchors in reality, that he have structure in his environment, and that he have authorities upon whom he can depend. Just as individuals differ in the extent to which they prefer to learn creatively, they also differ in the extent to which they require authorities.

I wish there were time to cite the research evidence and cases of individuals to show how a failure to accept this complex view of the learning process leads to inhumane treatment of gifted youngsters. Perhaps it can help you understand the panic and desolation of thirteen-year-old Alice when she transferred from elementary school where she had been permitted to learn both creatively and by authority to a junior high school where she had to learn primarily by authority. In elementary school, she achieved a straight "A" record and was regarded as creative, imaginative, and intelligent by her teachers. Alice's mother describes the situation as follows:

> "She hated junior high almost from the first day. It frightened her. She complained that she felt lost in it, that it was cold, impersonal. . . . The teachers are no doubt well-intentioned but they are too overworked to do anything but get angry, pressure, threaten. These methods have never worked with her. As a result, she lost interest in her work, lost all her self-confidence. . . . She has given up her drawing and writing. She says she can't create or be artistic while she is unhappy about her marks. I am heartsick about this whole situation because I know she is very bright and that she has the scholastic potential to do well in college. It would be a terrible waste of talent and of a good mind for the teachers to give up on her at this point. I believe I have reason to have faith in her. She thinks for herself; that's important. On a recent Iowa achievement test, she averaged at the 95th percentile for the eighth grade (98th percentile in reading and 99th percentile in vocabulary)."

Here we have a case which is just the opposite of the case of Bob which I have cited many times (Torrance, 1962) to show how a boy who had been considered a hopeless case throughout elementary school and into the ninth grade can regain confidence in himself and begin learning. Bob's English teacher encouraged him to take his tests over the poems and stories they read in class by illustrating them. His sensitive insights about what they had read—insights which he could not express in writing or orally—amazed the other members of the class and brought forth their praise. Soon he became interested in learning how to read, became a much happier and socially better adjusted person.

INTELLIGENCE TESTS AND CREATIVITY TESTS IN IDENTIFYING THE GIFTED

Our work with tests of creative thinking has caused some people to conclude that I advocate the abolition of intelligence tests and the substitution of creative or divergent thinking tests. The truth is that I have continually said that intelligence tests have long been very useful in guiding and assessing mental growth and intellectual potentiality and that they will continue to be useful. I have tried to show why we need to broaden our concept of "giftedness" from that of the "child with the high IQ" to *include also* the highly creative child and *other types*. I have spoken of the importance of giving greater emphasis to the fostering of original work at all levels, making this function at least as important as teaching information.

I have endeavored to present the creative thinking abilities as just one part of our expanded and expanding concept of the human mind and its functioning. Some of the misinterpretation of what I have reported may have come from the accounts of some of our partial replications of the Getzels and Jackson study (1962) in which we have contrasted a group of highly intelligent and less creative children with a group of highly creative but less intelligent children. Some have interpreted this to mean that high intelligence and high creative thinking ability are mutually exclusive, that one cannot be both highly intelligent and highly creative. This is certainly not true. I do not believe that I have ever failed to mention those who are high on both measures. In fact, if we identify a group of children as being either highly intelligent or highly creative, about 30 percent of them will be both highly intelligent and highly creative.

I believe that these facts do emphasize the need for more serious attention to the individualization of instruction, and to dissuade us from the vain hope of finding the one supreme educational method to which all children will respond. Perhaps the most that we can realistically hope for is to determine what methods are most effective with what types or categories of learners. Many convergent lines of research are beginning to make it clear, that when we change our methods of teaching, or the nature of our instructional materials, that children with different kinds of mental abilities become the star learners and non-learners. This occurs, even when we make no change in the methods and instruments of evaluation. Differences of even greater magnitude occur when we change these. Students who rank highest on a multiple-choice examination requiring recognition and memory may rank near the bottom of their class on an examination requiring decisions, supporting those decisions, and making creative applications of knowledge.

Let us turn now to a few examples of real live, gifted children, and see how our failure to accept a complex view of mental abilities leads to inhumane treatment of gifted children. Ted, who during his junior and senior high school years won eight major national and state awards for creative achievement in science, experienced his share of such inhumanities. It was not until after he entered senior high school that it was discovered that Ted's IQ and his room number had become transposed on his cumulative record during his elementary school years. Ted's mother and his older brother were aware that Ted was being treated as a mentally retarded child. He was always downgraded or ignored by his teachers. He was discouraged from doing whatever he wanted to attempt. Ted's science teacher in junior high school told Ted's brother that Ted had very little potential in science and should not be encouraged in his science interests. A college physics teacher in a nearby college who had been working with Ted, however, maintained that he wished his science majors knew as much about science as Ted did at the time he was in the seventh and eighth grades.It was also at this time that Ted won first place in his area and in the state science fair for his linear accelerator, with which he did biological research. Here is a case where teachers placed reliance upon the reality of the IQ on the cumulative record, rather than the realities of his actual achievement.

Many creatively gifted youngsters suffer inhumane treatment because their teachers refuse to believe that their creative achievements are their own, being blinded either by relatively low IQ's or some type of nonconforming behavior. Such has been the case of Dee, a gifted girl, just finishing junior high school. Her mother describes one such incident as follows:

"... When I got home from work yesterday, Dee greeted me with tears in her eyes—the history teacher again. This time she did an unforgivable thing. Before the whole class, while pounding on Dee's desk with her hand, she ridiculed Dee by swearing that Dee's homework was not done by her, and that it absolutely was not in her handwriting. . . . Dee has the ability to write with either hand. She has done this all her life. It is just as natural for her to switch hands when one gets tired as it is to breathe. The only difference in this instance was a slight change in style. She showed her homework to me while she was preparing it, and asked me how I liked her writing."

There are many kinds of giftedness, however, and whenever we fail to realize this, we are likely to contribute to the inhumane treatment of youngsters who have the potential for outstanding achievement. The case of Mark may prove to be one of this type. At any rate, Mark has always been classed as a "low achiever" and as "not interested in school"—a "no good." His arts and crafts instructor, however, believes that Mark is exceptionally gifted. Mark's mother wrote me as follows:

"The instructor tells us that Mark is an exceptionally talented craftsman, as well as an innovator of original ideas. He has recommended that Mark be sent to art school, and he predicts a promising future for this youngster as an artist or designer. On the other side of the fence, there is his counselor, a man thoroughly sold on verbal and word skills, who can see Mark *only* as a low-achiever. . . . His creative abilities and original ideas are recognized only by his arts and crafts instructor, so we are puzzled about what to do. The counselor tells us that the boy tests 'above average' on a standardized IQ test; the art instructor believes, from observation, that Mark is far above average in intelligence."

Such puzzles occur, I maintain, because neither the counselor, nor the art teacher accepts a sufficiently complex view of mental functioning. For a further documentation of cases which illustrate how an oversimplified view of giftedness can lead to an inhumane kind of education for the gifted, I would refer you to Hillel Black's article, "The Scandal of Educational Testing," in the November 9th *Saturday Evening Post*.

MORAL COURAGE AND SOCIAL ADJUSTMENT

On several occasions I have been accused of de-emphasizing the importance of social adjustment. Although this has never been my intent, I have pointed out that what is sometimes perceived as social adjustment may interfere with what I regard as a deeper kind of personal adjustment, a quality we usually talk of in terms of moral courage and honesty. Just as some children who are highly intelligent are not highly creative, some children who are highly adjusted, are not highly moral. In a peer-oriented culture such as ours, it is well to recognize the dangers of giving the greater rewards to those who accept the peer-value system and adjust almost automatically to the immediate group, almost without reference to moral values. The study by Getzels and Jackson (1962) indicated that in certain regards the highly adjusted adolescents are given greater rewards by the school culture than are highly moral adolescents.

In reviewing the Getzels and Jackson study (1963b), I expressed the opinion that their data on high moral standards and high adjustment dramatized one of the most serious defects of many programs of life-adjustment education. I had in mind those programs which stress only good manners, courtesy, conformity, obedience, industry, promptness, positiveness, and agreeableness, to the neglect of courage, independence in judgment, critical thinking, and high morals.

I have stressed the importance of courage and honesty because I believe that any conditioning to the contrary is inimical to creativity and to the development of the full potential of children. I think we must admit that there is much in our homes, schools, churches, and community organizations which conditions for dishonesty and results in the inhumane treatment of children. We find, for example, that parents and teachers in telling what they consider an ideal child, do not assign a place of great importance to courage, honesty, or independence in judgment. In a list of 62 characteristics, courage ranks 30th. In fact, it would appear that teachers in our culture consider it more important that their pupils be courteous than that they be courageous. It is more important that pupils do their work on time, be energetic and industrious, be obedient and popular or well-liked among their peers, be receptive of the ideas of others, be versatile, and be willing to accept the judgments of authorities than to be courageous.

In commenting on the fact that both parents and teachers rate "consideration of others" at the top of the list of characteristics they desire for children, I have always taken pains to state that I, too, place a great deal of value on being considerate of others. I have paused, however, to wonder how truthful we are in some of the things which we call "consideration of others." Some of our friends from other countries tell us that in our desire to appear considerate of them, we promise them things that we have no intention of giving. They tell us that it would be far more considerate if we would be honest rather than polite.

My contention is that we can have for children *both* a higher level of adjustment *and* a higher level of moral strength. Let us pause to examine one example of a gifted junior high school girl, whom we shall call Lena, which exposes some of the torture gifted children suffer when we give the greatest rewards to adjustment—actually coercion or surrender to the will of the teacher. Lena's mother describes the situation as follows:

> ". . . She is absolutely beside herself with this class in creative writing. She hates her teacher with a purple passion. The woman has a biting tongue, delights in making fun of all her students, all of her criticism is negative, and she has a one-track mind—patriotism. There has not yet been a chance to write anything of their choosing. They have spent the entire year writing essays for contests. Lena is so sick of her country and the flag and the DAR and RAD, etc., that she is ready to move to Russia.
> "Lena finally broke down and wrote one essay to please her. She set out with the intent to write one Mrs. W. would like— "I am the flame of freedom—I burn in the hearts of Americans—I warmed the soldiers at Valley Forge . . . etc. She read it aloud to us, the way Mrs. W. would read it. I almost lost my dinner. However, on THIS, she got an A—very

12

creatively done, the dear lady said. By the next time around, Lena said, 'I won't do that again—it was awful—it wasn't me writing it and I won't be untrue to myself—' So the child is constantly torn between her need to be a creative individual in her own right and this is the thing she talks and thinks about most—being herself, and the need to get a satisfactory grade from Mrs. W."

ACCUMULATION OF KNOWLEDGE AND CREATIVITY

Quite erroneously, some people have interpreted my interest in creative problem-solving activities in the classroom as a de-emphasis upon learning what is known from the past. Nothing could be further from the truth. In my own experiments involving the evaluation of creative ways of learning and in those which I have in any way supervised we have been concerned to see that the experimental methods or materials did not interfere with the achievement of the traditionally measured kinds of achievement. In *none* of these studies have the creative activities interfered with these traditionally measured outcomes. In some of these experiments (Sommers, 1961), students exposed to the experimental creative activities have shown significantly greater gains of the traditional, acquisition-of-knowledge type than their controls.

It would be foolish to ignore the accumulation of past knowledge. It would also be foolish for us to accept it as the final and exclusive truth. In some of my experiments, I have obtained findings which I believe tell us that it is not the amount of information we have that is important in creative problem-solving, but that the attitude we have towards this information makes a difference in how well we are able to use it. How we store information is important. I believe that both the record of my research and my interpretation of the results place me strongly behind the President of my University who made the following statement when he welcomed the 1963 freshmen:

"Welcome into the community of people trying to save what is known and desperately seeking to answer questions my generation could not answer" (Wilson, 1963).

It should be obvious to all that it is impossible to prepare today's school children for all of the demands that they will meet, for all of the changes they will experience. It is utterly foolish to think that we can impart to children all the facts and skills they will need. The information and skills for doing this simply do not exist. It seems to me that the only solution to this overwhelming problem is to develop in today's school children the motivations and skills to continue learning the rest of their lives. I do not see how this can be interpreted as excluding the dissemination of what was known in the past. My plea, especially for gifted children, is that we move out of the shallows, into the depths of learning and experiencing, from the acquisition of knowledge, to doing something with the knowledge that is acquired.

ORIGINAL ANSWERS AND CORRECT ANSWERS

One newspaper columnist (Weider, 1963) attacked me for advocating emphasis on original rather than correct answers. He wrote:

"Torrance, who draws public pay for this work, says questions should be asked which call for original answers—not the "right" one. (Like, if two and two make four, when do they not?)"

My own students know that this does not represent my viewpoint. In a day when it has become an educational sin to ask memory questions on examinations, my students know that I am one teacher who is not afraid to say that there are some facts that are so important and so well established that they should be remembered. These important, firm facts give them anchors against which to evaluate their original answers, and provide them with a source from which to generate original answers. I am simply opposed to exclusive attention to the one *correct answer*. There is a place for both original answers and correct ones.

I think gifted children suffer most when we confuse the acquisition of knowledge, and other types of solid educational achievement with mere conformity. You will recall the case of Ted with his nationally recognized creative achievements in science and his low grades in high school. His scores on the mathematics and science College Board Examinations, however, were outstanding, and his scores in subjects such as English above average. When educational achievement is regarded as a bookkeeping system, attention must be centered upon doing those things which count in the teacher's grade book. Gifted children frequently have more important things to learn and to do. This is reflected in Elizabeth Drews' (1961) comparison of three types of gifted high school students: the creative intellectuals, the high-achieving studious type, and the social leaders. Of these three groups, the creative intellectuals had the lowest teachers' grades but turned in the highest performance on difficult achievement examinations covering a broad range of knowledge. She found that just before examinations, the social leaders were studying and reading for the first time, but reading those things which count in the teachers' grade book. The high-achieving studious individuals were studying as usual and generally studying what they had been assigned. The creative intellectuals, however, were likely to be reading a book on philosophy or a college textbook, activities which have little or no "pay off" in the teachers' grade book.

This confusion of solid achievement with conformity behavior is also reflected in the already mentioned case of Dee. At the time Dee was in the third grade, her teacher reported to her mother that Dee was failing third grade. She explained that she could not understand why, since Dee was intelligent and imaginative. She could stand up in front of the class and tell stories which would grip the attention of the class for hours. In her arithmetic bee, Dee challenged the class' best arithmetic student and beat him soundly, yet Dee was failing third grade.

There just may be something inhumane about the one correct answer approach as it was applied to Bob, once regarded as gifted. Bob was a happy child who wanted to go to school more than anything. Even before he started to school, many people had noted his penetrating questions and conclusions, and generally assumed that he was in the third or fourth grade. Bob's first grade teacher believed in correcting everything that he did. She even corrected and graded his drawings. His mother was saddened when he brought home failing papers, in which he had changed the teacher's dittoed drawing or had added cowboy boots and hats to the drawings that he had been given to color. Apparently Bob was thoroughly confused by this one correct answer approach, and is now suspected as being mentally retarded. He is so energetic and alive at home and produces such clever ideas, that his mother finds it difficult to believe that he is mentally retarded.

DIVERGENT AND CONVERGENT BEHAVIOR

Another frequent misinterpretation that some people in some mysterious manner manage to place on our work is an advocacy of nonconforming behavior with a disregard for conforming behavior. This would be a ridiculous position to take. Successful creative work must usually take place within certain limits of conformity. In groups, conformity to certain values earns for one a kind of license to be nonconforming, usually in productive ways. I think Harold Benjamin's statement on this issue of divergency and conformity reflects my position quite accurately:

"How much uniformity does this society need for safety?

"It needs only that uniformity which the achievement of its greatest goals require. It demands security of life and health for its people. It demands wide opportunities for its people in work and play, in song and prayer. It must provide each individual with maximum aids to the development of his powers to contribute in every way possible to the great goals of his people. . . .

"How much deviation does this society require for progress?

"It requires just as much deviation, just as many uniquely developed peaks of ability, just as much idiosyncracy as the attainment of its goals will allow and need. All societies are wasteful of the capacities of their people. That society which comes closest to developing every socially useful idiosyncracy in every one of its members, will make the greatest progress toward its goals" (Benjamin, 1956, pp. 36–37).

In other words, we need and can have both divergency and conformity.

Perhaps the fundamental reason why the creatively gifted child so frequently evokes punishment upon himself and sometimes, pity is that he is divergent—different. Even when he is different in ways which are defined as socially and morally desirable, the divergent characteristic calls forth fear. He may work, or study, too hard and learn more than he should. He may be too honest, too courageous, too altruistic, or too affectionate, as well as too adventurous, too curious, or too determined. Parents do not want their children to be considered different, or unusual, and teachers endeavor to make them conform to behavioral norms, and become socially well-adjusted.

Being different does not seem to bother very young children, but year by year they seem to become increasingly more afraid of being themselves. The awesomeness of being different is well understood by most children by the time they reach the fourth grade. Children have been told this in many ways. My realization of its impact upon children became clearest to me when we asked children to write imaginative stories about animals and people with some divergent characteristic.

Most revealing are the stories about the flying monkey who might be regarded as a symbol of the "gifted child." In the stories of children, the parents of the flying monkey are upset when they learn that their baby monkey can fly. They may send him to another part of the jungle; they do not want him and reject him. They may think that he is mentally ill and take him to a doctor. Or, the mother may have the father give the young monkey "a good talking to" and tell him that the other monkeys will think he is "crazy in the head," if he continues to fly. They tell him that others will fear him and that he will have no friends. They may teach him to hide his wings, or camouflage them so that others will not know that he can fly. Or, they may cut off his wings. He is warned of all kinds of punishment and destruction. It is always the good little monkey who gives up his flying, and other divergent behavior. Even when the monkey's flying ability is used for the good of others, such as obtaining the top bananas for the other monkeys or saving their lives by flying them out of a burning jungle, he may still be ridiculed and punished.

RESPONSIVE AND STIMULATING ENVIRONMENTS

On a number of occasions, I have said that the creative child needs a responsive environment rather than *just* a stimulating one. I did not mean to infer by this that the creative child does not also need stimulation nor that some children might not need a stimulating environment more than

15

a responsive one. I think perhaps my greatest discomfort comes from the interpretation that some people have placed on my use of the term "responsive environment." People frequently ask, "Well, what you mean by a responsive environment is nothing but a *laissez-faire* or permissive environment." What I mean by a responsive environment is quire different from *laissez-faire* and permissiveness. What I have in mind calls for the most alert and sensitive kind of direction and guidance. It means building an atmosphere of receptive listening, relieving the fears of the over-taught and overguided, fending off devastating disparagement and criticism, stirring the sluggish and deepening the superficial, making sure that every sincere effort brings enough satisfaction to assure continued effort, heightening sensory awareness, and keeping alive the zest for learning and thinking.

TREATING BOYS AND GIRLS ALIKE OR DIFFERENTLY

On several occasions I have stated that our misplaced emphasis on sex role differences takes a heavy toll on the creativeness of both boys and girls and causes them to fall far short of their potentialities as human beings. This has been interpreted as meaning that I am advocating that boys and girls be treated alike, that I would make sissies of boys and tomboys of girls. Again, this is far from my intention. What I have been concerned about is the fact that we make taboo or place off limits certain areas of thinking and experiencing for both boys and girls. It seems to me that this reduces unnecessarily the freedom of both boys and girls.

Misplaced emphases on sex differences come into sharpest focus in studies of creative thinking, because creativity, requires both sensitivity or openness, and independence in thinking and judgment. In our society, sensitivity is a feminine virtue while independence is a masculine value. Thus, it is only a divergent personality who maintains both the sensitivity and independence of mind necessary for a high level of creative thinking. I fail to see how sensitivity can really make one less male or how independence of mind can make one less female. Yet there are important differences in the roles which the sexes must play in our society, differences which we would like to preserve.

I think the following excerpts from a letter I received recently from a parent helps us to understand the problem:

> "I'm sure you realize that most parents would rather their son be a typical boy, to all outward appearances anyway, than a creative person, especially if as a creative person he would wind up being one/nth less masculine.
> "Similarly most parents patiently tolerate the tomboy stages their daughters pass through, just so long, and then begin to quake if the latter don't begin to cast around for a suitable husband, before they get half through their teens. If creativity appears and looms as incompatible with the time-honored behavior of girls, 'To heck with creativity!' is the attitude of parents."

CHAOS AND DISCIPLINE

Perhaps the misinterpretation of my work which has disturbed me most is that creativity leads to lawlessness, delinquency, disorder, and chaos and that I have a disregard for discipline, organization and order. One newspaper columnist, (Weider, 1963), in ridiculing the NEA pamphlet (Torrance 1963a), wrote as follows:

"After all, why stunt a behavior pattern? Come to think of it, a little trespassing, vandalism and some thievery now and then may encourage arson, more rape and a greater frequency of murders.

"How else can a return to savagery be accomplished more quickly? Follow Torrance! No need to fear brainwashing—let's have no brains to wash."

Apparently, this columnist failed to read the following statement which I made in the very pamphlet which he attacked:

". . . It is important that creativity be energized and guided from birth. If it is stifled early, it will only become inactive, if it survives at all. It is true that vigorous creative imagination can survive early stifling and opposition; but if it learns only to act without direction, it becomes dangerous to society and perhaps to civilization."

Although Barron (1963) and others are doubtless correct when they say that highly creative people have a greater tolerance for disorder and complexity than their less creative colleagues, this does not mean that they can tolerate chaos nor that they do not also like order and organization. They can be tolerant of disorder because they have an exceptional capacity to synthesize relatively unrelated and even discordant elements into new combinations and unities. If the disorder or complexity is too great, however, it becomes stressful and even the highly creative mind is unable to function effectively. My point is that order, discipline, organization, guidance, purpose, and direction are necessary, even for creative behavior, and are not incompatible with creativity. The order, discipline, and organization, however, must be flexible enough to permit change and to allow one thing to lead to another.

CONCLUSION

In conclusion, I would like to reiterate my contention that a more humane kind of education for gifted children demands that we adopt a more complex picture of the human mind and personality and that we spend less energy in trying to oversimplify them. In their education and guidance there is a place for:

. . . *both* creative learning and learning by authority
. . . *both* intelligence tests and tests of creative thinking
. . . *both* moral courage and social adjustment
. . . *both* the mastery of what is known and the creation of new knowledge
. . . *both* original answers and correct ones
. . . *both* conforming and nonconforming behavior
. . . *both* a responsive and a stimulating environment
. . . *both* a respect for the common humaneness and sex differences of boys and girls
. . . *both* discipline and creative behavior!

References

1. Barron, F. *Creativity and Psychological Health*. Princeton, N.J.: D. Van Nostrand Co., 1963.
2. Benjamin, H. *The Cultivation of Idiosyncracy*. Cambridge, Mass.: Harvard University Press, 1956.
3. Black Hillel. "The Scandal of Educational Testing." *Saturday Evening Post,* November 9, 1963, 72–76.
4. Drews, Elizabeth M. "A Critical Evaluation of Approaches to the Identification of Gifted Students." In. A. Traxler (Ed.) *Measurement in Today's Schools*. Washington, D. C.: American Council on Education, 1961, pp. 47–51.

5. Getzels, J. W. and P. W. Jackson. *Creativity and Intelligence.* New York: Henry Holt and Sons, 1962.
6. Sommers, W. S. "The Influence of Selected Teaching Methods on the Development of Creative Thinking." Doctoral Dissertation. University of Minnesota, 1961.
7. Torrance, E. P. *Guiding Creative Talent.* Englewood Cliffs, N.J.: Prentice-Hall, Inc. 1962.
8. ———— *What Research Says to the Teacher: Creativity.* Washington, D.C.: National Education Association, 1963. (a)
9. ———— "Essay Review: 'Creativity and Intelligence.' " *School Review,* 1963, 71, 112–115. (b)
10. ———— *Education and the Creative Potential.* Minneapolis: University of Minnesota Press, 1963. (c)
11. Weider, Brayton. "Off the Beat." Corvallis (Oregon) *Gazette Times,* August, 1963.
12. Wilson, O. M. "Welcome to 1963 University of Minnesota Freshmen." Address delivered September 26, 1963, University of Minnesota, Minneapolis, Minn.

3. THE NECESSARY AND SUFFICIENT CONDITIONS OF CREATIVITY

Ralph J. Hallman

The purpose of this paper is to present a conceptual scheme for systematizing the extensive and diverse research data which this decade has produced in connection with the problem of creativity.

THE STATUS OF THE DATA

The data regarding creativity now exist in the form random, unrelated insights or as outright disagreements and contradictions. The disorganized state of this evidence prevails largely for reasons. In the first place, a wide variety of disciplines have investigated the creative process and have tended to emphasize their seperate interests. Philosophers, psychologists, scientists, artists, writers, engineers, and businessmen have contributed information, and this information reflects a particular concern. For example, the philosophers tend to discover the grounds for creative productions among the final powers operating in the universe, the psychologists, among the dynamisms of personality functions; the scientists, among the self-regulating forces of protoplasm or of matter; the artists and writers, among the products which they create; the engineers and politicians, among the externally defined needs which they confront; the businessmen and managerial officers, among the interpersonal relations of their organizations.

In the second place, the structure of the creative experience itself is very complex and therefore can accommodate widely diverse approaches. It involves components which are unrelated to each other except in this one circumstance. They bear no necessary relations to each other in the external world, that is, outside the bounds of the creative process. To be sure, the creative act is a single event, a highly integrated movement involving the total organism such that during the experience all boundary lines fade, distinctions blur, and the artist experiences himself as one with his materials and his vision. Yet, the creative act is multifaceted as well. It includes psychological, environmental, cultural, physical, and intellectual aspects. The evidence clusters around one or another of these aspects or around one of the methodological approaches to the problem.

For example, a large body of evidence has accumulated in connection with the effort to identify the particular *personality traits* which make for creativity. The assumption is that the creative process can be fully accounted for by providing an exhaustive list of such traits. The psychiatrist, the clinician, and the factor-analyst have shown great interest in explaining creativeness by means of traits. For example, Guilford's psychometric method has identified in the creative personality such traits as sensitivity to problems, fluency, flexibility, originality, ability to transform meanings, and ability to elaborate (*19*). Fromm speaks of four traits: capacity to be puzzled, ability to concentrate, capacity to accept conflict, and willingness to be reborn every day (*13*). Rogers has a similar list: Openness to experience, internal locus of evaluation, and ability to toy

Reprinted by permission of the author and *Journal of Humanistic Psychology,* Vol. 3, No. 1, Spring, 1963.

with elements (*46*). Maslow has perhaps the most extensive list (*33*); the creative personality, he says, is spontaneous, expressive, effortless, innocent, unfrightened by the unknown or the ambiguous, able to accept tentativeness and uncertainty, able to tolerate bipolarity, able to integrate opposites. The creative person is the healthy, self-actualizing person, Maslow believes. Others who have identified creative traits are Barron (*5*), Meier (*36*), Whiting (*60*), Angyal (*3*), Mooney (*38*), Lowenfeld (*28*), and Hilgard (*23*).

Another body of data has been collected to prove that creativity can be fully explained as a series of *chronological stages,* each stage of which makes its unique contribution to the total process. Wallas (*58*) provides the classical statement of this position, and he has been followed by Patrick (*41*) and Spender (*52*) in connection with creativeness in poetry; Hadamard (*21*) and Poincaré (*42*) in mathematics; Arnold (*4*), Patrick, and Montmasson (*37*) in science. Others who define creativity in terms of serial stages are Ghiselin (*16*), Vinacke (*57*), and Hutchinson (*24*).

A third cluster of evidence surrounds the definition that creative activity involves an interchange of energy among *vertical layers* of psychological systems. Creativeness consists in a shift of psychic levels. Most writers identify two psychological levels and refer to them variously as the primary and secondary processes, the autistic and the reality adjusted, unconscious mechanisms and conscious deliberation, free and bound energies, gestalt-free and articulating tendencies. These writers include Freud, Ehrenzweig *10*), and Shcneider (*48*). Maslow adds to these two levels a third one called integration (*30*). Murray also speaks of three levels, the physical, mental, and superordinate-cultural creations (*39*). Taylor's list of five levels moves away from the notion that levels are defined as psychic systems: these are the expressive, productive, inventive, innovative, and emergentive (*55*).

Yet a fourth set of data regards creativeness as *types of thinking* and seeks to distinguish those forms of thinking which are creative from those which are not. It is generally agreed that creative thought consists of certain integrating, synthesizing functions; that it deals with relational form rather than with individual instances; that it discovers new forms which can accommodate past experiences. It involves a real fusion of forms and not merely a juncturing. Spearman refers to creative thinking as the education of correlates (*51*); McKellar, as autistic, prelogical, and imaginative (*35*); Vinacke, as imagination rather than voluntary, rational operations (*57*); Bartlett, as divergent autistic thinking as distinguished from closed systems (*6*). Bruner's book *On Knowing* makes the same distinction (*8*).

A fifth type of evidence consists in the great numbers of *personal reports* from creative artists and scientists which are available. These vary from descriptions of private experiences, as in the case of Nietzsche (*40*), to public policies as taught by Reynolds (*44*), and to such heterogeneous collections as the recent one by Ghiselin (*16*). A complete survey of evidence would need to include such other problems as motivation for creativity, the kinds of creative acts, the concept of genius, and cultural influences.

We can conclude, I believe, that there is some advantage in viewing this valuable but disorganized evidence from the point of view of some conceptual system. The formal structure of such a system would need to reflect the necessary and sufficient conditions of creativity. These criteria would eliminate the less relevant data which have become associated with creativeness, and would unify into a consistent framework the great number of unrelated discoveries which have been made.

I propose, then, that on the basis of evidence now available a tentative statement can be made regarding these conditions. I propose that the creative act can be analyzed into five major components: (1) it is a whole *act,* a unitary instance of behavior; (2) it terminates in the production of *objects* or of forms of living which are distinctive; (3) it evolves out of certain *mental processes;* (4) it co-varies with specific *personality transformations;* and (5) it occurs within a particular kind of *environment.* These may be expressed in abbreviated form as the act, the object, the process, the person, and the environment. A demonstration of the necessary features of each of these factors can employ both descriptive and logical procedures; it can refer to the relevance of empirical evidence, and can infer what grounds are logically necessary in order to explain certain facts.

THE CRITERION OF CONNECTEDNESS

Descriptively, the first criterion can be called the condition of *connectedness.* Observers who have collected evidence about this aspect of creativeness agree that some form of combinatorial activity is requisite to creativity. Logically, a demonstration of this criterion employs the category of *relation* as a principle of explanation. But it may be more meaningful to refer to it as the concept of metaphor. This category isolates the relation of similitude rather than of difference as basic to connectedness. It is implied by the most fundamental characteristic of human creativity, namely, the requirement that man work with materials which he himself has not created. Lacking the omnipotence and omniscience of God, man cannot create out of nothing. He cannot create in the sense of bringing something into being from what previously had no existence. This condition therefore imposes upon him the need to create by *bringing already existing elements into a distinctive relation to each other.* The essence of human creativeness is *relational*, and an analysis of its nature must refer to the connectedness of whatever elements enter into the creative relationship. The analysis must demonstrate that though man does not create the components, he can nevertheless produce *new connectections among them.* It must prove that these connections are genuinely original and not simply mechanical. Logically, this means that connectedness comprises relationships which are neither symmetrical nor transitive; that is, the newly created connections as wholes are not equivalent to the parts being connected. Neither side of the equation validly implies the other, for the relationship is neither inferential nor causal; rather, it is metaphoric and transformational.

Let us refer to the research literature for descriptive materials which both logically require this criterion and also provide evidence for its validity. This criterion appears under a variety of names, but it does invariably appear. It is described variously as a combination, composition, configuration, novel relationship, constellation of meanings, new organization, purposive pattern formation, complete relatedness, integration, oneness, fusion, and education of correlates.

All forms of creativity, Bruner says, grow out of a *combinatorial* activity (*8*), a placing of things in new perspectives. Arnold refers to this criterion as the combining of past experiences into new patterns, into *new configurations* which in some manner satisfy the creator and perhaps society (*4*). For McKellar, it is a *fusion* of perceptions which have long lain dormant (*35*); for Gerard, an act of *closure,* a restructuring of the field of perceptual experience (*14*); for Taylor, the molding of experiences into *organizational patterns* which are new and different; for Poincaé, the production of combinations, of *ordered wholes* (*42*); for Kubie, the discovery of *unexpected connections* among things, a fusion produced by the free play of unconscious symbolic processes (*26*); for Murray, a *compositional* process which results in some new object, experience or image (*39*); for Rogers, the emergences of novel *relational products*. Ghiselin concludes from his studies of the creative work of artists, scientists, musicians, and writers that the most necessary requirement of creativity is that it present a *new configuration,* a new constellation of meanings which have no specific precedent (*16*).

These writers may locate connectedness either in the act of perception, in intellect, in personality development, or in the object. But all agree that it is necessary. There is one refinement to this statement: creativity is both a combination of elements into new relations, and a *re-combining* of them. This means that creativity is not merely the capacity to connect elements in a new way, but to transplant these new combinations onto previously unrelated materials. It is the capacity to regard life metaphorically, to experience even orderliness as plastic, to shift intellectual processes from one formal system to another. It is, as Rogers puts it, to remain in process, to discover structure *in* experience instead of imposing structure *upon* experience. Thus, the criterion of connectedness expresses the meaning that creativeness deals largely with relational structures; it implies a fusion of elements into these new structures rather than a mechanical arranging of them; it means that connections are actually produced and are not found.

THE CRITERION OF ORIGINALITY

Descriptively; the second criterion can be called the condition of *originality;* empirical observations identify this quality as being essential to the *products* which have emerged from the creative process. Logically, it requires the category of *singularity* as a principle of explanation, though the psychologist may prefer the term "individuality." This category, I shall argue, specifies four qualities which any item must have if it is to exist as an idiographic, nonclassifiable object, that is, if it is to be genuinely original. These are novelty, unpredictability, uniqueness, and surprise; they refer to the same fundamental characteristic of originality, but from the frames of reference of philosophy, science, art, and psychology respectively.

These four aspects of originality distinguish the authentically creative from the more mechanical arrangements. Logically, this means that they define what is meant by a class of objects as well as by a singular item. The completely idiographic instance logically equates with a class concept, and it functions similarly in syllogistic reasoning. Both the completely original individual and the universal are idiosyncratic and not further classifiable; these four qualities confer this uniqueness.

First, then, novelty means newness, freshness, inventiveness; it is universally recognized by writers in the field as an indispensable quality of originality. Creativity is the fusion of perceptions in a *new* way (McKellar), the capacity to find *new* connections (Kubie), the emergence of *novel* relationships (Rogers), the occurrence of a composition which is *new* (Murray), the disposition to make and recognize *innovations* (Lasswell), an action of mind that produces *new* insights (Gerard), the molding of experiences into *new* organizations (Taylor), the presentation of *new* constellations of meanings (Ghiselin). This meaning has been expressed by Wilson and his co-workers (*62*) in terms which can be handled more efficiently by the statistical method; these are cleverness, remoteness of association, and uncommonness of response. Guilford briefly considers the possibility that originality may relate more closely to the personality trait of unconventionality than to qualities of newness. That is, he considers whether originality is a function of temperament instead of the objects produced, but he carries this no further than speculation.

Second, originality means unpredictability. This factor refers to the relationship of the created object to other states of affairs in the real world, and asserts that creativeness uncouples such objects from causal connections. It asserts the incompatibility of creativity and causality theory. Generally, philosophic and scientific systems assume orerliness and necessity in the cosmos; they accommodate the concept of originality only with difficulty, for the creation of originals violates necessity and demands freedom. Creativity produces qualities which never existed before and which could never have been predicted on the basis of prior configurations of events. Metaphoric activity intrudes upon logical-causal necessity.

Third, originality means uniqueness. It asserts that every instance of creativeness differs from every other instance, that products which are original have no precedents. Original creations are incomparable, for there is no class of objects to which they can be compared. They are untranslatable, unexampled.

Fourth, originality means surprise. Just as novelty describes the connections that occur in the creative act, unpredictability to the setting of the new creation in the physical environment, and uniqueness to the product when regarded as valuable in its own right, so surprise refers to the psychological effect of novel combinations upon the beholder. Surprise serves as the final test of originality, for without the shock of recognition which *registers* the novel experience, there would be no occasion for individuals to be moved to appreciate or to produce creative works.

The element of surprise has been observed by creative artists and scientists in themselves, by experimental psychologists, and by clinicians. There is general agreement that recognition must be sudden and unexpected in order to achieve fullness of surprise. Fromm holds that the capacity to be aware, to respond freely and spontaneously, reduces tendencies to project and to distort and consequently permits the surprise response (*13*). Schachtel agrees that originality produces emotive shock and that it erupts with suddenness in conditions of unfettered and open encounter with the world (*47*). Getzels and Jackson find that surprise takes the form of unexpected endings to plots, of incongruities, and of humor (*15*). Bruner regards effective surprise as the very essence of creativity itself (*8*).

I shall leave open the question whether originality requires the production of a tangible object. Those who emphasize craftsmanship demand an object; others, as Maslow, believe that creativity can express itself in a style of living.

THE CRITERION OF NONRATIONALITY

Descriptively, the third criterion may be designated as the condition of nonrationality. Even those research workers who are not psychoanalytically oriented agree that certain *unconscious mental processes* are responsible for the metaphoric function of fusing images into new creations. Logically, this criterion depends upon a category of *causality* as a principle of explanation. The psychological version of this process includes references to the primary processes, to motile rather than bound energy, to various stages of creativity, to psychological levels of creativity, or to types of mental processes.

This criterion describes the metaphoric, symbolizing processes which produce new connections. I refer to it as nonrational because the combinatorial activity occurs in the form of unconscious operations; it does not belong to the rational mind, nor is it consciously controlled. Rationality divides and distinguishes; it focuses upon differences. Metaphoric activity unites and relates; it flourishes upon similarities, and transpires among the primary processes. Non-rationality is not merely a condition of novelty; it is a cause. The relationship between such processes as condensation, symbolization, displacement, and neologisms and the production of new connections is a causal one. It is the very nature of unconscious (or preconscious) levels of the mind to function metaphorically. The mechanisms which constitute the unconscious operations make this inevitable. Unless they function, no new connections can occur. Thus, there is an invariant relationship between the two.

The nonrational processes function by imposing upon ideas and images the quality of plasticity. Metaphor gives plasticity to language, and makes poetry possible; it gives plasticity to thinking, and makes scientific inventions possible; it gives plasticity to perceptual forms, and makes art possible. Metaphor disengages our belief attitudes from the conditioning induced by logical inference and presents new belief possibilities. It softens the discursive tendencies of language, and consequently allows new meanings to be fashioned. With the inferential limitations lifted from language and with causal connections uncoupled from objects, these become malleable and therefore make possible new visions, unexpected views of the world and of experience. The nonrational mechanisms which produce these new visions constitute the energy system of creativity, and operate similarly in all creative individuals whether they be scientists, artists, or housewives.

Inspection of the research literature indicates that at least three conceptual schemes have been devised for explaining the creative process. The first conceives of creativity as a sequential *series of stages* of activity, the second as vertical *levels* of psychological functions, and the third as *types* of mental processes. These three schemes agree upon one major fact: that segment or level of the creative process which is invariably associated with the creation of novelty is nonrational. It lies below the surface of consciousness; it resists rational analysis; it dissolves under logical examination.

The classical statement of the theory of stages was first formulated by Wallas in 1926; he identifies four distinct stages and calls them preparation, incubation, illumination, and verification (58). The second and third stages actually produce the new connections, the novel relationships, and these transpire in the form of nonrational operations. The incubation stage, for example, consists of spontaneous, uncontrollable events which cluster themselves seemingly in accordance with their own autonomous laws. It involves the relaxation of conscious thinking operations and the inhibition of logical control. Maslow refers to this process as voluntary regression (31), Ehrenzweig as surrender of the ego (10), and Rogers as openness to experience (46). The stage of illumination remains even more of a mystery. Being singular, unpredictable, idiosyncratic, it resists formal description. Writers from Plato to Lu Chi in ancient China to Nietzsche have remarked about the unexplainable nature of inspiration. Patrick has been most diligent in trying to prove the theory of four stages (41). Poincaré and Hadamard (21) agree that the four stages adequately account for mathematics creations. Arnold (54), Patrick, and Montmasson 37) discover the same four stages in connection with scientific inventions. Patrick and Spender (56) believe that poetic creativeness occurs in sequential stages. Other writers who explain the creative process in this fashion were mentioned above (57).

The evidence that nonrationality serves as a necessary condition of creativity becomes more conclusive when it is examined from the point of view that it consists in the interchange of energy among vertical levels of the psyche. This theory accepts the distinction between the primary and and the secondary processes, between the unconscious (or preconscious) and conscious functions, between autistic and reality-adjusted thinking, and it asserts that though the actual creative process involves a shift in psychic levels, the shift must always occur in such manner that the metaphoric fusion of elements shall transpire in the unconscious levels and be projected upwards into consciousness. Each level contributes to the creative process. The unconscious supplies the surge and the power, the imagery and the concreteness, the ambiguity and conflict, the actual connectedness. The rational level provides the elaboration, the testing, the gestalts, the socially derived approvals. Again, other writers who have developed this theory are mentioned above.

The third description of the creative process conceives of it in terms of types of mental operations. According to this definition, the creative act is one which combines forms of thought into new relationships. Creative thinking is only one of several kinds of operations included in the higher mental processes; it is usually distinguished from other kinds of thinking largely in terms of its nonrational aspects. As has been mentioned, Guilford, Vinacke, McKellar, Rapaport, Bartlett, and Bruner make this distinction. In every case it is the nonrational, the autistic, the metaphoric, the internally oriented, the spontaneous and involuntary, the integrating, unbound energies which are active in producing new connections. These differ from the conscious, the inhibitory, the rational, controlled, purposive, reality-oriented processes which, to be sure, play their part in creativity; but their function is one of elaboration and testing, not fusing. It is the fantasy-dominated forms of thought which contain clues to mind's creative capacities. These nonrational processes account for the seeming effortlessness and the spontaneity of creative activity; they explain the autonomy, the quality of "otherness," of being visited by a daemon or a voice. They account for connectedness. And they account for the direction which creative movement assumes.

THE CRITERION OF SELF-ACTUALIZATION

Descriptively, the fourth criterion can be called the condition of self-actualization, a pattern of personality growth which clinicians and analyst have studied. Logically, this criterion rests upon the category of *change* as an explanatory principle. Perhaps the psychologist prefers to speak of it in terms of motivation as the energy source for change, and of growth in the direction of psychological health as the goal toward which this energy is directed. This category must account for change as transformation and as transcendence.

This criterion asserts that creativity involves a fundamental change in personality structure, and that this change occurs in the direction of fulfillment. It distinguishes between those personality involvements which remain merely perfunctory and nonproductive and those which prove to be genuinely creative. It distinguishes between energy transformations which are habitual, tension-reducing, and repetitive and those which are tension-organizing, forward-pointing, and growth-oriented. It implies that though all personality change may not terminate in growth, all instances of personality growth are possible grounds for creativeness. It implies that though many forms of energy exchanges may be necessary in order to account for human behavior, only those kinds which eventuate in the realization of potentialities lead to creative acts. Thus, it identifies creativity with self formation, and therefore implies that unless significant transformation occurs in personality during an activity, that activity will fall short of the creative.

This criterion seems to be logically necessary. Personality dynamics can best account for the unique qualities of experiences and of products. It can best serve as the unifying agency for the entire creative process. Since this process in every instance has been analyzed into either discrete stages of activity, or sharply differentiated strata of psychic levels, or into distinct types of mental functions, some explanation must be given as to why such diverse operations mesh so efficiently and move forward in the creative act so effortlessly. A unifying principle is necessary, and the factor of personality-in-motion can serve as this principle.

Empirically, this criterion is supported by the great wealth of data which has been reported. Maslow (32) has spoken most forcefully on this theme. He equates creativity with the state of psychological health, and this with the self-actualization process. There is no exception to this rule, he says; creativity is a universal characteristic of self-actualizing people. This form of creativeness reaches beyond special-talent creativeness; it is a fundamental characteristic of human nature. It touches whatever activity the healthy person is engaged in.

This criterion also asserts a connection between motivation and creativity, for the self-actualizing person is characterized by an unusually strong motivational drive. These impulses energize the individual in such manner that he is impelled to act, to express, to perform; and they also produce personality transformations. The creative person, driven by an urge which eventually takes full possession of him, cares less about mundane things, spurns conventional attitudes, rejects security. These drives are pervasive, persistent; they resist deflection. Thus, a large body of literature has accumulated around this problem of motivation of creativity.

The Freudian theory that the creative urge grows out of substitute gratifications for incestuous and parracidal desires experienced during pregenital stages is still widely supported. Oriented to the past, our present responses are conditioned by past experiences; they are a form of tension reduction. Relief of tension both provides pleasure and insures reinforcement. Followers of the Freudian school are Brill (7), Engleman (11), Deri (9), Van der Sterren (56), Macalpine (29), Weiss (59), and Sterba (54). A major variation of this theme is that creative motives are efforts to make restitution and atonement for objects and persons destroyed during agressive fantasies. Segal (49), Fairbairn (12), Levey (27), Grotjahn (18), and Sharpe (50) concur in this analysis. They agree that creativeness stems from the efforts of the infant to restrain his destructive tendencies. This theory accounts for the urgency and the power which lie behind motivation. Some of Freud's followers reject the view that creative power is an alibi for thwarted sexuality. They associate it with some compensating force; Adler as compensation for organ inferiority (1); Rank, for man's mortality and finitude (43); Jung, for feelings of finitude as well (25). These writers emphasize creativity as a process of will affirmation, of indivuation, of self formation.

Thus, strong motivational drives have important effects upon creative activity. They energize the organism and impel it into creative expression. McClelland (34) describes other effects: motives relate, unify, and integrate the diversity of needs and goals in behavior. They provide organization, orientation, and direction; they introduce directional trends, create need-related imagery, increase interest in future possibilities. We recognize these effects as identical with the metaphoric process. Allport (2) points out the relationship of motives to emotions and asserts that they too serve a unifying, selective function. Further, strong motives sensitize the individual to a greater number and variety of environmental cues, and they push the level of aspiration upward. The highest aspiration involves self-actualization, which constitutes both the goal of life and its motivational wellspring. The theory of motivation as goal seeking completes the analysis of this fourth criterion. In the sense that personality transforms itself in the process of achieving the goal of mature growth, there is established a connection between creativity and self-actualization.

THE CRITERION OF OPENNESS

Descriptively, the fifth and final criterion can be called the condition of *openness*. It designates those characteristics of the environment, both the inner and the outer, the personal and the social, which facilitate the creative person's moving from the actual state of affairs which he is in at a given time toward solutions which are only possible and as yet undetermined. These conditions, or traits, include sensitivity, tolerance of ambiguity, self-acceptance, and spontaneity. Since these are passively rather than actively engaged in the creative process, this criterion may be explained logically within the category of *possibility*. But again, the psychological meaning of this category may best be expressed under the concept of deferment, as distinguished, for example, from closure; of postponement as distinguished from predetermined solutions.

Defined as traits by most psychologists, these conditions are learned and are not aspects of man's inheritance; they are environmental factors. They characterize both the individual and society; they describe such social organizations as schools and families, and they refer to personalities. The term "openness" is meant to encompass all such traits; however, I am proposing that this general category can be further subdivided into four distinguishable but closely related clusters of environmental factors. These are listed in the preceding paragraph. The larger category of openness is borrowed directly from Rogers: "This is the opposite of psychological defensiveness, when to protect the organization of self, certain experiences are prevented from coming into awareness except in disturbed fashion. . . . It means lack of rigidity and permeability of boundaries in concepts, beliefs, perceptions, and hypotheses" (*45*).

Sensitivity refers to a state of being aware of things as they really are rather than according to some predetermined set. The creative person is sensitive to the world of objects, to problems, to other people, to gaps in evidence, to unconscious impulses. The following are some of the research workers who agree that sensitivity is a condition for creative work: Angyal (*3*), Fromm (*13*), Mooney (*38*), Guilford (*20*), Stein (*53*), Lowenfeld (*28*), Greenacre (*17*), and Hilgard (*23*).

The ability to tolerate ambiguity is another trait which has been commonly accepted. It is the ability to accept conflict and tension resulting from polarity (*13*), to tolerate inconsistencies and contradictions (*33*), to accept the unknown, to be comfortable with the ambiguous, approximate, uncertain. The creative person can postpone decisions and accept the abeyance as pleasantly challenging. Zilboorg (*63*), Wilson (*61*), and Hart (*22*) concur in this analysis. Flexibility is an extension of the traits of sensitivity and tolerance of ambiguity. These latter traits allow the individual to change and to take advantage of change. Flexibility means being able to toy with elements, to operate without being anchored to rigid forms, to escape traditional solutions, to be playfully serious, to perceive meaning in irrelevancies.

The third set of meanings contained in the criterion of openness points to the need of the creative personality to have a sense of personal destiny and worth which will allow him to accept himself as the source of values. It is obvious that anyone who tolerates uncertainties and conflicts for long must enjoy an anchorage within some value system apart from the conventional order, and this would need to be himself. The forward-pointing search for possibilities which characterizes the creative process implies an acceptance of self as a source of judgment. The new creations exist at first in the future and in tentative form; they exist as possibilities. If they become original creations, they must then take on the values which the individual assigns to them. Since the creative person must speculate, test, modify, postpone completion of his work, he needs to rely upon his own sensitivity for guidance.

Finally, the fourth set of meanings connected with openness relates to spontaneity. This quality gives the creative act the feeling of being free, autonomous, undetermined. It allows creative behavior to be unbound and uncoupled from previous causal conditions. It produces the response of wonder and awe. It is responsible for the quality of freshness, of being born anew every day, of childlike naïveté, of naturalness and simplicity.

SUMMARY

This paper has submitted no new evidence about the creative process. Rather, it has suggested one possible way for organizing in a meaningful way the great amount of material which has already accumulated. It proposes five necessary and sufficient conditions for creativity as a basic framework which can encompass relevant data. These have predictive value. When all five are present, creativeness must of necessity result.

References

1. Adler, Alfred. *Problems of Neurosis* (London: Routledge, 1959).
2. Allport, G. W. *Patterns and Growth in Personality* (New York: Holt, Rinehart, and Winston, 1961), p. 198.
3. Angyal, Andras. A Theoretical Model for Personality Studies, in *The Self*, ed., C. E. Moustakas (New York: Harper and Row, 1956), pp. 44–57.
4. Arnold, J. E. Creativity in Engineering, in *Creativity: An Examination of the Creative Process*, ed., P. Smith (New York: Hastings House, 1959), pp. 33–46.
5. Barron, F. Needs for Order and Disorder as Motives in Creative Activity, *The Second Research Conference on the Identification of Creative Scientific Talent*, ed., C. W. Taylor (Salt Lake City: University of Utah Press, 1958), pp. 119–128.
6. Bartlett, Frederick. *Thinking: An Experimental and Social Study* (New York: Basic Books, 1958).
7. Brill, A. A. Poetry as an Oral Outlet, *Psychoanalytic Review*, Vol. 18, No. 4 (Oct., 1931), pp. 357–378.
8. Bruner, Jerome S. *On Knowing* (Cambridge, Mass.: Belknap Press, 1962).
9. Deri, F. On Sublimation, *Psychoanalytic Quarterly*, Vol. 8, No. 3 (1939), pp. 325–334.
10. Ehrenzweig, Anton. *The Psychoanalysis of Artistic Vision and Hearing* (London: Routledge, 1953), p. 193.
11. Engleman, A. A. A Case of Trensexion upon Viewing a Painting, *American Imago*, Vol. 9 (1952), pp. 239–249.
12. Fairbairn, W. R. D. Prolegomena to a Psychology of Art, *British Journal of Psychology*, Vol. 28 (1938), pp. 288–303.
13. Fromm, Erich. The Creative Attitude, in *Creativity and Its Cultivation*, ed., Harold H. Anderson (New York: Harper and Row, 1959), pp. 44–54.
14. Gerard, Ralph W. What is Imagination?, in *Selected Readings on the Learning Process*, ed., T. L. Harris and W. E. Schwan (New York: Oxford University Press, 1961), pp. 81–89.
15. Getzels, J. W. and Jackson, P. W. *Creativity and Intelligence* (New York: John Wiley and Sons, 1962), p. 37.

16. Ghiselin, Brewster ed., *The Creative Process* (New York: New American Library, 1952), p. 21.
17. Greenacre, P. Childhood of the Artist, in *The Psychoanalytic Study of the Child,* Vol. 12 (New York: International Universities Press, 1957), pp. 47–72.
18. Grotjahn, M. *Beyond Laughter* (New York: McGraw-Hill, 1957).
19. Guilford, J. P. A Psychometric Approach to Creativity, Mimeographed, University of Southern California, Mar., 1962.
20. Guilford, J. P. Traits of Creativity, in *Creativity and Its Cultivation,* pp. 142–161.
21. Hadamard, J. *The Psychology of Invention in the Mathematical Field* (New York: Dover Publications, 1954).
22. Hart, H. H. The Integrative Function in Creativity, *Psychiatric Quarterly,* Vol. 24, No. 1 (1950), pp. 1–16.
23. Hilgard, E. R. Creativity and Problem-Solving, in *Creativity and Its Cultivation,* pp. 162–180.
24. Hutchinson, E. D. *How to Think Creatively* (Nashville, Tenn.: Abingdon Press, 1949), p. 25.
25. Jung, C. G. *Psychology of the Unconscious,* trans. B. M. Hingle (New York: Dodd, Mead, 1916), pp. 62–86.
26. Kubie, L. S. *Neurotic Distortion in the Creative Process* (University of Kansas Press, 1958), p. 50.
27. Levey, H. B. A Theory Concerning Free Creation in the Inventive Arts, *Psychiatry,* Vol. 2, No. 2 (May, 1940), pp. 229–231.
28. Lowenfeld, Viktor. Current Research on Creativity, *Journal of the National Education Association,* Vol. 47 (Nov., 1958), pp. 538–540.
29. Macalpine, I. and Hunter, R. Rossini. Piano Pieces for the Primal Scene, *American Imago,* Vol. 9 (1952), pp. 213–219.
30. Maslow, A. H. Creativity in Self-Actualizing People, in *Creativity and Its Cultivation,* pp. 83–95.
31. Maslow, A. H. Emotional Blocks to Creativity, *Journal of Individual Psychology,* Vol. 14 (1958), pp. 51–56.
32. Maslow, A.H. Personality Problems and Personality Growth, in *The Self,* pp. 232–246.
33. Maslow, A. H. *Toward a Psychology of Being* (Princeton, N.J.: D. Van Nostrand, 1962), pp. 129–130.
34. McClelland, D. C. *Personality* (New York: William Sloane, 1951), p. 485.
35. McKellar, Peter. *Imagination and Thinking* (New York: Basic Books, 1957).
36. Meier, N. C. Factors in Artistic Aptitude, *Psychology Monograph,* Vol. 51, No. 5 (1939), pp. 140–158.
37. Montmasson, J. M. *Invention and the Unconscious* (London) K. Paul, French, and Trubner, 1931).
38. Mooney R. L. Groundwork for Creative Research, in *The Self,* pp. 261–270.
39. Murray, H. A. Vicissitudes of Creativity, in *Creativity and Its Cultivation,* pp. 96–118.
40. Nietzsche, F. Ecce Homo, *The Philosophy of Nietzsche* (New York: Modern Library, 1927), pp. 896–897.
41. Patrick, Catherine. Creative Thought in Artists, *Journal of Psychology,* Vol. 4 (Jan., 1937), pp. 35–73.
42. Poincaré, H. *The Foundations of Science* (New York: Science Press, 1913).
43. Rank, Otto. *Art and the Artist* (New York: Alfred A. Knopf, 1932).
44. Reynolds, Sir Joshua. *Discourses on Art* (Chicago: Packard and Co., 1945), p. 164.
45. Rogers, C. R. *On Becoming A Person* (Boston: Houghton Mifflin Co., 1961), p. 353.
46. Rogers, Carl R. Toward a Theory of Creativity, in *Creativity and Its Cultivation,* pp. 69–82.
47. Schachtel, E. G. *Metamorphoses* (New York: Basic Books, 1959), p. 242.
48. Schneider, D. E. *The Psychoanalyst and the Artist* (New York: Farrar Straus and Giroux, 1950), p. 58.
49. Segal, Hanna. A Psychoanalytic Approach to Aesthetics, *International Journal of Psychoanalysis,* Vol. 33, (1952), pp. 196–207.
50. Sharpe, Ella. Certain Aspects of Sublimation and Delusion, *International Journal of Psychoanalysis,* Vol. 11 (1930), pp. 12–23.
51. Spearman, C. E. *The Creative Mind* (New York: Appleton-Century, 1931), p. 83.
52. Spender, S. The Making of a Poem, *Partisan Review,* Vol. 13, No. 3 (Summer, 1946), pp. 294–308.
53. Stein, M. I. Creativity and Culture, *Journal of Psychology,* Vol. 36 (Oct., 1953), pp. 311–322.

54. Sterba, R. and E. Beethoven and His Nephew, *International Journal of Psychoanalysis,* Vol. 33 (1952), pp. 470–478.
55. Taylor, I. A. The Nature of the Creative Process, in *Creativity: An Examination . . .,* pp. 51–82.
56. Van der Sterren, H. A. The "King Oedipus" of Sophocles, *International Journal of Psychoanalysis,* Vol. 33 (1952), pp. 343–350.
57. Vinacke, W. E. *The Psychology of Thinking* (New York: McGraw-Hill, 1952).
58. Wallas, G. *The Art of Thought* (New York: Franklin Watts, 1926), p. 85.
59. Weiss, J. Cezanne's Technique and Scotophilia, *Psychoanalytic Quarterly,* Vol. 22, No. 3 (1953), pp. 413–418.
60. Whiting, C. S. *Creative Thinking* New York: Reinhold, 1958).
61. Wilson, R. N. Poetic Creativity, Process, and Personality, *Psychiatry,* Vol. 17, No. 2 (May, 1954), pp. 163–176.
62. Wilson, R. C., et al. The Measurement of Individual Differences in Originality, *Psychological Bulletin,* Vol. 50, No. 5 (Sept., 1953), pp. 262–370.
63. Zilboorg, G. Psychology of the Creative Personality, in *Creativity: An Examination . . . ,* pp. 21–32.

II

THEORY AND POLICY

4. FRAMES OF REFERENCE FOR CREATIVE BEHAVIOR IN THE ARTS

J. P. Guilford

If my interpretation of this situation is correct, we have gathered here a group of individuals representing the various arts, who desire to further their understanding of what it means to be creative and to give thought to procedures for investigating creative performance in the arts. The title chosen for this conference, "Creative Behavior in the Arts," by its appropriate emphasis on "behavior," implies that many of the problems encountered in the pursuit of these objectives lie in the realm of psychology. We have also in the gathering a group of psychologists, and there is rather obvious expectation on the part of organizers of the conference that there shall be fruitful intercommunication, cross fertilization of ideas, and, hopefully, some hybrid offspring with superior qualities.

As a psychologist who has devoted quite a number of years to investigations pertaining more or less directly to the potential understanding of creative behavior in general, I shall offer some suggestions that I hope will be helpful. I have chosen to emphasize frames of reference that I have found very useful in connection with the investigation of creative thinking and creative production. I shall speak first of the needs for frames of reference and how they facilitate progress in research. I shall describe two major frames of reference or theoretical models that I have found exceedingly useful and meaningful and show how they are readily adaptable to investigations of creative behavior in the arts.

NEEDS FOR FRAMES OF REFERENCE

Whether or not anyone here decides to adopt the frames of reference that I shall describe, I should like to emphasize that any serious investigator, in basic science or in technology, will find a good frame of reference very helpful. A frame of reference may be as broad as a philosophical point of view or as circumscribed as a limited scientific theory. The kind that is close to a scientific theory is most useful to the investigator of some particular domain such as creative behavior. The advantages are the same as those of a scientific theory. Why do we need scientific theory?

Without scientific theory, the investigator has no major goals or directions; it is a case of the proverbial "ship without a rudder." It is not enough just to have a strong desire "to do research." Undirected effort is often futile. Such an investigator is likely to pick away at minor problems, here and there, as fancy of the moment dictates or as opportunity comes his way. Only

Reprinted by permission of the author. Paper presented to the Conference on "Creative Behavior in the Arts" sponsored by the University of California at Los Angeles, Feb. 18–20, 1965.

more or less by chance is he likely to work on significant problems and to make a lucky strike, if he ever does.

A scientific theory is a source of significant problems, each problem a question, to which an answer is sought. Progress depends very much on being able to ask questions and to ask the right questions and the significant questions. Theory generates questions and also provides a basis for determining whether questions, however generated, are significant ones. Obtaining answers to questions by way of empirical testing, known as research, should be expected either to support the theory or not to support it. In the latter case, a change in theory may be called for. The need to change a theory is no disgrace. In research, one cannot afford to be afraid of making mistakes. Such fears put a damper on creative production. Correction of mistakes at least holds the prospect for real progress. Finding out what is not true is often as informing as finding what *is* true. And, very often, two alternative, positive, hypotheses can be tested, in which case either outcome is a positive gain.

REQUIREMENTS FOR A GOOD FRAME OF REFERENCE

A good frame of reference for an investigator's purpose has three important specifications; it should be comprehensive, it should be systematic, and it should be basic.

When I say that a frame of reference should be comprehensive, I do not mean that it should be of the broad, philosophical type. It should be sufficiently restricted to generate questions that can be answered by empirical tests by empirical procedures. But it should not be so circumscribed that one loses sight of the larger picture, for all phenomena have significant ramifications. Understanding one item in a complex of items depends in part upon knowing interrelationships. Keeping a broader view is needed to ensure that some item, perhaps an important one, if not a crucial one, may not be overlooked.

Some investigators, in their legitimate efforts to simplify things, in their dutiful application of the principle of parsimony, are likely to eliminate from possible view some of the phenomena that should come within the scope of their observations. Too many psychologists, at least, have overdone the urge to simplify, with the result that significant phenomena have been excluded from consideration. I urge you not to make the same mistake.

A good frame of reference is systematic. The only hope of human understanding of natural phenomena is the fact that there are regularities in nature. Such regularities are what we are seeking within the sphere of our investigations. They offer the possibilities of principles and scientific laws. Principles and laws provide a shorthand type of apprehending information, enlarging the scope of our understanding and our powers to operate with phenomena. In the pursuit of further simplification and at the same time larger grasps of information, model building becomes possible. Model building is theory construction.

It appears to be in the nature of human thinking to resort to one or more of a few standard types of models, which can be quickly pointed out. In the psychological development of children, Inhelder and Piaget (1964) point out that there is growth in conceptions of what they call "seriation." By seriation they mean the arrangement of items of information in linear order, each item related to the next in line in the same manner, e.g., larger than, harder than, or more beautiful than. In the adult, particularly the educated adult, thinking in terms of abstract dimensions becomes more or less natural. Thus, we have dimensional models, which are most widely applied in mathematics and in the physical sciences.

Inhelder and Piaget (1964) also point to a parallel development in the recognition of classes and of classes within classes, in other words, hierarchical systems or models. Such models have been relatively more common in the biological sciences, in the classification schemes of Linnaeus. They are not unknown in psychology and in psychiatry.

A third type of model, not nearly so well known, has been called "morpho-logical," by the astronomer Zwicky (1957). Basically, this type of model is a cross classification of phenomena, in intersecting categories. The chemist's periodic table introduced by Mendeleev is a good example, in which the chemical elements are arranged in rows and columns, each row and each column representing a different category. It could also be referred to as a "logical matrix." An ordinary matrix, as in mathematics, has two dimensions. There is no reason for not extending the model to three or more dimensions, if necessary. I have advocated the use of the morphological type of model in psychology and later I shall give an example of a three-dimensional one.

A fourth type of model owes its origin most largely to the communication engineers and to the fields of cybernetics and computer technology. It is well-named as an "operational" type of model, for it conceives of events in terms of an interconnected series of transmissions of information. In the course of time, there have been some steps in this direction made by psychologists in attempting to account for sequences of events in behavior. But for the most part, the operational model utilized by psychologists has been an over-simplified one constituted of stimulus and response. Taking their cues from computer technology and the efforts to stimulate human thinking and problem solving by means of computers, some psychologists are now proposing more complex and more descriptive operational models. I shall present an example of this kind of model.

When I say that a model should be basic, I am thinking in terms of basic science. Many of the problems with which art teachers are concerned are educational in nature and therefore technological rather than scientific in the basic sense. But the models of basic psychology should be relevant in educational investigations, just as chemical models are relevant in the studies of pharmacology or of petroleum engineering. There is no particular harm in developing models that may appear to represent phenomena more directly or more completely in a technological setting, but basic scientific models should carry the technological investigator a long way and serve certain of his purposes very well. In the present context, what I am suggesting is that the investigator into the realm of creativity in art could find certain psychological models quite useful; including their concepts and principles.

TWO PSYCHOLOGICAL FRAMES OF REFERENCE

I shall present for your consideration two psychological models, one in the operational category and the other morphological. They are not at all in the form of alternative models between which a choice has to be made. Being different in type, both can be applied and they are quite consistent with one another, in fact quite supplementary. They merely serve somewhat different purposes, they imply different kinds of problems and approaches, but share many of the same concepts and principles.

The model to be mentioned first is an operational one. The reason for mentioning it first is that it comes closer to a general description of psychological events with which all of you have had personal acquaintance. For the same reason, there has been some historical precedent. The model in question attempts to depict in very general form the events in problem solving. I might have said "events in *creative* problem solving," but that would be somewhat redundant. After a number of years of considering the relation of creative thinking to problem solving, I have come to the conclusion that wherever there is a genuine problem there is some novel behavior on the part of the problem solver, hence there is some degree of creativity. Thus, I am saying that all genuine problem solving is creative; I leave the question open as to whether all creative thinking is problem solving; it may be. At any rate, the relationship is so close that a problem-solving model is very relevant here.

The other model is more abstract but it is more basic and of greater consequence. It is of the morphological type. It arose out of some 20 years of efforts to analyze intelligence into its component abilities and is known as the "structure of intellect." Concepts arising out of the second model have been very serviceable in filling out the first, as we shall see.

The Problem-Solving Model. . Three progenitors of the problem-solving model will be mentioned. One was designed to describe a quite general sequence of events in problem solving; one to present an outline of the steps in creative production; and one more specifically for the steps in an ordinary invention, such as comes to the attention of the patent office. John Dewey (1910) offered the first attempt of such a model, when he pointed out the following steps in typical problem solving see Fig. 1): awareness that a problem or a difficulty exists; analysis of the problem, leading to understanding of its nature; suggestion of possible solutions; and testing the alternative solutions by a process of judgment and accepting or rejecting solutions.

Graham Wallas (1926) suggested four similar steps: preparation, which involves collecting information that may be needed; incubation, which means a temporary pause or relaxation of effort; inspiration, or the moment of insight or flash of genius; and evaluation, with elaboration of the created product.

Rossman (1931) considered what the typical inventor goes through in the total process of arriving at a new invention and concluded that there are seven steps: a need or difficulty is observed; the problem is formulated; available information is surveyed; solutions are formulated; solutions are critically examined; new ideas are formulated; and the new ideas are tested.

Similarities among these three operational models, evidently developed independently, should be obvious, supporting the earlier assertion of the strong connection between problem solving and creative production, if, indeed, they are not one and the same. I should say that the major difference is the mention of incubation in the Wallas model. I consider this a logical error, for incubation is a state or condition rather than a psychological operation. This is not to deny the role of incubation, or to degrade it, but to place it in proper perspective.

The model for problem solving . . . was developed, taking into account the traditional models but also the structure-of-intellect theory and some of the more recent findings of neurology, experimental psychology, and communication theory. It is consequently somewhat elaborate, yet embodying simple principles. We are not concerned with all the detailed features of the model here. Those features most pertinent to our present needs will be explained.

In common with earlier models, the upper row of rectangles indicates a temporal sequence of events moving from left to right, with the sensing and understanding of the problem (cognition) being followed by generated solutions (production). The main difference is the addition of a repeated cycle of cognition and production, as suggested by the Rossman model. Such cycles could go on and on, of course, but one repeated cycle is sufficient to demonstrate the principle of repeated attempts at understanding and solution generation. Missing from the direct sequence is the step

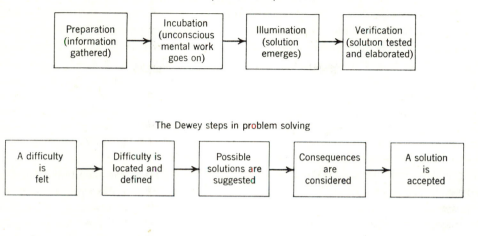

The Wallas steps in creative production

| Preparation (information gathered) | → | Incubation (unconscious mental work goes on) | → | Illumination (solution emerges) | → | Verification (solution tested and elaborated) |

The Dewey steps in problem solving

| A difficulty is felt | → | Difficulty is located and defined | → | Possible solutions are suggested | → | Consequences are considered | → | A solution is accepted |

The Rossman steps in the course of a typical invention

| Need or difficulty observed | → | Problem formulated | → | Available information surveyed | → | Solutions formulated | → | Solutions critically examined | → | New ideas formulated | → | New ideas tested |

Figure 1. Three traditional conceptions of the sequence of events in creative production, problem solving, and invention.

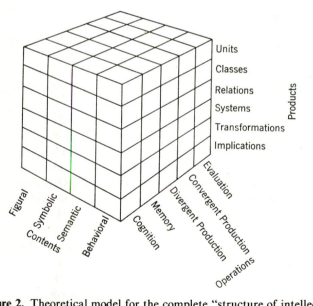

Figure 2. Theoretical model for the complete "structure of intellect."

of evaluation, which is put to one side (below the main stream), and which is repeated at every stage to indicate that there is continual self checking of behavior. Although evaluation may play its heaviest role after production, it can undoubtedly influence other operations at any time.

A novel addition is the memory-storage panel, placed at the bottom of the scheme to indicate that what happens at any moment along the course of problem solving can be and probably is influenced by what the thinker has in his memory storage. Most of the generated information in connection with production, also in connection with cognition and evaluation, comes from that source. New information that the thinker solicits and absorbs from his environment has at least a little time in memory storage before it is utilized. I shall ask you to put into your memory storage for use a bit later the fact that there are four major kinds of operation involved in the model—cognition, memory, production, and evaluation.[1]

The second important feature of the model that should engage our attention is the fact that there are four distinct kinds of information represented in memory storage, for this has far-reaching consequences. The four kinds of illustrated information are segregated for easy classification. First, at the extreme left we see some visual forms, having different visual properties of shape, size, and so on. Such information is concrete, much as we perceive it through the visual channel.

Next, to the right of the visual-figural information is a set of information called "symbolic," for the reason that when the individual processes information arising from stimuli such as letters, numbers, and musical notations, it is not the visual-figural properties with which he deals, but rather something for which those signs stand, as he has learned in his culture. The term "symbolic" here should not be extended too far. It does not include such things as Freudian symbols or national flags and the like. I shall give a different account of such symbolism later.

The third kind of information is touched off in our nervous systems by familiar objects of printed or spoken words that are meaningful to us. A printed word has shape, which is a figural property; it is a certain sequential coination of letters, which is a symbolic unit; and it carries to the person who can read the word the communication of an idea, which is semantic. These three kinds of information are often distinguished by those who write about language and by others.

The fourth kind of information, behavioral, is used by everybody every day but without the realization that it represents a distinct kind of information. It is information involved in the understanding of one person by another, often without the medium of verbal communication. The cues are in the form of facial expressions, bodily postures, tone of voice, and bodily movements. We implicitly recognize this kind of information when we say "Actions speak louder than words," or "It is not so much what you say as how you say it."

Information and Fields of Work. The four kinds of information were forced upon our attention in the Aptitudes Research Project at the University of Southern California, by findings concerning intellectual abilities. It has been demonstrated repeatedly that it takes quite different abilities to deal with or to process the four different kinds of information, even when performing the same operation—cognition, memory, production, or evaluation. There are parallel sets of abilities for dealing with the different kinds of information. But more of that later; here it is desirable to point out some of the consequences of all this for different kinds of work in everyday life, and more particularly in the various arts.

[1]Further details concerning the operations represented in this model may be found in . . . [Guilford (1964)].

Figural information is the psychological meat of those whose occupation calls upon its members to deal with concrete problems. Of the non-artist groups, the mechanic, the athlete, the aircraft pilot (especially of small aircraft), and the inventor of gadgets come first to mind. Artists of various kinds are very much concerned with figural information of one kind or another. At this point we must bring in a new distinction, for concrete information can be of auditory or of kinesthetic origin as well as visual. The field of visual-figural abilities has been rather extensively explored, with almost no investigation of abilities in the auditory or the kinesthetic modes of information.

Obviously, among artists dependent upon visual-figural information are painters, sketchers, sculptors, designers, and all their variations. Artists dependent upon auditory-figural information are musical composers, arrangers, and musical performers. The poet should be mentioned, to the extent that rhymes and rhythms have auditory properties. Kinesthetic information is of significance for the choreographer and the dance performer, although visual information also plays a role for these groups.

Symbolic information is the meat of the mathematician, the modern logician, the cryptographer, the linguist, and the chemist. With symbolic information defined in the limited way that it is in connection with the problem-solving model, there is little to offer in the way of applications in fields of art.

Semantic information being so much connected with words, and words with communication, occupations that deal very much with verbal counication are heavier processors of semantic information—scientists, writers, speakers, lawyers, and teachers, for example. Among artists whose mode of expression is verbal are writers of various kinds of output—fiction, non-fiction, poetry, plays, librettos, and lyrics.

Behavioral information is of relatively great importance to people who deal directly with other people, who must understand them and possibly attempt to control them. Among such occupations we can list politicians, statesmen, salesmen, policemen, teachers, social workers, and psychiatrists. Among the artists who deal heavily with behavioral information are writers of psychological novels and dramas; directors of drama, and actors; cartoonists and portrait painters; and sculptors (such as Michaelangelo or Rodin).

I do not wish to leave the impression that any one artist or type of artist deals in only one kind of information. Many artists often process more than one kind of information in the pursuit of their creative productions. The painter or the composer or the sculptor or the choreographer may first conceive of his theme in semantic form, then proceed to translate it into figural form. Only the modern type of painter may entirely lack semantic information in his product.

The four kinds of information are like four different languages and there is the possibility of making translations from one to another. There are limitations to translating, however, for "vocabularies" are not complete and fully parallel in all four of the languages. Each artist may find it much easier to think in terms of one of the languages and may know another language so poorly that he cannot succeed in making the translation. Problems of translation must surely come into the sphere of investigation in the psychology of the arts.

The Structure-of-Intellect Model. Fig. 2 presents a view of the structure-of-intellect model, a three-dimensional matrix or morphological model; a cross-classification of human intellectual abilities, known and yet to be demonstrated. Each cell represents a unique kind of ability or intellectual skill, of which 120 are hypothesized by the theory and 70 have been demonstrated.

When first conceived in this form, less than 50 such abilities had been demonstrated. The model has since served as the very useful source of suggestions as to where to look for new kinds of abilities, and further explorations are in progress. I mention this in support of an earlier statement about the advantages of having a productive theory or frame of reference.

In this model you will recognize the four kinds of information or content already discussed, also the four kinds of operations mentioned in connection wlth the problem-solving model. But here are represented *five* kinds of operations. The reason is that a distinction has to be made between two kinds of production abilities—*divergent* production and *convergent* production. Both have to do with the retrieval of information from memory storage, but convergent production occurs under severe restrictions. Starting with the given information, there is only one right or conventionally acceptable answer. The best examples of this kind of production are found in mathematics and logic. In divergent production, a variety of solutions or ideas is possible, under the freedom offered by the problem and the relaxed judgment of the thinker. The arts are notorious for such latitudes and they thus offer opportunities and challenges to the divergent thinker.

The entirely new concept in the structure-of-intellect model, not explicitly demonstrated in the problem-solving model (but actually illustrated there), is that of *products.* Psychological products are the special forms in which information is processed; as units, relations, classes, systems, transformations, and implications. Each and every separate item shown in memory storage . . . or, rather, the information that it stands for or implies, can be taken as a unit. A figural unit may be a letter, a geometric form, or the outline of a familiar object. A symbolic unit may be a familiar syllable or word, a bar of music, or a code letter or word. Concepts are semantic units; so are what are popularly called "ideas." Behavioral units are states of mind—perceptions, feelings, intentions, and the like. Examples of systems are the two theoretical models of which I have been speaking, although there are many simpler instances . . . when we analyze them to find the interrelationships among their parts. Examples of other kinds of products will come out in subsequent discussion.

Divergent-Production Abilities. Let us concentrate a while on the abilities in the divergent-production operation category, for it is believed that they play important roles in creative thinking. It should be kept in mind that the operation of production is a matter of generating items of information by retrieval or recall of those items from memory storage. The chances are that, to solve a new problem, those items of information must be recalled in new connections or in revised form, and this is where novelty comes in.

Before the divergent-production category of abilities was recognized, a number of abilities were found and described under the headings of fluency, flexibility, and elaboration. One test of fluency asks the examinee to produce items of information in response to given information as rapidly as he can. For example, in the verbal or semantic category, we ask him to list as many things as he can that are white, soft, and edible. For a parallel figural ability, we ask him to sketch simple objects or designs, each containing a circle or some other prescribed element. In these tests, units of information are being produced.

In another verbal-fluency test we ask the examinee to produce a list of four-word sentences. In such a task, the generation of a sentence means the organizing of production of a semantic system. In a parallel figural test, we give the examinee a set of elemental figures, such as a circle, a rectangle, a triangle, and a trapezoid, which he is to combine in various ways to produce more complex objects, in other words, figural systems.

In one verbal test for flexibility, we mention a very familiar object such as a newspaper, asking the examinee to suggest several unusual uses to which it can be adapted, all different. In a parallel figural test, we present a small set of figures that differ in several respects, each with some degree of complexity, asking him to form as many classes as he can, of three figures each. Similarities in terms of different attributes permit the regrouping of the figures in different ways. At first glance these two tests do not appear to be parallel, but psychologically they are; they both require the examinee to go from one class to another. Each unusual use of a newspaper (such as "to swat flies," "to light a fire," or "to wrap garbage") reclassifies it according to some particular property just as regrouping figures does in the other test. The product involved is that of class and the flexibility is shown in readily going from one class to another. You may have heard that one of the common diseases of the uncreative person is a "hardening of the categories."

For another kind of flexibility in the semantic context, we give a test called Plot Titles. Giving the examinee a very short story plot, we ask him to suggest alternative, appropriate titles. We may or may not instruct him to make the titles clever; some of them will be clever and some not. The number of clever answers is the score. Clever titles involve a playful shifting of views of the facts of the given story, in other words, revisions or transformations, which show up in titles in the form of puns, alliterations, and other literary tricks.

In the figural category of information, we give a Match Problems Test. This is based upon the familiar game that starts with a layout of adjacent squares or triangles, each side of which is a movable match. The examinee is told to remove a specified number of matches to leave a specified number of squares or triangles and to solve each problem in as many different ways as he can. Here, again, the examinee must be flexible. He must be able to take new looks at his problem and to strike off in new directions. The "new look" means a revision or a transformation. Being ready to transform given information and to revise our strategies accordingly is an important contribution to creative thinking. Transformations enable us to use information that is retrieved from memory storage in new ways, thus contributing to creative resourcefulness.

Ability to elaborate upon information has long been recognized as an important contributor to artistic production. The artist typically generates schema or systems first, to which he gives flesh and blood later. There are always finishing touches needed to round out the final product. We get at the elaboration ability in the semantic area in a test that calls for elaboration of a plan, for which only an outline of major steps is given. The number of detailed steps given in limited time is the score. In the structure-of-intellect theory, elaboration has been recognized as a matter of producing implications. That is, the details given to round out a scheme are implied by the scheme itself, and one added detail may lead to another. Where one item of information leads naturally to another, we have an implication. A more recently developed test of semantic elaboration is called Possible Jobs. Given is a relatively simple but realistic picture, such as a setting sun to which the examinee is to respond by listing occupations or groups of people for which the design may serve as a symbol. This test serves to measure the same ability as the Planning Elaboration test.

In the figural context, we offer simple lines or outlines of objects, asking the examinee to add lines of his own, as in our test called Decorations. Outlines of pieces of furniture and of clothing are presented and the number of appropriate additions is the score, where "appropriate" is given a very liberal interpretation. The same outline objects are presented twice, so there is added room for divergent production. As in the verbal tests, the lines are added by implication from what is given.

No examples were given for tests of divergent production involving symbolic information for the reason that this category of information is of little or not relevance for art. Remember that I ruled out of the symbolic category the kinds of symbolism that are so common in art. I now suggest that such symbolism really belongs under the heading of the product category of implications. The Possible Jobs test is an example. As in this test, symbolism in art often crosses the boundaries of information categories, hence involves the translation problem.

Nor were examples given for divergent production of *behavioral* information. At this point in time we are still in the hypothesis stage, for although the structure-of-intellect model predicts such abilities, we have only recently started research designed to test the hypothesized abilities. As a matter of fact, we have only recently demonstrated that there are *any* abilities for dealing with behavioral information at all. But a study testing the hypothesis that there are six abilities for cognition of behavioral information has just recently been successfully completed, giving strong faith in the expectation of other behavioral abilities, including those hypothesized for divergent production.

A word should be added regarding evaluation abilities, in view of the importance given to that concept in creative thinking and problem solving. I must confess that, although we have demonstrated a dozen evaluation factors, the rather limited kinds of tests that demonstrate those abilities suggest that only logical criteria are involved, for example, criteria such as identity and logical consistency. I am sure that the criteria of what is good and satisfying in art go well beyond those criteria. Psychologists have shied away from questions of value, but such problems must be faced, for, involving human behavior as they do, they should be challenges to the investigating psychologists as well as to investigating artists.[2]

SUMMARY

This paper has stressed the importance of having a frame of reference or theory as a source of significant problems in the conduct of research. It has suggested two psychological models that should serve the investigator in the area of creative artistic behavior; a model for the operations involved in problem solving, in which creative components are characteristic, and a model for the whole range of intellectual abilities, among which are many that are apparently relevant for success in creative artistic production. The concepts and principles offered by these models should be quite adaptable and serviceable in pursuing further understanding of the creative artist and his behavior.

References

Dewey, J. *How we think*. Boston: D. C. Heath, 1910.
Guilford, J. P. Creative abilities in the arts. *Psychol. Rev.*, 1957, *64*, 110–118.
Guilford, J. P. Three faces of intellect. *Amer. Psychologist*, 1959, *14*, 469–479.
Guilford, J. P. The psychology of creativity. *Creative Crafts*, 1960, *1*, 5–8.
Guilford, J. P. Creativity in the visual arts. *Creative Crafts*, 1962, *3*, 2–5.
Guilford, J. P. Basic problems in teaching for creativity. Unpublished paper presented at the Conference on Creativity and Teaching Media, held at La Jolla, California, Aug. 31 through Sept. 3, 1964.

[2]Further information concerning the structure of intellect may be found elsewhere (Guilford, 1959; Guilford and Merrifield, 1960; Guilford and Hoepfner, 1963). For further thoughts on the psychology of creativity in the arts, see other sources (Guilford, 1957, 1960, 1962).

Guilford, J. P. and Hoepfner, R. Current summary of structure-of-intellect factors and suggested tests. *Rep. psychol. Lab.,* No. 30. Los Angeles: Univ. Southern California, 1963.

Guilford, J. P. and Merrifield, P. R. The structure of intellect model: its uses and implications. *Rep. psychol. Lab.,* No. 24. Los Angeles: Univ. Southern California, 1960.

Inhelder, B. and Piaget, J. *The early growth of logic in the child.* New York: Harper and Row, 1964. (Trans. by E. A. Lunzer and D. Papert.)

Rossman, J. *The psychology of the inventor.* Washington, D.C.: Inventors Publishing Co., 1931.

Wallas, G. *The art of thought.* London: C. A. Watts, 1926, 1945.

Zwicky, F. *Morphological analysis.* Berlin: Springer-Verlag, 1957.

5. CREATIVE THINKING AND CONCEPTUAL GROWTH

J. Richard Suchman

The terms "creative thinking" and "conceptual growth" may have different meanings for different people, so I shall begin by defining them in the sense that they will be used in this paper.

Creative thinking has two defining characteristics. First, it is autonomous; that is, it is neither random nor controlled by some fixed scheme or external agent, but is wholly self-directed. Secondly, it is directed toward the production of a new form—new in the sense that the thinker was not aware of the form before he began the particular line of thought.

Conceptual growth is the expansion, elaboration, or other modification of a conceptual framework to provide meaning for a greater sector of experience. Through conceptual growth, more units of experience become meaningful, and more meaning is found in each unit. It is a step toward a more unified system of ideas at a higher level of abstraction, or toward a broader system of ideas at the same level.

CREATIVE THINKING AND EDUCATION

The question to be considered in this paper is just what role creative thinking has, or can have, in the process of conceptual growth. This question is particularly germane today because educators and psychologists are more concerned than ever with the development of thinking abilities, and because a growing number of experimental curriculum programs are based to some extent on a "discovery method" of teaching. In an age when the knowledge of mankind far exceeds the ability of the individual to keep track of it, much less to retain it, we are beginning to place a new premium on the ability to process information and abstract ideas from it, rather than simply to store it up.

Since Dewey's time we have paid lip service to the teaching of thinking as an educational objective, but in today's classrooms, pupils are still rewarded for how much they retain. The minds of pupils are still treated like little black boxes with informational inputs fed in at one end by the teacher and outputs tested at the other end. And the measure of quality is how well the outputs correspond to the inputs. How many teachers teach with the expectation that they can get more out of a box than they put in? Where I went to school it was automatically assumed that nobody could ever get 100 on a test.

Where creative thinking is used to further conceptual development we have what is usually called the discovery method. The popular idea of this method is that if you let a person have something of a free hand in obtaining and processing data, he will see new relationships, abstract concepts, generalize, and formulate principles, by himself without having these structured for him by somebody else. Hardly any person who has tried to get students to think their way inductively from data to concept would ever claim that all learning can or should take place in this manner,

Reprinted by permission of the author and *Gifted Child Quarterly,* Vol. 6, No. 3, 1962.

or that it is always the most efficient method when it can be used. But creative thinking has been employed in a wide range of teaching situations with marked success and there are instances where discovery is the only means by which a person can obtain a particular concept.

THE PROCESS OF CONCEPTUAL GROWTH

Bruner's (1958) studies of concept attainment have shown us much about the range of cognitive strategies that people use in solving problems where the solution requires the attainment of a concept. He has shown us that individuals use different strategies depending upon such conditions as the time limitations, the importance of speed, the importance of not making errors, etc. One strategy relies heavily on memory, another on luck, and still another on having lots of time. People are constantly adjusting their strategies of data intake even in the middle of a problem. This is a form of creative an adaptive flexibility that enables the learner to adjust his patterns of data intake and processing to correspond to his changing cognitive needs.

Inhelder and Piaget (1958) have identified developmental trends in the way that children pursue the casuality of physical events through the manipulation of apparatus. These investigators have also been concerned, like Bruner, with the strategies of concept attainment and particularly the kinds of changes that take place in these strategies as children grow older. They introduce the term operation which stands for a unit of action or thought, a tentative move that is reversible. An operation can be done and undone. They found that about the time the child enters elementary school he begins what is called operational thinking. He stands back from his environment and manipulates it experimentally, performing one operation after another on one part of the environment at a time. He observes the effects of these operations by comparing and relating them to each other. From these comparisons he begins to construct groupings and correspondences which in turn lead to conceptual models of causality. Creative thinking plays a central role in operational thinking as Inhelder and Piaget describe it.

Inhelder and Piaget also introduce two other concepts that help in the analysis of the process of conceptual growth. Assimilation refers to fitting a set of patterned stimuli into one's existing conceptual system. Sometimes percepts must be analyzed or distorted before they can be assimilated. If they cannot be assimilated they remain discrepant and as such are disturbing. They produce tensions. The only recourse one has is to adjust the conceptual system until it accomodates to the discrepant event. In other words, one creates a new conceptual category so that the event can be assimilated. It is only through successive accommodations that conceptual growth can occur. It is hard to imagine accommodation not involving some degree of creative thinking.

It is important to note that both Bruner and Piaget allowed their subjects to operate autonomously in an environment where one could perform operations and obtain a feedback of data immediately. They were able to see that under such conditions individuals over a wide range of ages can expand conceptual structures through self-directed operations.

CREATIVE THINKING IN THE
RESPONSIVE ENVIRONMENT

Two experimental teaching techniques that are currently being developed and tested make extensive use of creative thinking. One is a method devised by O. K. Moore at Yale for teaching pre-school children to read; the other is our Inquiry Training program at Illinois. Moore (1960) allows his subjects to manipulate freely the keys of an electric typewriter. The teacher says the name of each letter the cbild strikes and of course the child sees each letter as it is imprinted on the paper. No goals are set, no instructions given. Every time a child performs an operation by hitting a letter or a group of letters, he gets a response. When he hits groups of letters that are words, he is given the sound of the whole word. Through this method (which I have drastically oversimplified) three- and four-year-olds learn to read and type incredibly well and very quickly.

The key to Moore's approach is the responsive environment. He gives the learner freedom to operate in his own way, at his own pace, without any extrinsic rewards and pressures. The environment is highly responsive to each action the child performs. Moore opens the door to creative thinking by maximizing the child's autonomy and the feedback data he gets from his operations.

The Inquiry Training method (Suchman, 1961) is a variation on this same idea. Our subjects have mostly been sixth graders and they work in groups. They are shown short motion pictures of physics demonstrations which are designed to puzzle them. To these children the demonstrations are discrepant events. The children are asked to find an explanation of the episode by gathering information through question-asking. They are not permitted to ask for explanations, only data. They must then use the data to piece together their own explanations.

The key elements of this approach are once again the responsive environment and the freedom given the children to operate within it. They may seek assimilation of the problem episode in any way they wish. The data they obtain, the sequence in which they obtain them, and the hypotheses they formulate and test are all selected and used by the children themselves.

As yet we do not have clear evidence regarding the effects of the inquiry method on conceptual growth. There are many other variables that effect learning which we have had difficulty controlling. Furthermore, the exposure to the inquiry method has been brief—one hour a week for twenty-five weeks. Our subjects have been able to learn at least as much through inquiry as through traditional didactic methods.

The effects on motivation were much more marked. The children became quite actively involved in their investigations and maintained a high level of interest and excitement throughout the 25–week period of training. They also became more fluent in their production of questions and more precise and analytical in their probing. There was much less willingness to accept the perceptual whole as valid data. They tended instead to analyze the events and to test the relevance of each variable they could identify. This ability to analyze frees the child from the grip of his Gestalts and permits him to identify variables which can then be isolated and manipulated experimentally. In this manner relationships between variables can be discovered. A conceptual model of casuality can then be constructed and used for explaining, or in Plaget's terms, assimilating the original discrepant event.

CREATIVE THINKING IN A
PROGRAMMED ENVIRONMENT

Creative thinking can also be used in a selective way as part of an otherwise structured teaching program to help the student over certain crucial and difficult conceptual hurdles. The method used by the UICSM Project at Illinois—also known as the Beberman Mathematics Project—is an example of this (Beberman, 1958). They take the position that there is little point in talking about, let us say, the commutative principle unless the pupils have an almost intuitive understanding of just what the principle is. Too often when this is taught through a verbal didactic method the pupils acquire merely a superficial, mechanistic understanding. They know what they have to do to get the answer but they haven't the faintest notion of why. Beberman's method literally engineers the students into discovering the principle themselves.

His classes are given a series of mathematical operations to perform which can be done with simple arithmetic. The problems are arranged in order of increasing difficulty in that the numbers get larger and more difficult to handle arithmetically. However, it is possible to discover a short-cut that simplifies the calculations. By discovering this short-cut the pupil has discovered the commutative principle.

This is quite a different use of creative thinking than the loosely structured responsive environment technique. The learning situation is deliberately contrived to pressure the learner into being creative. The cognitive strain in each successive problem is greater than in the previous one and gradually builds up to intolerable levels. The necessity to reduce this strain becomes the mother of the invention of short-cuts.

In Bruner's terms, Beberman rigs the payoff matrix in such a way that the children become willing to take risks in trying out new ideas in place of the safer but more laborious method.

The commutative principle doesn't just drop into the child's lap the minute he starts to look for another approach. He works for it. He gets ideas and tries them out. He examines what he has done in previous problems. He is more likely to discover a principle by comparing problems and their solutions than by focusing on only one. Finally, somewhere along the line he notices something he hadn't noticed before and this will lead him to see the principle. But he is more likely to make such a discovery if he invents, experiments and makes comparisons.

SUMMARY

Teaching methods which permit the learner to operate autonomously in the search for new understandings utilize creative thinking to promote concept development. It has been widely observed and reported that children enjoy learning when they can think creatively. Discovery builds the self-esteem of the discoverer, who also develops a sense of autonomy and intellectual potency. According to Hunt (1961) there is intense excitement and pleasure in data processing itself.

But how does creative thinking serve the cognitive processes of learning? Conceptual growth—unless it is mediated entirely through verbal structuring—growth out of transactional episodes between the learner and his environment. The learner gathers data which he tries to assimilate by means of his existing concepts. Where the data cannot be assimilated, he either breaks them down into more basic units that can be assimilated, or he modifies his conceptual structure to accomodate the data. In this way concepts are modified and expanded to make room for discrepant events.

In any act of inquiry the quest for data takes the form of operational sequences. The ordering of these sequences according to a plan or system constitutes a strategy. Bruner found strategy to be a significant variable in his concept attainment experiments. The learner shifts and adjusts these strategies to maximize one or another objective in accordance to the kinds of results that offer the most reward. But the individual learner brings to any problem a unique constellation of abilities and concepts as well as a characteristic approach to concept attainment.

Thus his strategies must suit not only the problem and the kinds of solutions being rewarded, but they must also be attuned to his own individual cognitive and motivational characteristics. He must use the right strategy for him at any given instant. To learn how to do this well he must have freedom to adjust strategies of data collection and processing. Since he cannot be taught a single standard strategy that will work well under all circumstances, he must have a chance to work out his own ideas and discover for himself what works best in each situation. In short, he must have many opportunities to use creative thinking in the process of conceptual growth.

One way to promote the use of creative thinking as an aid to conceptual growth is to make the teacher's role less directive and more responsive, to have the learner focus on a problem, and allow him to gather data freely with the help but not the direction of the teacher. Another way is to present children with problems of data processing that impose so much cognitive strain that the learner tries to invent systems of handling the data more efficiently. If these systems have general validity they must represent some lawful properties of the environment. The discovery of such properties is the fundamental purpose of inquiry.

There are no doubt many other possibilities for facilitating conceptual growth by capitalizing on the creative thinking of the learner. Many of these have been and will continue to be invented by teachers who experiment with teaching techniques. Teachers who do this discover very rapidly what is effective and what is not . . . because there is no environment quite as responsive as a room full of children.

References

Beberman, M. *An Emerging Program of Secondary School Mathematics.* Cambridge: Harvard Univ. Press, 1958.

Bruner, J. S., Goodnow, Jacqueline and Austin, George A. *A Study of Thinking.* New York: John Wiley and Sons, 1956.

Hunt, J. McV. *Motivation Inherent in Information Processing and Action.* University of Illinois, Urbana. (Mimeo) 1961.

Inhelder, Barbel and Piaget, Jean. *The Growth of Logical Thinking from Childhood to Adolescence.* New York: Basic Books, 1958.

Moore, O. K. "Orthographic Symbols and the Preschool Child." Proceedings of the Third Minnesota Conference on Gifted Children. Minneapolis, 1960, pp. 91–101.

Suchman, J. Richard. "Inquiry Training: Building Skills for Autonomous Discovery." *Merrill-Palmer Quarterly,* Vol. 7, pp. 147–169. (July 1961).

6. SOME GUIDING PRINCIPLES IN EVALUATING EXCELLENCE

E. Paul Torrance

At various times during my research on creativity and giftedness I have reached several conclusions that I believe deserve to be applied rather generally to evaluating excellence. At the times these conclusions were reached, I was concerned with problems of identifying creative and/ or gifted children and young people. However, as I have become involved in problems of admission to graduate study, the appointment of new faculty, promotion and salary raises of faculty members, membership on the graduate faculty, criteria of creative achievement, and the like, it has seemed to me that these guiding principles might be useful in almost any kind of excellence evaluation. Thus, I shall summarize these conclusions I have reached on the basis of my research—or at least positions I have taken concerning some of the critical issues in excellence evaluation.

Creativity, a Distinguishing Characteristic

As I have continued to study and think about the whole realm of human achievement, I have held to the conviction reached early in my research that *creativity is a distinguishing characteristic of human excellence in every area of behaviour*. Creativity has long been recognized as essential in medical and scientific advances, invention, excellence in the arts, and the like. (Torrance, 1962, 1972). Creativity is an essential element in all genuine breakthroughs in science, literature, and the arts. I have insisted that creativity is also essential in excellence in human affairs.

I have never contended that creative ability be made the sole basis for identifying gifted children and young people nor that creativity be the sole criterion of outstanding achievement. However, I would argue strongly that creative ability *always* be one of the bases for identifying gifted children and young people and that the creativeness of one's achievements be one of the criteria used in evaluating the excellence of the achievement. Similarly, I would not advocate that creativity be the sole basis for evaluating students applying for admission to graduate study, faculty members being considered for membership on graduate faculties, appointees to college and university faculties, candidates for promotion, and the like. However, I would insist that it should be one of the criteria considered in making such evaluations.

Different Kinds of Excellence

I have held that it is important for human survival and the attainment of a healthy society to *evaluate and reward many different kinds of excellence*. James S. Coleman's studies of adolescent societies published in 1961 showed how narrow were the bases of excellence evaluation in American high schools. In some schools it was athletic prowess among boys and good looks or social skills among girls. Getzels and Jackson's study published in 1962 showed how teachers favour children who show excellence in intelligence over those who show excellence in creativity and favour those who show excellence in social adjustment over those who manifest excellence in moral courage.

Reprinted by permission from *Creativity Newsletter,* (Aligarh Muslim University, India) 1974, 4:1.

Study after study (Torrance, 1965) has shown that when different kinds of excellence are encouraged and evaluated in a classroom a different group of star performers or learners emerges. Perhaps this state of affairs is best symbolized by a generalization that I discovered in 1959 and which has continued to hold good since that time, namely, that if we identify as excellent or gifted those who rank in the 20 per cent on a test of intelligence or scholastic aptitude we will miss 70 percent of those who rank in the upper 20 per cent on a test of creative thinking. Some readers may recall that McNemar, in his 1965 presidential address before the American Psychological Association, ridiculed these findings as follows:

> The argument against the IQ is now being reinforced by the claim that the selection of the top 20% on IQ would mean the exclusion of 70% on tested creativity. This startling statistic, which implies a correlation of only .24 between IQ and creativity, is being used to advocate the use of creativity tests for identifying the gifted.

The correlations in the samples from which this generalization was derived were in fact somewhat lower than .24. In none of my discussions back in the 1960's was there any advocacy on my part for replacing measures of intelligence with measures of creativity. My plea, as was the case with Calvin Taylor (1968) and others, was to consider a wider range of abilities or kinds of excellence both in identification and in programme development.

Taylor's (1968) Multiple Talent Approach to Teaching considers not only excellence in academic and creative areas but also in planning, communicating, forecasting, and wisdom in decision making. Taylor has shown that as more of these talents are considered, we have an increasing number of gifted people. Taylor, Lloyd and Rollins (1971) maintain that as a natural by-product of the multiple talent development approach students acquired as much or even more information than they did in traditional classrooms. Students use their various talents to process and thereby acquire knowledge. They acquire a wider array and type of knowledge and do more things with this knowledge. They work at and beyond the fringe of knowledge. They project beyond present knowledge if they have a chance to use their forecasting talents to consider what might happen in the future.

EVALUATIVE CRITERIA RELEVANT TO PURPOSE

I have maintained that the *criteria used in evaluating excellence should be relevant to the purpose of the evaluation* rather than determined by some antiquated and irrelevant set of criteria. In some of my earlier contacts with special programmes for gifted children, I thought it almost tragic to identify children as gifted on the basis of their performance on intelligence tests and then expect them to excel in creative thinking. I would have considered it just as tragic to have identified children as gifted on the basis of creative ability and then to have provided them an educational programme devoid of opportunities to use and develop their creative potentialities.

Even in the evaluation of instruments to assess excellence, I have found myself the victim of the application of irrelevant criteria. Permit me to offer one example. Perhaps the most frequently quoted validity study of the *Torrance Tests of Creative Thinking* (TTCT) is one by Harvey, Hoffmesiter, Coates, and White (1970). They sought to test the validity of the TTCT with a group of 64 educators (male and female) against criterion measures such as Supernaturalism, Moral Relativism, Dictation of Classroom Procedures, Need for Structure-Order, Dogmatism, Authoritarianism, Curricular Traditionalism, Disciplinarianism, Encouragement of Student Exploration, Concreteness-Abstractness of Beliefs, and Belief System Classification. These investigators ignored the fact that the criterion measures are quite unrelated to theoretical rationale of the TTCT and that they were correlating personality variables with mental ability variables. Even so, it is interesting to note that Harvey and his associates obtained significant positive relationships between the creativity measures and Moral Relativism, Fostering Student Independence, and Fostering Exploration and significant negative relationships between creativity measures and Supernaturalism, Dictation of Classroom Procedure, and Need for Structure-Order. This is precisely what I would have predicted. Yet the results of this study are frequently cited as the sole basis for judging the TTCT to be without validity, rejecting research articles submitted for publication in refereed journals, and rejecting dissertation proposals using the TTCT.

I have also seen graduate students seeking admission victimized by the same kind of application of irrelevant criteria. Similarly I have seen candidates for promotion and for appointment on university faculties and candidates for admission to the graduate faculty victimized by the use of irrelevant criteria. Let me offer one example of this from what happened to the recommendation of a certain department in a large southern university for a new appointment at the associate professor level. The Department had worked very hard in formulating the criteria of selection and used a very elaborate system of evaluation and re-evaluation in selecting the appointee. The person selected by the Department met almost all of the criteria for the position and met them to a much higher degree than did any of the more than 50 other applicants. He has done some exceptionally imaginative and creative work, has an outstanding publication record in the most prestigeful refereed journals in his special field, and was highly recommended by some of the most prestigeful figures in his profession. He is going in a direction that I believe will give us the most important breakthroughs in the field of evaluating the mental and emotional functioning of children since Alfred Binet.

The committee appointed by the Provost to make the final decision concerning this appointment rejected the Department's recommendation. Among the reasons given for this decision was the invocation of such irrelevant criteria as the following:

Too many publications were co-authored. (The fact was that the majority of the candidate's articles listed the appointee as sole author. Some of the others were co-authored with his wife who is a partner in much of his independent research. A couple were team efforts.)

Too much of his research is on the same topic and related to his job. It does not reflect really independent effort. The entire history of invention and discovery indicates that almost all great breakthroughs have occurred in the context of group or team interaction. All of the most successful deliberate procedures for facilitating creative problem solving (Gordon, 1961; Osborn, 1963; Parnes, 1967) involve group interaction as an essential element. The productive, creative person is interdependent rather than independent.

The evaluating committee alleged that the candidate would have gotten more rigorous training in the Psychology Department at Columbia University than in Teachers' College, Columbia University. Even if the training in the psychology had been more rigorous, the trouble is that it would have been irrelevant and the candidate would have been incompetent to fill the position under consideration. Rigour in itself has little relevance to excellence evaluation.

The candidate was faulted for changing his major three times during his graduate career. The candidate's initial purpose in enrolling for graduate study was to become a school psychologist. When he received his M.A. degree his major was labelled as "Educational Psychology." In his doctorate, his major was labelled as "Measurement and Evaluation," a special area within educational and school psychology. The particular combination of studies of the candidate happened to be ideal for the position for which his appointment had been recommended. My contention, however, is that number of changes in jobs, graduate and undergraduate majors, and colleges is an irrelevant criterion of excellence. My own longitudinal studies of creative achievement (Torrance, 1971a) indicate that number of changes is positively and significantly related to intelligence, creative abilities, quantity and quality of creative achievement, and creativeness of future aspirations.

The evaluating committee complained that the candidate had made too many P (for passing) grades. The fact is that the key for interpreting the transcript indicated clearly that P was the only passing grade given in these courses. The unwarranted assumption, of course, is that graduate school grades are a good criterion of excellence in evaluating candidates for appointment at the associate professor level. A number of recent studies have shown that there is practically no relationship between college grades in such areas as medical practice, research in government laboratories, the National Space Agency, and the like (Taylor, 1972).

Thus, we see in just these few evaluative comments on one case for appointment to a university faculty the application of a variety of irrelevant criteria and numerous outright erroneous assumptions.

My real point is that we need to validate the criteria we use in identifying gifted students, admitting graduate students, awarding doctorates, appointing faculty members, and promoting them.

EXCELLENCE IN RACIAL AND ETHNIC MINORITIES

In evaluating excellence among racial and ethnic minorities, especially disadvantaged groups, it is important to give attention to those kinds of excellence that are encouraged and valued by the particular culture to which the person belongs.

It was not until I started working with disadvantaged black children in Georgia that I began to really understand how important it is that we stop trying to identify a universally gifted type child and begin looking for those kinds of giftedness that are valued by the particular subculture in which the child has been reared. From these experiences, I have taken the position that we should no longer insist on cultivating *only* those kinds of excellence that the dominant, affluent culture values. We should look for and encourage talents of the type that are valued in the various disadvantaged subcultures of our country. Since children tend to develop along the lines that are encouraged, the gifted children of a subculture are likely to be those who have developed to a high level those talents that are valued in that particular subculture.

Let me cite two illustrations—a positive one and a negative one. The positive illustration comes from a recent report (*Atlanta Constitution,* April 11, 1974, p. 4–B) by the associate dean of student affairs of the Harvard Medical School, Mary Howell. Her report gives evidence that ethnic minorities, women, and the poor have been the ones who have challenged medical myths and promoted new medical school programmes and innovations in medicine.

On the negative side I would like to cite a recent study by Caplan (1973) into the causes of the failure of so many of the federally-supported Youth Development Programmes. Many people had been saying that these programmes failed because the participants were unmotivated and unskilled. Caplan concluded that the programmes failed because the participants were highly motivated and highly skilled. These youths were, like most people, motivated to do the things that they can do best. The trouble was that the skills that they had mastered are those that insure their success within the ghetto community. Unfortunately the skills that make a person gifted on the street—hustling, rapping, signifying, gang leadership, psyching out people, fighting, athletics, etc.—may make him a failure as a mechanic, dishwasher, or maintenance man. The more talented is the young person in his own culture the more challenging is the problem of providing him meaningful, useful job training.

Caplan's conclusion is in line with my position that the education of racial and ethnic minorities and the poor should be based upon their strengths instead of their deficits (Torrance, 1973).

CREATIVITY, A MULTIVARIATE PHENOMENON

Creative ability is not a univariate phenomenon. Just as a person can attain excellence in an almost infinite number of ways, he can behave creatively in an almost infinite number of ways. Thus, to evaluate creative excellence or potentiality for such excellence, there is the problem of sampling adequately this universe of possible ways of behaving creatively. In assembling the TTCT I made a deliberate attempt to sample this universe as well as possible within the constraints of requirements in practical, educational situations. The TTCT tasks (Torrance, 1974) were devised so that they reflect different aspects of creative behaviour, that is, kinds of cognitive-affective functioning that facilitate effective creative behaviour. This was accomplished primarily by (1) analyzing the behaviour of eminent creative people as recorded in autobiographies and biographies as well as laboratory studies of the creative problem solving process and trying to identify the most important component skills and (2) subjecting scores derived from a variety of test tasks to factor analysis and selecting tasks that are factorially different. In summary, the criteria for selecting specific tests and testing materials were as follows:

(a) They must have relevance to creative theory.
(b) They must have relevance to adult creative behaviour in the "real world."
(c) They must sample different aspects of creative thinking.
(d) They must be attractive alike to children, adolescents, and adults.
(e) They must be open-ended so that a person can respond in terms of his experiences whatever these may have been.
(f) The instructions and response demands must be adaptable to the educational range from kindergarten through graduate school and professional education.
(g) They must yield data that can be scored reliably for such qualities as fluency, flexibility, originality, and elaboration.
(h) The testing materials, instructions for administration, time limits, and scoring procedures must be such that the use of the standard batteries in schools is feasible.

My associates and I have at various times assembled test batteries that are more appropriate than the basic battery for a particular age, ability, socio-cultural, educational or occupational group.

I believe that there are justifications for each of the above specifications but I shall discuss only one of these, that the *test tasks must be open-ended so that subjects be able to respond in terms of their experience whatever they may have been.* I realize that this stipulation results in certain difficulties in scoring. However, I believe that this is the nature of productive thinking, certainly divergent thinking. Furthermore, I believe single-answer formats would inescapably be biased in favour of some particular group. I believe that it has been my insistence on open-ended tasks that has been responsible for the fairly consistent finding that the TTCT has little or no racial, ethnic, or socioeconomic status bias (Torrance, 1971b).

ENVIRONMENTAL INFLUENCES AND EXCELLENCE

I hold that educators should be *concerned about those potentialities which, if given a chance, would result in excellence and which can be modified through educational experiences.* Rather early in my research it became clear that some children are treated in such ways that they sacrifice their creativity. I maintained that this did not detract from the value of either the test identifying this potentiality nor that of the potentiality. It also became clear that adults fail to recognize the value of many children's creative potentialities because these very potentialities make problems for the adults and may even be used against the adults if not guided along constructive lines. As time has elapsed, it has become clear that educational experiences can make a difference in the development and/or functioning of these abilities (Torrance & Torrance, 1973).

Only recently has the issue of heritability of the creative thinking abilities become fairly clear. A study by Pezullo, Thorsen, and Madaus (1972) found no evidence of hereditary variation in either the figural or verbal forms of the TTCT. Their subjects were 37 pairs of fraternal and 28 pairs of identical twins carefully selected and tested. These investigators found that short term memory (Jensen Level I abilities) has only a moderate index of heritability, .85. The heritability index for the figural and verbal measures of the TTCT approached zero. Another twin study by Richmond (1968) similarly found no evidence of heritability for the abilities assessed by the TTCT. Davenport (1967), using the Getzels and Jackson (1962) measures of creativity, did find weak evidence for heritability on most of the test tasks. The indications were so weak, however, that Davenport concluded that there was a wide range within which experience could influence the creative thinking abilities.

STATES OF CONSCIOUSNESS AND PERFORMANCE

Along with numerous others such as Gordon (1961), Maslow (1971), and Gowan (1972), I have attributed an important role in outstanding creative achievement to emotional, non-rational factors. In education and in evaluating abilities and achievement we have generally been pre-occupied with the fully conscious, the logical, the intellectual. This does not mean that states of consciousness other than ordinary waking consciousness have not existed in classrooms and testing situations. We have simply ignored them and pretended that they were not operating. We have organized our thinking, teaching procedures, and evaluation methods to deal with perhaps less than one-half of the brain power available. Certainly the history of invention, scientific discovery, literary and artistic creativity, and the like are filled with examples of breakthroughs that occurred in such states of consciousness as regression, meditation, reverie, daydreaming, internal scanning, hyperalertness, the hypnogogic, and the like. I believe that any serious effort in excellence evaluation must give serious consideration to the ability to use varying states of consciousness to go beyond what one is able to attain through conscious, logical efforts. States of consciousness other than ordinary awareness must be deliberately exploited.

SUMMARY

In summary, I would like to suggest the following guiding principles be considered in developing evaluation programmes where excellence, giftedness, and outstanding achievement are in question:

(1) Creativeness should always be one of the criteria considered, though not the sole criterion.
(2) Different kinds of excellence (multiple talents) should be evaluated.
(3) Evaluative criteria should be relevant to the purpose of the evaluation. Where possible, these criteria should be validated for the kind of excellence under consideration.
(4) Where racial and ethnic minorities are involved, attention should be given to those kinds of excellence that are valued by the particular subculture of the persons being evaluated.
(5) Creativity is a multivariate phenomenon and different kinds of creative thinking abilities should be samples in making an evaluation.
(6) Open-ended tasks should be a part of excellence evaluation since such tasks permit the respondent to use his experiences whatever they may have been.
(7) Attention should be given to those kinds of excellence that can be influenced by the environment.
(8) Various states of consciousness should be permitted and encouraged to facilitate optimal creative functioning.

References

Caplan, N. Street skills of many hard-to-employ youths may hinder success in job training programmes. *Newsletter* (Institute for Social Research, University of Michigan), 1973, 1 (19), 5, 7.
Coleman, J. S. *The Adolescent Society.* New York: Free Press, 1961.
Davenport, J. D. *A Study of the performance of monozygotic and dyzogotic twins and siblings on measures of scholastic aptitude, creativity and achievement.* (Doctoral dissertation, University of Maryland)` Ann Arbor, Michigan: University Microfilms, 1967. Order No. 68–3350.
Getzels, J. W., and Jackson, P. W. *Creativity and Intelligence.* New York: John Wiley and Sons, 1962.
Gordon, W. J. J. *Synectics.* New York: Harper and Row, 1961.
Gowan, J. C. *Development of the Creative Individual.* San Diego, Calif.; Robert R. Knapp, 1972.
Harvey, O. J., Hoffmeister, J. K., Coates, C., and White, J. A partial evaluation of Torrance's tests of creativity. *American Educational Research Journal,* 1970, 7, 359–372.
Maslow, A. H. *The Farther Reaches of Human Nature.* New York: Viking Press, 1971.
Osborn, A. F. *Applied Imagination.* (3rd. Ed.) New York: Charles Scribner's Sons, 1963.
Parnes, S. J. *Creative Behaviour Guidebook.* New York: Charles Scribner's Sons, 1967.
Pezzullo, T. R., Thorsen, E. E., and Madaus, G. F. The heritability of Jensen's level I and II and divergent thinking. *American Educational Research Journal,* 1972, 9, 539–546.

Richmond, B. O. Creativity in monozygotic and dyzogotic twins. Paper presented before American Personnel and Guidance Association, Detroit, April, 1968.

Taylor, C. W. Be talent developers as well as knowledge dispensers. *Today's Education,* 1968, 57 (9), 67–69.

Taylor, C. W. Can organizations be creative too? In C. W. Taylor (Ed.) *Climate for Creativity.* New York: Pergamon Press, 1972. Pp. 1–22.

Taylor, C. W., Lloyd, B., and Rollins, J. Developing multiple talents in classrooms through the implementation of research. *Journal of Research and Development in Education,* 1971, 4 (3), 42–50.

Torrance, E. P. *Guiding Creative Talent.* Englewood Cliffs, Prentice-Hall, 1962.

Torrance, E. P. Different ways of learning for different kinds of children. In E. P. Torrance and R. D. Strom (Eds.), *Mental Health and Achievement.* New York: John Wiley & Sons, 1965. Pp. 245–252.

Torrance, E. P. Is bias against job changing bias against giftedness? *Gifted Child Quarterly,* 1971, 15, 244–248. (a)

Torrance, E. P. Are the Torrance tests of creative thinking biased against or in favour of disadvantaged groups? *Gifted Child Quarterly,* 1971, 15, 75–80. (b)

Torrance, E. P. Predictive validity of the Torrance tests of creative thinking. *Journal of Creative Behavior,* 1972, 6, 236–252.

Torrance, E. P. Assessment of disadvantaged minority group children. *School Psychology Digest,* 1973, 2 (4), 3–10.

Torrance, E. P. *Norms-Technical Manual: The Torrance Tests of Creative Thinking.* Lexington, Mass.: Personnel Press/Ginn and Company, 1974.

Torrance, E. P., Torrance, J. P. *Is Creativity Teachable?* Bloomington, Indiana: Phi Delta Kappa, 1973.

"Challenging myths: Minority medical students have best growth abilities." *Atlanta Constitution,* April 11, 1974. P. 4–B.

7. DEVELOPMENT OF PROVISIONAL CRITERIA FOR THE STUDY OF SCIENTIFIC CREATIVITY

Norman Frederiksen,
Franklin R. Evans, and William C. Ward
Educational Testing Service

Research in the area of creativity has been handicapped by the lack of reliable and valid criterion measures. Much of the work on creativity has employed tests developed by Guilford and his collaborators to measure divergent production—tests such as Consequences and Brick Uses. Often these tests have been used as criterion measures. The use of a test which was developed to represent one cell in the structure of intellect—the divergent production of semantic units as a dependent variable interpreted as creativity is not consistent with Guilford's intention and could produce misleading results. Not that it is never appropriate to use Consequences as a dependent measure; it would be highly appropriate to do so when one is trying to increase ideational fluency by training procedure. But creative performance involves behaviors that are much more complex than ideational fluency, and the two things should not be confused.

A quite different approach to the study of creativity was that of MacKinnon and his collaborators, who studied the characteristics of persons of acknowledged creativity in comparison with those in the same field with lesser degrees of creativity. The method was to secure nominations by members of a profession (such as architects) of those who were most creative, and to invite these and other architects to Berkeley for a period of assessment. Differences found between the most creative people and those of lesser eminence were interpreted as characteristics of creative individuals. The main trouble with this approach is that the characteristics required to attain recognition by one's peers are not necessarily the same as are required to do creative work. In order to be *eminent,* it may be necessary for the scientist to be a good promoter as well as a good scientist.

The approach we are using is to develop tests of creative performance that may be characterized as intermediate or provisional criteria, using simulations or job samples of the work of a research psychologist (since that is the area we know most about). Such criterion tests, we hope will elicit interestingly complex behaviors that have a high degree of face validity. If the reliability and validity of such tests can be demonstrated, they should be useful in investigating correlates of various aspects of creative behavior and serving as dependent variables in experiments having to do with situational variables that might influence creativity. It seems feasible to focus the tests and experiments at the level of a second-year graduate student, a time when the student has mastered a significant amount of information but he has not yet become too specialized, and he still may be available (for a fee) to serve as a subject.

In this paper we propose, first, to describe the one such measure for which we have accumulated a fair amount of information about validity and reliability; and second, to describe more

Reprinted by permission from *Gifted Child Quarterly,* Vol. 19, No. 1, 1975. Paper presented at the Annual Meeting of the American Educational Research Association, New Orleans, February 26, 1973. The research was being supported by the Graduate Record Examination Board.

generally the battery of tests that is being developed and how they will be used in research on scientific creativity.

The **Formulating Hypotheses** (FH) test was designed to measure one aspect of scientific creativity: the interpretation of data, i.e., the ability to conceive of hypotheses that might account for research findings. Each item of FH consists of a graph or table showing findings from a research study. The sample item we have been using is a graph showing yearly rates of death from infectious diseases and rates of death from diseases of old age. The finding is stated as follows: "Rate of death from infectious diseases has decreased markedly since 1900, while rate of death from diseases of old age has increased." S is instructed to write hypotheses (possible explanations) that might account for, or help to account for, the finding.

The form of the test used in a recently-completed study* included seven items. They dealt, for example, with data showing that time lost from strikes was greatest in the summer months, and that World War II Navy recruits tested in June and July earned higher test scores on aptitude tests than those tested in other months. Ten minutes per item were allowed.

Five scores were obtained: (1) Number of Hypotheses proposed, (2) Number of *Acceptable* Hypotheses (a subset of *1*), (3) the Average Judged Quality of the hypotheses, (4) the Average Scale Value of the hypotheses (another quality measure based on a scoring method that minimized the influence of such factors as handwriting and quality of writing), and (5) the Average Number of Words per response.

Subjects were about 400 undergraduate students at two eastern colleges. They were first given tests of vocabulary and ideational fluency. Then the FH items were administered. A random third of the subjects received feedback after each FH item in the form of lists of model hypotheses which were of high quality. A second third were given models illustrating quantity rather than quality of hypotheses. The remaining subjects were given no models.

The median correlation between items for the Number of Hypotheses score was .39, and the reliability for the five-item posttest was .80. Reliabilities for the other four scores were as follows: Number of Acceptable Hypotheses, .67; Average Judged Quality, .60; Average Scale Value, .48; and Average Number of Words per Hypotheses, .87. Thus, scores of satisfactory reliability can be generated from a free-response test like FH—scores that reflect quality as well as quantity of performance.

Evidence for the independence of these scores for their construct validity was sought through Multivariate Analysis of Variance. The MANOVAs showed highly significant ($p<.001$) relationships involving both fluency and vocabulary. Ideational fluency was related to the *quantity* of hypotheses produced (Number of Hypotheses and Number of Acceptable Hypotheses), while vocabulary was related to *quality* scores (Average Judged Quality, Average Scale Value, and Number of Acceptable Hypotheses). Moreover, feedback treatments produced significant effects ($p < .001$). The quantity model led to higher scores on Number of Hypotheses and Number of Acceptable Hypotheses, and a lower Number of Words per item, while the quality model resulted in higher scores on Average Judged Quality. These results indicate that meaningful and discriminable indices of quality and quantity of ideas can be derived from the FH test.

The **Formulating Hypotheses** test used in the study just described did not involve data from psychological investigations; it was a more general test intended for undergraduate students. Our

*Frederiksen, N., and Evans, F. R. Effects of models of creative performance on ability to formulate hypotheses. *Journal of Educational Psychology,* 1974, *66,* 67–82.

56

next effort was to develop a similar test made up of items based on psychological studies found in the literature. Items were chosen to vary systematically along two dimensions. One of these concerned the degree of rigor exhibited by the study described; some items represented results from controlled experiments, while others concerned uncontrolled field investigations. Second, items were taken from each of three general areas of psychology: 1) personality-social, (2) learning-educational, and (3) experimental-physiological. This design should make it possible to discover to what extent one's ability to suggest explanations for research findings is dependent on the field from which the problem is drawn, or on the match of this field to the individual's area of specialization.

This version of the test has been administered, using item-sampling procedures, to about 80 graduate students in education. Most of the data have not yet been analyzed, but, at least so far as number of hypotheses is concerned, an interesting effect of item type has emerged. Students were able to produce more hypotheses to account for findings from the personal-social and learning-educational areas than for those from experimental-physiological areas, particularly when interpreting uncontrolled or poorly controlled studies. We won't know, however, until we've tested individuals with other areas of interest, whether this finding represents a main effect for item type (findings in the personality and learning areas being open to a broader variety of interpretation) or one part of an interaction of item type with the subject's area of interest (education students presumably know more about personality and about learning than they do about physiological processes, while another group of students might show a different and equally plausible pattern in relation to their areas of knowledge.) Completing this design will of course be of great importance for our further test-development activities; it remains to be seen whether one version of the FH test will be sufficient for measuring students from all areas of psychology, and perhaps from closely related social science fields as well; or whether tests will need to be tailored for individuals of different specialities within the field of psychology.

Another concern being investigated has to do with the meaning and generality of quality scores on the FH test. The instructions we have been using ask the student to produce as many reasonable hypotheses as he can to account for each finding; it is not surprising that most students seem to interpret this request as emphasizing the quantity, not the quality, of ideas they can produce. We are currently giving one FH test with instructions emphasizing quantity and another with instructions emphasizing quality to the same set of students, in order to discover whether it is possible to get a good measure of each of these attributes from a single testing or whether different instructions are required to get good measures of quality and quantity of ideas.

We are also engaged in the development of a number of new tests, each intended to sample one aspect of the scientist's productive thinking efforts. This developmental effort is a "bootstraps" operation: Obviously the task would be much more simple and straightforward if we had a coherent, believable theory of scientific creativity from which to sample processes for study. Just as obviously, such a theory is something whose development we hope to contribute to, not something sitting on the shelf. What we have to work with, instead, are suggestions as to processes provided by several sources. Various theories concerning steps in the creative process have been surveyed, beginning with the classic four-state model for creative problem solving suggested by Wallas in 1926: *preparation, incubation, illumination, verification.* Flanagan's study of scientists' job performance, using the critical incidents technique, has also been helpful. Guilford's structure of intellect, finally, has been a useful heuristic device. Our approach involves using such sources for suggestions as to possible components of creative scientific thinking; developing one or several measures of each hypothetical component; and then discovering empirically whether the suggestion was a good one—that is, whether reliable dimensions of creative performance that are discriminable from (though not necessarily independent of) other such dimensions can be found. The following measures are the ones under consideration for the first round of this developmental effort; for each, we have given here just the name of the test and an excerpt from the instructions.

Notice that we have chosen names that describe the operation required; we are trying to avoid titles that claim more for the test than we can justify.

Measuring Psychological Constructs. "For each construct, list as many different methods as you can think of for eliciting the behavior implied by the construct, so that it can be observed and measured."

Formulating Research Ideas. "You are at a point in your training where you must choose an area of specialization, and you have narrowed your choice down to two. Your advisor has suggested that, in order for you to get a better impression of the nature and variety of research projects you might engage in, you write down as many research ideas as you can think of in each area. Write titles or brief descriptions of as many research projects as you can think of."

Personnel Selection Problem. "Your boss has asked you to make a list of all the personal characteristics you can think of that might be associated with success in doing the work of a plumber."

Analyzing Psychological Constructs. "There are many constructs in psychology that are usually treated as though they are unitary but may on close examination be found to consist of a number of separate and relatively independent parts. For each construct write names (or short descriptions) of all the parts you can think of that might be identified."

Evaluating Hypotheses. "Here is a list of five hypotheses to account for the finding reported. Which one do you consider the best, i.e., most likely to account for the finding? Rank-order the remaining hypotheses."

Evaluating Proposals. "As a class exercise, you have asked each of your students to write a brief description of a proposed experiment of his own design. For each paper, write your suggestions to the student regarding how the design or methodology might be improved."

Ideational Fluency in Psychology. "Write as many words or phrases as you can think of that have been used to describe personality traits."

Scanning Speed." "You are interested in articles dealing with the effects of anxiety on learning motor skills. Scan the following titles and check the articles that seem relevant and that you might want to read."

This list is long, but it is only a beginning; some of these measures will undoubtedly fall by the wayside, while the need for others will become clear. The hope is that repeated cycles of brainstorming and of empirical tryouts will lead to a relatively compact set of measures, each somewhat distinct from the remainder in the aspect of scientific thinking it requires, and the whole providing a representative sample of those thinking processes psychologists and others must go through in their productive thinking efforts. We may, at the end, be uncertain which of these processes deserve the label "creative"; we may even scrap "creativity" in favor of "productive scientific thinking." In any case, such a battery should provide a vehicle to help in bridging the gap between the simple cognitive abilities, such as those appearing in the structure of intellect, which we may understand but whose usefulness in the world is unclear; and complex cognitive performances whose importance is clear but whose interpretation is far beyond us for the present.

III

DEVELOPMENTAL CHARACTERISTICS

8. FACTORS THAT AID AND HINDER CREATIVITY

J. P. Guilford

In the part of our current *Zeitgeist* pertaining to psychology and education, no word has had a more dramatic rise in popularity than "creativity." After generally ignoring the subject, psychologists have come to realize their backwardness in knowledge of this subject. Employers have been asking for more inventive scientists, engineers, and managers. Special courses on how to think creatively have been springing up by the score. Special institutes are being held on the subject. Teachers and educators are asking how they can make courses more stimulating and how they can arouse more productive thinking on the part of the students.

The interest is international, as well it might be. The whole world faces two very critical problems—how to feed its exploding population and how to keep the peace. It has been estimated that in the next 20 years we shall need three times the number of scientists and engineers we now have, and they shall have to exercise all the ingenuity of which they are capable. We are reminded by the scriptures, however, that man does not live by bread alone. There is, I think, a very noticeable resurgence of interest in the arts in all their forms. We wish to walk in beauty as well as in peace, freedom, and dignity. There is also good reason to desire increased creativity to achieve aesthetic goals.

INVESTIGATION OF CREATIVITY

My topic suggests that I give most consideration to the abilities and other traits of individuals that make some of them creative and some not. Knowing these traits should help us to recognize which persons are likely to have the potentialities of becoming creatively productive. The same knowledge should help us in taking steps that should increase creative output in ourselves and in others, and other steps that may remove obstacles in the way of creative productivity. Our primary concern, then, will be the basic facts concerning the nature of creative thinking and of the more creative persons, with reference to the application of this information.

Serious investigation of creativity by psychologists began only in recent years. For centuries the common idea had been that only the exceedingly rare person is genuinely creative and that creativity is a divine gift. As such, it was not to be investigated, or at best, there was little hope of understanding it. Even after Darwin came upon the scene, when creativity came to be regarded as some kind of rare, hereditary blessing, there was still little incentive to attempt to understand it because there was thought to be little that one could do about it. In addition to being very rare, the highly creative person's behavior is sometimes eccentric. This has sometimes branded him as

Reprinted by permission of the author and *Teachers College Record*, Vol. 65, 1962.

being abnormal and even pathological. Mental pathology was similarly avoided as a subject of study by scientific investigators for a long time.

Creativity became an object of scientific study primarily because of the general interest in individual differences. This approach recognizes that individuals differ psychologically in traits or attributes that can be conceived as continua or dimensions—that there can be varying degrees of a quality possessed by different individuals. This concept was eventually applied to creativity, but in serious ways only about a dozen years ago. This new way of looking at the matter permitted us to think that not only a few peculiarly gifted persons but individuals in general possess some degree of the same creative trait or traits.

This conception has opened the door to many kinds of research. We need no longer study creativity by catching the rare persons who are recognized as having creativity to high degree; a multitude of subjects is now available to investigators. We can discover the various aspects of the phenomenon called "creativity." We can find out the conditions under which creative performance occurs or does not occur.

As in the case of all psychological characteristics that make up personality, we may be forced to recognize that heredity establishes limits of development for an individual. But there is considerable faith among educators that rarely does an individual realize full development in any respect and that there is generally considerable room for improvement. This faith should also be applied to the creative aspects of personality.

BASIC TRAITS AND CREATIVITY

There are a number of approaches to the investigation of the traits or characteristics in which creative individuals are most likely to excel. Some investigators appear to regard the phenomenon of creativity as a single dimension of personality. It is my view that the creative disposition is made up of many components and that its composition depends upon where you find it. Practically all investigators recognize that there are many potentially contributing conditions.

When the problem is approached from the standpoint of individual differences, the most natural scientific technique to apply is that of factor analysis. This is the approach that my associates and I have taken almost exclusively in the Aptitudes Project at the University of Southern California.

According to our original hypotheses (7), we expected to find the more creative individuals to think with greater fluency, with more flexibility, and with greater originality. The tests designed to measure fluency present very simple tasks, and the quantity of output determines the scores. When told to produce a list of items of information of a certain kind, how many responses can the examinee give in a limited time? Quality does not count, but, of course, the responses must be appropriate.

Flexibility in thinking means a *change* of some kind—a change in the meaning, interpretation, or use of something, a change in understanding of the task, a change of strategy in doing the task, or a change in direction of thinking, which may mean a new interpretation of the goal.

There has been some debate concerning the meaning of "originality." In our research and in that of others, originality means the production of unusual, far-fetched, remote, or clever responses. But there are some who say that an idea is not original or novel unless no human being has ever thought of it earlier. This conception is worthless to the scientist because there is no way of knowing that an idea has never existed before. It is somewhat better to say that a novel idea is a new one so far as the particular individual who has it is concerned. But unless we know the individual's past history of thinking, we cannot be sure of meeting this criterion either.

Fortunately, we can resort to empirical signs of novelty in terms of the statistical infrequency of a response among members of a certain population that is culturally relatively homogeneous. This gives us some workable operations for applying the criterion of unusualness. The index of unusualness can therefore be purely objective. As for the far-fetched or remote associations and the clever responses, we have as yet no way to avoid some degree of subjectivity of judgment in assessing test performance to obtain an index of originality.

Another somewhat popular criterion of an original idea is that it is socially useful. Those who deal with practical affairs may be appropriately concerned about this aspect of produced ideas. But such a criterion involves us in values in a way that science cannot deal with directly; hence, the criterion of social usefulness can be quickly dismissed by the psychologist. This does not mean that as a person he is unconcerned about social usefulness. It does mean that as a scientist he cannot afford to be so concerned and so restricted.

FLUENCY FACTORS

We shall now give closer attention to the various factors of fluency, flexibility, and originality. It turns out that in verbal tests alone there are three differentiated fluency factors (9). Ideational fluency has to do with the rate of generation of a quantity of ideas. The idea produced may be as simple as a single word, as complex as the title for a picture or a story, or as phrases and short sentences that convey unitary thoughts. In a test, we may ask the examinee to list all the things he can think of that are solid, flexible, and colored. He may respond with *cloth, leaf, rose petal, hair, skin, leather,* and so on. Any response that fulfills the specifications is accepted and counts toward the total score. In other tests, we may ask the examinee to list the consequences of a certain action or event, the various uses of an object, or some appropriate titles for a given story. In all such tests, there are strict time limits.

It is easy to see where an operation such as that in tests of ideational fluency fits into problem solving of many kinds. Perhaps a problem situation, when interpreted in a certain way, calls for an object with a certain set of specifications in order to solve it. Once these specifications are realized, the person who can list pertinent possibilities most rapidly could, other things being equal, solve the problem most quickly.

Many a problem calls for a running through of the likely possibilities during the earlier stage of interpreting or structuring it as well as during the stage of finding solutions. This process also probably depends in some degree upon ideational fluency. Of course it is not necessary to run through *all* the logical possibilities in solving a problem. One can ignore the less promising ones. This point will be touched upon later.

Another kind of fluency is called "associational fluency." It pertains to the completion of relationships, in distinction from the factor of ideational fluency, which involves giving ideas that fit a class. As a test of associational fluency, we may ask the examinee to list all the words he can think of that mean the opposite, or nearly the opposite, of the word "good." He may respond with

61

bad, poor, sinful, defective, awful, terrible, and so on. This ability is most obviously of use to the creative writer, who wants to find quickly a variety of verbal expressions without having to resort to a thesaurus.

The factor of associational fluency may have more general utility—for example, whenever we apply thinking by analogy as our strategy in solving problems. Thinking of a correlate is the completion of an analogy. Many solutions to new problems are achieved by the practice of thinking by analogy. The success of certain kinds of engineers in their work has been predicted to a small extent by means of a test of associational fluency as found by Saunders (*21,* 1956).

A third kind of fluency is called "expressional fluency." It has to do with the facile construction of sentences. We ask the examinee to write as many four-word sentences as he can, all different, with no word used more than once. We may give the initial letters of the four words, the same four being specified for each sentence—for example, "W_____ c_____ e_____ n_____." To this task, he may reply "We can eat nuts." "Willie comes every night," "Wholesome carrots elevate nations," "Weary cats evade nothing," and so on. You will probably not be surprised when I tell you that in a ninth-grade sample, the girls obtained a higher mean score than the boys.

We do not know yet how much generality to attach to this factor, whether it is limited to tasks such as the writing of sentences or whether it is so broad as to pertain to organizing ideas into systems. If it is as broad as the latter suggestion, it should be of considerable consequence, perhaps in something as important as the trial-and-error development of a scientific theory. The factor has been found significantly related to ratings by psychologists of the creative performances of military officers.[1]

FLEXIBILITY FACTORS

One type of flexibility we first recognized as "spontaneous flexibility" because the tests that measure it do not even suggest that the examinee be flexible (5). Without his knowing it, he can make a good score if he varies his *kinds* of responses. If we tell the examinee to list all the uses he can think of for common brick, the total number of uses listed is a good score for his status on the factor of ideational fluency. But we also score his performance in terms of the number of times he changes *category* of uses. For example, the person who responds with *build a house, build a school, build a factory,* etc., does not change his class of uses. Another person who responds with *make a paper weight, drive a nail, make baseball bases, throw at a cat, grind up for red powder, make a tombstone for a bird,* etc., changes class with each new response. He shows much more flexibility.

The person who makes a low spontaneous-flexibility score is rigid in the sense that he perseverates within one or a very few classes. As there are several kinds of flexibility in thinking, so there are several kinds of rigidity. When someone tells you that a certain person is rigid, beware of overgeneralization of the term. We do not find in normal (nonpathological) people a very general trait of rigidity vs. flexbility. We find several. This does not say that there are no individuals who are rigid in just about every respect, but the general rule is that they may be rigid in some respects and not in others, at least so far as thinking is concerned.

[1]From an unpublished study conducted jointly by the Aptitudes Project at the University of Southern California and the Institute for Personality Assessment and Research, University of California, Berkeley.

A new hypothesis may be considered in connection with the factor of spontaneous flexibility. Some advisers on how to think creatively suggest that in starting to solve a new problem, we keep our thinking at a rather high level of abstraction. We think of it first in very general terms. Thus, the person who goes from class to class in the Brick Uses test is operating within the frame of reference of a much broader class within which there are subclasses. A higher level of abstraction may mean thinking in terms of broader classes. This has the effect of broadening the scope of the scanning process in searching for information. Going from one class to another in the Brick Uses test also means considering all the properties of a brick—its weight, its color, its texture, and so on. These are abstractions all lying within the class of the total nature of a brick. This is reminiscent of a stock method of practicing creative thinking, a method known as "attribute listing" and advocated by Crawford (*3*).

A second kind of flexibility has been called "*adaptive* flexibility" for the reason that in tests in which it was first found, the examinee, to succeed, must make changes of some kind—changes in interpretation of the task, in approach or strategy, or in possible solutions. Our current interpretation of the factor of originality is that it is adaptive flexibility in dealing with verbal information.

We have a kind of test, called Plot Titles, in which the examinee is told a very short story and that he is to suggest as many appropriate titles for the story as he can. One of the stories is about a wife who is unable to speak until a specialist performs the appropriate surgery. Then her husband is driven to distraction by her incessant talking until another surgeon eliminates his hearing, when peace is restored in the family.

The number of commonplace titles given to the story may be used as a score for ideational fluency. Such titles include,

A man and his wife
Never satisfied
Medicine triumphs
A man's decisions
Talking and hearing

The number of responses rated as "clever" serves as a score for originality. Such titles are exemplified by

The deaf man and the dumb woman
Happiness through deafness
Operation—peace of mind
Yack, yack, hack

Several other types of tests serve to indicate individual differences in the factor of originality.

ELABORATION

In the course of our investigations of abilities involved in planning (*1*), we found another kind of ability we have called "elaboration." In one test, given the bare outlines of a plan, the examinee is asked to produce the detailed steps needed to make the plan work. The more details he adds, the better is his score. We believe that the unique feature of this ability is that in tests for it, one item of information leads to another as a kind of extension or completion. In more technical language, we say that the examinee is producing a *variety of implications*.

It was eventually recognized that the abilities of fluency, flexibility (including originality), and elaboration are similar in that the tests of them call for a variety of answers. There is no right or fully determined answer in connection with the information given in the item. There are now parallel tests in which each item *does* have one right answer because it is fully determined by the information given or because there is one conventionally accepted answer. A distinction has therefore been made between *divergent* thinking and *convergent* thinking to represent the two classes of abilities. The abilities of which I have been speaking thus far belong in the divergent-thinking category. Because the individual has to generate his answer or answers, starting from given information, in both categories of abilities, we speak of divergent-*production* factors vs. convergent-*production* factors, respectively.

QUANTITY VS. QUALITY

Several questions arise concerning the relationship of quantity and quality of production. One debated and investigated hypothesis is that "quantity breeds quality." This hypothesis holds that if a person produces a greater total number of ideas, he also produces a greater number of high-quality ideas in a limited time. Another view is that a mental set for quantity is inefficient because if a person spends his time producing a lot of low-quality responses, he cannot produce so many good ones.

There is another aspect of this controversy. When a person is set to give "good" answers, he is applying judgment or evaluation as he goes along. On the one hand, it is believed that an evaluative or critical attitude is generally inhibiting to the flow of ideas, good and poor alike. On the other hand, it is believed that the application of evaluation as one proceeds has a selective effect, holding back the low-quality responses and letting the high-quality responses come through.

The well-known brainstorming technique, attributed to Alex Osborn (*18*) and employed by many others, conforms to the first of these two schools of thought. One of its chief claimed virtues is that the separation of production and evaluation—in other words, suspended judgment—is better procedure. As originally applied, of course, brainstorming has other features, which includes thinking in small groups rather than thinking by individuals in seclusion.

The experimental results bearing upon the issue of suspended judgment are somewhat mixed. Meadow *et al.* (*16*) report that with suspended judgment, the production of "good" answers was a little more than doubled. The problems were to suggest unusual uses for a wire coat hanger and for a broom. The criteria for "good" responses were "unique" and "useful."

In our Aptitudes Project (*2*), we gave the Plot Titles test with and without the specific instruction to give clever titles. It was expected that the instruction for clever titles would entail more evaluation. The effects of this instruction were shown by a reduction in the number of low-quality responses, an increase in the number of high-quality responses, and a higher average rating of degree of cleverness.

Hyman (*13*) found that his subjects generated 68% more responses under quantity instructions, but that this increase in "good" responses, where "good" meant uncommon and of "high quality," failed to keep pace with the total output. Hyman is probably right when he concludes that quantity may breed quality for some types of problems but not for others. It is also probably true that the *kind* of evaluative attitude applied by the thinker has much to do with the quantity and quality of responses he produces.

Divergent thinking is a matter of scanning one's stored information to find answers to satisfy a special search model. Evaluation comes into the picture in determining whether or not the produced information fits the search model. Relaxed evaluation would permit a broadening of the base of the search, whereas an evaluative attitude with some degree of strictness should narrow the search. In doing so, however, it may lead more efficiently to good answers. This should depend upon the clarity and accuracy of the search model. If the thinker has a good search model, the application of evaluation while he thinks should be helpful.

But if evaluation is of a more vague kind, such as that involving a fear of being unconventional, a fear of thinking socially unacceptable thoughts, or a fear of being wrong, it should be definitely better to suspend judgments based on such criteria. Evaluation incident to an overly strong desire for a quick solution would also be handicapping. But evaluation for the sake of efficient scanning, where there is good strategy in the scanning process, should be beneficial.

Hyman (13) has found that a general critical attitude can have rather broad transfer effects in solving problems. A group of engineers, in Hyman's experiment, read some previously given solutions to a certain practical problem under the instruction to list all the good points that they could see in those solutions. A second group was instructed to list all the faults they could see in the same solutions. Later, in solving the same problem and in solving a new one, the uncritical readers suggested solutions of their own that were rated higher on the average than those of the critical group. Thus, very general critical attitudes must be taken into account.

GROUP VS. INDIVIDUAL THINKING

The question of group thinking vs. individual thinking has received a great deal of attention. The virtue claimed for group thinking in brainstorming is that one person stimulates another. In support of this hypothesis, Osborn (19) reports that about a third of the ideas produced in group brainstorming are of the "hitchhiking" type. In such a case, one person's idea is based upon another person's idea.

There are results which do not support his hypothesis, however. Taylor *et al.*(23) found a larger number of unrepeated ideas produced by individuals working alone than by those working in groups, where both kinds of thinkers were working under the condition of suspended judgment. Taylor points out that the group condition may have the effect of channeling thinking in similar directions, reducing the variety and therefore the quantity of unrepeated ideas.

Perhaps neither the group nor the isolation condition is best under all circumstances or for all individuals. It is quite possible that both can be applied to advantage. The preference of the thinker should have something to do with the choice of condition. A great deal is made of the point that the highly creative person is an independent thinker and that his creation may be a highly personal thing. Torrance (21, 1959) found that the more highly creative child (as indicated by his test scores) in a small group often works by himself or is somehow induced by the others to do so.

Whatever the outcome of brainstorming sessions in particular instances, experiments show that courses on creative thinking that are heavily weighted with brainstorming exercises seem to leave the students with beneficial results, and these results have some degree of permanence (15, 20). How much of the improvement to attribute to the brainstorming technique and to which aspects of it the improvement should be attributed are open questions.

CONTEXT OF CREATION

From the discussion thus far, one may conclude that creative performances are to be identified psychologically as a small number of divergent-production operations. Two different qualifications must be introduced. One exception is that two of the factors that we in the Aptitudes Project regarded from the first as being pertinent to creative thinking fall outside the divergent-production group. The other exception is that I have not yet told the whole story regarding the divergent-production factors. I shall make good on the latter omission first.

I have repeatedly stated that the tests on the factors thus far described are *verbal* tests. They pertain to verbally stated information. There are other kinds of information, and the question comes up whether the same person is usually equally creative in handling different kinds of information, material, or content. From our analytical results, we can say that it can happen, but we should rarely expect the same person to be equally capable of creativity in science, in the arts, mathematics, administration, and musical composition. Highly creative individuals in many of these different areas may have outstanding qualities in common, but psychological study indicates that they also have some marked differences.

In the area of divergent-production abilities alone, we find that individuals may be uneven in handling verbal vs. concrete vs. symbolic material. Symbolic material is the kind with which the mathematician deals—numbers and letters. Fluency, flexibility, and elaboration in dealing with concrete (perceived) material are probably of greater importance to the inventor of gadgets, the painter, and the composer, whereas the same kinds of abilities for dealing with verbal material or content are more important for the creative writer and the scientist. In other words, there are parallel abilities for dealing with concrete (or figural) material, symbolic material, and verbally meaningful (or semantic) material.

One of our earlier hypotheses (7) was that the unusually creative person has a high degree of sensitivity to problems. One person notices something wrong or in need of improvement, whereas another fails to observe defects, deficiencies, or errors. The observation of imperfections starts the creative person on his way to creative production. The observation of inadequacy of solutions also keeps the creative thinker at work on his problem (17).

Factor analysis has consistently upheld this hypothesis by finding an ability common to a variety of tests calling for the noticing of defects and deficiencies in such things as common household appliances, social customs, or in solutions to problems. Such an ability, however, seems to fit better in the general category of evaluative factors than it does in that of divergent production.

Not being satisfied with things as they are is a matter of evaluation. We hear a great deal about the "divine discontent" of the creative person. It is said that Thomas A. Edison frequently admonished his workers with the comment, "There must be a better way. Go and find it." The uncreative, in contrast, are often willing to settle for half-way measures and tolerably successful solutions to problems.

Another of our initial hypotheses was that many an invention or new idea is the revision of something that is already known. But the revision is not an obvious one. It takes quite a change in the meaning, interpretation, or use of an object to achieve such an innovation. One of our tests, designed for such an ability, asks which of five objects or their parts could be most reasonably adapted to be used to start a fire when there are available the following items: a fountain pen, an onion, a pocket watch, a light bulb, and a bowling ball. The accepted answer is "pocket watch,"

66

since the cover of the watch face could be used as a condensing lens. Since this and other such tests call for one best answer, this factor falls logically in the convergent-production category. The feature that makes a contribution to creativity is that a *transformation* must occur; objects must be redefined. Individuals who are clever at improvising seem to show this kind of ability.

There are other abilities outside the divergent-production category that make some contribution to creative performances in their own ways. We have seen that one of the evaluative abilities—sensitivity to problems—has a function in getting the creative thinker started. Other evaluative abilities should have their uses, whether judgment is suspended or not, in determining whether the products of thinking are good, useful, suitable, adequate, or desirable. If the creator is to finish his job, he will eventually appraise his product, and he will revise it if he feels that revision is called for.

COGNITION AND MEMORY

Thus far I have spoken of three major categories of intellectual factors—abilities of divergent production, convergent production, and evaluation. There are two other major categories—cognitive abilities and memory abilities—all distinguished from those in the first-mentioned categories and from each other. Cognitive abilities have to do with discovery recognition, or comprehension of information in various forms. Memory abilities have to do with storage or retention of information.

Many people, including some teachers, have for some reason disparaged memory and memory abilities. Some of them, who emphasize the importance of thinking, seem wrongly to believe that good thinking and good memory are incompatible qualities, perhaps even negatively correlated. Actually, good memory contributes to good thinking.

It is not a good, well-stocked memory, as such, that is bad, for even the most creative people have given due credit to stored information. It is the way in which storage is achieved and organized that makes the difference between the graduate who is sometimes described as "merely a walking encyclopedia" and the graduate who has a usable and fruitful fund of information. Memory abilities thus make their indirect but important contribution to creative performance.

The question often arises concerning the relation of creativity to intelligence. In connection with this question, the usual conception of "intelligence" is that which is measured by such tests as the Stanford Binet, the Wechsler scales, or the California Test of Mental Maturity.

In discussing abilities related to creativity, I have referred to them as intellectual factors. It is very doubtful whether these abilities, particularly those in the divergent-production category, are represented to any appreciable degree in standard IQ tests. IQ tests were designed to predict success in school learning, particularly in reading, arithmetic, and the subject-matter or informational courses. But we now know that there are many other kinds of intellectual abilities.

Studies of groups of research scientists and engineers (*22*) show that such groups have high average scores on IQ tests. They would need to have higher-than-average IQs to have passed all their academic hurdles, most of them including the PhD. But only a fraction of these are outstanding for creative performance. But within groups of scientists and engineers, the correlation found between IQ-test scores and creative performance is usually rather low. This is due in part to the restriction of range of IQ within such groups. The evidence seems to indicate that although the qualities in traditional IQ intelligence may be of some help to the creative scientist or engineer, they are by no means sufficient.

The low correlation between creativity and IQ is also found at younger age groups. In high school students, Getzels and Jackson (*21*, 1959) found that if the highest 20% of the subjects on IQ were selected as "gifted," 70% of those who stood in the highest 20% in terms of divergent-thinking tests would have been missed. Torrance (*21*, 1959) has reported a similar finding in the elementary grades. In both instances, it was reported that the teachers knew their high-IQ students better and liked them better. The high-creative without high IQs were often regarded as nuisances, and they were somewhat estranged from other students. Those with both high IQ *and* high creativity were recognized as having unusual but sound ideas, to be good in planning and improvising, and effective in getting attention (*21*, 1959).[2]

NON-APTITUDE TRAITS

The assessment of traits of temperament, interest, and attitude in connection with creativity has been approached in various ways. One approach has been to find the most outstandingly creative individuals in different professional groups, such as architects, writers, and scientists, and to assess them quite thoroughly by methods that are available. If a creative group differs systematically from the general population or, better, some group outside the profession but matched with it for age, sex, and educational level, it is concluded that this creative group stands apart or is distinguished by the personality trait or traits in question.

There are obvious dangers in drawing conclusions from studies of this kind, unless an appropriate control group has been used. When it is found that creative architects, scientists, mathematicians, and writers alike tend to score highest on theoretical and esthetic interest on the Allport-Vernon-Lindzey *Study of Values,* this may occur just because any high-IQ group would do the same (*14*). When it is found that the creative males tend to score relatively in the direction of femininity on the masculinity-femininity scale of the *Minnesota Multi-phasic Personality Inventory* scale, we remember that Terman and Miles (*24*) found that as members of the two sexes are more intelligent and better educated, they respond more alike to test items on masculinity vs. femininity. Nor should it be surprising that the creative groups just mentioned should tend to score high on the Strong *Vocational Interest Blank* scales for architect, psychologist, and author-journalist.

A somewhat better approach is to obtain two samples from the same profession, composed of highly creative and less creative individuals, respectively. The groups can then be compared with respect to various assessed qualities. Sometimes the groups are distinguished on the basis of judgments by their teachers (*4, 12*). In still other studies, subjects of mixed occupations but similar in IQ and educational level have been tested with measures of creative aptitude and of non-aptitude traits (*10*).

NON-APTITUDE DIFFERENCES

We have had to recognize that creative occupational groups share parallel but different exceptional abilities. We should expect the various groups to show some non-aptitude qualities in common and also to show some differences. One difference, for example, has been noted between creative students of art and of science. The more creative art student has been reported to be more

[2]For systematic treatments of a unified theory of intelligence see references (*8, 11*).

of an observer than a participant in what is going on (*12*). The more creative science student is reported to be more of a participant than the less creative student (*6*). Such observations should prevent our generalizing conclusions obtained from one creative group to all other creative groups.

There are many ways in which creative people of many groups are alike, however. There is general agreement that the highly creative person, particularly the original person, is self-confident. Which comes first, originality or self-confidence? It is a little like the old hen-and-the-egg problem. Probably, it works both ways: Originality yields success and hence self-confidence, and self-confidence leads the individual to attempt to solve problems where others would give up. In some instances, self-confidence goes over into conceit, as we have all been aware. Sometimes this is fed by the adulations of admirers. Sometimes it may suggest an underlying hypersensitivity to criticism.

Along with self-confidence, there is usually self-assurance or social boldness. The creative person is especially confident about his own judgment and his own evaluations of his work. He is often described as an independent thinker, which includes having an independent set of values. If he thinks his product is good, he discounts the criticisms of others and may disparage their judgments.

Not only is he more or less independent of other people's judgments, he may be self-sufficient in that he can take people or he can let them alone. He is likely to find ideas more important than people, though he is not necessarily a social recluse. These qualities do not add to his popularity with others, so he is in danger of becoming estranged from his parents, his teachers, and his peers. Contributing to this state of affairs also is a lack of mutual understanding. The creative child and his associates may need special counseling to help smooth over some roughness in interpersonal relationships. This can be done without curbing development along creative lines.

We have found that young men who stand high in one or more kinds of fluency are likely to be somewhat impulsive, cheerful, and relaxed. Those who score high in tests of originality tend to have strong esthetic interests, and they like to indulge in divergent thinking. They do not feel much need for meticulousness or for discipline. Somewhat surprisingly, they show no particular dislike for conventional or socially approved behavior nor do they show signs of neuroticism.

One of the striking traits found by Getzels and Jackson (*21*, 1959) among high school students who stand high in divergent-thinking tests is a strong sense of humor. This is shown particularly in the kinds of stories they tell in response to pictures. For example, one picture showed a young man working at his desk at six-thirty in the morning. A bright but less creative student wrote the following kind of story: "This young man is very ambitious to get ahead. He comes early every morning to impress his boss so he will be promoted." A more creative student told the following kind of story: "This picture is the office of a firm that manufactures breakfast cereals. It has just found a formula to produce a new kind of cereal that will bend, sag, and sway. The man is a private eye employed by a rival firm to obtain the formula. He thinks he has found it and copies it. It turns out to be the wrong formula, and the competitor's factory blows up."

Such stories usually involve some novel twist or transformation, such as the expression regarding the cereal that will "bend, sag, and sway." Many stories derive their humor from such a source. The person who makes up such stories is exhibiting verbal or semantic transformations, which is a sign that he has a fair degree of the factor of originality. Since this is a semantic ability, and since Getzels and Jackson's tests were verbal, we may well question whether the affiliation of humor and the ability to produce transformations extends to other kinds of content, figural or symbolic. It is probably true, however, that creative painters, composers, and mathematicians also experience a certain amount of enjoyment, if not amusement, in playfulness with their own kinds of materials.

FINAL SUGGESTIONS

Although the temperament and motivational qualities can help us somewhat in identifying potentially creative people, no one of them is a dependable sign, nor would all of them collectively be sufficient. Neither do these qualities help us very much in understanding the nature of the creative processes. On the whole, we have less chance of changing individuals with respect to these qualities in order to increase their creativity, except for changing certain attitudes.

Our chief hope, then, of either identifying the more creative persons or enhancing their creative performances lies with the aptitude factors. If we regard the intellectual factors as distinct but somewhat generalized thinking skills, this statement seems more reasonable. We develop skills by practicing them. The question, then, is one of what kinds of practice can best be applied and under what conditions.

An understanding of the nature of the skills is one of the most important steps either for the teacher or the student. When we know what kind of skill is to be developed, we have a more clearly defined goal toward which to work. Torrance (21, 1959) reports that even after 20 minutes of instruction on the nature of divergent-thinking processes, grade-school children showed a clearly observable improvement in performing tasks of this type.

Although special courses on creative thinking have proved beneficial, our whole educational system can be of greater help by giving more attention to this subject. There is abundant opportunity to teach almost any subject in ways that call for productive thinking rather than rote memory. Even the multiplication tables can be taught in ways that give the pupil insight into properties of the number system.

In some experimental courses at the University of Illinois in which mathematics is taught from the lower grades on by what is called a "discovery" method, instead of telling the child the axioms and other principles of mathematics, the teacher lets him discover them for himself by exposing him to appropriate examples. Also at the University of Illinois, science is being taught to children by a discovery method. Some natural phenomenon is demonstrated without explanations to the class, perhaps in motion-picture form. From then on, it is a matter of the students asking questions, with minimum information being given by the teacher, until the student develops his own satisfactory hypothesis.

Education in this country has unfortunately been too much dominated by the learning theory based upon the stimulus-response model of Thorndike, Hull, and Skinner. People, after all, are not rats (with a few exceptions), and they are not pigeons (with similar exceptions). Let us make full use of the human brains that have been granted to us. Let us apply a psychology that recognizes the full range of human intellectual qualities. We must make more complete use of our most precious national resource—the intellectual abilities of our people, including their creative potentialities.

References

1. Berger, R. M., Guilford, J. P., and Christensen, P. R. A factor-analytic study of planning abilities. *Psychol. Monogr.*, 1957, 71, (Whole No. 435).
2. Christensen, P. R., Guilford, J. P., and Wilson, R. C. Relations of creative responses to working time and instructions. *J. exp. Psychol.*, 1957, *53*, 82–88.
3. Crawford, R. P. *Techniques of Creative Thinking*. New York: Hawthorne Books, 1952.
4. Drevdahl, J. E. Factors of importance for creativity. *J. clin. Psychol.*, 1956, *12*, 21–26.
5. Frick, J. W., Guilford, J. P., Christensen, P. R., and Merrifield, P. R. A factor-analytic study of flexibility in thinking. *Educ. psychol. Measmt.*, 1959, *19*, 469–496.
6. Garwood, D. S. Some personality factors related to creativity in young scientists. Unpublished doctoral dissertation, Claremont Graduate School, 1961.
7. Guilford, J. P. Creativity. *Amer. Psychologist*, 1950, *5*, 444–454.
8. Guilford, J. P. Three faces of intellect. *Amer. Psychologist*, 1959, *14*, 469–479.
9. Guilford, J. P., and Christensen, P. R. A factor-analytic study of verbal fluency. *Rep. psychol. Lab.*, No. 17. Los Angeles: Univ. Southern California, 1957.
10. Guilford, J. P., Christensen, P. R., Frick, J. W. and Merrifield, P. R. The relations of creative-thinking aptitudes to non-aptitude personality traits. *Rep. psychol. Lab.*, No. 20. Los Angeles: Univ. Southern California, 1957.
11. Guilford, J. P., and Merrifield, P. R. The structure of intellect model: its uses and implications. *Rep. psychol. Lab.*, No. 24. Los Angeles: Univ. Southern California, 1960.
12. Hammer, E. F. *Creativity*. New York: Random House, 1961.
13. Hyman, H. *Some experiments in creativity*. New York: General Electric, Relations Services, 1960.
14. MacKinnon, D. What do we mean by talent and how do we use it? In *The search for talent*. New York: College Entrance Board, 1960.
15. Meadow, A., and Parnes, S. J. Evaluation of training in creative problem solving. *J. appl. Psychol.*, 1959, *43*, 189–194.
16. Meadow, A., Parnes, S. J., and Reese, H. Influence of brainstorming instructions and problem sequence on a creative problem solving test. *J. appl. Psychol.*, 1959, *43*, 413–416.
17. Merrifield, P. R., Guilford, J. P., Christensen, P. R., and Frick, J. W. A factor-analytical study of problem-solving abilities. *Rep. psychol. Lab.*, No. 22. Los Angeles: Univ. Southern California, 1960.
18. Osborn, A. F. *Applied Imagination*. New York: Charles Scribner's Sons, 1953.
19. Osborn, A. F. *Development of creative education*. Buffalo, N.Y.: Creative Education Foundation, 1961.
20. Parnes, S. J., and Meadow, A. Evaluation of persistence of effects produced by a creative problem solving course. *Psychol. Reports*, 1960, *7*, 357–361.
21. Taylor, C. W. (Ed.) *Research Conference on the Identification of Creative Scientific Talent*. Salt Lake City, Utah: Univ. of Utah Press, 1956, 1958, 1959.
22. Taylor, D. W. Thinking and creativity. *Ann. N.Y. Acad. Sci.*, 1960, *91*, 108–127.
23. Taylor, D. W., Berry, P. C., and Block, C. H. Does group participation when using brainstorming facilitate or inhibit creative thinking? *Admin. Sci. Quart.*, 1958, *3*, 23–47.
24. Terman, L. M., and Miles, Catherine C. *Sex and Personality*. New York: McGraw-Hill, 1936.

9. THE USE OF DEVELOPMENTAL STAGE THEORY IN HELPING GIFTED CHILDREN BECOME CREATIVE

J. C. Gowan

INTRODUCTION

It is sometimes said of our profession, that we are practitioners without rationale. This paper is an effort to provide some logical reasons for some specific procedures with gifted children. To start, the following three postulates are regarded as obvious:

1. Creativity is the objective of talent development;
2. The dynamics of developmental process is necessary for this development;
3. Developmental Stage theory is a necessary part of developmental dynamics.

These, in my view are the new thrusts in the area, and failure to pay attention to them will slow our progress, and miseducate us so that we will be less able to deal with the challenges of the future. The central theme here is the exploration and development of the increasing powers and abilities of the human mind.

Secondly, the procedures by which such issues should be implemented include, in my view, three that I am not sure are being emphasized enough by the LTI institute. They are respectively a) the use of guidance, b) the use of paraprofessionals, and c) the use of "hands-on" research experimentation (as in Joe Renzulli's "Type III" enrichment). Again I have neither the time or option to dwell on these matters.

I am also not happy about the maladroit phrasing of the subject assigned to me which is "Psychoanalytic Perspectives on the Gifted/Talented." Being an iconoclast and not hung up on sex, I have little inclination to worship Freud, though I do recognize the basic nature of some of his developmental concepts. I believe that science rests on the progression of ideas, not cultism, and am therefore far more sympathetic to the views of Erikson, Kris, Maslow, Kubie and Reich. The enunciation of affective developmental stages by Erikson in his famous "Eight Stages of Man" (Erikson 1950) is, in my view, a landmark. Similarly, Maslow (1954) explored the positive side of mental health, particularly its higher reaches. Kris (1953) and Kubie (1958) have helped us understand the relationship of the cognitive ego to the "collective preconscious" from which creativity appears to come. And Reich (Mann 1973) has extended psychoanalytic theory to larger issues of cosmic energy flow. I have entitled this paper, therefore, "The Use of Developmental Stage Theory in Helping Gifted Children Become Creative." In my view, this hits all the bases by using updated neo-psychoanalytic theory to undergird developmental process, and then applies this new knowledge to the specifics of helping gifted children actualize their creative potential.

Accordingly, we shall proceed with I) General Developmental Stage Theory, II) Suitable Modifications for the Gifted Child, III) Three Paramount issues for educators for the gifted, namely:

1. Stage 3 (age, 4–6), Creative Fantasy or Magic Nightmare,

*Prepared for LTI class use, Summer, 1979. This article contains author's material from the following copyrighted sources: (Gowan, 1960, 1972, 1974, 1978a and b.)

2. Stage 4 (age, 7–11), Teaching to avoid the creativity drop,
3. Stage 5 (age, teens), Establishing Verbal Creativity at Adolescence.

I. GENERAL DEVELOPMENTAL STAGE THEORY

1. The Theory Summarized

Introduction

In *The Development of the Creative Individual* (Gowan, 1972) and *The Development of the Psychedelic Individual* (Gowan, 1974) the theme of both books centered around our version of periodic developmental stage theory (see figure 1). The central issues of this theory are as follows in summary form:

a. combination of the cognitive stages (Piaget) and the affective stages (Erikson) into unified form
b. extension of the five Piagetian stages into eight,—the three new ones being: creativity, psychedelia, and illumination.
c. Periodicity of three in table, which results in similarities between stages 1, 4, 7, etc.
d. reinforcement of concept of discontinuity, succession emergence, differentiation, and integration as components of escalation
e. significance of "dysplasia" (malformation in development) as splitting of cognitive and affective stage levels in malfunctioning individuals
f. emphasis on self-actualization as escalation into higher developmental stages.

In this paper, after detailing the significance of these six issues, we shall discuss newer developments, since publication of the books, which throws further light on the theory, and which updates it particularly in respect to higher developmental processes.

In *The Development of the Creative Individual* (1972), the writer stated the new hypotheses as a set of theorems:

1. Developmental process is best understood by conceptualization of the Erikson-Piaget-Gowan periodic table of developmental stages, consisting of triads, in which each developmental stage has a cognitive and affective characteristic (see Table I). Using the earlier 5-stage Piagetian model, the age stage range for the two components, independently arrived at by Erikson and Piaget, are remarkably coincident.

2. Each stage has a special affinity for another three removed from it. Stages 1, 4, 7 are noticeable for a thing-oriented, sexually latent aspect, dealing with the world of experience. Stages 2, 5, 8 are ego-bound, ego-oriented and ego-circumscribed. Stages 3 and 6 are times for love and creativity.

3. Within each stage, development occurs through cycles of escalation. Escalation is described as an aspect of developmental process which involves increased complexity and embraces five attributes: succession, discontinuity, emergence, differentiation and integration. Succession implies a fixed order within a hierarchy of developmental stages. Discontinuity involves an ordered and discrete sequence of equilibriums like a series of stairs. Emergency involves budding and the making of the implicit, explicit in the flowering of characteristics unseen before. Differentiation

TABLE I
The Erikson-Piaget-Gowan Periodic Developmental Stage Chart

ATTENTIONAL MODES		LATENCY	IDENTITY	CREATIVITY
DEVELOPMENTAL LEVELS		3 it, they — THE WORLD	1 I, me — THE EGO	2 thou — THE OTHER
INFANT	ERIKSON (Affective)	TRUST vs. MISTRUST	AUTONOMY vs. SHAME & DOUBT	INITIATIVE vs. GUILT
INFANT	PIAGET (Cognitive)	SENSORIMOTOR vs. CHAOS ①	PREOPERATIONAL vs. AUTISM ②	INTUITIVE vs. IMMOBILIZATION ③
YOUTH	ERIKSON (Affective)	INDUSTRY vs. INFERIORITY	IDENTITY vs. ROLE DIFFUSION	INTIMACY vs. ISOLATION
YOUTH	PIAGET-GOWAN (Cognitive)	CONCRETE OPER'NS vs. NONCONSERVATION ④	FORMAL OPERATIONS vs. *DEMENTIA PRAECOX* ⑤	CREATIVITY vs. AUTHORITARIANISM ⑥
ADULT	ERIKSON (Affective)	GENERATIVITY vs. STAGNATION	EGO-INTEGRITY vs. DESPAIR	
ADULT	GOWAN (Cognitive)	PSYCHEDELIA vs. CONVENTIONALISM ⑦	ILLUMINATION vs. SENILE DEPRESSION ⑧	

from J. C. Gowan, DEVELOPMENT OF THE PSYCHDELIC INDIVIDUAL. Copyright, J. C. Gowan, 1974.

refers to the attribute which clarifies, fixates and metamorphosizes the emphasis in successive developments. Integration summates the other attributes into a higher synthesis with greater complexity.

2. The Literature of Developmental Stage Theory

The earlier literature on developmental stage theory, particularly that of Piaget on cognitive stages and Erikson on affective stages was thoroughly covered in our earlier efforts (Gowan, 1972, 1974), so that no further reference need be made to these pioneers. It is also appropriate to mention in this regard the Developmental Guidance of Blocher (1966), the developmental vocational choice stages of Ginsberg (1951) which correspond to our 4, 5, and 6th stages respectively, the adolescent developmental tasks of Havighurst (1964), and the Maslow hierarchy (1954), all of which predated our efforts. We now turn our attention to other work corroborating these views but of later date.

First to be mentioned is the doctoral thesis of P. K. Arlin (1975) which predicted a developmental cognitive stage following formal operations. Indeed, Epstein in the 1977 *NSSE Yearbook,* p. 344, declares: "We therefore predict a hitherto unknown stage of intellectual development." Arlin called her stage "problem-finding" which is one of the chief discriptors of what we have called "creativity." It should be remembered in this regard that perhaps one of the reasons why Piaget was unable to discover stages beyond formal operations was that he was testing his own three children; and when they reached adolescence, they would no longer submit to this daily drudgery.

J. Weinstein and Alfred Alschuler at the University of Massachusetts have reported on "Levels of Self-Knowledge," four of which bear uncanny resemblance to our stages 4, 5, 6 and 7 and are in roughly the same age bracket. They say that "What one does not do at a given stage that he can do at the next higher stage tells us an important story." In analyzing students' stories, they report as follows:

4. CONCRETE OPERATIONS: Stream of consciousness reporting of separate images with no casuality, nothing but separate feelings, and no overall start and finish;

5. FORMAL OPERATIONS: Report of feelings with start and finish of story and a moral, casual outcome, however, no pattern across situations.

6. CREATIVITY: Strong personal feelings in report of personality characteristics and personal style of which the story is an example, but outcome is fatalistic, working out the same across different situations;

7. PSYCHEDELIC: Choice, responsibility and autonomy enter reports, with the individual able to change his response pattern.

While there are differences here, the developmental trend of these stages clearly follows periodic developmental stage theory.

3. Acceleration versus Escalation

A very complex question, on which the final answers are not yet in concerns the issue of whether acceleration of (gifted) children in any stage can produce escalation into the next stage. The trouble is compounded by the fact that it is possible that gifted children may automatically escalate into a higher stage at an accelerated pace, or alternatively, they may require special educational intervention to do so. Although acceleration is one of the few areas in gifted child education where the research is all positive (Gowan and Demos 1964:182ff), we should perhaps pause before we accelerate to ask what are we accelerating into. Perhaps an even better question is, "Will acceleration produce escalation into the next higher stage?" Unfortunately, the research here is not so clear-cut.

Webb (1974) in a study of "Concrete and Formal Operations in Very Bright Six- to Eleven-Year Olds" found that "No child showed any trace of (our stage 5) until he reached close to age eleven years." Brown (1973) showed similar results for stage 4 (and years). These results are reported by Epstein (1977:347) who concludes that while the rate of maturation in a new stage can be affected, there seems little evidence of accelerated escalation.

Keating (1976:98) in an article, "A Piagetian Approach to Precocity," as a result of his own work, plus a review of Webb, Lovell and DeVries, suggests a somewhat more complex interpretation in which "the brighter individual would be at an advantage in moving through the successive stages more quickly." He concludes: "Precocity across stages is clearly present, but perhaps not as pronounced as that within stages."

Defending the concept of "advance organizers" on school learning in accelerating escalation into higher cognitive stages Ausubel (1978:256) says:

> Working with 6- and 10-year-old children Lawton (1977b) found an acceleration and facilitated effect from advance organizers on the learning of subject matter in that advance organizers significantly accelerated "a move from the level of pre-operations to that of concrete operations." In other cases it facilitated the more complete understanding of "concrete operations . . . at least within the context of a social studies unit" (Lawton & Wanska, 1977b).

4. Psychomotor, Moral and Conative Components

There is not a priori reason why the components of developmental stage theory should be restricted to cognitive and affective. Indeed, in line with Bloom's Taxonomy one would expect as psychomoter addition. This segment has now been found owing to the work of Simpson (1966) and Harrow (1972). The efforts of Kohlberg in the moral development area, (Kohlberg and Mayer 1972) are so well-known as not to require further comment. Less known, but equally important is the research of Perry (1968) in the conative area. An excellent compendium of these various components is found in the master's thesis of Simpson (1977:359ff) in an article "Developmental Process Theory as Applied to Mature Women". Of particular interest to developmental stage theorists is the synoptic table which accompanies this article. The correspondence of age ranges from these five different viewpoints is a validating aspect of the construct.

More recently, a Canadian psychologist, H. Koplowitz, (Brain/Mind Bulletin, Oct 2, 1978) has proposed that the usual Piagetian cognitive stages are transcended by at least *two* higher ones: a) a *systems* level "in which the individual understands complementarity, homeostasis, and interdependence," and a *unitary operational thought*, in which the individual understands "that the way the universe is perceived is only one of many possible constructs". These two stages are again chief discriptors of the creative and psychedelic stages we had earlier enunciated.

Other hints of the possibility of higher cognitive stages may be found in the work of Gruber (1973), and Vygotsky (1974) on which Arlin and Epstein built.

5. Escalation*

Developmental stages are characterized by escalation, which involves five separate but interrelated aspects known as succession, discontinuity, emergence, differentiation, and integration: the concept of developmental dysplasia arises from a failure to escalate.

The objective of escalation is creativity, which is emergent in the personal "unfoldment" of the individual as part of his developmental process. This unfoldment is as natural as the budding and blossoming of a rose, if proper conditions of sunshine, soil and moisture are present. Once a certain developmental stage has been reached, creativity is a direct outcome of self-awareness.*

The construct of escalation is helpful in understanding the process of development. "Escalate," a recently coined word, means to raise the level of action by discrete jumps; it derives from moving up an escalator, a flight of stairs or a ladder. When one shifts gears in an automobile, one escalates; this is not just a matter of going faster—more properly, one engages a different service of power.*

Succession

The term "succession" implies that there is a fixed order or hierarchy among developmental processes. The ordered hierarchy in turn implies a continual rise in the level of action at each stage. The order is invariant, although the time sequence is organismic and not strictly chronological.

The concept of succession implies that the track of development is fixed, in that a given stage follows and never precedes another. The rate of succession through stages and the extent of development at any stage, however, is flexible since these are influenced by the nature of the organism and its environment.

Discontinuity

The concept of discontinuity parallels that of succession. One cannot imagine a flight of locks in a canal as other than a succession of discontinuities, each with the water level at equilibrium. The order is invariant. One could not have the first lock, then the fifth, then the fourth, third and second. As a flight of locks contains water at various stages of equilibrium whereas a waterfall does not, so this discontinuity of ordered sequences allows for equilibrium at various stages as a smooth growth curve does not.

Emergence

Emergence, or the debut of new powers, is the third aspect of escalation. As the child progresses from one stage to another in the developmental sequence, qualities which were implicit or covert in a previous stage become explicit or overt in the next or following stage. This bringing out or manifestation of emergent characteristics, some of them unexpected or unrecognized at the earlier level, is seen in many phases of development as the budding or preparation for the next phase.

Differentiation

Differentiation refers to the escalatory attribute which clarifies, "fixates" and modifies the emphasis in developmental processes. It resolves or fixates in the sense that "focusing in" on an object by a zoom camera lens clarifies the optical field.

*Sect. 5 is from Gowan 1974.

Developmental processes which are loose and inchoate at early stages tend to become bound, defined and fixated at higher stages. The increase in specialism and specificity results in part from the accumulation of habits and conditioned responses. Fixation is more complex, however, than mere conditioning; it involves selection of tempos, pacing, and the development of likes and dislikes of objects and processes. Experiences become organized into value systems which determine choice into similar patterns. A girl at the heterosexual stage of development will be attracted to boys in general; later she will love a particular boy. Fixation not only means that the attribute will be held more tightly, but that it will be apprehended in the same manner each time. The habituation of response tends to put an end to creative play variations on that response; we learn to do something well in a certain way, and it becomes more certain that we will do it in that way without variation. The process is analogous to "type casting" in the theater.

Integration

Integration, the final attribute of escalation, synthesizes the others. It is in some respects the mathematical integral of the previous aspects. A mathematical integral of an algebraic function is a related function of the next higher degree with the addition of a constant which must be determined by observation, thus giving two sources of extra freedom and one of greater complexity. It is not surprising that a higher synthesis, greater complexity and new degrees of freedom are characteristic properties of the concept of integration.

The tasks of a stage are not simple accretions of the previous stages, but are interconnected to form a meaningful unit (like the rafters of a roof) which unites into a gestalt called by Piaget *"structures d'ensemble."* This is more characteristic of our concept than his "integration" which simply refers to reemphasis. Following are some familiar examples of integration:

(1) The child's interest in various parts of his body seen during stage two (autonomy) now becomes integrated in stage three (initiative) into a narcissistic love of his whole body. The energy of the parts becomes bound into energy for the whole.

(2) In the transformation from child to adolescent, there is increase in complexity of emotion, and such emergent qualities as genital sexual drives, greater capacity for tenderness and feeling and more intellectual range, all of which form a newer synthesis of previously identified aspects and permit new degrees of freedom and choice.

Integration also embraces a higher synthesis of already delineated elements; hence it summates the concept of escalation. Who among us has not felt the thrill of driving a geared car on an open road and shifting into overdrive as the highway clears ahead? The car goes faster with less effort, because the gear ratio has been changed and the engine labors less per mile per hour traveled. We can do this and experience the consequent sense of freedom and elation at high speeds only on an excellent road. We feel this way even though there is no more potential power in the auto than there was at rest or backing up a steep grade. We are in a sense self-actualizing the automobile for we are using it at its utmost at the task for which it was built. This top efficiency at any stage of development is reached only through a harmonious psychic-biologic relationship resulting from excellent mental health on the part of the individual which enables him to integrate his total potential or, as we say in current slang, to "put it all together."

6. Dysplasia (Mal-Development)

Dysplasia, a word borrowed from W. T. Sheldon, will here be used to show a split in developmental levels in which the affective level is ahead of the cognitive level. The concept involves developmental lag or arrest so that in some part of his development the individual is behind schedule. The effects of developmental dysplasia are that the individual tends to accept the achievements of any one stage as comprising the totality of self, and further potentialities of higher stages are not discerned or appreciated.

The most common adult dysplasia (the so-called "7–5" dysplasia) characterizes the average intellectual who is in the generativity (seventh stage) affectively, but still (since not creative), in the formal operations stage cognitively. Dysplasias are difficult to remediate, almost always on the cognitive side, and never of more than two levels. While further information on the area is available elsewhere (Gowan 1974: 166ff), we may summarize here that a cognitive dysplasia prevents affective development from advancing more than two stages beyond the cognitive arrest. Hence when arrest occurs in cognitive development, affective development is eventually blocked also.

We do not have space at hand to go fully into the guidance implications of dysplasias. Suffice it to say, that they are the cause of most absences of creativity in gifted adults; and hence are the targets of most counseling for the gifted. Prevention of dysplasias is also much more fruitful than their remediation.

II. SUITABLE MODIFICATIONS FOR THE GIFTED CHILD

Concern for the qualities of exceptional human beings arises out of an exceptional concern for the qualities of all human beings. Thus a developmental program for actualizing the talents of gifted children arises out of sound knowledge of developmental stage theory, and the ability and motivation to apply it to the special problems of the gifted. Since developmental stage theory is discontinuous (as befits the carrying over of the discontinuity found in physical science to behavioral areas), guidance and help over these discontinuities is necessary. Not only will there be acceleration in the developmental stages for the gifted child (with consequent social dislocation), but the child to become an actualized creative adult must escalate to higher stage levels than Piagetian formal operations.

This brings us to two major departures in the guidance of gifted children: (1) guidance is distributed over a wider temporal span, starting earlier and extending later in the lifetime of the individual; and (2) guidance is distributed over a wider personnel span, embracing not just the ordinary guidance workers but literally all persons who come in contact with the exceptional child, from his parents onward. It should come as no great surprise to us to find that the guidance of gifted children follows the general guidelines that the remedy for their problems is to start as early as possible, and involve them with as many types of guidance workers as possible, enlisting the home whenever feasible.

Developmental and differentiated guidance for the gifted has recently received some attention in a symposium issue of *The Gifted Child Quarterly,* (Fall, 1977), and in a new book specifically on the subject, (Colangelo and Zaffram, 1979). From Gowan 1960:

Side by side with these developments has come a growing consciousness of the importance of guidance for the gifted. Just as it was once thought that the able needed no curriculum modifications, so it has been said that they are bright enough to find their way unaided by guidance services. What is conveniently forgotten is that the able may have special problems, which it takes individual guidance to handle. Some of these may be:

1. They may be faced with an embarrassment of riches in trying to make wise occupational and educational choices.

2. There may be problems attendant upon upward social mobility.

3. They may become aware of developmental tasks before they have the physical resources to solve them.

4. They may have more need than usual to develop the specialized interests which go with certain professional occupations.

5. There may be problems connected with the lack of adult model figures.

One of the problems which many gifted youngsters face in connection with guidance has been expressed with some humor by a gifted student as the perennial question of "How far out beyond the safety railing can I lean without going over the cliff?" Gifted students are bright enough to know that they deviate in characteristics considerably from the norms and to see that, in consequence, many generalizations that apply to the average student do not apply to them. The problem for them is to discriminate between those situations which apply equally to all persons, regardless of ability, and those which apply to them only with diminished force. For example, the gifted student frequently finds that he can take one or two courses in excess of the requirements and that he does not need this or that prerequisite. It takes a wise counselor to help him discriminate between those experiences he can safely telescope and those that he should undertake in as full measure as the next student.

The major function of the guidance person working with the able youth is twofold: first, to assist in personality development and the removal of emotional or environmental handicaps; and second, to aid and advise in the maximizing of achievement and college placement which will facilitate his progress to a professional career. Both of these matters are complex enough to require separate analysis and hence will not be developed here. It should be emphasized, however, that these tasks should be prosecuted with positive, agressive action in place of the all too current passivity about able youth which infects many guidance offices. It is not enough to measure the function of the guidance office against the comparison of the mental health and scholastic achievement of these able youngsters with the norms; instead we should strive to prepare these outstanding representatives for the really grueling task ahead of them. If our intellectual leaders are to keep pace and be found in the frequencies demanded by modern conditions, we need not only to deliver a much higher percentage of our able youth to the door of the university but to ensure that they have the motivation and mental health to graduate. This means a program of college-going for able youth involving the encouragement, the motivation, the strengthening of curriculum, and the upbuilding of achievement on a level not approached by our high schools at present. It means a change of attitudes in students, teachers, parents, and the public regarding the importance of high school scholarship, the desirability of taking more than four "solids" per year, the need for new prestige symbols in adolescent groups, the decrease of community anti-intellectualism, the fostering of the conservation principle in young human talent—all matters of social values with which the guidance worker is concerned. While these issues are matters of community concern, they can be raised and fought for if professional educators are truly social leaders. A program for scholarship in the senior high school extending through the three years—not just the senior year—with prestige and other rewards for the participants and with good publicity regarding effective college placement and the various scholarships and awards which come to students is one way of starting such a program. Needless to say, such a job is a full-time task in the average high school and can scarcely be accomplished if the counselor is so burdened with the problems of the lower 10 per cent that he has no time for the able.

III. THREE PARAMOUNT ISSUES FOR EDUCATORS OF THE GIFTED

We have earlier listed three paramount issues for teachers of the gifted, which indeed are respectively the principal educational tasks for stages 3, 4, and 5 (see figure #1). They are respectively 1) Creative Fantasy or Magic Nightmare (initiative period 4–6), 2) Teaching to Avoid the Creativity Drop (industry period 7–11), and 3) Establishing Verbal Creativity (formal operations in the teens). Each of these tasks is directly concerned with the preservation and stimulation of creativity, and failure in any one of them at its appropriate level will probably result in a sterile and non-actualized gifted adult. While such failure is not crucial for the average person, it *is* crucial for the gifted child, both as a source of anxiety and mental ill health in him personally, and as a waste of talent socially.

The key concept in all these issues is the elicitation of right hemisphere imagery, either through the indirect method of stilling the overriding left hemisphere functions of a) receiving incoming precepts and b) internal discourse, or through the direct method of stimulation of the right hemisphere while the left is operant. It has been known for some time that art, music, and spatial units of curriculum would tend to accomplish this, but it may be that newer and better curriculum methods will allow other areas such as science and perhaps mathematics also to assume this function.

(From Gowan 1978a):

Right-hemisphere Imagery is the vehicle through which incubation produces creativity. In his famous paradigm of creative process, Graham Wallas (1926) identified four components: preparation, incubation, illumination, verification. By incubation, he meant any technique of relaxation of the conscious cognition (left-hemisphere function), such as, but not confined to, dreams, daydreams, fantasy, hypnosis, meditation, diversion, play, etc., which allows subliminal processes (right-hemisphere functions) to operate. He saw preparation (academic discipline), as the necessary, and incubation (relaxation), as the sufficient condition for creative insights to emerge.

Whereas most functions of the left hemisphere are concerned with convergent production as described by Guilford, functions of the right hemisphere are principally concerned with divergent production. These functions involve imagery through which incubation produces creativity.

A more practical question than "Where does imagery come from?" is "Under what conditions does imagery occur?" It is now quite obvious that, while imagery occurs spontaneously under hypnosis, and in trance, dreams, hypnogogic and hypnopompic states, as well as in other natural and induced altered states of consciousness, it can be found also in the more normal states, such as, daydreaming, fantasy, meditation, creative spells, relaxation, sensory deprivation, and the like, where the ego and full memorability are present. The key elements in the situation appear to be a) lowering the sensory input and b) stopping the internal verbal chatter; both of these point to allaying the overriding function of the left hemisphere: From the above it appears that right-hemisphere imagery goes on all the time and that it is merely necessary to pay attention to it. Learning of how to do this is obviously a new educational challenge, if we are to educate both halves of the brain and hence stimulate creativity in young people.

1. Magic Nightmare or Creative Fantasy, (age 4–6)

Creativity is expressed in stage spurts, the genesis occurring in the third (initiative—intuitive) period when (from Gowan 1972)

the child is drawn oedipally to the parent of the opposite sex. He may be plunged into a creative fantasy conceptualization of his world through which, with parental help and love, he gains some control over the new forces in his environment or, without parental help, he may experience a magic nightmare when the environment controls him, and he is powerless.

The creative fantasy is apparent in the third stage when an able and healthy child receives the full affectional approach of the opposite sexed parent. Hence, creative individuals tend to have oedipal and electral complexes. Boys who are affectionally close to their mothers and girls who are unusually close to their fathers during the years from four to seven tend to become more creative than others of similar ability. The child in this period responds to the warm affection of the opposite sexed parent by freely enlarging the bridge between his fantasy life and his real world. The affectionate adult who values the child's ideas stimulates and encourages the child to produce ideas and show off intellectually. The emotional support encourages the child to draw freely from past experiences, and to retrieve half-forgotten ideas from the preconscious. Thus he becomes able to dip further into this area and produce more creative ideas than another child whose efforts might be inhibited by his parent's disapproval or negative judgments.

The child's successes in winning the affection from the opposite sexed parent gives some semblance of reality to the oedipal fantasies of this period. The bridge between fantasy and reality becomes strengthened while at the same time the child feels "in control," and he grows in the power to discriminate between what is and what is longed for. This control is perhaps what Kris meant by "regression in the service of the ego." This kind of creativity is exhibitionistic, with intrusive, phallic qualities characteristic of the stage. Because more boys are close to their mothers during this period (closer than girls are to their fathers) may be one explanation why there later are more creative men than women in the world of adults.

At this time the child discovers his individuality in a world of powerful and forbidding adults. He recognizes his wants and impulses and senses the strength of his will which can be satisfied either through action or fantasy. Each may lead to pleasure or pain, to joy or guilt, and to growing power and success or to helpless immobilization. For the child this period can be a creative fantasy or a magic nightmare, on the one hand a full expression of the Sullivanian "good me" and on the other a frightening experience of the "not-me," the resolution depending upon the degree of control he can exert as compared with the controls exerted upon him by the significant adults in his life.

Some of the best loved and most enduring fairy tales throughout the world center around this theme of a child imprisoned in a magic kingdom, surrounded by powerful good and evil personifications, who later prove to be impotent. In *Alice in Wonderland, Through the Looking*

82

Glass and *The Wizard of Oz* a powerful like-sexed figure (the Queen of Hearts, the Red Queen, and the Wicked Witch of the West) attempts to immobilize the child protagonist. After a series of scary adventures aided by weak, male, nonhuman models (the White Rabbit, the White Knight, and Dorothy's three companions), the child triumphs over and reveals the actual impotence of the magical figure. Alice says: "You're nothing but a pack of cards", and herself becomes a Queen in *Looking Glass*; Dorothy discovers that even the kindly Wizard of Oz is a fake after destroying the Wicked Witch of the West, and finally gets back to Kansas on her own. The discovery that adults do not actually have the magic power ascribed to them by the child signals the transformation from the magic nightmare of the third stage where everything is in terms of badness-goodness to the forkaday world of the industry stage where facts come into their own.

2. Teaching to Avoid the Creativity Drop.

The drop in creativity in most children at about the fourth grade level is well documented by Torrance (1962) and others, although no reason other than a cultural one has been given. We suggest that this drop is due to the extinction of right hemisphere imagery due to overteaching of left hemisphere functions of reading, writing and arithmetic which occurs at that time, and the lack of stimulation of right hemisphere functions cause by the lessening or absence of music and art for the curriculum, and the lack of other right-hemisphere stimulation procedures. While *The Gifted Child Quarterly* for Spring 1979 is entirely devoted to a number of such procedures including meditation and guided fantasy, we would like here to concentrate on elementary science as perhaps more easy and appropriate a tool.

Let us accept the stipulation that the teaching of science to elementary school children will increase their vocabulary, experience, categorizing ability and familiarity with the size, form, shape and texture of matter,—all aspects of Piagetian conservation in the concrete operations period. It may also motivate interest. All of the above are even more true of gifted children, but such results all involve a quantitative change. It is here suggested that in the case of gifted children at least, there may be qualitative escalation in line with developmental stage theory, (Gowan 1972), in the direction of formal operations and creativity. To put it more pungently, science may be used as a tool to preserve right hemisphere imagery and prevent the Torrance drop in creativity, (1962), about age ten caused by over-teaching of left-hemisphere activities such as the three 'r's" to the extinction of right hemisphere function.'

To be sure, Suchman's "Inquiry Training" (1967), promised certain results closely approximating creative and divergent production, and other types of Socratic instruction (such as SMSG) have also in past years addressed this issue. What is new at present is a better understanding of developmental stage theory, coupled with a better understanding of the differential function of the cerebral hemispheres. Let us develop background on these matters.

Piaget's formal operations period as described in the literature is primarily Guilfordian convergent production, which in turn is primarily left hemisphere function. Since it has been shown elsewhere (Gowan 1978:) that right hemisphere imagery is the vehicle through which incubation produces creativity, some very important implications immediately follow.

The first is that perhaps formal operations as described is not what formal operations should be with optimum symbiotic functioning of both hemispheres. We shall return to this thesis later. The second is that if right hemisphere imagery is so important, we ought to find out more about it and then learn to stimulate it educationally. Let us pursue this thesis further.

The seat of this imagery appears to be in the Wernicke area of the right cerebral hemisphere (Jaynes 1976:109). While it was once thought that special means were necessary to elicit it, it has lately appeared that the process (like the shining of the stars) goes on all the time, but during our waking hours under most circumstances is overlain by the more cognitive processes of the generally dominant left hemisphere. These involve the handling of incoming perceptual information, and its processing into thought and action via language, and the continual stream of internal discourse which accompanies consciousness. Remove both of these activities from left hemisphere function through relaxation, meditation, hypnosis, fantasy, day-dreaming, sensory deprivation or similar state and the imagery of the right hemisphere is brought at once to focus. Indeed, Wallas (1926) in his paradigm for creativity called this aspect "incubation," and indicated that it is the sufficient (whereas preparation is the necessary) condition for creative illumination.

But right hemisphere activity need not be indirectly stimulated by removing left hemisphere function in an altered state of consciousness: art and music teachers have long advocated that their efforts directly stimulate the creative imagery of the right hemisphere (Williams, 1977). We now have bolder statements that science, if properly taught in an empirical discovery-oriented manner may also stimulate right hemisphere imagery. Perhaps the most authoritative statement on the subject is by Professor E. S. Ferguson in *Science* (1977) who says in part:

> Many features and qualities of the objects that a technologist thinks about cannot be reduced to unambiguous verbal descriptions. They are dealt with in his mind by a visual, non-verbal process. His mind's eye is a well developed organ that not only reviews the contents of his visual memory, but also forms such new or modified images as his thoughts require.

Better elementary science teaching can (in the case of gifted children at least) produce qualitative differences which accelerate the escalation of the Piagetian cognitive stages. If care is given to manipulation and discovery in the laboratory, such qualitatively different teaching can preserve right hemisphere function with its incubative imagery, which results in creative production. Not only can the new teaching accelerate the stage change, but it may actually be able to produce a more complete formal operations stage, where both sides of the brain engage in symbiotic operation, rather than the left side alone (with the resultant creativity drop which Torrance has noticed about the tenth year).

Table II, (Structure of Intellect Products in Concrete Operations Level Teaching) illustrates this point neatly. Usual teaching goes down the column in a manner stimulating left (but not right) hemisphere function. Thus when it finishes in verbal analogies, the child is brain-washed

TABLE II
SOI Products in Concrete Operations Level Teaching

	Hemisphere	Classroom Procedure (Unit)	SOI Product
conventional teaching (left-hemisphere oriented)	left	Vocabulary	units
	left	categories, attribute finding, combinations	classes
	left	Verbal analogies	relations
needed science teaching (right hemisphere oriented)	right	(general systems analysis)	systems
	right	(invert, maxify, minify, reverse, change, etc.)	transformations
	right	(remote associates, "What would happen if . . . ?")	implications

into left hemisphere formal operations. What should happen is a concomitant teaching to stimulate right hemisphere operation, by going from the bottom up. It is, however, much harder for teachers to devise units of this type.

A second theme is that creative production is a more realistic objective in qualitatively different science teaching for the gifted than it is for average children, since in this case we are not merely teaching for consumer science knowledge but for preparation for creativity in later life. Paul Brandwein in *The Gifted Child as a Future Scientist* (1955) was the first to appreciate this fact, and his little classic should still be required reading for science teachers. More recently Washton (1967) has indicated that creativity is a major objective in science teaching.

A third theme, much more recent in discovery, is that direct cognitive stimulation of the right hemisphere may be made in science as well as in art and music, if spatial and empirical methods are adopted. Such stimulation results in the education of imagery, which is necessary for scientific creativity as well as for other types. Indeed, it may be useful to ask the question: "How do major adult scientists create, as indicated by their own statements?" One of the best sources of such information is Ghiselin (1952) in a book called *The Creative Process*. Koestler (1964) in *The Act of Creation* also investigated such statements.

We lack the space to quote this impressive testimony, but it is to the effect that even in science it is imagery not logic which produces creative discovery. The great Einstein, himself, says:

> Words or language do not seem to play any role in my mechanisms of thought. The psychical entities which seem to serve as elements in thought are certain signs, and more or less clear images, (Ghiselin 1952:43).

3. Establishing Verbal Creativity at Adolescence

Since images are so much more understandable than verbal concepts, let us contrast the image of a sleepy peddler driving his shambling horse, with that of a trotting jockey deftly spurring his thoroughbred to victory in a close race. It would be completely inappropriate for the peddler to whip his horse up to a faster pace; it would be entirely inappropriate for the jockey not to do so. In the latter case, the racehorse has the ability to reach running excellence, but needs the guidance and coaching of an expert driver to excel in a way in which only racing trotters can. As educators we are involved in an exact analogy in attempting to spur gifted adolescents into verbal creativity, which other more average children are unable to reach. The driver in this case is a dedicated language arts teacher; the race involves the competition of other gifted classmates in a segregated seminar; the spur and whip are the disciplines of constant requirements for daily writing in a journal, and also in more formal themes and papers.

It is here in the lack of escalation from formal operations to creativity that most gifted children fail to make the jump, and hence are lost to creative adult function. The toll is especially heavy on adolescent girls because of the combined sanctions imposed on creative expression by parents, teachers and peers. We have devoted the entire attention of *The Gifted Child Quarterly* for Spring 1979 to this problem; the main constituents of the solution are 1) a dedicated teacher, 2) a segregated seminar, 3) maintenance guidance, and 4) continual pressure to produce creative writing via a journal.

In the struggle to produce creative adults out of gifted children, these are the three times and places where the major defections occur. As educators, we can bring a much higher percentage of children through to adult creativity by more careful attention to these critical phases.

CONCLUSION

What ideas stand out in this presentation?

1. Giftedness is mere *potentiality*. A gifted child can be defined as one who has the potential for verbal creativity. A talented child can be defined as one who has the potential for non-verbal creativity. In each case it is the *actualization* of the potentiality, not the potentiality itself, which is important. (We would never brag about a potentially good football player). This is why the name of the game we are trying to play is "How to make the gifted child creative."

2. To make the gifted child creative, we must understand developmental stage theory with its blending of Piaget (cognitive) and Eriksonian (affective) levels, and then apply these principles to guiding the development of the gifted child. This development demands that right hemisphere functions not be lost so that some imagery may be preserved.

3. There are three developmental stage levels where the baby can be thrown out with the bath water. We have discussed them under the headings 1) creative fantasy of magic nightmare, 2) teaching to avoid the creativity drop, and 3) establishing verbal creativity.

4. The continued understimulation of the potential talents of gifted students is stupidity of the same order as running a car on the freeway in low gear or using a racehorse to pull a dump cart. It destroys the capability of the agent, and it wastes the resources of the environment. The memorable achievements of mankind consist in actualization of his potential not their denial.

Epilogue*

I dreamed I was walking through an enormous field of wild red roses. "How many roses are there here?" said a voice. "Oh, at least a million," I answered. "Are there any sports among them?" the voice queried. "Yes, here is one," said I, appropriately sighting one which had flecks of white on its petals. "And how many such sports do you think there are here?" asked the voice. "Oh, probably a thousand, if one assumes that once every thousand roses there is some mutant variation." "And could these mutants be developed into distinctive colors and patterns?" inquired the voice. "Of course, for that is the way our domestic varieties originated," I replied. "Ah," said the voice, "but you had to have a gardener who believed in the possibility of such development and then set about to accomplish it." "That is true," I agreed.

There are many more children than roses, and they are much more important. Do some of them have talents and potential in exotic abilities which we do not even understand, and so cannot begin to stimulate? The gardener has produced a domesticated rose much bigger and more beautiful than the wild variety; could we do the same with children? But who will be the gardener for humanity? What are the talents of man? Are we sure we know them all? What if any are the boundaries of his abilities? Or are they as evanescent as was the limit of the four minute mile? What might we accomplish if we truly educated our children for the maximation of all talents which they possess?

A century ago lightning calculators were exhibited as side-show freaks. Since my dream I am haunted by the nagging possibility that some children possess similar exotic talents, which, because they are not appreciated by society, are not cultivated or stimulated, and we are therefore back looking at the wild rose mutation, rather than visualizing what it might become with husbandry. What are some of the possible powers of mankind?

*From Gowan 1978b

Could empathy, for example extend to telepathy? Could spatial visualization extend to non-spatial visualization? Could intellectual accretion and learning become telescoped into instantaneous knowledge and understanding? Some otherwise saintly and truthful mystics have told us that this is so. And it might not be amiss to check out this possibility.

Hunt and Draper (1977:20) tell us of the powers of the electrical wizard Nicola Tesla:

> He was conscious of certain phenomena before his eyes which others could not see. He envisioned objects and hypotheses with such reality and clarity that he was uncertain whether they did nor did not exist.

Before we regard Tesla's powers as miraculous or his biographers as liars, let us remember that when a picture of the scene is chromokeyed behind a newscaster as he describes a news event, we do not react in disbelief, nor do we when we see a virtual image in a holographic display. Science has sanctified these miracles, so we believe them though most of us cannot explain their technology. If geniuses like Tesla are forerunners, then it might be useful to recognize the possibility of such unusual talents and begin to study how to develop them in others.

In conclusion, let me go back to the speech of Huxley's minister of education (1963:208): on the child and his potentialities:

> How does he do his thinking, perceiving and remembering? Is he a visualizer or a non-visualizer? Does his mind work with images or with words, with both at once, or with neither? How close to the surface is his storytelling faculty? Does he see the world as Wordsworth and Traherne saw it when they were children? And if so, what can be done to prevent the glory and the freshness from fading into the light of common day? Or in more general terms, how can we educate children on the conceptual level without killing their capacity for intense non verbal experience? How can we reconcile analysis with vision?

Here are the problems of education consequent upon the differential functions of the right and left hemisphere posed clearly a decade before psychology discovered the difference. As Dr. Parnes has clearly told us, problem finding is the necessary precursor of problem solving. Today we have found that El Dorado exists; we also have a map for getting there; we have less than a quarter of a century left to make the immense journey.

References

Arlin, Patrica, "Cognitive Development in Adulthood" *Developmental Psychology* 11:601-6, 1975

Ausubel, D. P. "Defence of Advance Organizers", *Review of Educational Research* 38:2:251-9 Spring, 1978

Blocher, D. *Developmental Counseling*. New York: Ronald Press, 1966

Brown, Ann, "Conservation of Number . . . in Normal, Bright and Retarded Children, *Child Development* 44:376-9, 1973

Colangelo, N. and Zaffram, R. T. (Eds.) *New Voices in Counseling the Gifted*. Dubuque, Ia.: Kendall/Hunt Publishing Company 1979

Epstein, H. T. "Growth Spurts" (p. 343–57) in *Education and the Brain*. Chicago: National Soc'y for the Study of Education Yearbook, 1977

Erikson, E. *Childhood and Society*. New York: Norton Press, 1950

Ferguson, E. S. "The Mind's Eye: Non-Verbal Thought in Technology" *Science* 197:827–36, Aug 26, 1977

Ghiselin, B. *The Creative Process*. New American Library, 1952

Ginsberg E. and others. *Occupational Choice: An Approach to a General Theory*. New York: Columbia Press, 1951

Gowan, J. C. "The Organization of Guidance for Gifted Children" *Personnel and Guidance Journal* 39:275–79, Dec. 1960

Gowan, J. C. *Development of the Creative Individual.* San Diego: R. Knapp Pub. Co. 1972

Gowan, J. C. *Development of the Psychedelic Individual.* Buffalo: The Creative Education Foundation, 1974

Gowan, J. C. "Incubation, Imagery and Creativity" *Journal of Mental Imagery* 2:23–43, Spring, 1978a

Gowan, J. C. "Education for the Gifted in Utopia" *Mensa Research Journal* 8:2:2–11, Fall, 1978b

Gowan, J. C. and Demos, G. D. *The Education and Guidance of the Ablest.* Springfield, Il.: C. C. Thomas Pub. Co. 1964

Gruber, H. E. "Courage and Cognitive Change in Children and Scientists", in Schwebel M. and Raph, J. (Eds.) *Piaget in the Classroom.* New York: Basic Books, 1973

Harrow, Anita, *A Taxonomy of the Psychomotor Domain.* New York: McKay Co. 1972

Havighurst, R. J. "Youth in Exploration and Man Emergent" (p. 215–36) in Borow, H. *Man in a World of Work.* Boston: Houghton-Mifflin, 1964

Hunt, I. and Draper, W. W. *Lightning in His Hand.* Hawthorne, CA: Omni Publications, 1964

Huxley, J. *Island.* New York: Harper & Row, 1962

Jaynes, J. *The Origins of Consciousness in the Breakdown of the Bicameral Mind.* Boston: Houghton-Mifflin, 1976

Keating, D. P. *Intellectual Talent: Research and Development.* Baltimore: The Johns Hopkins University Press, 1976

Koestler, A. *The Act of Creation.* New York: Macmillan, 1964

Kohlberg, L. and Mayer, Rochelle, "Development as the Aim of Education," *Harvard Educational Review* 42:449–496, Nov. 1972

Kris, E. "Psychoanalysis and the Study of Creative Imagination", *Bulletin of N.Y. Academy of Medicine* (p. 334–51), 1953

Kubie, L. *Neurotic Distortion of the Creative Process.* Lawrence: University of Kansas Press, 1958

Mann, W. E. *Orgone, Reich & Eros.* New York: Simon & Schuster, 1973

Maslow, A. *Motivation and Personality.* New York: Harper Bros. 1954

Perry, W. G. *Forms of Intellectual and Ethical Development.* New York: Holt, Rinehart & Winston, 1968

Piaget, J. *The Psychology of Intelligence.* London: Routledge & Kegan Paul, 1950

Simpson, J. "Developmental Process Theory as Applied to Mature Women," *Gifted Child Quarterly* 21:3:359–71, Fall, 1977

Simpson, E. J. *The Classification of Educational Objectives: Psychomotor Domain.* Urbana: University of Illinois Press, 1966

Suchman, J. B. "Creative Thinking and Conceptual Growth" (p. 89–95) in Gowan, J. C. Demos, G. D. and Torrance, E. P. (Eds.) *Creativity: Its Educational Implications.* New York: J. Wiley, 1967

Torrance, E. P. *Guiding Creative Talent.* Englewood Cliffs, N.J.: Prentice-Hall, 1962

Vygotsky, L. "The Problem of A ge-periodization in Child Development", *Human Development* 17:24–40, 1974

Wallas, G. *The Art of Thought,* London, C. A. Watts, 1926

Washton, N. S. "Teaching Science Creatively: A Taxonomy of Pupil Questions", *Science Education* 5:428–31, 1967

Webb, R. A. "Concrete and Formal Operations in Very Bright 6 to 11 Year Olds", *Human Development* 17:292–300, 1974

Williams R. "Why Children Should Draw: *Saturday Review* (p. 11–16) Sept. 3, 1977

10. CROSS-CULTURAL STUDIES OF CREATIVE DEVELOPMENT IN SEVEN SELECTED SOCIETIES

E. Paul Torrance

Theorists and researchers in the field of human development have for hundreds of years been divided on the issue as to whether it is healthy for intellectual development to be continuous or discontinuous and in stages. Such educators as Pestalozzi and Froebel argued strongly for the concept of continuity of growth while Freud, Sullivan, Erikson, and others have emphasized the concept of stages of development. When various aspects of mental development have been studied empirically and quantitatively, the occurrence of stages has been revealed. These discontinuities have generally been accepted as inevitable and healthy in spite of the fact that they are quite frequently accompanied by behavioral problems, difficulties in learning, emotional disturbance, and other symptoms of poor mental health.

For many years psychologists and educators have observed a rather severe discontinuity in creative functioning and development at about ages nine and ten (fourth and fifth grades). Seldom was any attempt made to quantify and document this discontinuity. Perhaps it was too obvious to require such documentation. Near the end of the Nineteenth Century, however, researchers began documenting this slump in creative thinking. Examples are found in the research of investigators such as Kirkpatrick, Simpson, Torrance and Hiller, Axtell, and others. At the same time other investigators documented other discontinuities of development that are logically related to the one in creative thinking. Barber and Calverly found that at this fourth grade stage, children are more suggestible; McConnell found that they possessed greater visual perceptual suggestibility; L'Abate found an increase in uncertainty behavior; Barkan detected an increase in perfectionistic tendencies; and Boland found a decrease in willingness to take a dare.

Original data have been cited to support the existence of important discontinuities in education and in society at about the time a child enters the fourth grade in our dominant, advantaged culture of the United States. Parents become greatly concerned about the problems exhibited by children at this stage of development, as measured by the number of letters written to the investigator. Statistics concerning mental health and psychoeducational clinic referrals in Atlanta, Los Angeles, and Minneapolis show sharp upswings in the number of referrals during the fourth and fifth grades.

In an attempt to investigate the universality of the slump in creative development and functioning at the fourth-grade level, cross-sectional studies of creative development were conducted in each of seven different cultural groups. It was thought that data thus derived would help resolve the issue as to whether the fourth-grade slump in creative development is culture-made or natural and inevitable. The cultures selected for study were as follows:

1. An advantaged, dominant subculture in the United States (a suburban, all white school in the Minneapolis, Minnesota, area).
2. A disadvantaged, minority subculture in the United States (a segregated, Negro school in Georgia).

Reprinted by permission from *Educational Trends*, Vol. 8, No. 1, January-October, 1973.

3. An almost primitive culture with a reputation for suppressing creative functioning and development and resisting change (mission and government schools in Western Samoa).
4. A European culture with a history of creative achievement and known to be relatively low in peer-orientation (two schools in West Berlin, Germany, one in a workman's neighborhood and another in an advantaged, surburban neighborhood).
5. A European culture with a history of limited creative achievement (two schools in Norway, one in an isolated mountain village and rural area and another in a suburban area near Oslo).
6. Another English-speaking culture with a reputation for strong authority control and weak peer-orientation (an urban and rural school in Western Australia).
7. An underdeveloped and emerging culture made up of many rather distinct sub-cultures with different languages (seven schools in New Delhi, India, each representing a different culture).

METHODS

The basic plan of this set of cross-cultural studies of creative development called for the administration of figural and veral batteries of creative thinking ability in each of the seven cultures to samples of children from the first through the sixth grades. The cultures were chosen on the basis of known differences in the way they deal with creative behavior and encourage or discourage the characteristics judged to be essential to the development of creative personalities.

In addition to the basic data—responses to the battery of creative thinking tests by samples of 500 to 1,000 children from grades one through six in each of the seven cultures—supplementary data were collected to help in understanding and interpreting performance on the tests of creative thinking. Except in Norway, teachers were interviewed concerning their classroom practices, their philosophy of education, and their concepts of what kinds of behavior should be encouraged and discouraged among children. Except in Western Samoa and Australia, the fourth and fifth grade children wrote imaginative stories concerning animals and persons with divergent characteristics. Children in each of the samples indicated their occupational choices or aspirations. In some instances, special analyses were made of the children's literature in the culture with special reference to the characteristics encouraged and discouraged in the stories.

In all seven samples, three figural and six verbal tests were used for assessing the creative thinking abilities. In most instances, the verbal tests were not administered below the third grade. These batteries had been developed by the investigator and are now available rather generally for research purposes. The tests were translated by language experts into the native languages or dialects of the subjects. In all instances subjects were encouraged to respond in the language and dialect in which they felt most comfortable. In most instances, responses were translated into English and the translated rezponses were scored. Most of the test booklets were scored three or four times. The final scoring was accomplished by a single person, however, using the most up-to-date scoring concepts uniformly.

Data collection was accomplished in 1960 and 1961, in almost all cases near the end of the school year for the children concerned. (For children in Minneapolis, Minnesota, the end of the school year meant May and in Norway it meant June; in Western Samoa and in Western Australia it meant November). The final scoring and statistical analysis of the data were accomplished during the summer and fall of 1967.

RESULTS

Evidence was presented to support the argument in favor of a high degree of commonality in the dominant, advantaged culture of the United States. On the Ideal Pupil Checklist, the rank-order correlations among different groups of teachers in such diverse localities as Minnesota, California, New York, Georgia, Mississippi, and Michigan are all quite high (.95 and higher). When the rankings obtained from data supplied by 1,512 teachers in the dominant, advantaged culture of the United States were correlated they were moderate or low. The rank-order coefficients of correlation between each of the cultures from whom data were obtained and the U.S. comparison group and expert ratings of the ideal creative personality are as follows:

Comparison Group	Rank-Order Coefficients of Correlation	
	U.S. Teachers	Expert Panel
U.S. Comparison Group	.96	.43
U.S. Negroes	.78	.21
Western Australia	.85	.19
Western Samoa	.56	.17
West Germany (Berlin)	.81	.37
India (New Delhi)	.81	.11

From the rank-order coefficients of correlation between the rankings by teachers of the six groups and the rankings of the expert panel, the predicted levels of creative functioning would be as follows:

1. U.S. Dominant, Advantaged Culture.
2. West Germany, Inner City and Suburban.
3. U.S. Negroes, Disadvantaged Culture.
4. Western Australia, Urban and Rural.
5. Western Samoa, Urban Mission and Remote Government Schools.
6. India, Christian Mission, Muslim, Sikh, and Nationalistic Schools.

This prediction is borne out quite well in the data obtained in this study on the level of creative functioning of fourth-grade children. The mean scores of the fourth-grade level on each of the measures were converted to standard or T-score equivalents for each of the cultures. (Standard scores were based on U.S. Comparison Group data for the fifth grade). The sums of these standard scores were then obtained and the following rankings resulted:

	Total
1. U.S. Comparison Group	350
2. West Germany	341
3. U.S. Negro	307
4. Western Australia	305
5. India	298
6. Western Samoa	295

It will be observed that only one small error in prediction occurred, giving a rank-order correlation of .97 between the predicted rankings and the actual rankings.

Figure 1 presents more information concerning the relative standing of the seven cultures at the fourth-grade level on the seven creative thinking variables. It will be noted that the rankings shift somewhat from variable to variable. In the discussion, it will be argued that these shifts can be explained logically on the basis of the way children at about the fourth-grade level are treated in the culture and in terms of what kinds of behavior are encouraged or discouraged throughout the culture.

In a number of ways, the creativity level of a culture as a whole may be distorted by using only the fourth-grade data. In order to make use of all of the data from the creative thinking test performances, an overall creativity index was developed for each of the seven groups. All mean raw scores at each grade level were converted to T-score equivalents based on the U.S. Comparison Group data for the fifth grade. A mean figural and a mean verbal score were then computed for

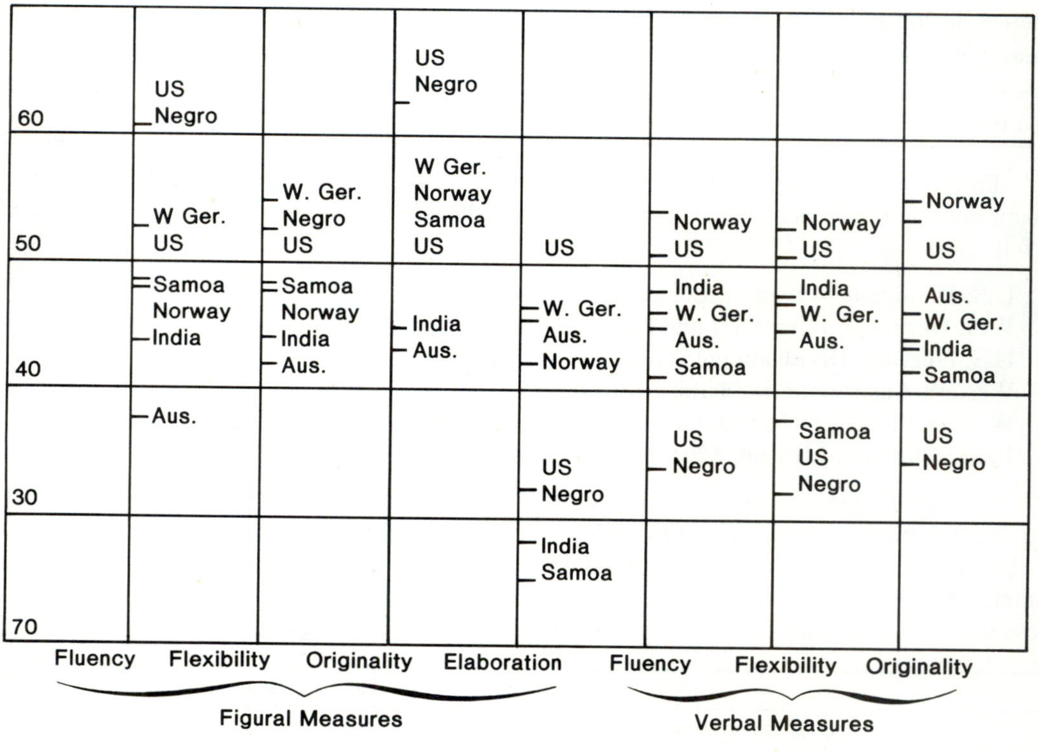

T-score	Figural: Fluency	Flexibility	Originality	Elaboration	Verbal: Fluency	Flexibility	Originality
60	US Negro		US Negro				
50	W. Ger. / US	W. Ger. Negro / US	W Ger. Norway Samoa / US	US	Norway / US	Norway / US	Norway / US
40	Samoa Norway / India	Samoa Norway / India / Aus.	India / Aus.	W. Ger. Aus. Norway	India / W. Ger. / Aus. / Samoa	India / W. Ger. / Aus.	Aus. / W. Ger. / India / Samoa
30	Aus.			US Negro	US Negro	Samoa US Negro	US Negro
70				India Samoa			

Fluency   Flexibility   Originality   Elaboration   Fluency   Flexibility   Originality

Figural Measures   Verbal Measures

Figure 1. Relative standing of fourth graders in seven different cultures on each of seven measures of creative thinking.

each of the seven cultures. The creativity index is the sum of these two means. This procedure resulted in the following mean score and rankings:

Rank	Culture	Figural	Verbal	Total
1	U.S. Comparison Group	47.3	49.9	97.2
2	West Germany	45.3	47.2	92.5
3	Norway	43.1	45.2	88.3
4	Western Australia	39.4	42.7	82.1
5.5	U.S. Negro	42.9	37.1	80.0
5.5	India	37.3	42.7	80.0
7	Western Samoa	40.4	38.9	79.3

Going back to the rankings derived from the rank-order correlations obtained between the rankings of the teachers of the characteristics of the Ideal Pupil Check-list with the rankings obtained by the expert panel with the productive, creative person as the criterion, a rank-order correlation was run against the above rankings (omitting Norway, of course). A rank-order coefficient of correlation of .96 was obtained.

In obtaining the data concerning occupational choices and aspirations, it was hypothesized that the freedom to grow creatively will be influenced by the freedom of children to consider a diversity of occupations and to consider the creative occupations as possibilities. There are many alternative methods of obtaining an index of this freedom, but the one chosen for this study is the sum of the percentage of all children in the sample choosing occupations outside of the twenty-five most popular occupation or occupations in visual art, music, dance, and drama. The following rankings and indexes resulted from this procedure:

Rank	Culture	Index
1	U. S. Comparison Group	47
2	West Germany	30
3	Australia	21
4	Norway	14
5.5	U.S. Negro	10
5.5	India	10
7	Western Samoa	7

It will be noted that the rankings obtained here are with one minor exception identical with the rankings based on the total performance of all grades on the creative thinking tests. The rankings for Norway and Western Australia are reversed. The rank-order coefficient between the two sets of rankings is .96.

The overall indexes in standard or T-score units also provide a helpful way of examining the continuity and discontinuity phenomena. These data are summarized in Table 1. Speaking in rather general terms, the U. S. comparison group showed decreases in both the figural and verbal measures between the third and fourth grades and showed some recovery between the fourth and fifth grades.

TABLE 1
Comparison of the Mean Figural and Mean Verbal Scores for Each Culture at Each Grade Level Expressed in Standard (T-Score) Units

Culture	1st Gr. Fig.	2nd Gr. Fig.	3rd Gr. Fig. Verb.		4th Gr. Fig. Verb.		5th Gr. Fig. Verb.		6th Gr. Fig. Verb.	
U. S. Comp.	43	48	47	54	44	46	50	50	51	50
Germany	43	41	43	42	46	42	59	49	40	57
Norway	40	44	43	41	44	49	46	45	43	46
Australia	39	40	36	40	39	42	41	44	41	45
U. S. Negro	33	43	46	37	48	36	. .	36	. .	40
India	32	34	36	42	42	42	43	40	37	48
West Samoa	36	40	40	38	42	37	42	39	43	41

The German children experienced a slight slump in the second grade on the figural measures and reached an apex in the fifth grade. Their most serious decrease occurred between the fifth and sixth grades on the figural measures. During this period, however, there was a considerable increase in performance on the verbal measures.

The Norwegian children experienced a slump in figural performance in the sixth grade and one in verbal performance in the fifth grade.

The Australian subjects showed a fairly severe slump in figural performance in the third grade but showed no slump in verbal performance.

The U. S. Negro children showed no slump through the fourth grade on the figural measures but data for the fifth and sixth grades on the verbal tests were not obtained. There was little increase or decrease in verbal performance until the sixth grade.

The subjects in India showed their slump in figural performance in the sixth grade. As with the Negro group, there was little change in the level of verbal functioning until the sixth grade at which time there was an increase of almost a standard deviation.

Among the Western Samoans, there was little growth reflected on the figural measures except between the first and second grades. At no time was there much growth on the verbal measures.

It is interesting to note that the children in some cultures tended to perform at a relatively higher level on the figural tests, while those in other cultures performed at a relatively higher level on the verbal ones. The German, Norwegian, Australian, and Indian groups tended to perform somewhat better on the verbal than on the figural measures while the Samoan and Negro children functioned at a higher level on the figural measures.

In almost all of the seven groups, the mean developmental profiles show significant departures from linearity. In the more disadvantaged cultures such as Western Samoa and the U. S. Negro groups, the departure from linearity seems to have resulted from a lack of growth. In most cases, however, the departure from linearity seems to have been associated with sharp decreases in performance at some grade level, the grade level varying from culture to culture but generally occurring at about the end of the third or beginning of the fourth grade. When specific groups within the larger samples are studied separately, continuities and discontinuities of development occur with considerable clarity. This is illustrated by Johnson's analyses of development in the mission schools with their discontinuities in contrast to the highly continuous culture of the isolated government schools where traditions are staunchly maintained and a recently acquired alphabet has had little impact. It is also illustrated in the analyses of Prakash in India. Where British and American influences have been strongest, the discontinuities are clearest. Where the native culture and language predominates, the continuities are clearest.

DISCUSSION AND CONCLUSION

The combined evidence presented in this report support the idea that cultural factors strongly influence the course of creative development, the level of creative functioning, and the type of creative functioning that flourishes most. In some cultures, development is relatively continuous. In others, there is little growth during the elementary school years. In most, however, there are discontinuities. In general, these discontinuities occur at about the beginning of the fourth grade or the end of the third grade; in some groups, discontinuities do not appear until the sixth grade. There are a number of indications that these discontinuities occur within a culture whenever children in that culture are confronted with new stresses and demands. When Christian missions and similar groups establish schools in underdeveloped areas, they apparently bring both a stimulating and a disrupting influence on development, producing discontinuities in creative development.

The anthropologically oriented interviews with the teachers of the subjects of this study, the analyses of the imaginative stories written by the subjects, the studies of the children's literature and folk stories of the cultures, the Ideal Pupil Checklist data supplied by the teachers, analyses of the occupational choices and aspirations of the subjects and the independent studies of other investigators of the particular cultures under study provide many possible explanations of the findings of this study. At a gross, general level, the occupational choice data and the teachers' responses to the Ideal Pupil Checklist seem to be related to the overall level of creative functioning of the children within a culture. This does not mean that other clues given in these studies are not as powerful, but these data were collected from all or almost all of the cultures in a rather uniform manner and it is possible to derive meaningful indexes from them. When the composite rankings of the teachers of six of the seven cultures were correlated with the rankings of an expert panel in terms of the ideal, productive, creative personality, we can order the cultures in terms of the creative functioning of the children of that culture rather accurately (rank-order coefficient of correlation, .94). When we derive an index from the percentage of occupational choices and aspirations outside a list of the 25 most popular occupations with children in the United States and add to it the percentage who express a desire to be visual artists, actors, musicians, dancers, and scientists, the resulting index also makes possible a rather accurate ordering of these cultures in terms of the creative functioning of the children in those cultures (rank-order coefficient of correlation of .96).

When we seek greater precision and attempt to explain differential level of functioning on the figural and verbal measures of fluency, flexibility, originality, and elaboration, we have to look more closely at the above data and at other characteristics of the cultures involved. The more highly developed cultures such as the U. S. Advantaged culture, West Germany, Australia, and Norway stand separately from the more underdeveloped cultures such as the U. S. Negro group, Western Samoa, and India on elaboration. In the more developed cultures, complexity and elaboration are required for satisfactory adjustment. In the less developed countries, such complexity of thinking might be maladaptive. Something simpler is frequently more effective in these cultures.

Except for India, children in the underdeveloped countries performed quite poorly on the verbal tests. Western Samoa has had a written language for only a few years and textbooks and books of all kinds are still quite rare. In the U. S. Negro culture, numerous studies have also pointed to the lack of books, lack of perceptual awareness, gross deficiencies in all kinds of verbal skills, and the like. In India, however, there is great emphasis on language. Even for a marginal adjustment in a metropolis such as Delhi one must know two or more languages. The school curriculum is overloaded with languages and instruction frequently is conducted in two or more languages. Thus, there is great emphasis on verbal development.

The U. S. Negroes are among the best on figural fluency and originality and lower than any other group on the verbal measures. Where words are not required they can produce many ideas quickly and can make the mental leaps that make it possible for them to get away from the obvious and commonplace. Yet they have serious difficulty in elaborating these ideas and in expressing ideas in words. The Australians show up as inhibited in the figural fluency, flexibility, and originality, yet they rank rather high on figural elaboration even though they produced few ideas. In the United States, this characteristic has been associated with what occurs among pupils taught by high controlling teachers. The data supplied by the teachers themselves and by independent observers do indeed characterize Australian teachers as highly controlling.

Throughout the interview data supplied by the teachers and the independent cultural studies, there were indications of differential treatment for boys and girls. A thorough study of sex differences and the relationship of these differences to the differences in treatment should be made. Already, an examination of the data from the U. S. comparison group suggests a general superiority of boys over girls on figural elaboration and the verbal measures in the upper grades. In two independent studies in India, Prakash (1966) and Raina (1966) found that boys excelled girls on almost all measures, especially the verbal one.

References

Axtell, Joan. Discontinuities in the perception of curiosity in gifted preadolescents. *Gifted Child Quarterly,* 1966, 10, 78–82.

Barber, T. X. and Calverley, D. S. Hypnotic-like suggestibility in children and adults. *Journal of Abnormal Social Psychology,* 1963, 66, 589–597.

Barkan, M. *Through Art to Creativity.* Boston: Allyn & Bacon, 1960.

Boland, Genevieve. Taking a dare. *Pedagogical Seminary,* 1910, 17, 510–524.

Erikson, E. H. *Childhood and Society.* (2nd ed.) New York: W. W. Norton. 1963.

Froebel F. *The Education of Man.* (Trans. from the German by W. N. Hailman) New York: Appleton-Century-Crofts, 1911.

Kirkpatrick, E. A. Individual tests of school children. *Psychological Review,* 1900, 5(7), 274.

L'Abate, L. Sanford's uncertainty hypothesis in children. *ETC: A Review of General Semantics,* 1957, 14, 210–213.

McConnell, T. R., Jr. Suggestibility in children as a function of chronological age. *Journal of Abnormal Social Psychology,* 1963, 67, 286–289.

Prakash, A. O. *A Study of the Creative Thinking Abilities of Indian Children.* Master's research paper, University of Minnesota, 1966.

Raina, M. K. A study of sex differences in creativity in India. Research paper, Regional College of Education, Ajmer, India, 1966.

Simpson, R. M. Creative imagination. *American Journal of Psychology,* 1922, 33, 234–243.

Sullivan, H. S. *Interpersonal Theory of Psychiatry.* New York: W. W. Norton, 1953.

Torrance, E. P. *Rewarding Creative Behavior.* Englewood Cliffs, N.J.: Prentice-Hall, 1965.

Torrance, E. P., and Gupta, R. *Programmed experiences in creative thinking.* Minneapolis: Bureau of Educational Research, Universiy of Minnesota, 1964. (Mimeo).

IV

CAN CREATIVITY BE INCREASED BY PRACTICE?

11. CREATIVE TEACHING MAKES A DIFFERENCE

E. Paul Torrance

A few years ago, it was commonly thought that creativity, scientific discovery, the production of new ideas, inventions, and the like had to be left to chance. Indeed many people still think so. With today's accumulated knowledge, however, I do not see how any reasonable, well-informed person can still hold this view. The amazing record of inventions, scientific discoveries, and other creative achievements amassed through deliberate methods of creative problem-solving should convince even the most stubborn skeptic. Both laboratory and field experiments involving these deliberate methods of improving the level of creative behavior have also been rather convincing. In my own classes and seminars I have consistently found that these deliberate methods can be taught from the primary grades through the graduate school with the effect that students improve their ability to develop original and useful solutions to problems. The evidence is strong that creativity does not have to be left to chance.

I have similarly maintained that the development of the creative thinking abilities does not have to be left to chance. Here I find myself in a distinct minority. Indeed, some educators believe that it would be extremely dangerous to educate children to be creative while they are still children. They argue that the emphasis must be on obedience, conformity, discipline, and fundamentals like the three R's. One educator sought to clinch his argument by saying, "A child has to know the three R's in order to do anything! Isn't it enough that schools teach him to read, write and figure? Let him dash off on his own errands later; let him specialize in college!" Such a statement, of course, reflects a gross misunderstanding of the nature of creative thinking. The development of the creative thinking abilities is at the very heart of the achievement of even the most fundamental educational objectives, even the acquisition of the three R's. It is certainly not a matter of specialization.

For years, students of creative development have observed that five-year olds lose much of their curiosity and excitement about learning, that nine-year olds become greatly concerned about conformity to peer pressures and give up many of their creative activities, that the beginning junior highs show a new kind of concern for conformity to behavioral norms with the consequences that their thinking becomes more obvious, commonplace, and safe. In 1930, Andrews published data to document the drops at about age five. Even earlier, the drops at about ages nine and thirteen had been documented and have been further supported in the Minnesota Studies of Creative Thinking (1962).

Reprinted by permission, Bureau of Educational Research, University of Minnesota, 1964. The Florence S. Dunlop Memorial Lecture, Ontario Council for Exceptional Children, Point Credit, Ontario, Canada, October 30, 1964.

Those who have commented on the drops in creative thinking ability and creative behavior in general have almost always assumed that these were purely developmental phenomena. (For example, Wilt (1959) observed that creativity may all but take a holiday at about age nine or ten and returns only for a few after the crisis has passed. She concludes that about all that can be done is to keep open the gates for its return. Rarely, however, has anyone taken a contrary stand. One of these rare individuals, Susan Nichols Pulsifer (1960), has taken such a stand concerning the abandonment of creativity at about age five. She maintains that it is not a natural developmental change but is due to the sharp man-made change which confronts the five-year old and impels him by its rules and regulations.)

If our research at the University of Minnesota has contributed anything to thinking about this problem, it has come from my unwillingness to accept the assumption that the severe drops in measured creative thinking ability are purely developmental phenomena that must be accepted as unchangeable. As we entered into our longitudinal studies, it seemed obvious to me that many children needlessly sacrificed their creativity, especially in the fourth grade, and that many of them did not recover as they continued through school. It also seemed to me that many of our problems of school drop outs, delinquency, and mental illness have their roots in the same forces that cause these drops.

It will certainly take a great deal more research than we now have before very many people will be convinced about this matter. Personally, I consider the accumulated evidence rather convincing. One of the first positive bits of evidence came from my experiences in studying the creative development of two fourth-grade classes taught by teachers who are highly successful in establishing creative relationships with their pupils and who give them many opportunities to acquire information and skills in creative ways. There was no fourth-grade slump in these classes, either in measured creative thinking abilities or in participation in creative activities.

A somewhat more convincing line of evidence has come from our studies of the development of the creative thinking abilities in different cultures. As we have obtained results from the administration of our tests of creative thinking in diverse cultures, we have found that the developmental curve takes on a different shape in each culture and that the characteristics of the developmental curve can be explained in terms of the way the culture treats curiosity and creative needs.

For purposes of illustration, let us examine the developmental curve for non-verbal originality in the United States, Western Samoa, Australia, Germany, India, and in United States Negroes. There are no drops in the developmental curve for Samoan subjects. The level of originality begins in the first grade at the lowest level of any of the cultures studied but the growth is continuous from year to year. The second greatest continuity in development is shown by the U.S. Negro sample, although some of the specific cultural groups in India show curves almost identical to those of the Samoan subjects. Through the fourth grade, German and Australian children seem to show about the same level and pattern of development. Pressures towards standardization and conformity apparently occur quite early and continue for the Australian child but not for the German child. The overall pattern of growth among the children in India is much the same as in the United States, especially in the mission schools and public schools.

What are some of the things which make a difference? This is the search in which my staff and I have engaged for the past five years. We have studied the development of the creative thinking abilities in a variety of schools in the United States and in other countries. We have tried to discover what are the factors in nature and society which influence this development. We have conducted both laboratory-type experiments and field experiments in an attempt to see what effect certain changes in teaching procedures will have. We have tried to create various kinds of instructional materials which will have built into them many of the principles which have been discovered through this research.

These and other experiences have left me with the firm conviction that teaching can indeed make a difference insofar as creative development is concerned. Methods, materials, attitudes, relationships with pupils, and other aspects of teaching have been shown to make a difference. Yesterday I stated that I believe creative needs and abilities are universal enough to make creative ways of learning useful for all children, though not an exclusive way of learning for any children. Yet I am convinced that some children who do not learn in other ways will learn if permitted or encouraged to learn in creative ways. In other words, for these children learning in creative ways truly *makes the difference!*

WHEN DOES CREATIVE LEARNING OCCUR?

You may be asking, "How can I tell that creative learning is taking place?" I do not believe this is difficult. This summer I asked 200 students in my class in "Creative Ways of Teaching" to list within a five-minute period all of the signs they could think of to tell whether creative learning is taking place. When I analyzed their lists, I found that altogether they had listed 230 different signs I would accept as valid indicators that creative learning is occurring in a classroom or other learning situation. Since a person can be creative in an infinite number of ways, it is not surprising that a list of 230 signs was produced within a five-minute period. You might be interested in some of these signs. I have them arranged alphabetically, so let us examine the A, B, C's of creative learning, remembering that there are also D, E, F's and so on.

Absorption—there is absorbed listening, absorbed watching, absorbed thinking, or absorbed doing—sometimes irritating but searching for the truth
Achievement—there is a feeling of moving forward towards goals, getting things done
Acceptance—of individual differences in preferred ways of learning, differences in learning rates, faults, etc.
Admission—of errors, mistakes, and failures
Alert—listening and observation, intense awareness of the environment
Aloneness respected—there are times when the best learning can be done outside of the group but with purpose
Animation—there is movement, aliveness and spirit in whatever is done
Analogizing—there is play with various kinds of analogies as ways of stating and solving problems
Arguments—differences are permitted and used to correct mistaken ideas and find more creative productive solutions
Art media are used to develop and elaborate ideas and to give them concreteness
Atmosphere is tingling with excitement and communication of ideas

Behavior problems rare
Bells frequently unheard or unnoticed
Bodily involvement in writing, speaking, thinking, etc.
Boldness of ideas, drawings, stories, etc.
Brainstorming possible
Bulletin boards contain pupils' ideas
Bursting out to complete the teacher's sentence or to communicate some new idea or discovery
Busy hum of activity

Change of pace and approaches to learning or problem-solving
Challenging of ideas
Charged atmosphere
Changes in plans to permit one thing to lead to another
Checking many sources of information and ideas
Choice making
Close observations possible
Colorful, bold art work
Communication of ideas and feelings
Comparisons and contrasts are made
Community used
Combination activities cutting across the curriculum
Composing own songs
Consideration of apparently unrelated ideas and showing relationships
Concentration on work, not easily distracted
Conflicting ideas leading to new ideas
Continuation of activities after the bell
Continuity of activities, one thing leading to another
Control freedom
Curiosity evident in questions, experimenting, manipulating, and reading to find out.

WHAT DIFFERENCE DOES CREATIVE TEACHING MAKE?

Even from this partial list of signs of creative learning, logical reasoning would lead us to expect that changes will occur in the lives of the children who participate in such learning. In our experimental work we have usually been concerned about some effect of creative teaching on classes, schools, or school systems. From these studies, we know that creative teaching seems to result in increased creative growth as measured by changes in performance on tests of creative thinking ability, creative writing, and the like; increased participation in creative activities on one's own; increased liking for school; and changed career aspirations. These experiments do not tell us what differences creative teaching makes in individual lives over extended periods of time.

To obtain some exploratory data to develop some clues about this matter, I asked my California students to recall instances in which they had allowed or encouraged children, young people, or adults to express themselves creatively and then observed that the experience made a difference in achievement and behavior. These students included teachers, administrators, and school psychologists at all levels of education from nursery school to college and adult education. Of the 165 students present when this request was made, 135 or 82 per cent were able to recall such instances.

Only a few of these respondents denied that creative teaching can make a difference. In these rare instances the denial seems to stem from the mistaken notion that all changes in behavior and achievement are of a developmental nature and independent of teacher influence. For example, one teacher wrote as follows:

> "Right now, I can't really remember any particular child whom I've encouraged and where there has been a noticeable change. I have always felt that any change at the end of kindergarten year was due mainly to the natural development growth for the five-year old. . . ."

This attitude is encountered frequently among teachers and developmental psychologists who have accepted the view that developmental processes are set, genetically determined, and unchangeable. I believe that this view results from a misinterpretation of developmental studies. These studies describe the developmental processes which occur when children experience only what the environment happens to provide. Recent studies are showing that the developmental processes can be quite different when children experience guided, planned experiences designed to lead to certain kinds of development.

Let us examine some of the changes mentioned most frequently by the 135 students who responded to my request to recall an incident in which creative teaching had made a difference:

From non-readers to average or superior readers

From vandalism, destructiveness and lack of school achievement to constructive behavior and improved achievement

From emotionally disturbed and unproductive behavior to productive behavior and even outstanding school achievement

From estrangement and lack of communication to good contact with reality and sensitive communication with others

From social isolation and rejection to social acceptance and productive group membership

From fighting and hostility to improved speech skills and lack of hostility

From bitter, hostile sarcasm to kindly, courteous, thoughtful behavior

From apathy and dislike of school to enthusiasm about learning

From lack of self-confidence and self-expression to adequate self-confidence and creative expression

From mediocrity of achievement among gifted pupils to outstanding performance

From diagnoses of mental retardation to diagnoses of normal or superior mental functioning

From a troublesome student to outstanding job performance

I was interested to note that some of these experienced teachers indicated that it was only a knowledge that teaching can make a difference that sustains them in their teaching roles.

Let us examine now a few examples which illustrate some of the different kinds of changes attributed to creative teaching.

From Non-reader to Reader. The most frequently mentioned type to change mentioned by the 135 respondents is from non-reader to reader, usually accompanied by improved behavior and achievement in general. Some of these changes occur in the primary grades, while others do not occur until the intermediate grades or the junior high school years. The following anecdote describes the occurrence of such a change during the second grade:

> "In second grade we do lots of creative writing and I usually type the children's stories and let them illustrate them. John, a dreamy lad, artistic, sloppy, and a very slow reader, disturbed me by never getting more than a sentence or so written. Usually that was lost in the crumpled welter in his desk by the time the next chance to work on it came around. John was a "poor listener" and took offense over nothing. He often cried because he thought he was being slighted. (The sociogram showed him not so much rejected as ignored.)
>
> "One day I let him dictate to me and I typed his story as he talked. He wanted to tell the story of the *Spider*—from a TV horror story. I was tempted to censor this, but fortunately kept my mouth shut. John's story was long. It was a problem to take the time to do it all, but I did, while the class carried on. His choice of words, sentence structure, use of suspense, etc. were very vivid, imaginative, mature. When I read the story to the class, the reaction was one of wild enthusiasm. John was starry-eyed. He learned to read the story, did many more, and learned to read other things. His behavior improved and he made friends."

From Destructive Behavior to Constructive Behavior. Destructive behavior on the part of a child or adolescent is especially disturbing to teachers, classmates, and administrative and custodial personnel. Students describing the consequences of creative teaching indicate that destructive behavior can be transformed into positive, creative energy and generally constructive behavior. The following is an account of one such instance:

"The principal, the janitor, the teachers all worked on the problem of John, the vandal. He was reported as being the culprit of many a weekend shambles at our school, but no one could prove anything. He couldn't stay still very long; his iron muscles seemed to need to move every minute; he was as strong, at 12 years, as most grown men. He was almost a permanent fixture in the office because of undesirable behavior. He was skilled, a *natural*, in things mechanical. He liked to boss and was often swaggering and bully-like in his playground behavior. The consensus as a result of brainstorming, was that John did not feel he belonged. The problem was how to make him feel he *did* belong.

"He was appointed by the Student Council (in which he could never be an officer, because of their strict code of grades and behavior) to be a chairman of the Lunchroom Committee. He organized a team of boys; they spent half their noon recess cleaning, moving tables, helping the janitor. He began to notice the litter which collected in certain windy corners of the schoolyard. His 'gang' cleaned it up. He helped park cars for Back-to-School-Night. One woman ran her car into a deep ditch, when she did not wait for John to show her the way. The way he directed her, telling her how to cramp the wheels and when was a marvel. She would have had to have a tow-away, except for his know-how. He had organized the entire parking area without a hitch, where the drivers followed his directions, and all this done as well as an adult could have done it.

"Happily, as John became 'part' of the school, the vandalism became less and less. Reports came to us that he threatened (and coming from this boy that was no mean threat) others who tried to destroy school property. Happily, he began to take an interest in school work. His father told us that John had at last said, 'I like school.' He said John had learned to read things around the house, in the neighborhood, at the store, and on trips for the first time in his life. His art work (racing cars, car engines and antique cars) was excellent. We all hope some of this progress will continue when he leaves us this fall to go to junior high school.

From Trouble Maker to Star Learner and Teacher. In the case of John, ability for verbal learning is perhaps limited although his capacity for art, mechanics, and leadership may be outstanding. Thus, the development of his potentialities might take a direction quite different from that reported for David, a younger learner:

"David had been a problem in kindergarten. He knew it and acted it out in the first and second grades. He had thoroughly convinced everyone he was a problem by the time he entered my third grade.

"A thatch of yellow hair, crystal clear blue eyes—as he walked along the path to school all he needed was a fishing pole over his shoulder to be the perfect Huckleberry Finn! He intrigued me and interested me beyond words—there must be a key to David, and I must try to find it.

"I set the stage in every possible way so he would do a few things at least that we could praise—this was a shock to him and he didn't know quite what to do with praise! . . . By Christmas time we had arrived at the point of mutual respect for one another.

"At Christmas in our room we take a trip around the world and explore the Christmas customs of the children in our countries. This year we had decided to go by plane. We had a representative from the airlines as a guest speaker—telling about tickets, traveling by plane, and showing some slides of various countries.

"The day came when each child was to make his ticket for the country he wished to visit. I was surprised as I watched David—usually he was one of the last ones to start, but this time he was well on his way immediately. As I 'toured' the room, I noticed David's ticket would be for Sweden. This surprised me as he had brought many things from Mexico in for Sharing Time, and I had rather thought his ticket would be for Mexico. The 'Captain' for the trip arranged his 'passenger' list by countries. David was the only one for Sweden. This seemed to please him, and as time passed we were all amazed at the responsibility he assumed in finding things to present about 'his country.'

"We found that he had chosen this country because his favorite grandmother had come from Sweden. . . . He found it necessary to write five or six letters to her for various items of information. I was surprised at the neatness and the care with which he did the job—would that he had done many of his other papers in like manner!

"He wrote some wonderful factual stories about Sweden. His Swedish fairy tales were really something! He often found expression at the easel—and such vivid colors.

"The day when the class were his 'guests' in Sweden he told of the customs and even taught us a game the Swedish children play. He also taught us to make little 'goodie' baskets they hang on their Christmas trees.

"Our children come to school by bus, but the two weeks before Christmas David walked nearly every morning because he wanted to get there early so he could get extra painting or writing done. As he was telling me goodbye on the last day of school before the holidays, he said, 'Gee, Miss T., this is the neatest Christmas I've ever had—I feel like I've almost been to Sweden.'

"I had found my 'key' to David. He needed to find out things and tell them—sometimes do a bit of embroidery on them—sometimes do a bit of dreaming and make-believe on them. He liked his real world much better too.

"This did change David—he no longer needed to be the 'bad boy'—he adjusted to the praise and found it 'fun' (as he said) to write stories, draw pictures, etc. of his 'secret world.' He was so busy doing this he didn't have time to revert to the 'old' David."

From Estrangement and Retardation to Adjustment and Achievement. A number of the anecdotes related by the respondents involved children who seemed to be estranged and out of contact with reality and regarded as mentally retarded. The following account of Jamie at the time he was in the fifth grade falls into this category:

"Jamie lived on another planet. He seemed to feel no need to relate to the world around him. As he entered the fifth grade, the children thought of him as a 'dumb kid.' In a flexible individual reading program I was able to let him skip around in the book as the spirit moved him and report in the way he was able through drawings. He completed one fourth grade and two fifth grade readers during the year and I feel he is ready to face any sixth grade reading material.

"At the same time in a 'slow' math class he was exposed to an imaginative teacher. By allowing him to use his interest in motors to develop a math project he was able to show a real flair for teaching others and his classmates discovered that Jamie had brains!"

WHAT MADE THE DIFFERENCE?

The incidents I have just reported provide many provocative ideas about what makes a difference. In some ways, the teacher provided a responsive environment—one which involved a sensitive and alert kind of guidance and direction, the creation of an atmosphere of receptive listening, responding to children and young people as they are or might become rather than as they have been told that they are, fighting off ridicule and criticism, and making their efforts to learn worthwhile.

Now, I would like to give you a list of the factors mentioned most frequently by my students in "Creative Ways of Teaching."

Recognizing some heretofore unrecognized and unused potential
Respecting a child's need to work alone
Inhibiting the censorship role long enough for a creative response to occur
Allowing or encouraging a child to go ahead and achieve success in an area and in a way possible for him
Permitting the curriculum to be different for different pupils
Giving concrete embodiment to the creative ideas of children
Giving a chance to make a contribution to the welfare of the group
Encouraging or permitting self-initiated projects
Reducing pressure, providing a relatively non-punitive environment
Approval in one area to provide courage to try in others
Voicing the beauty of individual differences
Respecting the potential of low achievers
Enthusiasm of the teacher
Support of the teacher against peer pressures to conformity
Placing an unproductive child in contact with a productive, creative child
Using fantasy ability to establish contacts with reality
Capitalizing upon hobby and special interests and enthusiasms
Tolerance of complexity and disorder, at least for a period
Involvement
Not being afraid of bodily contact with children
Communicating that the teacher is "for" rather than "against" the child

PERMITTING CHILDREN TO WORK
ALONE AND IN THEIR OWN WAY

In learning and in doing creative work, many people are unable to function very well in a group. They seem to need to "march to a different drumbeat" and to work at their own pace. Much in established ways of teaching creates a set which makes this difficult. Even beginning teachers find it possible, however, to permit such divergency. The following story of Mark's report on Latin America illustrates this point and suggests a number of other ideas as well:

"Last year was my first year of teaching. I had a student, Mark, whom I immediately recognized as an extremely creative student, and someone for whom I had an enormous respect.

"The study of Latin America is a required part of our social studies curriculum for the sixth grade. I followed every step of what I had been taught in 'Teaching Social Studies in the Elementary School' . . . letting the class decide what you need to learn about a people and a country to understand them and their needs, and then a secretary wrote the names of the various Latin American countries on the board, so that the children could select the country's committee they would like to be on to prepare written reports. We decided that the major countries would need more on a committee . . . Ecuador came up, and two people volunteered and were given that country to research and do a project on. After all of the countries had been spoken for, I noticed that Mark had not made a choice.

"Talking with him, I learned that he had wanted Ecuador, as he had been reading Darwin's journals and was fascinated by the Galapagos Islands, but he hadn't wanted to work with anyone, so hadn't held up his hand. Well, I said that was all right, and that he could make up a separate report on the Galapagos Islands, which he agreed to do.

"Three weeks later, Mark had not begun his report, in the sense that he had nothing on paper. He was just too busy reading books, interviewing anthropologists at the University of California, and thinking. I tried very hard to help him get something on paper, but when I saw that he just was too interested in Darwin's discoveries and their implications and the evidence of it that remains to this day on the Islands, I decided Mark's assignment would be changed to an oral report. He reacted very favorably to this, delivering a magnificent account of what kind of person Darwin was, an account of the voyage of the *Beagle,* and then delivered a very instructive lecture on the various forms of a single species as they appear on the different islands, drawing pictures of the variants on the chalkboard, complete with describing the different environment a different island would offer and asking the other students in the class to guess what variant they would imagine would result!

"Mark got such a good feeling out this experience, I was able, when the next report came up, to talk with him in terms of being able to operate in more than one manner and thus be prepared to be flexible and able to choose—I put it to him in terms of baseball; that a player might be a right-hander but it would be to his advantage to also learn to bat left-handed so that he could be a switch-hitter—that he decided he would prepare a written report, which he did— a very good one, and in on time and beautifully done, even as far as presentation—right down to the bibliography.

"The point is, I think, that in honoring his involvement at a particular time in research, he learned to respect me enough to consider the advantages when the next report came around of knowing how to prepare and get in on time a written report."

If we examine the teacher's report of this episode closely, we find several factors involved. It is likely that one of the more salient factors contributing to the success of the teacher in working with Mark was her willingness to change or bend her planned sequence of experiences to permit Mark to function in such a way to achieve his potentialities. He was able to function in terms of his abilities and interests, without actually upsetting the curriculum or the classroom organization. We find, however, that the teacher had already recognized Mark's creative potential and that she had an enormous respect for him. She recognized that she would be bucking a strong force to divert him at this time from his interest in the Galapagos Islands; furthermore, she saw how he might be able to contribute meaningfully to the curriculum for the entire class. She had not counted upon his absorption being so great that he could not find time to write his report. She remained open and flexible, however, and saw that he might contribute most by giving an oral report, a challenge which he met with unexpected skill. Having achieved success and having achieved respect for his teacher, he was then ready to learn some of the more conforming ways of behaving in the educational environment. In fact, he was even able to include a very proper bibliography documenting his report. He has learned adaptive and constructive ways of behaving which will doubtless stand him in good stead throughout his educational career.

A CONCLUDING SUGGESTION

My final suggestion is one created by J. H. Mohrman, one of my students, at the end of the course on "Creative Ways of Teaching." I shall present it to you just as he presented it to me— A Checklist for Creative Teaching:

"There is a story, common in the Navy and Merchant Marine, of the young third mate who had a great admiration for the Master of the ship in which he sailed. He was, however, puzzled about one of the Captain's habits. Quite occasionally while they were at sea, the Captain would take a dog-eared piece of paper from his pocket and study it intently for a few minutes. Following this ritual, the Captain was his usual picture of calm, self-assurance. Although he was never able to learn what was written on the paper, the Third Mate felt that it must contain the ultimate secret of the Captain's success as a seafarer. On one voyage the Captain died while they were at sea, and the Third Mate was given the task of inventorying and packing the Captain's belongings. He was in a high state of excitement as he went about this task knowing that, at last, he would discover the secret written on the slip of paper which the Captain had guarded so jealously. With trembling fingers, the Third Mate removed the paper from the Captain's jacket pocket and opened it to find this "secret" written inside: 'Starboard is Right—Port is Left.'

"We are all somewhat like the Sea Captain, and occasionally need some simple reminder of the elementary principles that we all 'know perfectly well.' For many reasons; partly because we all need a crutch for our courage from time to time, and a stiffner for our resolve, or perhaps more likely, simply a reminder of our good intentions, I have prepared a check-list to keep handy in my desk drawer to remind myself frequently of at least some aspects of the creative process. We all tend to be creatures of habit and to have our judgment beclouded by our ingrained prejudices and predelictions, particularly with regard to what the 'good' pupil or the 'good' classroom is like. Because of the many possibilities for conflict with our own personalities and the creative personality, or some aspect of the classroom where creative learning is taking place, I hope that this simple 'Starboard is Right—Port is Left' type of list will keep us closer to the creative course."

Don't be too "threatened" by the exceptional child—or the unexpected response.
Pay attention to the "atmosphere" of the room.
Don't be too concerned about a higher noise level—if it's a "busy hum."
Remember the creative need to communicate—maybe that whisper is all right.
Don't be blinded by "intelligence" test scores—they don't tell the *whole* story.
Don't be afraid to wander off your teaching schedule—stay flexible.
Encourage divergent ideas—too many of the "right" ideas are stifling.
Be accepting and forgiving of the "mistakes."
Remember, the "obnoxious" child may simply be escaping from the tedium of your class.
Don't let your pride get in the way of your teaching.
Different kinds of children learn in different ways.
Let them "test their limits."
Don't let the pressure for "evaluation" get the upper hand.
Give them a chance to "warm-up" to producing ideas.
Respect the privacy of their responses (especially the less successful ones).
Criticism is killing—use it carefully and in small doses.
How about those "Provocative Questions?"
Don't forget to define the problem.
Don't be afraid to try something different.

"This list could, of course, be added to indefinitely—and I intend to. Also these items won't 'translate' properly for everyone, but it's at least a start, and it will have served its purpose if it helps only me."

I would urge you to create your own list to fit yourself. Each teacher's way of teaching must ultimately be his own unique invention. I wish for you the very greatest success in perfecting your own invention—your way of teaching.

References

Pulsifer, Susan Nichols. *Children Are Poets*. Cambridge, Mass.: Dresser, Chapman & Grimes, Inc., 1963.
Torrance, E. P. *Guiding Creative Talent*. Englewood Cliffs, N. J.: Prentice-Hall, Inc., 1962.
Wilt, Miriam E. *Creativity in the Elementary School*. New York: Appleton-Century-Crofts, 1959.

12. TEACHING FOR SELF-DIRECTED LEARNING: A PRIORITY FOR THE GIFTED AND TALENTED

Donald J. Treffinger

If you would ever like to start a lengthy and heated discussion among educators, one effective technique is to bring up the question of "educational goals." Because of the complex nature of our society, and the many goals and needs of our people, it is understandable (and probably desirable) that education serves many different purposes. While it would certainly seem fruitless to propose that any one set of goals should be considered especially important or "relevant", it does seem quite likely that there are some general purposes which would meet with approval from many parents, students, educators.

Usually, for example, a school's "philosophy", to inform us of the school's purposes or goals, includes some statements like these:

"Every pupil should have the opportunity to develop his or her full potential as a person."
"Our pupils should be able to make decisions effectively, to solve problems, and to think critically and creatively."
"The pupil should become an adult who knows *how* to think, not just *what* to think."

Many critics of education contend that frequently we are better at talking about these goals than we are at meeting them. We tell the public (and ourselves) that we want children to be able to use what is learned in school in solving many every-day problems. We speak of the "joy of learning" or our hopes that pupils will become "life-long learners". Especially for the gifted and talented, we speak of helping pupils learn how to assume the responsibilities of independent inquiry. But, all too often, the school experience primarily provides opportunities for just the opposite. We cannot really be surprised when our students act as if "they cannot handle" the demands of independent learning; ordinarily, we have not taught them how. Instead, pupils learn from the primary grades that *someone else* (usually the teacher, who is presumed to be the wisest person in the room, of course) knows best *what* the pupils should do, *how* and *when* it should be done, and when it has been *completed satisfactorily*. Instead of learning to be critical, imaginative, and independent, there is too often an emphasis on being obedient, cooperative, and dependent.

The principal concern of this paper is to suggest that a goal of primary importance in the education of the gifted and the talented is to *cultivate self-directed learning.*

This goal is especially desirable for the gifted and talented for several reasons. First, most research on the personal characteristics of gifted, talented, and highly creative individuals suggests that they are critical, independent of thought and judgment, self-starting, and perseverant (*e.g.,* Torrance, 1965; Feldhusen, Treffinger and Elias, 1969). Any teacher concerned with adapting instruction to provide for individual differences or learner characteristics should thus attempt to take these attributes into account. In addition, self-directed learning enhances the possibility of increased student involvement and strong, positive motivation for learning. Self-directed learning involves the learner's interests and motives in a way comparable to Bruner's (1961) ideas on

Reprinted by permission from *Gifted Child Quarterly,* Vol. 19, No. 1, 1975.

discovery or Torrance and Myers' (1971) concern for the intrinsic motives in creative learning. Finally, self-directed learning provides an effective way to realize other goals which are frequently discussed but seldom implemented or attained, such as helping the student apply what is learned in school to solving other, day-to-day problems and challenges.

SETTING ASIDE SOME MISUNDERSTANDINGS

Sometimes, especially in a world in which we are constantly confronted with new gadgets and ideas, it is very easy to feel confused. This can also happen in discussions of innovative approaches to teaching and learning.

In our case, there is a danger of confusing "self-directed learning," as used here, with our feelings about many other ideas which have received considerable attention: "open concept" education, "informal" education, "free" or "alternative" schools, or many others. Of course, it would be impossible to stipulate definitions of all these ideas and specify how they do or do not compare with "self-directed learning." Each of these ideas probably has some unique connotations for every reader. Given the nature of much of the publicity for many of these in recent years, the connotations may not be entirely favorable. Thus, it is necessary that we attempt to set aside some of the more common misunderstandings as soon as possible.

(1.) Self-directed learning is neither random nor disorganized. For some people, the first visit to an "open" or "individualized" school results in a perception of randomness and disorganization. This is especially true for adults, who still recall vividly their own school days of sitting quietly in rows of chairs arranged neatly by a stern teacher. Movement and activity of children in many schools today seems almost chaotic. It is too easy to conclude from such initial reactions that an emphasis on the individual needs and efforts of the learner leads to confusion and anarchy. Of course, this is not necessarily the case. Self-directed learning is concerned with creating an environment in which the learner manages and directs his or her efforts towards the attainment of specific goals. It does not involve (nor encourage) outlandish behavior at either extreme. We do not anticipate that teachers should herd children together and impose learning upon them with painful, brute force; neither do we anticipate a school of children screaming, shouting, writing on the walls, and swinging from the light fixtures. Encouraging self-directed learning involves planfulness and a great deal of organization; it is neither excessively rigid (as many teacher-centered ideas appear) nor wildly permissive (as some anti-traditional models appear).

(2.) Self-directed learning is not "unstructured." Many critics of education have seized upon the concept of "structure" and defined it as the arch-enemy of "real learning." This is a fallacy, for in one way or another, whenever *some* systematic effort at education is made, some variety of "structure" does occur. Our goal in creating an environment for self-directed learning is, therefore, to create a supportive structure, not to eliminate structure. We are concerned with designing and implementing an approach in which the structure works to the benefit of the student, rather than restricting or inhibiting the student's efforts. This effort requires that we consider the needs, interests, and personal characteristics of the learner, and that we seek to apply established principles of instructional design in order to establish conditions for effective, personal, creative learning by each student.

110

(3.) Self-directed learning is not so preoccupied with the individual that social outcomes are ignored. The goal of self-directed learning is to assist every learner to become an effective manager and director of his or her own learning. This certainly should imply that the learner will have opportunities to experiment and acquire skills in working with other people, as well as opportunities for independent study. Many parents and teachers are concerned that individualized instruction will place so much emphasis upon working *alone* that pupils will not learn how to work in groups or to get along with others. This *need not* occur; we are not striving to create a generation of hermits. It may be especially important for the teacher of the gifted and talented to provide alternatives for students with opportunities for cooperative efforts with other students (at a wide range of abilities). Self-directed learning emphasizes providing "full services" to meet the needs of each learner; it does not presuppose that all instruction will be carried out by students working alone.

(4.) Self-directed learning is not "selfish" in an unconstructive sense. Critics sometimes assert that an emphasis on self-directed learning risks the creation of students who cannot look beyond their own immediate needs and gratification. This misunderstanding is based upon an incorrect assumption about the learner and about the role of the teacher. We should recognize that gifted and talented students are curious about many problems and issues, capable of abstraction and generalization, and motivated by the unknown and the puzzling. It is therefore incorrect to assume that they would misuse the opportunity to manage and direct their own learning experiences. The teacher, not primarily concerned with imparting information in this approach, can direct his or her energies more effectively into guiding the students' efforts, helping them formulate new problems and questions arising from their work, and developing instructional materials to increase the number and kinds of alternatives available to students in the classroom. These efforts by the teacher, combined with the natural inclinations of the students, will help insure that students will address their efforts to goals and objectives that are neither "selfish" nor trivial.

(5.) Self-directed learning is not merely changing the rate of instruction, but involves a variety of cognitive and affective processes and outcomes. A common misunderstanding about "individualized" approaches to instruction is that the rate of presentation, rather than the nature of the outcomes themselves, is altered. In this view, the learner gets as much time as he or she needs to accomplish what would formerly have been "taught" by a teacher in a fixed period of time. When this misunderstanding occurs, students are merely given assignments or worksheets, one after another ("at their own pace.") The *outcomes* emphasized in those assignments may continue to be primarily knowledge and memory processes—the lowest level of the cognitive taxonomy (Bloom, 1956). Although it is important to allow students to pace their own work, attention must also be given to providing for such complex cognitive outcomes as critical and creative thinking, problem solving, and evaluative thinking and for affective outcomes, including attitudes toward learning, internalization, and commitment to ideals (Krathwohl, 1964; Mager, 1968).

(6.) Evaluation is not absent in self-directed learning. Another major misunderstanding among some proponents of "open" or "alternative" approaches to education is that evaluation is oppressive and discouraging to the learner. Some critics of "traditional" schools have proposed that all forms of evaluation should be abandoned. In a self-directed approach to learning, however, evaluation plays an important role. The focus of evaluation must be changed, however. We are most unconcerned with "passing judgment" and labelling the adequacy of the student's efforts.

Evaluation, when constructively viewed, is primarily a problem of identifying and using as effectively as possible every conceivable source of evidence for the learner's progress or success. Teachers, parents, peers, and older students may be involved in this process at various stages. "Evidence" may include test scores, but must also incorporate many other kinds of performances, including examples of successful accomplishment outside of the school setting. The learner himself should be actively involved in defining and conducting the process of evaluation (*cf.,* Hohn and Treffinger, in press).

(7.) **Self-directed learning does not "just happen," but involves skills which are acquired through planned instructional experiences.** This important misunderstanding has to do with the occasional urgings we hear to let learners work by themselves. This assumes that learners will eventually acquire on their own the ability to manage their own learning. There is no doubt that, under conditions we cannot prescribe with certainty, some learners *do* manage to become self-directing without any deliberate efforts on the part of the school or even despite our efforts to the contrary. That some survive does not warrant the conclusion that self-direction *will* eventually occur naturally among all students. Many students become so thoroughly dependent upon external rewards and structures that involvement in self-directed study at the college level becomes anxiety-producing and uncomfortable (*cf.,* Treffinger and Johnsen, 1973). The goal of fostering self-directed learning should thus require an active commitment by educators. Efforts must be made to provide opportunities for students to learn, gradually and systematically, how to become effective directors and managers of learning. The success of experimental efforts in improving children's creative thinking and problem solving abilities suggests that efforts in this direction can be worthwhile (Davis, 1973; Torrance, 1972).

(8.) **Fostering self-directed learning is not accomplished merely by providing "activities for students to do."** It is very easy for the teacher who is concerned with individualization to focus rather exclusively on assignments, projects, activities, reports, worksheets, and the like. It is very important to recognize, however, that such "things to do" do not necessarily help the student become more autonomous as a learner. The projects and activities which the learner conducts during any instructional episode represent only one part of the total instructional process; in order to foster self-direction, the learner must have opportunities for active participation in every phase of that process. This implies that the learner will be involved (in more than just a trivial way) in the planning of goals and objectives, in the diagnosis of individual needs, and in the evaluation process. To restrict the learner's involvement to carrying out instructional activities presented by the teacher is really to communicate to the learner: "Your job is to do what other people, who know better, tell you to do, when they tell you to do it, and how they tell you to do it." This message may well be over-emphasized for almost every school child; it seems particularly inappropriate, however, when we are attempting to foster self-management among gifted, talented, and highly creative learners.

FOSTERING SELF-DIRECTED LEARNING

What can the teacher do to foster self-directed learning among gifted and talented students? In order to propose a tentative answer to this problem, we can begin by examining a basic model of instruction (*cf.,* DeCecco, 1968; Popham and Baker, 1970; Kibler et al., 1974). This model is depicted in Figure 1.

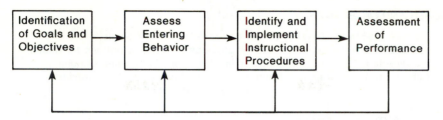

Figure 1. (A basic model of instruction)

This simple model illustrates four basic factors which can be used to analyze any instructional event or sequence. The initial step involves the identification of goals and objectives; the instructional process begins with decisions about what is to be learned. Next, the instructional planner must take into account the *entering behavior* of the learner. That is, adjustments must be made in our plans in order to account for the extent to which the learner may already have mastered the intended objectives, has attained or lacks the necessary prerequisites, or for particular personal characteristics, needs, or motives which may influence instruction. Next we proceed to *identify and implement appropriate instructional procedures.* At this stage, we are concerned with the actual ways in which the learner sets out to attain the objectives. The fourth stage involves *assessment of performance.* Here we are concerned with evaluation, or deciding whether the goal has been reached. (The *feedback loop,* represented by the arrows extending back in Figure 1 from the last stage to the first three components reminds us that failure to reach the goal has implications about the adequacy of the instruction, not just about the learner's success or failure.)

Self-directed learning may be fostered through deliberate efforts by the teacher in relation to each of these four components of the basic model of instruction. The self-directed learner can participate in goal-setting and defining instructional objectives, in diagnosis of entering behavior, in the selection and implementation of a variety of learning activities or procedures, and in the process of evaluation.[1]

The teacher, of course, does not simply decree that, on some specified morning in the future, all students will be responsible for becoming self-directed learners. Instead, the teacher may facilitate the development of self-direction in each of these four areas, through systematic efforts to provide the students with experiences involving increasing degrees and kinds of self-management.

A plan for teachers to facilitate the movement of gifted and talented students toward self-directed learning is proposed in Figure 2.

Within each of the four components of the basic model of instruction, four steps are suggested. The first step assumes the existence of a teacher-directed model of instruction. The next three steps represent gradual ways for the teacher to increase the learners' experience with self-direction. It is likely that, in each of these areas, most teachers already implement some of these steps, at least in part. The plan is intended to suggest, first, that movement towards self-directed learning must involve all aspects of the instructional process; second, that there may be varying degrees of self-direction which can be provided for the students to help them acquire confidence

---

1. Mosston (1972) has advanced a similar proposal, suggesting that as one's model of teaching changes from a "command" to a "discovery" approach, learners are increasingly and more directly involved in instructional decision-making in advance of, during, and after instruction.

GOALS AND OBJECTIVES

Teacher-directed:	Teacher prescribes for class or for pupils.
Self-directed, 1st step:	Teacher provides choices or options for pupils.
Self-directed, 2nd step:	Teacher involves pupil in creating options.
Self-directed, 3rd step:	Learner controls choices, teacher provides resources and materials.

ASSESS ENTERING BEHAVIOR

Teacher-directed:	Teacher tests and makes specific prescription.
Self-directed, 1st step:	Teacher diagnoses, provides several options.
Self-directed, 2nd step:	Teacher and learner use diagnostic conference, tests employed individually if needed.
Self-directed, 3rd step:	Learner controls diagnosis, consults teacher for assistance when unclear about needs.

INSTRUCTIONAL PROCEDURES

Teacher-directed:	Teacher presents content, provides exercises and activities, arranges and supervises practice.
Self-directed, 1st step:	Teacher provides options for learners to employ independently, with learner's own pace.
Self-directed, 2nd step:	Teacher provides resources and options, uses student contracts which involve learner in scope, sequence, and pace decision.
Self-directed, 3rd step:	Learner defines projects, activities, etc.

ASSESS PERFORMANCE

Teacher-directed:	Teacher implements evaluation and gives grades.
Self-directed, 1st step:	Teacher relates evaluation to objectives, gives student opportunity to react or respond.
Self-directed, 2nd step:	Peer-partners used in providing feedback; teacher-student conferences for evaluation.
Self-directed, 3rd step:	Student self-evaluation.

Figure 2. (Moving toward self-directed learning)

and specific skills of self-management; and third, that there is an important role for the teacher (albeit a unique and different role from traditional definitions) in even the most extensive implementation of self-directed learning, in which the learner *controls* most of the critical instructional decisions. We recognize that attainment of the third step of self-directed learning may not be easily reached by any classroom teacher, and that it may also require far-reaching alterations in our entire notion of how schools operate. Thus, the emphasis will be primarily upon helping students move toward self-direction, not to stress "plunging headlong" into the third step of self-directed learning.

Goals and Objectives

In teacher-directed instruction, the goals of the schools are probably defined (abstractly or very generally) by the school district's board, and, more practically, by the curriculum choices which are usually made by administrative staff or committees in response to state requirements.

114

At the most practical level, however, the actual decisions about curriculum are made by the teacher in each classroom, who determines what will be taught daily. The teacher may employ specific instructional objectives, or rely upon general lesson plans, textbooks, and resource or teacher's guides. The students are expected to accept and respond to the decisions made by the teacher concerning what will be studied, and the sequence in which it will be presented. In some cases, the teacher teaches the content to the assembled class as a group, or provides specific assignments for individual students.

Movement towards self-direction begins as the teacher, usually in response to recognition of differences among students in the class, introduces *choices* or *options* into the daily program of instruction. Frequently this may involve giving the students choices about *rate* or *sequence* (you may do A or B for a certain period of time . . .). Sometimes, however, a wider range of activities may be designed. Typically, however, the students are still involved in meeting objectives which have been established by the teacher. The second step towards self-direction involves the pupils in *creating* choices or options concerning what will be learned. The most common mechanism for implementing this step is for the teacher to discuss with the class topics or projects in which they are interested, followed by individual or committee efforts to conduct projects or activities on those topics. Another alternative at this step involves class discussion to select subjects for which the teacher plans or obtains special resources of self-instructional units (mini-courses, learning stations, learning activities packages, etc.). The teacher retains final authority and control, but the pupils are actively involved in the selection of objectives and subjects. The third step transfers the final authority for goals and objectives from the teacher to the learner. The teacher serves as a guide, to help the learner explore new areas, and to provide resources and materials to facilitate learning. The teacher may also be involved in determining the objectives, through group or individual discussion concerning topics identified by the learners, but the decision for selecting or creating objectives rests finally with the learner. (At the third step, the curriculum becomes entirely personalized for each learner, which might improve students' interests and accomplishments but infuriate curriculum authorities.)

Assessing Entering Behavior

Unfortunately, this component of instruction is frequently overlooked or handled very superficially even when it is under the direct control of the teacher. Most teachers, for example, do not distinguish between pre-testing and diagnostic efforts to identify the presence or lack of specific prerequisite skills. The pre-test, of course, should determine whether or not the learner has already met the planned objective. (We can only speculate about the number of hours spent "teaching" gifted children things they already knew.) It may be more important in many cases to determine whether the student knows what will be necessary to enable him or her to *learn* the new material. This assumes, of course, that the teacher has determined what those prerequisites actually are. In any event, let us assume idealistically that the teacher-directed approach implies that the *teacher* studies carefully all evidence concerning the learner's background, knowledge, abilities, motives, and personal characteristics. The teacher then prescribes (suggesting a process akin to the diagnosis and prescription of the physician) for the learner a specific set of objectives and activities.

In the first step towards self-directed learning, the challenge of *diagnosis* remains in the teacher's domain. The teacher assesses the important characteristics, formulates several alternative courses of action (or instructional prescriptions) and then confers with the learner to present and discuss the alternatives and their merits, in relation to the learner's entering behavior. The next step begins with a diagnostic conference, during which the teacher and the learner consider together possible goals and objectives, their necessary prerequisites, and the learner's needs, interests, and qualifications. Diagnostic tests may be employed individually by the teacher as appropriate. The learner has initial *input* for both diagnosis and prescription, although the teacher's responsibilities are still quite substantial. At the third step, diagnosis and prescription are under the control of the learner. Assessment of the possible goals and objectives, the necessary background or prerequisites, and the available resources, are made by the learner. Of course, the teacher remains the best possible outside resource to assist the student in many areas, and serves as a "consultant" to the student to help resolve uncertainties about the availability or advisability of certain choices. (Ultimately, of course, students could choose the teachers they found most helpful as resources or consultants, which could prove overwhelming to some teachers and quite threatening to others. The risks are always great!)

Planning and Implementing Instruction

When instruction is entirely under the control of the teacher, he or she presents content, provides problems and exercises, and arranges and supervises practice for the student. Teacher-controlled instruction may be expository, in which the teacher *tells* the students what they need to know in order to meet the objectives. Other methods of "delivering" instruction may also be teacher-centered, however. The teacher may employ a class discussion approach, individualized use of worksheets, learning packages, or programmed instructional units, all of which may be planned, distributed, and supervised very closely by the teacher. "Individualized" instruction may not contribute to the development of self-direction, but merely provide experiences one at a time which were previously presented to an entire class at the same time.

The first step in moving towards self-direction in planning and conducting instruction is for the teacher to increase the kind and number of alternatives for the learners to follow. This involves allowing each learner to work independently, at his or her own pace, and also to select from among several options. These options should provide opportunities for products to be created using many different media and for individual and group activity; providing such options implies differentiating objectives for each learner.

The second step is for the teacher to provide a wide variety of resources and alternatives, utilizing contracts with students to plan the instructional episode. The learner, through the contract, now has involvement in decisions pertaining to scope, sequence, and pace of instructional activities, as well as the availability of numerous options. The design and implementation of contract approaches to instruction has been discussed very effectively by Dunn and Dunn (1972).

In the final stage, in which the learner is the manager of his or her own instruction, control over instructional decisions has been transferred entirely from the teacher to the learner. The learner defines the projects and activities, in accord with his background and interests, to accomplish self-initiated goals and objectives. The teacher's role changes in this stage, from the planner and controller of instruction to a guide or facilitator of learning (cf., Rogers, 1969; Wight, 1970).

Assessment of Performance

In the traditional, teacher-centered approach to instruction, the teacher is primarily responsible for designing and conducting evaluation procedures, and for using those results to assign grades to students. This may involve testing, of course, but it should be concerned *with any form of evidence* that the learner has successfully attained a specified set of instructional objectives. When evaluation is teacher-centered, the student plays virtually no role in the process, except, of course, to provide the evidence to be used by the teacher.

In the first step towards self-direction, the teacher begins by clarifying the nature of the objectives, and the kinds of evidence that will be accepted in meeting them, and communicates that information to the students at the beginning of instruction; this may be the most important reason for specifying instructional objectives in explicit terms. In addition, however, the teacher should provide opportunities for the student to participate in the evaluation process, by using conferences and group discussion in which the students can see how the evidence of their success is obtained and used, and can contribute to the teacher's assessment of that evidence.

In the second step, the student's active role in the evaluation process can be extended, so that pupils take part in conferences with their teachers and participate actively in peer-partnership approach for feedback on group projects and activities (*cf.,* Mosston, 1972). Thus, the students learn to develop and apply criteria for evaluation of their own work individually and in group settings, as well as in cooperation with the teacher.

In the final step, the student becomes primary responsible for identifying and applying criteria for evaluation of his or her own work. At this stage, the student should be actively involved in identifying goals, objectives, and instructional procedures, and thus should be in an excellent position for assessing the evidence that the objectives have been attained. The teacher's role in the evaluation process at this stage is, of course, very different from teacher-centered evaluation. Rather than implementing the evaluation and assigning grades, the teacher becomes a resource, who may be used by the learner as necessary to facilitate effective identification and application of evaluation procedures. Thus, the teacher may assist the learner by suggesting sources of evidence that the student may have overlooked, by making tests and test scores available to the student as appropriate, and by being available to discuss problems and challenges in the evaluation and grading process with the student.

A FINAL NOTE

The proposals described here for helping gifted and talented students move towards self-directed learning represents a tentative plan, a set of hypotheses for systematic investigation and testing, rather than experimentally-derived conclusions. These proposals have been derived from research on the characteristics of gifted and talented students, and from studies of experimental programs for fostering creative thinking and problem-solving. It seems clear, after several years of study, that educational programs for stimulating divergent thinking, positive attitudes, and problem-solving skills are steps which are necessary, but not sufficient, in establishing an educational environment in which significant, creative learning occurs. We must take additional steps to make school learning more joyful, more applicable to the challenges of the day-to-day world, and more flexible in meeting the unique needs of every child. This requires that we do more than create new curriculum packages to insert in the school day, more than just "tinkering" with the curriculum. It seems quite likely that steps towards increased self-direction in any single aspect of the instructional process must also be accompanied by consistent, supportive changes in other phases. For example, as the learner's self-management increases in relation to defining goals and objectives and implementing instructional activities, changes must also occur in the evaluation process. The four components of the instructional process we have identified in this paper, with the stages for transition towards self-direction proposed for each component, may thus be importantly inter-related, so that progress in each area will be needed in order to reach our ultimate goal of a more creative learning environment for the gifted and talented.

Some of these proposals have been implemented in a variety of classes from third grade through graduate school. It may well be, of course, that the progress from teacher- to learner-directed instruction may differ somewhat for students at various ages. There may also be particular characteristics of learners which are systematically related to the degree or rate of progress toward self-management. These questions, still awaiting experimental investigation, should be addressed by researchers and classroom teachers who are concerned with the education of the gifted and talented.

References

Bloom, B. S. (Ed.). *Taxonomy of Educational Objectives. Handbook I: Cognitive Domain.* New York: David McKay, 1956.

Bruner, J. S. The Act of Discovery. *Harvard Education Review,* 1961, 31, 21–32.

Davis, G. A. *Psychology of Problem Solving: Theory and Practice.* New York: Basic Books, 1973.

DeCecco, J. P. *The Psychology of Learning and Instruction.* Englewood Cliffs: Prentice-Hall, 1968.

Dunn, K., and Dunn, R. *Practical Approaches to Individualizing Instruction.* West Nyack, New York: Parker, 1972.

Feldhusen, J. F., Treffinger, D. J., and Elias, R. M. The right kind of programmed instruction for the gifted and talented. *NSPI Journal,* 1969, 8, 6–11.

Hohn, R. L., and Treffinger, D. J. Student self-evaluation. Unpublished mimeograph, University of Kansas, 1974.

Kibler, R. J., Cegala, D. J., Barker, L. L., and Miles, D. T. *Objectives for Instruction and Evaluation.* Boston: Allyn & Bacon, 1974.

Krathwohl, D. R. (Ed.) *Taxonomy of Educational Objectives. Handbook II: Affective Domain.* New York: David McKay, 1964.

Mager, R. F. *Developing Attitude Toward Learning.* Palo Alto: Fearon, 1968.

Mosston, M. *Teaching: From Command to Discovery.* Belmont: Wadsworth, 1972.

Popham, W. J., and Baker, E. L. *Systematic Instruction.* Englewood Cliffs: Prentice-Hall, 1970.

Rogers, C. R. *Freedom to Learn.* Columbus: Charles E. Merrill, 1969.

Torrance, E. P. *Gifted Children in the Classroom.* New York: MacMillan, 1965.

Torrance, E. P. Can we teach children to think creatively? *Journal of Creative Behavior,* 1972, 6, 114–143.

Torrance, E. P., and Myers, R. *Creative Learning and Teaching.* New York: Dutton, 1971.

Treffinger, D. J., and Johnsen, E. P. On self-directed learning: When you say hello, do they write it in their notebooks? *Liberal Education,* 1973, 59, 471–479.

Wight, A. R. Participative education and the inevitable revolution. *Journal of Creative Behavior,* 1970, 4, 234–282.

13. DEVELOPING CREATIVITY TRAINING ACTIVITIES

Joseph S. Renzulli
Carolyn M. Callahan

Although research has consistently shown that almost all students can improve the quantity and quality of their creative output, many elementary and secondary school teachers experience a great deal of difficulty when they attempt to encourage youngsters to express themselves creatively. Part of this difficulty is due to group pressures toward conformity that typically exist among adolescents, but the problem is also a result of our failure to teach students the basic skills of creative thinking. All too often we have assigned students higher-level creativity tasks without first providing them with the underlying techniques that are necessary for more complicated assignments such as writing expressive poetry, creative stories, or imaginative essays. The purpose of this chapter is to point out some of the basic techniques for encouraging youngsters to think creatively. The first part of the chapter will deal with the general strategies for developing creativity training activities. This will be followed by brief descriptions of some specific activities that can be used to give students practice in creative thinking.

PRINCIPLES UNDERLYING CREATIVITY TRAINING

The Fluency Principle

Research in creativity training has shown that the more ideas a person generates, the more likely he is to come up with new and unusual ideas. For example, when a group of students was presented with the hypothetical problem of thinking up a name for a new breakfast cereal made from dandelions, almost all of the students called the cereal "Dandy Flakes." Since creative ideas are, by definition, unusual or infrequent solutions to problems, and since "Dandy Flakes," was the response given by more than 90 percent of the students, it was judged to be a relatively common response. The teacher then asked the students to think of five more possible names for the new breakfast cereal. Needless to say, several unusual names were created, and in many cases, students developed names that were unique to the group. For example, one student suggested manufacturing the cereal in the shape of lions or lions' heads and then calling the cereal "Dandy Lions."

This example helps to illustrate the fluency principle. Unless we encourage students to develop many ideas rather than just one, and unless we reward them for the sheer quantity of ideas that they produce, they may never get beyond the ordinary and the obvious. Fluency training activities such as the dandelion problem give students practice in the basic creativity technique of brainstorming. Such activities are good warm-up exercises for more complicated activities because they help youngsters explore various alternatives to problems and thereby free their thinking process from the restraints that usually hinder creativity.

Reprinted by permission from *Gifted Child Quarterly,* Vol. 19, No. 1, 1975.

The Principle of Open-Endedness

The principle of open-endedness is closely related to the fluency principle. Simply stated, it means that creativity training exercises should not have predetermined answers. A good deal of the "education game" that is played between teachers and students is based on the mental process of convergence. Teachers usually raise problems that have one predetermined solution and students are rewarded for speed and accuracy with which they converge on the solution. Such exercise provide students with very limited opportunities to let their minds range far and wide across a broad range of possible solutions to a given problem.

Open-ended activities also help students to develop the skills of self-evaluation. When an answer is either right or wrong, the final source of judgment always resides with an external authority—usually the teacher or a textbook. With the threat of evaluation and the fear of being wrong constantly hanging over their heads, it is little wonder that students are reluctant to take risks and to express thoughts and ideas that are somewhat unusual or divergent from the ordinary. Open-ended activities, on the other hand, provide youngsters with a psychologically safe atmosphere in which to express themselves. When there are no right or wrong answers to problems, and when students are given an opportunity to generate many possible solutions to a particular problem, a situation is created that enables students to review their own alternative responses and to select the response that they like the best. This is not to say that the teacher and other students should not have an opinion about a youngster's work. But the important thing to keep in mind is that the student himself has passed judgment on his own work and that his opinion is a valid one because it is based on his own standards and criteria for self-satisfaction.

Open-ended activities such as the dandelion problem can be used to create an atmosphere where students can develop free and open thinking without the usual restraints that frequently result from rigorous external evaluation. We can help youngsters become more creative thinkers by giving them numerous opportunities to practice on material which allows for many acceptable responses and then to bring their own judgmental processes to bear on the responses they produce.

The Principle of Environmental Relevancy

When students are engaged in creativity training, they should not be penalized for a lack of knowledge about a particular topic. In other words, creativity training activities should allow the learner to draw upon his own background and experiences. For example, if we asked youngsters to engage in "thing listing" by writing all of the things that they might find in a kitchen, they would not have to search through reference books in order to make several responses to this problem. Because this is an open-ended exercise that is based on experiences that are relatively common to all youngsters, it also helps to make adjustments for differences in background and ability level. Youngsters from affluent homes might list luxury items such as garbage disposals and microwave ovens, but even students from so-called disadvantaged homes will be able to respond within the limits of their own experience. And while less able students are likely to focus mainly on concrete items, brighter students may include certain intangibles on their lists such as pleasant aromas and warm atmosphere that they might associate with a kitchen.

As has been indicated above, the major purpose of warm-up activities such as the dandelion problem and thing-listing exercises is to give students practice in generating several ideas and solutions to a given problem. Unless these activities are relevant to a student's present background and immediate environment, the exercises are likely to become traditional search-for-information experiences. The major purpose of developing brainstorming skills can easily be lost if the student is asked to slow down divergent thinking processes in order to search out factual information. Thus, it is important in creativity training to develop exercises that are based on information that is relatively common to all members of a group and, at the same time, to select activities that are open-ended and that allow for many responses rather than just one or two.

The Principle of Enjoyment

Creativity training, like any other aspect of the teaching-learning process, can become a routine and dreary experience if we do not guard against the forces that tend to stifle enthusiasm and enjoyment. Even the most exciting activities can lose their appeal if they are administered in a mechanical fashion by teachers who are not themselves enthusiastic. One of the best ways a teacher can demonstrate her genuine interest in creativity is to become an active participant in training activities. When the teacher shows a willingness to reveal her own creative thoughts and ideas, when she contributes to class discussion on an equal basis with students, and when she is not afraid to operate in a free and open atmosphere, students will quickly develop trust in the teacher and security in situations where unusualness is rewarded rather than punished. It is one thing to tell students that we want them to strive for originality and "way out" solutions to open-ended problems, but it is much more effective to achieve trust by actually displaying the kind of behavior that she is attempting to elicit from students.

Whenever teachers and students are purposefully striving for unusualness, a good deal of laughter and humor is likely to be displayed. It is important for the teacher to be accepting of these reactions (especially laughter directed at the teacher's creative ideas) because humor is an important part of creativity. Attempts to suppress laughter will invariably result in a dampening of the free and open atmosphere that is necessary for the development of uninhibited expression.

Students will also derive more enjoyment from creativity training sessions if they have an opportunity to participate in planning the activities. While we hear a great deal of talk about cooperative planning, much of what goes on in classrooms is solely determined by the teacher. Once students have been exposed to a variety of creativity training exercises, they should be given a choice about which types of activities they would like to pursue. Since the objective of such activities is the development of creative thinking processes rather than coverage of subject matter, creativity training exercises provide an opportunity for students to deal with topics that are of interest to them. For example, adolescents can practice brainstorming by listing all of the possible names they can think of for musical rock groups. If students are interested in politics or ecology, they may want to write slogans or design symbols that promote their point of view. Capitalizing upon student interests will help to maintain enjoyment and enthusiasm and, at the same time, will shorten the communication gap that often exists between adolescents and their teachers.

CREATIVITY TRAINING ACTIVITIES

Creative Writing

As has been indicated, creativity training exercises are designed to help free students from the usual constraints that are placed on their thinking and thus prepare them for higher level assignments such as creative writing. Numerous activities can be developed around the brainstorming and thing-listing formats discussed above. In preparation for creative writing, students can develop lists of words that are related to given emotions such as fear, happiness, and sadness. They can also be given the stems of common similes such as "as big as _____" and "as quiet as _____" and asked to develop several colorful comparisons that will complete each simile. Similar exercises can be developed for analogies and metaphors. In each case, it is important for students to generate as many responses as possible for each item. Students can also be asked to apply the brainstorming technique to developing lists of synonyms and antonyms for given words. Additional word fluency exercises can be carried out by asking students to write specific ways of conveying a certain meaning. For example, there are several dozen specific ways of communicating the act of speaking (say, bellow, whine, mumble,), each with its own special meaning. Students will gain greater control over their writing when they learn to explore a wide variety of possible words to create a certain mood or feeling.

Word-listing activities can be used to help prepare students for writing poetry. Prior to introducing rhyming patterns in poetry, students can be asked to list all of the words they can think of that rhyme with a given word. This exercise will generate a great deal of excitement if carried out under mildly competitive conditions. Students can compete individually or in groups to see who can develop the longest lists of rhyming words. After they have completed their lists, they can be introduced to rhyming patterns such as those used in limericks and asked to use words from their lists to write original limericks.

One of the problems that teachers often face when attempting to develop creative writing abilities is helping students generate interesting ideas for their stories. Brainstorming and thing-listing exercises can be used to assist students in the process of idea finding. For example, students can be asked to list ten or twelve roles or characters in the first of four columns on a piece of paper. Each item should be numbered. Characters or roles might include spacemen, hippies, and deep sea divers. The second column should contain a list of places: the inside of a fall-out shelter, a jungle, an underwater cave. The third list should contain actions: swimming, building an igloo, chopping down a tree. The final column should contain objects: teapot, television antenna, broom. After all of the lists have been completed, the students should randomly select one item from each list by rolling a set of dice or using a spinner. The items selected from each of the four lists should then be used as the elements for a short story. By forcing relationships among things that may not logically be related to one another, some interesting and unusual stories are quite likely to be created. Students can use their lists several times, and the activity can be varied by placing certain specifications on one or more of the lists. For example, the list containing characters might be restricted to famous people or characters that students have encountered in their reading. The actions list can be restricted to occupations or recreational activities, and similar kinds of restrictions can be placed on the lists of things and places.

A similar technique can be used to help students develop interesting character sketches. Categories of physical characteristics such as weight, height, age, eyes, hair, and build can be written on a piece of paper. Students should be asked to list as many words or phrases as they can think of under each category. For example, under the age category, students might list *baby, girl, teenager, old man*. After students have listed as many words as they can under each heading, one item should be randomly selected from each list and the words used as the basis for a character sketch. Needless to say, some unusual and quite fanciful characters will emerge from this technique; however, it will help students break away from the formula-type of characters that often

122

result when students are not given practice in combining characteristics that are sometimes incongruous. The main purpose of this technique is to help youngsters stretch their imaginations by providing them with an exercise where unusual relations are forced together.

The brainstorming and word-listing techniques can also be used to help students develop the skills of descriptive writing. Students can be asked to list all of the words they can think of that are associated with each of the five senses. For example, under the sense of touch, they might include *smooth, rough, mushy.* After students have completed their lists, they can be asked to write descriptive paragraphs that highlight some of the words on their lists. The paragraphs might focus on one of the senses or a combination of two or more senses. Students can also be asked to brainstorm a number of topics for description—a rainy afternoon or the midway at a carnival—and then write a description that incorporates perspectives on the topic from each of the five senses.

Figural and Symbolic Creativity Activities

One way of capitalizing on student interests and special talents is to combine figural and symbolic activities with verbal activities. For example, students might be asked to design a camper or a recreation park using given size specifications. When the designs have been completed, a number of verbal exercises are natural follow-up activities. Students might be asked to write slogans to sell the camper, a technical description of the park that would be sufficient for the landscaper to lay out the park, a classified ad for the camper, a political speech that would convince the town council to provide the funds to build the recreation park, or even a simple description of the camper or recreation park. One might also make use of special interests in art or music by asking students to write descriptions of moods created by abstract paintings or music played on a tape recorder or record player.

The close connection between symbols, emotions, and propaganda might be the basis for a thing-listing activity in which students are presented with pictures of well-known symbols such as the peace symbol, hammer and sickle, star of David, or United Nations symbol. They may then be asked to write a list of their emotional responses first, followed by an essay on how these symbols have been or might be used for propaganda purposes.

The use of an activity where students can create closely related verbal slogans and symbols for a business, club, or school team will often motivate the child with little verbal fluency but some artistic ability to complete a verbal task by its close association with a symbolic task. It is, of course, important that the teacher reward both efforts in order to emphasize the need for a fluency of modes of expression as well as fluency within a given mode of expression.

SUMMARY

There are a number of general techniques for encouraging youngsters to think creativity. The four basic principles underlying creativity training have been discussed above. By way of summary the fluency principle states that the more ideas a person generates, the more likely he is to come up with new and original ideas. Open-endedness implies that creativity training exercises should not have predetermined answers. Instead they should enable students to generate many solutions to a given problem. Environmental relevancy emphasizes that students should not be penalized for lack of knowledge about a particular topic. The principle of enjoyment suggests that enthusiasm is an important part of creativity and that a free and open atmosphere is necessary for the development of uninhibited expression.

These principles and the specific suggestions which followed were not intended as cookbook recipes for creative thinking or as formulas which in and of themselves will lead to the creation of brilliant literary works. However, the principles and the activities which develop from them do serve a very important function in the development of the creative thinking processes. They free the student from the traditional modes of thinking which call for him to search for the one right solution and instead encourage him to explore many possible alternative responses, to draw upon his entire life experience in searching for responses, to evaluate his own responses, and to enjoy and feel confident in expressing his ideas to others no matter how real or unreal, true or fanciful, practical or whimsical those ideas might be.

14. GUIDING CREATIVE ACTION

Sidney J. Parnes

INTRODUCTION

This article is presented in two sections. Section A will attempt to provide you with an *experiential* understanding of the nature and possible use with gifted youngsters of the *Guide to Creative Action* prepared by myself and my colleagues, Ruth B. Noller and Angelo M. Biondi. (Scribner's, 1977).[1] If you are turned on by the experience, as many people are, you will almost certainly want to expose your gifted charges to this kind of thinking. Section B of the article will give you an introduction to this use of the *Guide*.

In the eventuality that you are left confused or uncertain by the experience in Section A, the guidelines in Section B will offer further explanation of the rationale for what you experienced, and will explain in greater detail how teachers and parents of the gifted can use the *Guide* and its companion *Creative Actionbook* in helping to fully develop the creative potential of their charges. The article draws or adapts from selected explanatory information in the *Guide,* as well as Correlated Session 15C, entitled, "Putting It All Together." That particular session, as explained further below, samples small bits of the extensive exercises of the *Guide* and *Actionbook* so as to provide one kind of an experiential mosaic of the processes dealt with in our program. You might later like to test out the impact of these creative processes with your youngsters in a similar or modified way you might even direct the very general approach used in Section A into a particular subject-matter area.

Students have reported significant transfer of our general creative problem-solving processes to all academic disciplines,—from English to Mathematics, from the sciences to Social Studies. Furthermore, faculty in these areas report the same effects, supporting the statistical findings of our research in a more generally-understandable and impressive way. Two examples of faculty observations, one from mathematics and the other from social studies are illustrative:

Mathematics: "The students who were taking Creative Studies seemed to do better on the examination in the sense that they apparently could analyze the questions, some of which were word problems and some of which were purely geometrical. Regardless of the type of questions, they seemed to be better able to analyze what was given, what had to be found, and were then enabled to work better from that. Not only were they better able to define the problem but they were more critical, too; where you gave them too much information, most of them spotted that. Obviously, you are teaching them to analyze things in ways that they have not been taught in other fields or other subjects."

Social Studies: "The first lesson plan I graded in my methods course was written by Karen ——————— and it was a very creative job. I thought that if the paper was typical, I could have a marvelous time with the class. Unfortunately it wasn't a typical paper, and Karen went on to distinguish herself as one of the best students I had. This year I taught Diane ——————— in

Reprinted by permission from *Gifted Child Quarterly,* Vol. 21, No. 4, 1977.

[1]The material in Section A will appear in a forthcoming book, *New Ways of Growth,* edited by Herbert and Roberta Otto.

methods and noticed the same extraordinary creativity that Karen had. Karen and Diane attribute their achievements to your class. They say that you gave them confidence in their ideas and convinced them to generate many ideas in response to a problem. The results are very salient."

SECTION A—AN EXPERIENCE IN CREATIVE PROBLEM-SOLVING

Introduction. In this section of the article, you yourself will have an opportunity to experience how your youngster can "turn on" their creative processes in a very deliberate manner, following a rationale that has been developed in our research and development since 1949. *You* will be in charge; *I* will merely offer stimuli that may increase the *probability* of your deriving some "aha's" from the exercise. Before we embark on the experience, let me first summarize the basic rationale for it, starting by what I mean by the "aha's" we are seeking; however, if you are "chafing at the bit" to get started, turn directly to *"Preparation."*

Let us start with the premise that the essence of creativity is the fundamental notion of the "aha"—meaning the fresh and relevant association of thoughts, facts, ideas, etc., into a new configuration,—one which pleases, which has meaning beyond the sum of the parts. Let us assume that the new connection, association, relationship that you make is harmonious, relevant, valuable, satisfying, pleasing, etc., to *you*. It might be something as simple as moving the body or the parts of the body in a spontaneous new way, in response to a sound or rhythm that you hear. The "aha" may be implicit in even such a momentary, fleeting relationship of elements as in that little spontaneous dance routine that so many of us have experienced.

The typical "aha" experience may be considered to be the result of the new connection of elements residing inside our mind and/or within our preceptual field. This new and relevant connection or *new and harmonious* connection often "just happens," accidentally or serendipitously. In earlier days, it was frequently thought that this was the *only* way it could happen—accidentally—i.e., one had to just wait and *let* it happen, like the famous "Eureka!" of Archimedes in the bathtub. However, what research of the last 25 years has made increasingly clear, is that there are many processes a person can use to help increase the *likelihood* that the chance connection will take place. Notice that I do not say processes that will *make* the connection happen, but only that will increase the *likelihood* or *probability* of it occurring.

If I were to say to you that one-half of eight is zero, you might scoff, shrug, be puzzled, or react in a number of ways. Think about it for a moment. If you happened to smile to yourself or "light up" inside just a little, it might have been because you experienced a bit of an "aha." You may have experienced a mild "eureka" similar in type, but not in intensity, to Archimedes' "aha" in the classic bathtub episode or to Sir Isaac Newton's in the classic instance of his insight into the law of gravity when the apple fell on his head. You may have structured "one-half of eight" in your mind to become "one-half of 8," and then "one-half of 8," and may have then suddenly seen "one-half of eight" to be "0"—the top or bottom half—or "zero." Of course, you might then also see it as something else, depending on how you view or interpret "one-half of eight" in your mind.

Notice that the word AHA reads the same backwards and forwards. Forward may suggest outward-oriented "ahas" on the environment—the "world"; backward may be thought of as inward "ahas" on ourselves. It is here that our courses and institutes may represent the synergistic synthesis of the inward-looking (often called "affective") programs like sensitivity training, awareness development, meditation, etc., and the outward-looking (often called "cognitive") programs like problem-solving, decision making, etc. Through the "inward-looking" processes we may better be able to sense problems or challenges—to become more aware in our lives; the "outward-looking" processes may help us to *cope* with these problems or challenges we uncover.

The problem-solving process per se is not substantially different in our programs—in terms of its steps or logical processes—from those of John Dewey, Graham Wallas, or any of the well-known problem-solving models, historic or modern. However, the plus ingredient that Alex Osborn introduced was the deliberate and exaggerated use of the imagination; this provided a powerful force when effectively harnessed within a total problem-solving model.

One might view the deliberate development of creative behavior in our programs as an exaggerated push for change: we "stretch" people beyond their normal limits in an oscillating process of imagining and judging, during all stages of problem-solving in piling up facts, in defining viewpoints of the problem, in generating ideas, in recognizing criteria, for evaluation, and in finding ways of insuring the successful implementation of ideas. Thus we provide practice in intensive stretching between conceptions and actions in this oscillating process. The result of this intensive practice is increased ability to take more factors into consideration, in a given time, in making decisions. This is what I will ask you to attempt in the experience I will provide, and that you can then do for your own youngsters.

Thus the problem-solving process becomes one of opening up the self to the fullest possible awareness of the storehouse of energy and resources within oneself—in one's vast mental library of life experience—as well as in the vast data of the external world. Problem-solving becomes the task of synergizing the greatest number of inter-connections and interrelationships among these vast resources, including the layer-upon-layer of primary information stored in our brain cells from birth and even from embryonic states. One searches for the kinds of synergistic connections that one can make toward the solution of one's problems, goals, wishes, aspirations, hopes and dreams for oneself or others in any subject area or endeavor.

In the experience I provide on the following pages, I will attempt to capsulize the kind of interactive programming we have created between creative problem-solving, synectics, sensitivity, art, fantasy, meditation, body awareness, etc., in one session that will experientially provide you with a brief montage of what our programs are designed to accomplish. You will probably need at least an hour for the experience to have significant meaning for you. It will be your personal experiment with the processes we suggest in your attempt to both cognitively and affectively deal with real concerns you may have.

Preparation

In getting ready for the experience, please gather several diverse odors. One might be a plant, another a spice, another a chemical, another a perfume. If you can get someone else to provide these odors for you in unlabeled containers or plastic bags, in such a manner that you cannot identify the items by sight, this would be preferable. Ideally, when I call for their use, you should not know what the item is that you are smelling. You will also need a pen, several sheets of paper, and a source of music, ideally music with a "descriptive" quality that will tend to stir you in some way.

The experience will serve as an example of one of infinite "compositions" that might be conceived by putting the pieces of the problem-solving process together in new and different arrangements, just as an infinite number of musical compositions can be generated by rearranging the notes within various frameworks. As I provide the stimuli for your thoughts, allow yourself to *be*; allow your thoughts to *flow* freely as each stimulus is presented, without analyzing or evaluating them in any way other than as the stimulus of the particular moment suggests.

If your time is limited to one hour, then pace yourself quite rapidly—a minute or so only on each response. I will present many diverse stimuli in an attempt to increase the probability of a greater number and intensity of personal *"aha's,"* or new connections. If you should happen to solve a problem ahead of my suggestions, it might be advisable not to dwell on it, but rather to record it and then move ahead to another challenge, continuing to follow the stimuli as provided. Also, if you find after getting started that you are making progress or accomplishing something important but that my stimuli are getting in your way, go right on without me. Remember that the objective is to *accomplish* something valuable to *you*. My stimuli are only designed to help increase the likelihood that this will happen.

Do not read ahead before completing each instruction, unless you are only interested in understanding what I am doing rather than experiencing your creative processes. If you should decide to read only and not to write as suggested, I urge you at least to *think* your responses to each instruction before reading on.

Lastly, please don't try to figure out why I am providing a particular stimulus as you respond to it. Just *respond,* spontaneously; then go back later and analyze, if you like, why the items were provided in the way they were. But respond to each first as you would to a musical composition. You might later like to analyze the arrangement of notes, the purposes the composer had in mind, etc. But you probably wouldn't want to do that kind of thinking as you were listening to the music for pure enjoyment. So just *experience* the process as it is laid out in this particular composition. If you are interested enough for detailed theory and explanations, you will find that elsewhere in my writings.

Remember, also, that this exercise is often given at the end of a creative studies course or institute, after intensive practice in processes designed to increase the flow of ideas. So don't be frustrated if you find the going slow or arduous. Just move along from item to item, trying always to *allow* your thoughts to flow wherever they take you in response to my stimuli. And if something is not clear to you, just take it for whatever sense it makes to you at that moment; respond to that without worrying "if you are doing it right." Good luck in your adventure!

The Experience

A. *Objective-Finding*
   1. List any thoughts you have in mind: challenges or problems you would like to solve; goals, objectives, aspirations you have; ideas you would like to use, etc. These may refer to work, home, school or social life. If ideas or solutions pop into mind, jot them down. Use the following as a check-list to spur your thoughts:
      a. What would you like to do, have, accomplish?
      b. What do you wish would happen?
      c. What would you like to do better?

128

d. What do you wish you had more time for? more money for? etc.?
e. What more would you like to get out of life?
f. What are your unfilled goals?
g. What angered you recently?
h. What makes you tense, anxious?
i. What misunderstandings did you have?
j. What have you complained about?
k. With whom would you like to get along better?
l. What changes for the worse do you sense in attitudes of others?
m. What would you like to get others to do?
n. What changes will you have to introduce?
o. What takes too long?
p. What is wasted?
q. What is too complicated?
r. What "bottlenecks" exist?
s. In what ways are you inefficient?
t. What wears you out?
u. What would you like to organize better?
2. List six or more roles you play in your life (example: daughter, politician, student, etc.)
3. List more thoughts that now pop to mind re your challenges, problems, goals, etc.
4. Think of a *non-verbal* message which you *might* give to someone you know. How might it be done? How might it feel as it is done?
5. Add more thoughts to the list you were making.
6. Choose (from your list) one problem, challenge, or idea you would most like to do something about.

B. *Fact-Finding*
1. List all you know about the problem, challenge, or idea chosen.
2. Record as much as you can in an attempt to produce a clear verbal picture of what is happening and/or what is not happening with regard to the chosen problem, challenge or idea. Answer the following questions: Who is and who is *not* concerned? What is or is *not* happening? When does this occur, and when doesn't it occur? Where does and does *not* this occur? Why does it happen? How does it happen?
3. Now introduce whatever emotions and feelings come forth to create an "interpretive painting" from the picture. Write more thoughts as they occur.
4. Smell deeply from the packages you assembled earlier. Deal with them slowly, reflecting, ruminating, as you breathe in the aroma from each one. Draw associations from these odors; do *not* attempt to *identify* the odors, but simply record what thoughts or memories the odors "trigger." The sense of smell is one of the most powerful triggers to awakening memories.
5. Connect to your earlier facts and interpretations whatever you can from the thoughts you just recorded.
6. List your *strengths,* without being modest. Brag a little, about *all* aspects of yourself, your personality, your abilities, etc., that are positive forces for you.

7. Now add new thoughts that may have surfaced—to the facts you were listing.
8. Look around you; taste, touch, listen, smell—then add more thoughts that are triggered from your memory bank—facts which are related but which you may have forgotten.

C. *Problem-Finding*

1. List as many questions as possible surrounding the situation you described. Try to start the questions with the words, "What ways might I . . ."—"What might I do to. . . ." If "Should I" or "Do I" questions come to mind, change them to "What ways might I decide . . ." or "What ways might I find out . . ." etc.
2. Stop a moment and ask, "What is the *real* problem?"—the *essence* of it? "What is my basic objective?" "What do I want to accomplish here?" Ask "Why " of each question you have listed. ("Why do I want to do this?") As a result of these questions you ask yourself, try to restate and broaden your problem. For example, if you asked "Why" of the problem, "How might I catch the mouse?" it might lead to the restatement, "How might I *get rid* of the mouse?" Try, similarly, to find problem statements (questions) that allow you the largest number of possible approaches. Try paraphrasing, changing the verbs in your statements, etc. Keep listing as many additional "What ways might I" questions as you can about the situation.
3. Now think of a "peak" experience in your life. Close your eyes, and relive that experience in your imagination.
4. List additional "What ways might I . . . ?" questions suggested by the peak experience you visualized.
5. Break down some of the above questions into sub-problems,—additional aspects, parts, stages, operations, etc.,—in order to obtain more "In what ways might I . . ." questions.
6. Draw a personal symbol to represent yourself.
7. Now write additional "What ways might I . . . ?" questions, connecting aspects of the symbol to the situation you are defining.
8. Select the "What ways might I . . . ?" question which looks most promising or most interesting for the moment.

D. *Idea-Finding*

1. Deferring judgment as fully as you can and allowing your ideas to flow freely—without any evaluation at the moment—list as many ideas as you can as leads to attacking the problem or challenge you just chose.
2. Now magnify, rearrange, etc., in seeking additional ideas. Ask yourself what would happen if you made it bigger, smaller, reversed elements or positions, etc. As you imagine these changes, do not evaluate the ideas that occur. Just continue to jot them down.
3. Look for strange analogies to situations you are working on, in searching for additional ideas. (Example: if the situation has to do with the home, think of a "circus" or a "battleship" and try to draw relationships from another "world.")
4. Play some music that has a "descriptive" quality which will tend to stir some response from you. As you listen to it, concentrate on the music and forget about what you have been writing. This will allow you to "incubate" on the problem. Move with the music—physically move in a new way. Make new "physical connections," if only with your head, fingers, toes, etc.

5. As the music concludes, write more ideas that now come to mind.
6. Close your eyes, and think of your own "personal paradise."
7. Write more ideas, connecting aspects of your personal paradise with the problem you are working on.
8. Try to "force" relationships with what you see, feel, hear, smell, taste, in your present environment—triggering and listing additional ideas.
9. Choose from your total list the ideas which look most promising, interesting, exciting, etc., and/or which you *like* best to use at this time. The choice may be totally a "gut-level" one, even if you have no awareness of how the idea can be implemented.

   NOTE: If your original problem statement was quite broad, you may find that your ideas listed are really "sub-problems." For example, consider the problem "in what ways might I become a more effective person?" You might list ideas such as "become a more outgoing person," "find new interests," etc. In cases like this you could choose one of these "approaches" at a time, and then probe for more *specific* ideas ("In what ways might I find new interests," etc.)

E. *Solution-Finding*
1. List evaluative criteria: ways to decide how "good" or "bad" the idea is; elements which might make it fail, or those which might make it better; who and what might be affected; etc.
2. In your imagination, be something in the situation other than yourself; become another person, thing, animal, etc., imagining fully, empathizing; then add additional criteria from the new connections that you may have made.
3. Glance over the criteria you have listed, and bring them to the fore-front of your awareness.

F. *Acceptance-Finding*
1. Mentally apply the criteria to the ideas you chose earlier, deciding upon the best idea or combination of best ideas. If you have selected a "gut-level" idea which doesn't generally meet the criteria, "tailor" it to fit the criteria—or fantasize it working, then adapt the fantasy to reality by modifying it as necessary.
2. Produce a free flow of ideas for gaining acceptance and putting your idea to use—ideas which make new connections toward aiding in implementation, insuring success, improving the original idea, showing its advantages, gaining enthusiasm of yourself or others, overcoming objections, anticipating possible misconceptions, etc.
3. Close your eyes and concentrate on physically relaxing yourself from the top of your head to the tips of your toes, thus providing another moment of "incubation." You may want to tense your muscles as you explore which ones need to be more relaxed. Tense them; then relax them fully.
4. Now list additional ways of getting your idea to work—but with an emphasis on *specifics,* and those which are *verifiable* or *demonstrable.* For example, change "cut down on smoking," to "smoke one cigarette less each succeeding day until I've stopped entirely." The checklist, "who, what, when, where, why, how," may again help at this point. (Who might help? Who else? What resources might I use? What special times? Occasions? Places? etc.?)

5. Now spell out in writing a final plan *for the moment,* listing as many *specifics* as possible, including first steps you will take, schedule, follow-ups, etc.

6. Fantasize putting this plan into action, as you would like to see it happen; visualize every detail—experience in your imagination every expression, feeling, reaction, etc.

7. Now bring into the "picture" an unexpected development; then, using your imagination, "watch" the consequences.

8. Add further ideas to the plan in order to take into account what you just "saw", in order to further insure the effectiveness of your plan.

9. Now visualize and list new challenges which might result from implementing the plan.

10. As a final step for now, review in your mind any new connections which you have made as a result of the new challenges you just listed. Adapt the details of your plan accordingly. Then "incubate" further on the plan and continue extending your effort toward meeting the challenges which you have just been considering, as you put your plan into action—remembering always that "nothing is final!"

Summary. Hopefully you were able to gain some new insights into the concern you chose to deal with. And, hopefully, you can understand better what the *Guide to Creative Action and Creative Actionbook* are all about. As a summary of where to find further development of the specific processes you experienced, the following may be useful to you. It shows specific sessions where we particularly emphasize certain abilities.

The ability to sense problems—See Unit 1, Session 1.

The ability to define problems—See Unit 2, Session 2.

The ability to defer judgment and break away from habit-bound thinking—See Unit 3, Session 3.

The ability to see new relationships—See Unit 4, Session 4 and/or Unit 13, Session 13.

The ability to evaluate in full light of the consequences of one's actions—See Unit 5, Session 5 and Unit 11, Session 11, Part 2.

The ability to implement ideas—See Unit 6, Session 6.

The ability to observe carefully and discover the facts—See Unit 8, Session 8.

The ability to use checklists to discover new ideas—See Unit 10, Session 10.

The ability to refine strange ideas into useful ones—See Unit 11, Session 11, Part 1.

The ability to use a methodical approach to problem-solving—See Units 7, 9, 12, 14 and 15 of Sessions 7, 9, 12, 14 and 15, respectively.

Section B will now give you more understanding about the material and how you might use it most effectively.

SECTION B—THE INSTRUCTIONAL MATERIALS

Guide to Creative Action provides the most pertinent learning and instructional guides, as well as reference materials, that have emanated from a quarter century of research and development in the stimulation of creative behavior at State University of New York in cooperation with the Creative Education Foundation. The book includes:

(1) detailed explanations of 225 hours of instruction

(2) guides to several hundred practice exercises

(3) some twenty-five of the most significant articles on the development of creative behavior

(4) information on several hundred methods and programs for stimulating creative behavior

(5) an annotated listing of 175 films on the subject

(6) information on scores of tests of creative ability

(7) over 100 questions and topics for research

(8) a bibliography of almost 2,000 books on creativity in the past twenty-five years.

Indexed for easy reference, this volume is a convenient mini-encyclopedia of creativity-development, a combined "source book and guide" for the deliberate cultivation of creative behavior. Introductory sections attempt to relate the contents of the volume to the burgeoning literature, research, and developmental efforts in the subject of creativity. Headnotes accompanying readings in Part 3 allow teachers and students, as well as general readers, to select pertinent materials.

The *Guide* and *Actionbook* may also serve as a home-study program or as a review source for students. Detailed explanations of the various uses of the book are provided at the beginning of its Part 2.

The material is organized so that the instructor can draw all background material, examples, and exercises directly from the *Guide* and its companion, the *Creative Actionbook*. The *Actionbook* is designed to be used in the creative problem-solving programs outlined in the *Guide*. It contains classroom or self-study exercises and materials that are explained in the *Guide* and is designed to be used in conjunction with the latter—not alone.

Part 1 of the *Guide* contains four chapters designed to provide background understanding of the philosophical, psychological, and sociological bases for a program for deliberate development of creative behavior. (If you already have this background, you may move right on to Part 2 of the book.) The first chapter deals with an overall orientation to our program. Chapter 2 provides a fuller perspective of the program within the realm of developing human potential. In Chapter 3, a more detailed rationale is provided for programs designed to deliberately cultivate creative behavior. Chapter 4 provides a summary of research on our developing program. It is drawn from various research reports over the years of scientific evaluation of the program.

The thesis presented is that a prime "medium" for instruction is the imagination of the individual. It is commonly accepted that any instructional medium must first engage the student and capture his or her attention. What could possibly capture one's attention faster or more completely than personal realization of the power to discover—to create knowledge. Thus each has a "built-in-medium" for the teacher or facilitator to use—imagination, the nucleus of the student's mental energy.

This self-fulfilling approach does not minimize the need for subject matter. We can give individuals the opportunity to grow creatively within their milieu, rather than only outside it. The mastery of subject matter can be provided concurrently with opportunity and exercise for creativity development. The teacher can learn to utilize more fully the medium of the student's imagination. Educators have too frequently been accustomed to pouring in from without, rather than drawing out from within, as the word "educate" literally means. We can cultivate talent in the way soil nurtures a seed. It provides for the growth of the seed; it does not tell the seed what to become.

Underlying all of our program's approaches is the basic objective of getting the student to interrelate more freely and effectively both what she or he already knows and what she or he acquires through the senses, so as to be able to find relevancy where it was not seen before. Hundreds of examples and exercises designed to help toward this end are suggested in Part 2 of the *Guide* as part of the program presented therein.

Many educators have revised the material to suit their own purposes more directly. This is encouraged, and the material is designed to lend itself to that end. Paul Torrance reports that the program or its modifications have been among the most popular approaches used in elementary and high school attempts to teach children to think creatively. Moreover, he points out that twenty of twenty-two scientific studies using the program or modifications of it have resulted in successes— the highest percentage of success for any of the more popular programs and methods he studied. (The full reference for the study is: Torrance, E. P. "Can we teach children to think creatively?" *Journal of Creative Behavior,* 1972, 6(2), 114–143.)

Part 2 of the *Guide* provides the actual detailed instructional program for cultivating creative behavior. Teachers are urged to read the introductory pages to Part 2, which provides important information on use of the instructional materials. The following headings will provide a notion of the kind of detailed explanations offered for helping teachers apply the material more effectively: using unit outlines; alternation between individual, team, and group involvement; peer-tutoring; sessions emphasizing awareness-development; film sessions; modifications; timing of sessions; flexible program schedules; expansion or shortening of sessions; progress-testing exercises; guests as resources; room arrangements, materials and supplies; grading plans and evaluation; readings; outside projects; alternate ways of using program materials (in creativity courses, for training of specific mental abilities and in other subjects); and references for further study.

Part 3: The authors of the readings presented in Part 3 need little introduction to the serious reader concerned with creativity and problem-solving. They will be recognized as some of the leading opponents of the growing movement that focuses on the nature, nurture and application of human creativity.

The thirteen articles following the opening one by J. P. Guilford are a response to his statement that "an informed people, with skills in using this information, is a creative, problem-solving people." They relate to cognitive creative problem-solving methods and programs available to users who wish to push for deliberate solutions to problems. J. H. McPherson's selection puts them into perspective. He points out that the problem-solving method(s) selected will be contingent upon (1) the nature of the problem to be solved, and (2) the unique nature of the individual(s) attempting the solution. Appendix A in the book augments McPherson's thrust with an extensive, representative listing of programs and procedures (with references for each) used in developing problem-solving effectiveness.

Lewis Walkup was impressed by the way in which creative individuals seemed to have discovered and then intensely developed the ability to visualize mentally in the areas in which they were creative. He further observed that creative outcome seemed to depend largely upon the degree the mental images could be manipulated and the skills by which the individual could sense the properties of the new combinations of things. Thus articles 15–18 deal with visualization, the second important emphasis in this section.

The third emphasis in Part 3, highlights the *Human Potential Development Movement* and its concern with the fact that the normal productive person seems to be functioning at approximately 10 percent of his or her capacity. Herbert Otto's article traces the development of 300 growth centers around the nation beginning with the 1962 Esalen Institute at Big Sur. The centers serve to bring to popular awareness the many kinds of human-growth programs described in articles 19–22.

The conscious integration of the human-development principles with creative-development programs has generated impactful advances toward greater human fulfillment. When Alex Osborn was first channeling his efforts toward helping individuals create ideas, he noted that the techniques had a very positive effect on individual personalities. It seemed that as individuals became increasingly aware of their creative potential, they achieved a new level of confidence which enabled them to cope more adequately.

The two final articles in Part 2 focus on highly challenging programs geared to assist the individuals to deepen contact with their greater potential as they prepare to cope with the geometrically expanding problems of today's life. Because of their current embryonic stage of development, readers may find the material contained here less immediately applicable.

The articles in Part 3 relate to and extend or reinforce the various sessions of the program. Titles and brief headnotes provide for quick selection of appropriate readings to amplify particular sessions.

Appendices A-F provide the information mentioned earlier on related methods and programs, films, tests, research questions, and bibliography.

Self-study explanation. Appendix G provides further detailed session-guides for teachers using the material for the first time, as well as a self-study explanation for students using it outside of class. Full explanation is provided for the student who may be working through the material alone. It has been subjected to extensive programming research as described on pages 23 and 24 of the *Guide.* "The results finally demonstrated that the revised material could be adequately understood and successfully followed by students working alone."

In the introduction to Appendix G, suggestions are provided for making the self-study approach more palatable and effective by such patterns as team study. "Study with someone you like so that the experience is an enjoyable one. Some students have made pleasant study-dated out of the session assignments. It might be a good idea to form small student 'clubs' for working on the material." Suggestions are offered for making such team study most effective.

Age Levels. Although the material was formally tested with average college-bound high-school seniors, it should certainly be usable as is by gifted high-school or even junior-high students. Many teachers have already used it in this way, and many more have adapted it successfully at lower levels, all the way down to the primary grades; parents have done likewise in many different and effective ways with youngsters of all ages.

If you become involved with these creative problem-solving processes and apply *deliberate* creative effort on your part toward stimulating *deliberate* creative thinking on the part of your youngsters, you may derive new satisfaction from your responsibilities. You may experience the delight that one teacher enjoyed when a youngster exclaimed, with eyes twinkling, "I've been *thinking*!"

V

CURRICULUM

15. ASSESSING CREATIVITY ACROSS WILLIAMS "CUBE" MODEL

Frank E. Williams

Until now little has been done in devising a satisfactory way to assess a combination of cognitive and affective factors related to creative behavior which can be easily used by classroom teachers. And translating findings from creativity assessment into practical classroom practices by teachers desiring to make conscious efforts to develop student's creative behavior has been practically unheard of until the present gifted movement began in 1975. Of the six general areas of multiple abilities considered legitimate for funding gifted projects, the one area of creative productive thinking has until now remained rather barren and neglected in terms of valid assessment and treatment procedures. Educators working in gifted programs have been plagued with difficulties in locating curriculum materials and tests when attempting to identify, implement, and evaluate projects in the area of creativity. Yet, this is one of the main ability areas strongly advocated by federal, state and district policies governing defensible and differentiated programs for gifted students.

During this current resurgence of gifted education many former models of learning have been revitalized for sake of expediency in order to offer defensible programs for gifted, talented and creative students. Bloom's taxonomy (1956), Guilford's structure of intellect (1955), Parnes' creative problem solving and brainstorming (1964), Piaget's stage theory of intellectual development (1953), Rath's higher thinking processes (1966), Taylor's multiple talents (1968), Taba's teaching strategies (1966), and Williams cognitive-affective interaction model with teaching strategies (1969) are the most popular and practical delivery systems for present gifted programs. All are older models initially designed from theoretical research studies on child growth and development. None were ever conceived as learning models for gifted students, but were to provide better instructional techniques for all students in school classrooms. Of these models, only one offers educators a complete diagnostic-prescriptive instructional delivery system including teaching strategies across basic content producing specific cognitive-affective student outcomes in the divergent area of creativity. This is Williams model with accompanying materials which now includes assessment instruments for measuring those divergent behaviors research has shown most important to the creative process.

The Williams model[1], provides continuity within a delivery system for coordinating those creative abilities of students by strategies teachers can use for teaching the basic skills and content. It is based upon the importance of developing pupil-teacher interactions with the curriculum by dealing specifically with those cognitive and affective behaviors vitally responsible for encouraging

Reprinted by permission from *Gifted Child Quarterly*, Vol. 23, No. 4, 1979.

1. Williams, Frank E. *Total Creativity Program* kit, Educational Technology Inc., 140 Sylvan Ave., Englewood Cliffs, New Jersey 07632

and releasing creativity which have become well known from long standing research evidence. Now it is possible to purposely program the on-going curriculum for developing and sustaining those divergent thinking and feeling processes most responsible for the creative process. These can be measured by a combination of cognitive and affective instruments, pre and post treatment with gain scores computed to show each student's progress. Thus, a delivery system now exists consisting of definable, developmental and measurable factors purposely aimed at encouraging creativity among students in school classrooms. This article shall discuss the instruments now available measuring both those cognitive and affective factors of divergent thinking and feeling which can be administered for not only gifted students but for all typical, average learners.

As can be seen from the Williams model, eight pupil behaviors shown in Dimension 3[2] are student outcomes from implementation of the model consisting of 4 cognitive and 4 affective

DIMENSION 3
Pupil Behaviors

Behavior	Meaning
COGNITIVE—INTELLECTIVE	Generation of a quantity
FLUENT THINKING	Flow of thought
To think of the *most*—	Number of relevant responses
FLEXIBLE THINKING	Variety of kinds of ideas
To take *different* approaches—	Ability to shift categories
	Detours in direction of thought
ORIGINAL THINKING	Unusual responses
To think in *novel* or *unique* ways—	Clever ideas
	Production away from the obvious
ELABORATIVE THINKING	Embellish upon an idea
To *add on* to—	Embroider upon a simple idea or response to make it more elegant
	Stretch or expand upon things or ideas
AFFECTIVE—FEELING	Expose oneself to failure or criticisms
RISK TAKING	Take a guess
To have *courage* to—	Function under conditions devoid of structure
	Defend own ideas
COMPLEXITY	Seek many alternatives
To be *challenged* to—	See gaps between how things are and how they could be
	Bring order out of chaos
	Delve into intricate problems or ideas
CURIOSITY	Be inquisitive and wonder
To be *willing* to—	Toy with an idea
	Be open to puzzling situations
	Ponder the mystery of things
	To follow a particular hunch just to see what will happen
IMAGINATION	Visualize and build mental images
To have the *power* to—	Dream about things that have never happened
	Feel intuitively
	Reach beyond sensual or real boundaries

2. See *The Gifted Child Quarterly*, Winter 1979, Vol. XXIII, No. 4, p. 750.

factors. Dimension 3 lists and defines these 8 factors. The 4 cognitive factors were derived from Guilford's divergent operations slab of the structure of intellect (cognitive-divergence). The 4 affective factors were derived from various studies on the traits and characteristics of creative persons, more primarily from MacKinnon and Barron's extensive studies on the temperament, dispositional factors among high creative individuals (affective-divergence).

It is important to point out that all 8 factors as pupil behaviors from the Williams model are divergent in nature but related to both cognitive and affective domains.

SUBJECTS

Subjects of this study were selected from 468 classroom students, grades 3 through 9, from four large gifted programs where the author had worked as a consultant during the past five years. The four project locations were Anchorage, Alaska (PACT project), Medford, Oregon (Southern Oregon Gifted Project), Great Falls, Montana, (PACE project), and Troutdale, Oregon (Reynold's G-T project). All subjects had met certain project criteria for being gifted students, and had been identified, selected and involved in a gifted program within their respective school districts. These subjects had demonstrated superior performance in either intelligence, academic achievement, creativity, and/or in the affective area of self concept. These were the four ability areas chosen by their respective projects as criteria for identification and selection into a gifted program. In short, these were gifted, and creative students, with strong feelings of self-worth.

From this large pool of gifted students, four groups were selected by a rank order of highest scores on four respective ability areas as classified by the Williams continuum diagram shown in the figure below.

Test scores, nominations and rating scales by teachers, parents and peers were used as identification and selection criteria for these four groups. On a variety of tests and scales, selected subjects for the four groups had attained scores averaging 1.2 to 1.7 standard deviations above the mean from published test norms for this grade level group. Classification of the four groups shown by the figure was determined from the nature of the test or scale used and how it is scored. For example, self concept scales are affective in nature but scored by correct answer keys, hence they yield an affective-convergent classification.

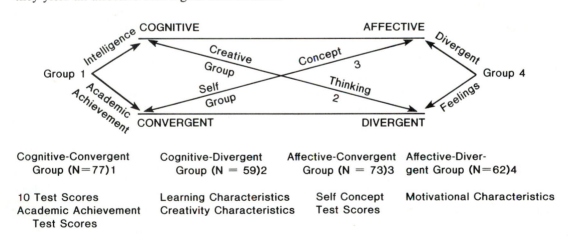

Cognitive-Convergent Group (N=77)1	Cognitive-Divergent Group (N = 59)2	Affective-Convergent Group (N = 73)3	Affective-Divergent Group (N=62)4
10 Test Scores Academic Achievement Test Scores	Learning Characteristics Creativity Characteristics	Self Concept Test Scores	Motivational Characteristics

METHODS

All four groups of subjects classified as shown in the figure were administered two test instruments. Both tests had been designed and validated to measure the 8 pupil behaviors in Dimension 3 of the Williams model. These test instruments are:

Drawing Test of Creative Thinking—measures the four cognitive-divergent factors from the Williams model; namely fluency, flexibility, originality, elaboration and title yielding these sub scores. This test is a revised form of the earlier figural Torrance Test of Creative Thinking consisting of two drawing exercises, completing a picture using a form and completing a series of pictures using a stimulus figure. Even though these drawing exercises are similar to the earlier Torrance Test of Creative Thinking, a whole new and simplified scoring procedure deriving weighted scores with norms have been devised by Williams based upon thorough analysis of test performance on over two thousand protocols. Both exercises elicit right brain visual perception classified to structure of intellect as divergent figural transformations (DST), except the title score which is left brain oriented classified to structure of intellect as divergent semantic transformations (DST). Hence, the test meets hemisphericity criteria for creativity requiring alternate modes or integrated styles of information processing through synthesis productions.

This modified form of the older Torrance Test of Creative Thinking was validated by a random sample of student subjects from the current study (N=67) by administering both creative thinking tests, the earlier figural form of the Torrance scored by his procedure and this later form scored by a new simplified scoring procedure. High creative scorers on both tests did discriminate significantly over low scorers. Both tests yield the same subscores of creative-productive thinking; fluency, flexibility, originality and elaboration as derived from the divergent slab of Guilford's structure of intellect model. However, the new Drawing Test of Creative Thinking can be more easily and quickly scored for use by classroom teachers.

How Do You Really Feel About Yourself Inventory [HDYRFAY]—measures the four affective-divergent factors from the Williams model; namely, curiosity, imagination, risk taking, and complexity. This test was initially validated against the original Torrance Tests of Creative Thinking, both figural and verbal, as a divergent production exercise. High scoring creative thinkers on the Torrance tests did discriminate significantly on the HDYRFAY as compared to low scoring individuals. High performers on the 4 cognitive-divergent factors of fluency, flexibility, originality and elaboration also scored high on the 4 affective-divergent factors of curiosity, imagination, risk taking, and complexity. Title scores likewise correlate high and significantly to verbal comprehension scores on academic achievement tests. This test exercise satisfies integrated brain functioning by requiring left brain verbal analysis alternating with right brain emotional, affective processing, and on structure of intellect is classified as divergent semantic units (DSU).

Both test instruments are now available in a newly designed *Creativity Assessment Test Packet* by Frank Williams published and distributed by DOK Publishers, Inc.[3]

Williams Scale

A third instrument has been designed and was administered to classroom teachers and parents of the four selected groups of subjects. This instrument is the Williams Scale, a scale for rating divergent thinking and feeling behaviors of children. It consists of an observational check

---

[3]Williams, Frank E., *A Creativity Assessment Packet*, DOK Publishers, Inc. 71 Radcliffe Road, Buffalo, New York 14214, 1979.

list of traits and characteristics across each of the 8 factors, both cognitive and affective, from Dimension 3 of the Williams model. For example, it defines fluent thinking and lists 6 trait characteristics of a fluent thinking person, or defines curiosity and lists 6 trait characteristics of a curious person. Each trait characteristic may be checked by 3 alternative boxes; often, sometimes, or seldom. In addition to the 48 trait characteristic items on the scale there are 4 open-ended items asking a parent and a teacher for their expectations of a school program for a gifted child and their expectations of the accomplishments of a gifted child in a school program. The entire Scale yields a weighted score of 100 points and has norms available. This Scale like the Drawing Test of Creative Thinking and the HDYRFAY are likewise available in the new Creativity Test Packet as indicated. Hence, the entire packet is a series of test instruments to be used across the Williams model for assessment and evaluation as the model is used for treatment.

RESULTS

The table on p. 141 reports means and standard deviations for each group of subjects as shown in the figure on p. 139 on all eight factors measured by the two test instruments administered. It should be noted that subjects in the cognitive-divergent and affective-divergent groups, Groups 2 and 4, attained the highest scores on most measured factors.

ASSESSMENT

Subjects initially scoring highest on cognitive-divergence and affective-divergence by scores on instruments and checklists, Groups 2 and 4, obtained higher scores on all factors of both the creative thinking drawing test and the HDYRFAY except title score on the drawing test. To test the statistical significance of these differences Chi-Square tests found 7 of the 9 factor scores for groups 2 and 4 (cognitive and affective-divergence) to be statistically significant beyond the .05 level of confidence. Flexible and original thinking along with curiosity and imagination yielded

Means and Standard Deviations of Selected Creative Thinking and Feeling Factors Across Four Groups of Gifted Students

Measured Factor	Group 1 Cognitive-Convergent		Group 2 Cognitive-Divergent		Group 3 Affective-Convergent		Group 4 Affective-Divergent	
	Mean	S.D.	Mean	S.D.	Mean	S.D.	Mean	S.D.
Fluency	8.4	1.6	9.3	1.4	8.7	1.7	9.0	1.3
Flexibility	5.7	2.0	7.1	2.1	5.9	2.2	7.0	1.9
Originality	26.4	2.1	30.3	2.4	27.9	2.6	30.1	2.7
Elaboration	24.3	4.9	27.1	5.2	26.1	4.7	28.8	5.0
Title	2.9	0.9	2.5	1.0	2.4	1.1	2.3	0.8
Curiosity	15.1	1.9	18.8	2.1	16.9	2.3	18.3	2.0
Imagination	14.7	2.1	19.0	2.4	16.8	1.7	18.4	2.2
Complexity	15.0	2.4	15.3	2.1	16.7	2.0	16.2	2.3
Risk-Taking	15.1	2.3	17.9	2.0	16.7	1.7	16.3	2.2

the greatest significant gains for groups 2 and 4 over groups 1 and 3. The data suggests two confirming facts. One, if you want to choose students who will do well on measures relating to creativity you assess certain creative thinking and feeling behaviors; not IQ, academic achievement nor self concept. For the latter are convergent abilities at least the way they are tested, while a majority of abilities necessary for creativity are divergent abilities. This study reveals eight predominantly divergent behaviors highly related to assessing creativity. Two, the importance of linking or connecting cognitive with affective styles of processing information under conditions calling for divergence appears to be generally more effective for eliciting creativity than under convergent, fixed-answer conditions.

In addition to data shown in the table on p. 141 on results of the two test instruments administered student subjects, correlations were obtained using the Williams Scale administered to parents and teachers of these same subjects. It is important to point out again that the 8 factors comprising the Williams Scale which is a rating checklist to be used by parents and teachers observing student behaviors at home and in school are the same 8 factors measured by the two test instruments reported on in Table 1 and developed as student outcomes by use of the Williams model. By analysis of teacher-parent pairs of Williams Scales for the same student, correlations obtained were .73 for upper grade students, .67 for elementary grade students, with an overall correlation across all pairs of .71, all significant at the .01 level of confidence. Such correlations indicate a significant relationship existed between teachers' rating and parents' rating of the same student on fluent, flexible, original and elaborative thinking along with curiosity, risk taking, complexity and imagination.

The last part of this correlation study asked the question did students as subjects in the study observed at home eliciting these processes as well as in school perform the same on tests which measure like processes? The top five ranked scoring students on the Williams scale by both parents and teachers were compared to the bottom five ranked scoring students by their scores on the Creative Thinking Drawing Test and on the HDYRFAY. A rank order correlation of .84 was obtained. These data confirm that students who are curious and flexible at home as observed by parents are also curious and flexible in school as observed by teachers and perform equally well as curious and flexible students on tasks measuring curiosity and flexibility.

CONCLUSIONS AND SUMMARY

Using gifted subjects scoring highest by tests, checklists, and nomination forms across the cognitive or affective domains under either convergent or divergent conditions; it appears from the study that both cognitive and affective divergers perform better on creative thinking and feeling tasks measuring cognitive and affective divergence. The evidence produced by this study indicates rather clearly that groups of gifted students classified by tasks of cognitive and affective convergence obtain lower scores than do groups of students classified by tasks of cognitive and affective divergence on measures of creative thinking abilities and on personality measures associated with creative behaviors. On measures of creative thinking, cognitive-divergent groups excelled over cognitive-convergent groups on the factors of flexibility and originality. On measures of temperament or dispositional factors, affective-divergent groups excelled over affective-convergent groups on measures of curiosity and imagination.

By use of the Williams model, there now is available a complete delivery system for school classrooms including test instruments, curriculum materials and teaching strategies for teacher's use when interested in developing the creative process within subject content areas of a school program. Although evidence of the study suggests that among exceptional students both convergent and divergent behaviors are involved in multiple ability giftedness, a style of information processing utilizing both cognitive and affective domains operating under divergent conditions seems to be most favorable for assessing creativity. Additional studies need to be conducted with different populations, especially a replicative study on typical, average students. For if accepting the premise that giftedness is a matter of degree not kind, perhaps these assessment instruments tested in this study used well with gifted students could likewise be used for most other students.

References

Williams, Frank E. *A Total Creativity Program* kit, Educational Technology Publications, Inc. Englewood Cliffs, New Jersey, 1972.

Williams. "A Magic Circle", *G/C/T Magazine,* Premiere Issue, Jan/Feb, 1978.

Williams. "Williams' Strategies Orchestrating Renzulli's Triad", *G/C/T Magazine,* Sept/Oct. Issue, 1979.

Williams. "Assessing Pupil-Teacher Behaviors Related to a Cognitive-Affective Teaching Model", *Journal of Research and Development in Education,* Vol. 4, No. 3, Spring, 1971.

Williams. *Classroom Ideas for Encouraging Thinking and Feeling,* D.O.K. Publishers, Inc. Buffalo, New York, 1969.

Williams. *Performance Levels of a School Program Survey [PLSPS],* D.O.K. Publishers, Inc. Buffalo, New York, 1979.

Williams. *Teachers Without Fear,* D.O.K. Publishers, Inc., 1977.

Williams. *Creativity Assessment Packet,* D.O.K. Publishers, Inc. Buffalo, New York, 1979.

16. TEN WAYS OF HELPING YOUNG CHILDREN GIFTED IN CREATIVE WRITING AND SPEECH

E. Paul Torrance

Children show their giftedness in many ways—some in one way and some in another. Many children show their giftedness first through creative writing and speech. If your child shows his giftedness in this way, you may be fortunate in many ways. First, even very young children gifted in this respect provide themselves and others with much pleasure. Second, the exercise of this talent provides an excellent means for developing the creative thinking abilities and a variety of skills in creative problem-solving.

Most of our studies have been concerned with ways in which schools and colleges can foster creative growth of various kinds. I believe, however, that through these studies we can suggest some rather positive ways by which parents can help children who are gifted in creative writing and speech. In this article, I shall discuss ten of them.

1. PROVIDE MATERIALS WHICH DEVELOP IMAGINATION

Parents can do much to provide materials which help *develop* the imaginative powers of children. Some parents will argue that there is no need for this, that their problem is to keep their children from being too imaginative. It is tremendously important, however, that parents keep alive imagination and fantasy until the child's intellectual development is such that he can engage in a sound type of creative thinking. I would like to place the emphasis upon the word *development*. Parents can use the child's natural inclination to engage in imaginative activity to bring about some of this development, and to bring it about in such a way that it will lead to this sound type of creative thinking which I have been talking about.

Perhaps I can best communicate what I have in mind by talking about some specific materials through books. One of my favorites is a series of books by an Italian artist and story-teller, Bruno Munari. They are now published in the United States by the World Publishing Company. An interesting one entitled, *Who's there? Open the Door?* is good for developing both the imagination and the evaluation of judgment abilities. The cover of the book is in the form of a big door with the eye of an animal peeking out. You can have the child guess all of the things he can think of that would be so big that it would take a room for them to stand up in. The child might guess an elephant, a camel, a giraffe, a pony and the like. You open the door and it's actually "Lucy the giraffe with a large crate come all of the way from Lisbon." It might also have been some of the other things guessed. You might accept such large ones as elephant, camel, and others. You might point out, however, that a pony would not take this much space. Next, the question becomes "What's in the crate?" Again, he might guess pony, bear, hippopotamus, pig, cow, and the like. It is actually "Peggy the zebra with a trunk come all the way from Paris." Again, other things similar in size to the zebra can be accepted and those larger and smaller can be eliminated. The

Reprinted by permission from *Gifted Child Quarterly,* Vol. 6, No. 3, 1962.

game continues. We have Leo the lion with a valise come all the way from London. Next we have "Romeo the cat with a package wrapped in tissue paper, come all the way from Rome." In the package we have "Bertha, the blackbird, with a basket come all the way from Berlin." In the basket we have "Dick, the cricket, with a small parcel come all the way from Dublin." In the parcel we have "a little ant with a grain of wheat for the winter."

With such materials you are doing more than developing the imagination, you are developing the ability to think in terms of possibles, to make judgments about size, and to gain a more accurate picture of the world in which they live. Incidentally, they might on later occasions be stimulated in their curiosity to ask about the places from which these animals and insects have been shipped: Lisbon, Paris, London, Rome, Berlin, and Dublin.

Another of the Munari books that I like is *The Elephant's Wish*. The story begins: "The elephant is bored with being a big heavy animal. He wishes he could be something else. What do you think he would like to be?" This starts the guessing game. The child is asked to look into the mind of the elephant, to imaginatively put himself in the place of the elephant and think what he would want to do if he were to be tired of being an elephant. Then he is given a look into the elephant's mind by the artist and author. "He wishes he could be a little bird who flies and sings." The bird, however, has his problems. "The little bird is bored with flying and singing. He is wishing too. What does he wish?" After some guessing on the part of the child, he can be given a look into the bird's mind. The bird "wishes he could be a fish and swim under water." But the fish is bored too. He is bored with swimming under water. What does he wish?" He wishes he could go on land. How tempting it must be to him to want to go on land! "He wishes he could be a lizard sitting on a stone in the sun." The story continues. The lizard wants to be a cow, a fat, lazy ox. The ox wants to be an elephant. Thus, we return to the place where we started. Everything wants to be something else. Our problem is to accept creatively our limitations and use our abilities and resources. If we do, we will not be bored. Life will always be exciting.

There are many others. One series is E. P. Dutton's *Imagination Books*. One is *Let's Imagine Thinking Up Things* by Janet Wolff and Bernard Owett. It is a kind of duplication of one of our tests of creative thinking. For example, the child is told, "Here is a circle. Let's imagine all the things the circle can be." The child can produce some either by drawing or in words. Some examples are given in the book. I might add that the examples given are some of the most obvious and unoriginal ones: a face, the sun, the top of an ice cream cone, a ball, money, a clock, a hoop, and the like.

Other examples are Alastair Reid's *Just Suppose*, Lenore Klein's *What Would You Do, If. . .* and the monthly magazine, *Highlights for Children*, which you may have in your doctor's or dentist's office. *The Poetry-Drawing Book* by Cole and Colmore provides another innovation in children's books. It provides poems for children to illustrate and color by themselves. These materials have not been subjected to very much scientific testing, but on the basis of what we know I would assume that they provide rather sound approaches.

2. PROVIDE MATERIALS WHICH ENRICH IMAGERY

To go very far in really developing imagination or creative thinking, a child needs a rich store of imagery. This, I might add, is important not just in developing a background for writing and speaking creatively but in scientific discovery and invention, art, and the like. There are many ways of doing this. One way is through the use of the well-known classical fairy tales, folk stories, myths and fables. I still think that the Mother Goose stories; the folk stories and fables of Italy, Germany, France, India, and other countries; the Greek and Roman myths; and the like have a very important role in developing this kind of imagery. Of course, it is also hard to beat the fact book of nature—the models of creation we have in animal and plant life. It is from this source that so many of our modern inventions come (Gordon, 1961).

3. PERMIT TIME FOR THINKING AND DAYDREAMING

Many parents keep their children so busy that they don't have time to think, much less speak and write creatively. Certainly many families would find life much more exciting and would enjoy much better mental health, if they reduced the number of activities in their schedule and gave more time for creative development. We become very disturbed, however, if children want to be alone or if they are not *visibly* busy. It is almost illegal to be busy thinking. This condition must be changed, if you are to foster creative speaking and writing in children.

I always find it very rewarding to hear stories like the following one by a graduate student. His children had always made good grades and had found school work easy before coming to the Twin Cities. Early in the school year, he found his eight-year-old son crying over his homework. He had been assigned to make up a story about a picture and couldn't think of one. He had never been asked to make up a story before. He was an outstanding reader, but making up a story was something new to him. The father was disturbed by his son's new school difficulty and decided to do something about it. The family instituted a story-telling session during the evening meal. The four-year-old led the way with some of the most delightful stories, but the mother and father also joined in. The father attests that this greatly improved mental health conditions in the family and helped his son hurdle what appeared to be a difficult handicap.

We do many things which discourage children from speaking creatively—or at all, for that matter. Typical is the story of a mother who was shocked that her five-year-old daughter asked to be permitted to eat alone in her room when Mrs. Green came to lunch (Miller, 1961). The child explained that she didn't like to talk with Mrs. Green.

When asked to explain, the child said, "Oh you know. She talks to me in a baby voice—and keeps asking me things and never gives me time to answer."

Then the mother recalled that every remark Mrs. Green made to the child was some little question she obviously did not expect answered. "Where did you get that pretty dress? What have you been doing today? What makes Julie grow so fast?"

As a result, the child clammed up tight. Then, Mrs. Green made matters worse by adding, "My Julie is a shy one, isn't she? Are you bashful honey? She doesn't talk much, does she?"

Many highly creative children appear to be either shy or show-offs. Shy children will talk freely with adults, if they are given time to answer questions—to take time to think and find words to express their ideas. The show-offs will find that their acting up is unnecessary, if they are accepted as persons in conversations with adults.

4. ENCOURAGE CHILDREN TO RECORD THEIR IDEAS

Children's stories, poems, songs are valuable—they are charming and delightful and can give others great pleasure and insight. Children need encouragement, however, to write down their ideas. They do not do so naturally. It is best done if some purpose is given to the writing. We found that children could be encouraged to do a great deal of writing on their own, through the use of a magazine in which we reproduced their stories, poems, inventions, opinions, drawings, and the like. Parents cannot easily provide such an outlet. They can, however, provide many good excuses for such productions—original greetings for birthdays, important family occasions, holidays, letters to friends and relatives, and so on. To encourage children to write poems or other creative productions whenever they have something to express, give them an attractive binder, folio, or the like in which to collect their writings. Forced writing will not help. The child needs to be warmed up to his creations whatever their nature might be. He needs only to feel free to do so when he has something to express. Such writings should be done to be read, heard, or used and not to be corrected or graded. They should be enjoyed.

5. GIVE CHILDREN'S WRITINGS SOME CONCRETE EMBODIMENT

In our work with children, I have learned that they are stimulated to greater heights in their creative thinking, if their ideas find embodiment in some concrete form. There is excitement in seeing one's ideas take form. Young children in kindergarten and first grade take great pride in the murals which they paint—and I have seen some wonderful ones done by them—the inventions which they contrive, the songs and poems they compose, and the stories they write. When children find that others value and do not disparage their productions, they take courage and are eager to keep building onto their ideas, improving them, creating new words, letting one thing lead to another.

Pre-school children have to tell their stories through drawings or by telling their stories and having someone else record them. In either case, their productions can be translated into some concrete form which will be appreciated. Their drawings can be placed in frames and given places of honor in the home. You can use attractive frames in which the pictures can be changed easily from time to time. These can give family and friends a great deal of enjoyment. Their drawings can also be used as designs in mother's ceramic work, sewing, and the like. I have a very treasured dinner plate which was designed by a four-year-old child. She drew a picture which she called "Snow Bubbles." Her aunt used it as the design for a set of dinner dishes for her family's Christmas gift. I liked it so much that she made a plate for me. The "Snow Bubble" title is a charming one and the dinner set is beautiful.

Children are natural story tellers and poets, and can compose charmingly and excitingly, if encouraged to do so. Seldom are these appreciated and given adequate treatment in publications. I would like to call to your attention two notable exceptions. One of these is an exciting little book by Susan Nichols Pulsifer entitled *Minute Magic* (1960). In this book, Mrs. Pulsifer presents a variety of poems by preschool children and describes her experiences in getting children to compose poems and songs. Mrs. Pulsifer joins me in contending that the drop in creative behavior which occurs at about age five is not a natural developmental change. Instead, she contends that it is due to the influence of other children, group activities, the imposition of correct techniques and facts, rules and regulations. She believes, as I do, that with wisdom the home and school can do much to reduce this discontinuity in development and lessen this serious loss of creativity.

Another example is the work of Kathleen Wrenn and her son Robert (1949). When her son was about two years of age, Mrs. Wrenn discovered that he was responding much more readily to suggestions that were sung to him than he did when the same requests were spoken. Soon, she discovered that he was responding by singing and rapidly developed a sense of rhythm and a singing scale. When Bobby was about four years old, the idea of making a book of songs began taking shape. These were simple songs about everyday happenings—songs about the fireman, the milkman, the zoo, balloons, traffic signals, and the church bell.

With new experiences, Bobby would think of ideas for songs and work them out. On one occasion, his mother asked him to put some leaves over the tulips planted in the yard so they would not freeze. He came back with the following idea for a song:

Here comes tne flowers out of the ground.
Spreading happiness all around.
Daffodils, hyacinths, tulips gay,
Oh, how I wish you were here to stay!

His mother suggested that "hyacinth" was a very difficult word for little children to sing and why not say "daisies" instead. His reply was, "I'm a little child aren't I and it's my word." (Yes, children dislike for others to tamper with their compositions and their reasons may be well-founded.)

One night Bobby lay for a long time listening to the sound of the rain on the roof. Then he called his mother to come quickly with a pencil and write down what he had been singing. This is what he was singing:

Pitter patter, pitter patter,
Hear the raindrops falling down.
Pitter patter, pitter patter,
Falling falling all around.

Dripping, dripping, dripping, dripping
I can hear them overhead.
Dripping, dripping, dripping, dripping,
On the roof above my bed.

I would like to submit that the use of devices such as the ones used by Mrs. Pulsifer and Mrs. Wrenn might do much to reduce the discontinuity in creative development between the home and the school. It does not mean fixating development at a pre-school level of maturity. It could mean increasing maturity.

6. ACCEPT THE CHILD'S NATURAL
TENDENCY TO TAKE A DIFFERENT LOOK

For some time I had been familiar with deliberate methods for increasing creativity by looking at something in a different way. Synectics (Gordon, 1961), for example, stresses the principle of making the unfamiliar, familiar or the familiar, unfamiliar. One idea was sparked when one member of the team tried to imagine himself as a drop of paint, struggling to get some kind of hold in a wall which had been painted and had not been scraped or cleaned. I noted, as I began to study the thinking of kindergartners, that children use the technique of synectics and of brainstorming spontaneously and naturally all of the time. This lesson was dramatized for me through a song composed by little Catherine Babcock, "Did You Ever Read a Clock Upside Down?" (with sound effects).

Did you ever read a clock upside down?
  Upside down!
Did you ever read a clock upside down?
It is very hard to do but I think you should
  Learn how to read a clock upside down.

Children think quite naturally in terms of analogy. They do not have to be *taught* the methods of synectics and bionics. Two interesting examples are given in a current advertisement of a new NBC program called "Exploring." A small boy is trying to tell us his foot has fallen asleep. He exclaimed, "Gee, my toes feel just like ginger ale!" Most people know exactly what he means. A little girl, discovering the woozy ribbons of color in a grease puddle, mournfully describes them as a "dead rainbow." Most people know exactly what she means, but do you know that many parents will "correct" such accurate and imaginative descriptions. If you take your cue from the amazing record of invention by the students of bionics and synectics you would do all you can to keep alive this habit of thinking by analogy. Fortunes are being made in this way!

7. PRIZE RATHER THAN PUNISH TRUE INDIVIDUALITY

Very early in our studies of creative thinking it became clear that children really prize their individuality. Just before Christmas I visited a class and admired their Santa Clauses. I commented quite informally that each one was so interesting, that no two were alike. Later in the year, they had prepared another exhibit of which they were very proud. Just as they had completed this, one little fellow said, "Dr. Torrance would like these. No two are alike!"

Not all kindergartners and first graders received this kind of encouragement for their individuality. One mother wrote me of her son's kindergarten troubles which arose over his desire to paint his dittoed horse striped like a "z-horse" instead of brown like all of the other children's. Another mother thinks that her son's learning problems began in the kindergarten over such a difficulty. Before he started to school, he was frequently mistaken for a third or fourth grader because of his penetrating questions and conclusions, his excitement in learning. In kindergarten, however, he began bringing home failing papers. To his teacher's dittoed drawing he would add cowboy boots and hats, or even change the teacher's drawings. Now, this boy's school performance is so apathetic that he is suspected of mental retardation.

Although such things, and worse, still occur in our schools, I believe and hope that they are becoming a rarity. If your child has a teacher who is a devotee of the dittoed drawing, as parents you may have to encourage original work, as Tommy's mother did. Tommy's story can be told through four drawings. Just before Easter, 1962, Tommy and his classmates were instructed to paint "nice" rabbits for their mothers. Tommy's coloring was not the smoothest possible, so the teacher was displeased and gave him another dittoed rabbit. Again, Tommy displeased the teacher who gave him another rabbit. By now, however, it was time to flit to another activity, so in desperation she told Tommy to take the rabbit home and paint it "nice" for his mother. When Tommy reached home he was almost in tears. How could he paint a rabbit "nice" for his mother! Quite wisely his mother gave him a blank sheet of paper and told him to draw whatever kind of rabbit he wanted. He drew a delightfully different rabbit which his mother loved.

8. BE CAUTIOUS ABOUT
EDITING CHILDREN'S WRITINGS

Adults sometimes think they can improve the writings of children by editing them—"correcting them," they say. Sometimes we think we are improving them when we really do not. In fact, we may spoil some of their beauty and honesty and this disillusions children. We learned a very painful lesson on this score in one of our studies which involved the production of a weekly magazine of children's writings.

I had instructed the editor to be careful to maintain the integrity of the children's ideas but to correct spelling, punctuation, grammar, and the like—errors which might prove embarrassing to the children when it appeared in the magazine. This was not enough caution, however, and the fifth graders let us know about it in no uncertain terms. One of them wrote as follows:

Dear Editors:
"I don't think that you should change our poems, stories, etc. I know you are trying to make them better, but sometimes the way people write things—no matter whether it makes sense or not—is the way people want them.
"In poems this is especially true. Sometimes certain punctuation marks express an awful lot.
"Please try and understand the way we feel about it."

It was the following paragraph in another letter which really sobered me:

"Dr. Torrance, you told us that our ideas are important. The way our stories and poems have been changed around makes us wonder."

This doesn't mean that children aren't willing to proofread and polish their creative productions for publication. They are. Nevertheless, the experience has taught me how easy it is for adults unknowingly to communicate to children that their ideas are *not* really important.

9. ENCOURAGE CHILDREN TO PLAY WITH WORDS

Children and adults enjoy word games and there are a number of good ones on the market in a number of forms. Almost all of them involve the creation of new relationships. Since the ability to see or to create new relationships is at the very core of every creative act, this can be an important skill to develop in children. These make interesting family entertainment and provide one way in which parents can help. One delightful book about word play is Alastair Reid's *Ounce Dice Trice* (1958).

10. LOVE THEM AND LET THEM KNOW IT

Children will never reveal their intimate imaginings unless they feel that they are loved and respected. As I observed teachers and pupils during my first year of study, I was almost immediately impressed by the obvious importance of the feeling of affection between teacher and pupils and the development of what I have chosen to call the creative relationship. I like to call it the creative relationship because it operates so much like the creative thinking process. I think it works the same way with parents and children. The adult has to be willing to let one thing lead to another in this relationship, to embark with the child on an untraveled pathway, not knowing where the relationship will lead. It is something that a parent or a teacher can desire fervently and for which they can work hard. Then suddenly, it seems to "just happen," but the teacher or parent has to be willing to let it happen, just as the inventor or scientific discoverer does when the solution to his problem "just happens."

For some time I had observed that a certain teacher seemed to have such a relationship with almost all of her pupils, especially Brian. One day she showed me this picture that Brian had drawn of her one day when he became angry with her. He did not show the picture to her until several days later. When she asked him what were all of the scattered lines in the background, Brian explained, "That's your brains. I was so mad with you that day I thought your brains had fallen out." I felt that this was a good test of relationship. The teacher was not threatened by it. She knows that Brian loves her and Brian knows that she loves him.

References

Babcock, Catherine Marly. *Did You Ever Read a Clock Upside Down?* Danbury, Conn.: Reeves Soundcraft Corp., 1962.

Cole, W. and Julia Colmore (Ed.) *The Poetry-Drawing Book.* New York: Simon & Schuster, 1960.

Gordon, W. J. J. *Synectics.* New York: Harper and Row, 1961.

Klein, Leonore. *What Would You Do If. . .* New York: William R. Scott, 1961.

Miller, Joyce. How to Talk to Children. *Home Life,* November 1961, *15(11),* 13.

Munari, B. *Who's There? Open the Door!* Cleveland: World Publishing Company, 1957.

Pulsifer, Susan Nichols. *Minute Magic.* Boston: Chapman and Grimes, 1960.

Reid, A. *Ounce, Dice, Trice.* Boston: Little, Brown, 1958.

Reid, A. *Supposing.* Boston: Little, Brown, 1960.

Wolf, Janet and B. Owett: *Let's Imagine Thinking Up Things.* New York: E. P. Dutton, 1961.

Wrenn, B. and Kathleen Wren. *Fun For Everybody: Songs for Children.* Cincinnati, Ohio: Willis Music Company, 1949.

17. ART AND MUSIC AS STIMULANTS TO RIGHT HEMISPHERE IMAGERY AND CREATIVITY

J. C. Gowan

Progressively in the last several decades, art and music have tended to drop out of the curriculum on the grounds that they were "frills". Recently, some very powerful new research and theory has surfaced which appears to indicate that art and music may be far more important than had previously been realized, since they may contribute to the development of right hemisphere imagery, and hence to creativity. This paper will try to describe the research and connect it to classroom implications.

First, we need to review a bit of physiology. The quotation is from Gowan 1975:261:

> The brain is composed of two cerebral hemispheres, each of which governs the motor activities of the other side of the body. The two hemispheres appear to work as dual controls, being joined by a massive conduit of nerves known as the *corpus callosum*. About 1950 Myers and Sperry discovered that if the *corpus callosum* were cut, each hemisphere could function independently as if it were a complete brain. This discovery led to a number of intriguing questions such as what are patients like who have had this operation? and are there differential hemisphere functions?
>
> Sperry and Gazzaniga (Gazzaniga, 1957) conducted tests to show the differential function in split brain patients. These showed that for some reason, the left side of the brain quickly assumed the normal functions of speech and writing, and that the right side was unable to speak and write. The right side, however, is not without intelligence. When a patient feels fruit with his left hand in a photographer's change muff in which there are (for example) two apples and an orange, he cannot say what the fruit is, but he can signal that the two apples are alike and the orange is different. The right hemisphere of such patients also handled spatial relations better than the left. It also appears from other research to handle holistic concepts and creative imagination better.

Whereas left hemisphere function is primarily Guilfordian convergent production, right hemisphere function is primarily Guilfordian divergent production. Thus right hemisphere imagery is the vehicle through which incubation produces creativity. The implications of this simple statement for educational change are enormous.

The seat of this imagery appears to be in the Wernicke area of the right cerebral hemisphere, (Jaynes 1976:109). While it was once thought that special means were necessary to elicit it, it has lately appeared that the process, (like the shining of the stars) goes on all the time, but, during our waking hours under most circumstances is overlaid by the more cognitive processes of the generally dominant left hemisphere. These involve the handling of incoming perceptual information and its processing into thought and action via language, and the continual stream of internal discourse which accompanies consciousness. Remove both of these activities from left hemisphere function through relaxation, meditation hypnosis, fantasy, day-dreaming, sensory deprivation or some similar state and the imagery of the right hemisphere is brought to focus at once. Since speech and writing are confined to the left hemisphere, most educational processes

---

For further discussion of the relation of right hemisphere imagery to creativity, see Gowan (1978).

educate only this half of the brain. Wallas (1926) in his paradigm for creativity, called this aspect "preparation", and clearly indicates that it is the necessary, but not the sufficient condition for creative illumination. The sufficient condition is, of course, incubation, which was Wallas' term for the relaxation which produced right hemisphere imagery.

We have a good repertoire of educational techniques of preparation (e.g. Williams, 1970; Meeker, 1969) but we lack equally strong techniques for incubation. *Thinking Creatively with Sounds and Words*, (Khatena and Torrance, 1973) is one of the few devices in this area.

It is already obvious that one of the imminent curriculum changes in schools for the gifted will be more attention paid to incubation techniques. These techniques relax the usually dominant left hemisphere function through dreaming, day-dreaming, drugs, fantasy, meditation, hypnosis, diversion, play and sensory deprivation. Left hemisphere cognitive function appears to require two conditions: a) continual sensory input, and b) continual internal discourse. Any of the previous techniques appear to allay left hemisphere function through cutting down one or the other of these dual inputs. While researchers have known about such techniques for a few years, their widespread use in schools had been handicapped because of the religious, moral, legal or social sanctions against some of them.

The previous approach has been mainly a negative one: cut out the activity of the dominant left hemisphere, and imagery will automatically appear in the right hemisphere (since it goes on there all the time, but is ordinarily not paid attention to). But the new approach is more positive: Find positive activities (i.e. art and music) which stimulate the right hemisphere directly, despite activity in the left. Let us follow this approach further.

The use of art and music education, not only for their own sake, but to stimulate right hemisphere activity, and hence improve creative function has been mentioned by a number of writers. Williams (1977) in an article on "Why Children Should Draw" points out that art stimulates a child's curiosity. He quotes Houston: "Verbal-linear-analytical intelligence is a small part of the intelligence spectrum. There is also visual-aesthetic-plastic (working with the hands) intelligence. . . ." This right-hemisphere intelligence is what in an earlier day Lowenfeld called "haptic", and what Prof. Ferguson (1977) calls "thinking with pictures" which he believes is an essential strand in the history of technology development, although presently neglected in scientific education.

Again to quote Williams:

> The differentiation of the brain into left and right hemispheres certainly plays a role in arts-centered learning. . . . A child without access to a stimulating arts program, according to Houston 'is being systematically cut off from most of the ways in which he can perceive the world. His brain is being systematically damaged. In many ways he is being de-educated'.

Williams then cites a number of elementary schools where an enriched arts program has improved general performance.

Jaynes (1976:364–9) devotes several pages to the importance of music, and musical instruction to stimulating the right hemisphere. After citing a number of authorities and facts in support of the special relationship of music to the right hemisphere, and hypothesizing (after experiments on neonates) that "the brain is organized at birth to obey musical stimulation in the right hemisphere", he concludes that the research points "to the great significance of lullabies in development, perhaps influencing the child's later creativity."

But it is in the difference between speech and song where we begin to pick up practical educational hints. Says the author (p 365) "Speech, as has long been known is a function primarily of the left hemisphere. But song . . . is primarily a function of the right." He then gives four illustrations, ending with daring the reader to think of a topic with which he is familiar, and then compose an extemporaneous song about it. The reason why this is next to impossible, he says is that the song is in your right hemisphere and the cognitive topic in your left.

Pointing out that "lateralization of music can be seen in the very young" (p 367), he describes an experiment with an infant showing that the right hemisphere area is activated upon hearing music. He continues (p 368):

> In the experiment I am describing, not only did the children who were . . . crying stop doing so at the sound of music, but they smiled and looked straight ahead, turning away from the mother's gaze. . . . This finding has immense significance for the possibility that the brain is organized at birth to obey stimulation in what corresponds to Wernicke's area on the right hemisphere. . . . It also points to the great significance of lullabies in development, perhaps influencing the child's later creativity.

One is certainly justified in extrapolating that perhaps the continuance of music educationand singing is of considerable importance in pre-school and elementary school in its effect in stimulating the use of right hemisphere function. The Greeks, as usual, were on good ground in stressing the importance of music, and in connecting it with the Muses.

The casual reader might allow that such things go on in music and the arts, but hardly in the world of science, where the logic of the left hemisphere should reign supreme. But curiously, it is here in the area of scientific invention that we find the strongest case for right hemisphere imagery. Indeed, we may go further and assert that in the case of every historic scientific discovery and invention which is researched carefully enough, we find that it was imagery, either in dreams or in a waking state which produced the breakthrough. We have the testimony of men such as Archimedes, Newton, Faraday, Agassiz, Hilprecht, Poincare, Mendeleev, Kekule, Loewi and others (Ghiselin, 1952; Gowan 1974) that this is so. Perhaps the most authoritative recent statement on the subject is that of Prof. E. S. Ferguson in *Science* (1977), who says in part:

> Many features and qualities of the objects that a technologist thinks about cannot be reduced to unambiguous verbal descriptions; they are dealt with in his mind by a visual, nonverbal process. His mind's eye is a well developed organ that not only reviews the contents of his visual memory, but also forms such new or modified images as his thoughts require.
>
> It is non-verbal thinking, by and large, that has fixed the outlines and filled in the details of our material surroundings. . . . Pyramids, cathedrals and rockets exist not because of geometry, theory of structures or thermodynamics, but because they were first a picture—literally a vision—in the minds of those who built them.
>
> Galton, speaking of "inventive mechanicians" observed that "they invent their machines as they walk" and see them in height, breadth and depth as real objects, and they can also see them in action." How to cultivate this "visualizing faculty" without prejudice to the practice of abstract thought in words or symbols was, to Galton, one of the "many desiderata in the yet unformed science of education".
>
> Much of the creative thought of the designers of our technological world is non-verbal, not easily reducible to words. Its language is an object or a picture or a visual image in the mind.

What research has now discovered is that imagery is the precursor of creativity in both the arts and sciences, that right hemisphere activity is the precursor of imagery, and that positive means of right hemisphere stimulation through art and music is equally as effective as other incubatory techniques for allaying left hemisphere function. Education is thus presented with a new and powerful tool in its efforts to make gifted children creative, and art and music education has received a research rationale of immense importance.

References

Ferguson, E. S. "The Mind's Eye: Non-Verbal Thought in Technology" *Science* 197:827–36, Aug 26, 1977.

Galton, F. *Inquiries into the Human Faculty and its Development*. London: Dent & Co., 1870, (reprint, N.Y.: Dutton, 1927).

Ghiselin, B. (Ed.) *The Creative Process*. Berkeley: Univ. of Calif. Press, 1952.

Gowan, J. C. *The Development of the Psychedelic Individual*. Buffalo: The Creative Education Foundation, 1974

Gowan, J. C. *Trance, Art & Creativity*. Buffalo: Creative Education Foundation, 1975.

Gowan, J. C. "Incubation, Imagery Creativity" *Journal of Altered States of Consciousness,* (in press), 1978.

Jaynes, J. *The Origin of Consciousness in the Breakdown of the Bicameral Mind*. Boston: Houghton-Mifflin Press, 1976.

Khatena, J. and Torrance, E. P. *Thinking Creatively with Sounds and Images*. Lexington, Mass.: Personnel Press, 1973.

Meeker, M. *The Structure of Intellect: Its Interpretation and Uses*. Columbus, OH: Merrill, 1969.

Wallas, G. *The Art of Thought*. London, C. A. Watts, 1926.

Williams, F. *Classroom Ideas for Encouraging Thinking and Feeling*. Buffalo: Dissemination of Knowledge Pub. 1970.

Williams, R. "Why Children Should Draw" *Saturday Review,* (9/3/77):11–16.

18. UTILIZING THE DIVERGENT PRODUCTION MATRIX OF THE STRUCTURE-OF-INTELLECT MODEL IN THE DEVELOPMENT OF TEACHING STRATEGIES

Charles E. Gray
Richard C. Youngs

RATIONALE AND OBJECTIVES

The investigation was initiated as a two-year developmental research project funded jointly by Illinois State University and the Office of the Superintendent of Public Instruction, Gifted Program Development Section. The project was conceived as a cooperative venture designed to narrow the gap between theory and application in an important area of education. Hence, one of the primary objectives of the project was to demonstrate the efficacy of cooperative undertakings between state agencies interested in stimulating and applying educational research.

The research project was based upon four important assumptions about creative problem solving and the creative learning process. The first assumption was that creative problem-solving is essential in dealing with the problems confronting individuals and groups in our pluralistic, dynamic, industrial society. Second, that creative problem-solving can be viewed as a logical process involving specific thinking operations. Third, that creative problem-solving can be learned and used by pupils as a heuristic method of thinking and dealing with problems. Fourth, that teachers can be trained to facilitate creative problem-solving on the part of their pupils.

There is little doubt that new and fresh ideas and approaches are needed in dealing with the multitude of problems confronting contemporary society. Unfortunately, the schools have been only minimally helpful in identifying creative talent or encouraging creative problem solving; in fact one noted scholar maintains that curiosity and free inquiry "are often brutally squelched" in the schools. (Torrance, 1964). If creativity is to be cultivated, the school is certainly a place where it could be done early in the child's life, continuously, and systematically. Also, in order to insure maximum transfer of learning, creativity should be facilitated in a variety of contexts which have personal meaning and relevance for pupils.

In a pedagogical context creative problem-solving can be viewed as the "creative learning process." Torrance defines this process in terms of the following operations and behaviors:

Involvement in something meaningful.

Curiosity and wanting to know in the face of wonder, incompleteness, confusion, complexity, disharmony, disorganization, or the like.

Simplification of structure or diagnosing a difficulty by synthesizing known information, forming new combinations, or identifying gaps.

Elaborating and diverging by producing new alternatives, new possibilities, etc.

Judging, evaluating, checking, and testing possibilities.

Reprinted by permission from *Gifted Child Quarterly,* Vol. 19, No. 4, 1975.

Discarding unsuccessful, erroneous, and unpromising solutions.

Choosing the most promising solution and making it attractive or aesthetically pleasing.

Communicating the results to others. (Torrance, 1970).

A key element in the creative problem-solving process is that of generating ideas—or hypotheses related to the solution of a given problem. In fact, ideation of this kind is more uniquely creative than any other type of behavior involved in the process. If teachers can learn how to facilitate the generation of multiple hypothesized unique solutions on the part of their pupils, they will have overcome one of the most frustrating obstacles to creative learning. Of course, ability to facilitate hypothesizing is not an end in itself—and must be learned in a context which clearly reveals its relationship to the total problem-solving process. However, if in learning how to facilitate hypothesizing the teacher has acquired a rationale and a repertoire of appropriate teaching strategies and skills, he is likely to have a degree of confidence in himself and to be reasonably well prepared to engage in the other phases of the creative problem-solving process. In addition, successful experiences with this newly acquired facilitating ability might very well affect in him a positive attitude toward the importance of instruction for creative problem-solving.

In summary, it is herein maintained that hypothesizing is both a central element of and crucial to the success of the creative problem-solving process; it is also the most uniquely creative type of behavior involved in the total process. When teachers have learned how to facilitate hypothesizing they will in effect have learned how to overcome pupil resistance and inhibition with respect to an important aspect of creative behavior; overcoming such barriers is also important to success with other aspects of the process.

The basic concern of the investigation was to determine the parameters of a training program which would efficiently train teachers to stimulate the generation of hypotheses on the part of elementary and secondary school pupils; and further, to develop a concise training program consistent with such findings.

DEVELOPMENTAL DESIGN

The training program was developed by means of a sequential training-instruction-feedback-revision cycle (see figure 1)*. The procedure involved first the training of a group of teacher education students, followed by an opportunity for them to apply their training in an instructional setting; subsequently their performance was carefully analyzed and appropriate revisions made in the training program. Thereupon, the cycle was repeated by training a new group of teacher education students using the revised program.

More specifically, the developmental cycle proceeded in the following manner: Selected university teacher education students in the junior participation program at University High and Metcalf laboratory schools were given either minimal instructions (*i.e.,* no training) or the initial phase of a trial training program (*i.e.,* consisting mainly of exposition, exercises, readings, and modeling). Consequently, they applied what they learned by actually engaging in instruction— they were given the opportunity to facilitate creative hypothesizing with micro-type groups of laboratory school pupils at given grade levels (*i.e.,* grades K, 3, 7, 10, or 12). The micro-teaching sessions were video-taped and systematically analyzed by means of the Expanded Interaction

*All figures except figure 5 have been suppressed. Available from author.

Analysis Category System (Amidon, 1969); hypotheses were quantified; laboratory school pupils were controlled with reference to creative ability (Torrance tests); and trainee attitudes toward creative behavior were measured on a pre-post treatment design. The collected data were subjected to a series of analyses and statistical tests for the purpose of identifying possible relationships between variables and determining possible effects of the training program.

Inferences derived from the analyses and procedures were incorporated into subsequent training programs. The cycle was repeated until a training program was developed which was concise, internally consistent, and enabled trainees to facilitate creative hypothesizing on the part of pupils at a level consistently and significantly better than the performance of non-trained subjects. (Gray and Youngs, 1971)

University teacher education students in the junior participation program in the University High and Metcalf laboratory schools were selected to participate in the research project in lieu of their "regular" participation program. Three criteria for selection of trainees were used:

1. Is their participation assignment at the appropriate grade level (*i.e.,* grade K, 3, 7, 10, or 12)?
2. Are they available at the appropriate times?
3. Are they willing to volunteer for a junior participation experience that will be somewhat different from that of their peers?

The target populations utilized for the trial instructional attempts of trainee subjects were University High and Metcalf laboratory school pupils at grades K, 3, 7, 10, and 12. Pupil subjects were organized into small micro-type groups for the trial instructional sessions. The criteria for selection in formulating the groups were availability, convenience, grade level, group size, creative ability, sex, and non-repetition.

DEVELOPMENTAL PROCESS: THREE PHASES

A. Phase I: First Training Program

The first training program was developed on the basis of (a) an analysis of the data collected from the no-training group, (b) findings and recommendations in contemporary literature on creative problem-solving, and (c) the advice of project consultants. (Gray and Youngs, 1971)

The dominant theme of the first training program was classroom climate, namely, ways and means of establishing the type of classroom atmosphere (or environment) which would be most likely to stimulate divergent thinking on the part of the pupils. In order to accomplish this objective the program included components designed to alleviate trainee apprehensions and uncertainties regarding the idea of divergent thinking as an ingredient of the problem-solving process in a classroom setting; and to equip the trainee with a repertoire of techniques which he could utilize in encouraging pupils to view learning tasks in imaginative and unusual ways. The program emphasized such climate-related topics as the following: (1) Avoidance of excessive evaluation, (2) Judicious use of silence, (3) Student-initiated talk and interaction, (4) Clarity and explicitness of communication, (5) Divergent questioning procedures, and (6) Probing questions. For each topic, instruction included a study of definitions and appropriate examples; this was followed by a sensitizing session (with trainees as pupils) wherein the investigator modeled the previously discussed types of teacher behavior in an effort to stimulate divergent thinking and elicit multiple hypotheses on the part of the trainees. Consequently, each trainee demonstrated his application of the teaching behaviors with a micro-group of pupils and viewed the video-tape of his performance. A schematic representation of the mode of instruction would be as follows:

| Definitions Descriptions | Examples Illustrations | Modeling (Sensitization) | Application (Instruction of Pupils) | Feedback (Video-tape) |

B. Phase II: Second Training Program

The second training program was developed on the basis of (a) an analysis of the data collected from the first training group (*i.e.,* trained using the first training program), (b) findings previously mentioned relative to the no-training group, and (c) the advice of project consultants. (Gray and Youngs, 1971)

The second training program retained the classroom climate theme of the first program with the addition of a set of instructional strategies designed to more efficiently stimulate hypothesizing on the part of pupils. Both the classroom climate and the instructional strategies components were integrated into a basic procedure for brainstorming hypotheses. The classroom climate component included such elements as: (a) Student talk—Quantity, (b) Teacher Talk—Phrasing, (c) Silence, (d) Student Talk—Dispersion, (e) Evaluation, (f) Respect, (g) Feedback Sensitivity, and (h) Student Talk—Ideas. The instructional strategies component included such elements as (a) Thinking Activities based on the Structure-of-Intellect model (Guilford, 1959, 1967, 1968), (b) Stating the Problem, (c) Brainstorming, and (d) Divergent Excursions (a type of questioning strategy designed to maintain focus on various aspects of the problem, stimulate divergent-type thought related to the problem, and kindle the generation of additional hypotheses). Instruction included direct presentation of content, demonstration of process, analysis of process, modeling, micro-teaching, evaluation of performance, recycling (if needed), and summation. In general, the mode of instruction was similar to that of the first training program.

C. Phase III: Third Training Program

The third training program was developed on the basis of (a) an analysis of the data collected from the second training group (*i.e.,* trained using the second training group), and a summer workshop group, (b) findings previously mentioned relative to the no-training and first training groups, (c) findings and recommendations in contemporary literature on creative problem-solving, and (d) advice of project consultants. (Gray and Youngs, 1971)

The third training program retained the major elements of the integrated brainstorming hypotheses procedures and the mode of instruction of the second program. The brainstorming hypotheses procedures included classroom climate and instructional strategy components and utilized the Structure-of-Intellect model as a theoretical base. The mode of instruction included direct presentation of content, demonstration of process, analysis of process, modeling, micro-teaching, evaluation of performance, recycling (if needed), and summation. Minor changes between the two programs consisted of a number of content adjustments, clarifications, and editorial refinements. Major changes included the following: (1) More thorough evaluation procedure for trainees (including minimum performance standard) (2) More complete recycling procedure for trainees (including diagnostic graphs), (3) Substantially revised presentation of the Structure-of-

Intellect model (Guilford, 1969, 1971). (4) Presentation of two complete creative problem-solving models (Gordon, 1961, 1969; Parnes, 1967, and Osborn, 1963). (5) More intensive use of video-tapes for analysis and evaluation. (6) Greater attention to the nature of hypotheses and hypothesizing. (7) Additional group work and participation of trainees in training sessions. The complete program is entitled, *Instructional Strategies for Creative Hypothesizing: A Training Program*. The following materials have been produced for use in the training of teachers: (1) Leader's Syllabus (Youngs and Gray, 1971), (2) Training Materials (loose-leaf notebook), and (3) a set of Divergent Transformation Activities (boxed).

DESCRIPTION OF FINAL TRAINING PROGRAM

A. Program Elements

The training program consists of the following four major elements: Classroom Climate, Divergent Transformation Activities, Brainstorming Hypotheses, and Divergent Operations Matrix (and Divergent Excursions). Each element will be briefly described below and in the following section they will be described more fully and related to one-another in terms of the total training program.

Classroom Climate. A set of classroom climate guidelines designed to facilitate and elicit divergent-type thinking and responses on the part of pupils (see figure 2).

Divergent Transformation Activities. Activities designed to provide students with practice in divergent transformation and to help create the type of classroom climate necessary for creative problem-solving (see figure 3).

Brainstorming Hypotheses. General divergent brainstorming procedures for eliciting a variety of unique possible solutions to problems.

Divergent Operations Matrix (and **Divergent Excursions**). Use of the Divergent Production section of the Structure-of-Intellect model as a means of developing a questioning strategy designed to stimulate divergent thinking and elicit hypotheses on the part of pupils. The questioning strategy is termed a *divergent excursion* and is employed at the point when hypotheses are no longer forthcoming in a regular brainstorming session (see figure 4).

B. Sequential Summary of Training Program

Training begins with a brief overview of the complete program. The trainees are then introduced to a set of guidelines for classroom climate in an expository-discussion session. This is followed immediately by a modeling session in which the instructor exemplifies classroom climate as he introduces the trainees to the Divergent Transformation Activities and encourages the production of divergent transformations. After the modeling session the trainees are asked to analyze both their experience with the activities and the instructor's application of the classroom climate guidelines.

The next portion of the training program is a video-taped session in which the instructor exemplifies classroom climate as he introduces a problem and engages in brainstorming hypotheses with the trainees (employing the Divergent Operations Matrix for Divergent Excursions when hypotheses are no longer forthcoming). In this session the instructor is actually modeling the basic creative hypothesizing teaching strategy, with the trainees in the role of pupils (see figure 5).

160

The Climate

Teacher—DIVERGENT QUESTION
Teacher—PROBE FOR DIVERGENCIES
Teacher—ACCEPTANCE/RESPECT
Teacher—SILENCE
Teacher—FEEDBACK SENSITIVITY
Pupil Talk—QUANTITY
Pupil Talk—DISPERSION
Pupil Talk—DIVERGENT

The Problem

How would you change your school or classroom to make learning more interesting?

The Brainstorming Procedure*

SEEK HYPOTHESES
EXTEND HYPOTHESES
LIST HYPOTHESES
USE *DOM* FOR DIVERGENT EXCURSIONS

Divergent Operations Matrix (DOM)*—For Divergent Excursions

	Units	Classes	Relations	Systems	Transformations	Implications*
Fig	Invent a classroom study space (i.e., desk, corral, etc.)	List different kinds of things to sit on.	List ways in which classroom furniture can be arranged.	How might the phys. facil. of schools be arr. for different types of learn.?	What other institutions have objects or facilities which are similar to those found in schools?	What if schools had no teachers, desks, book, etc.?
Sya	List symbols that characterize your school.	List symbols for types of schools.	Suggest relationships between two symbols common to education.	Suggest a simplified numbering, alphabet, or spelling system.	What else might a given educational symbol represent?	What if the symbol-X were eliminated?
Sen	List your educational needs.	List the educational needs for types of students.	List ways in which schools meet educ. needs of specific stu.	Outline a new system of education.	What other process is similar to the educational process?	What if classrooms were run like a family?
Beh	List ways you could gain recognition in school.	List types of behavior that would make school more pleasant.	List ways to establish rapport with teachers.	Outline kinds of classroom atmos. (or climate) which facilitate learning.	What other relationships are analogous to the teacher-pupil relationship?	What if all teachers were understanding?

(Return to Brainstorming as Soon as Practical)

Figure 5. Summary of brainstorming hypotheses procedure.

*J. P. Guilford, "Three Faces of Intellect," *American Psychologist*, vol. 14, no. 8 (August, 1959), pp. 469–479.

The video-tape is henceforth employed as a tool of instruction. It is subsequently viewed in its entirety twice as the trainees review, analyze, and summarize the essential elements of the creative hypothesizing teaching strategy.

During a playback of the first half of the video-tape the trainees are asked to analyze the instructor's application of the classroom climate guidelines. This is followed by a brief description of the Structure-of-Intellect model with particular emphasis on the Divergent Operations Matrix and the way in which it is related to the Divergent Transformation Activities, and the Divergent Excursion strategy employed in the video-taped session.

During a playback of the second half of the video-tape the instructor draws attention to how hypotheses were solicited; and, by means of an overlay of the Divergent Operations Matrix, points out specific instances where it was utilized for Divergent Excursions (*i.e.,* when hypotheses were no longer forthcoming).

At this point trainees are asked to review certain components of the training program—the general brainstorming procedures, the classroom climate guidelines, the Divergent Operations Matrix—and to note the inter-relatedness among the components. As a means of summarizing the complete process the video-tape is shown again in its entirety. At various points in the tape the instructor makes brief comments about: (a) the application of general brainstorming procedures, (b) the application of the classroom climate guidelines, and (c) the utilization of the Divergent Operations Matrix for Divergent Excursions. Also, trainees are provided with opportunities to identify video-tape sequences that exemplify the elements and/or strategies they have been learning, and to practice identifying and counting specific pupil hypotheses.

The trainees are now ready for the classroom application portion of the training program wherein they will be asked to change roles and apply, with small micro-groups of pupils, that which has been modeled for them by the training program instructor. Each trainee will be involved in two micro-sessions with a given group of pupils—one session using the Divergent Transformation Activities (for climate building and practice in divergent production), and a second session of brainstorming hypotheses (for applying brainstorming procedures and utilizing the Divergent Operations Matrix for Divergent Excursions). They are informed that the sessions will proceed in the same way as in the modeling sessions, with the second session video-taped. Prior to the application sessions the trainees are given an opportunity to examine the Divergent Transformation Activities, provided with a specific problem to pose in their brainstorming sessions, and given directions about analyzing and evaluating their sessions (including the counting of hypotheses and comparison with a minimum performance standard).

The trainees proceed to work with their micro-groups. In the first session they demonstrate the application of the classroom climate guidelines and the use of the Divergent Transformation Activities. Subsequently they evaluate their performance. In the second session (video-taped) they demonstrate the application of the classroom climate guidelines, the use of the brainstorming procedures, and the use of the Divergent Operations Matrix for Divergent Excursions (when hypotheses are no longer forthcoming). Subsequently they view the tape and evaluate their performance, tabulate the hypotheses elicited, and plot the hypotheses on a graph which indicates the minimum performance standard. If they meet the minimum standard they are asked to study the summary material on the complete creative problem-solving process (entitled, Hypothesizing in Perspective) and at this point their training is complete. If they fail to meet the minimum standard recycling is indicated; special recycling procedures are specified in the training program syllabus.

In addition to producing a useful product in the area of creative problem-solving, the project has stimulated thought and served as a catalyst for a number of potentially significant undertakings at Illinois State University and elsewhere.

B. Recommendations for Further Research

As indicated above, both the educational applications of the Structure-of-Intellect model and the teacher training techniques developed by the project are being considered (or utilized) for other or related investigations. With respect to the final training program the investigators are interested in applying it on a large scale in the training of teachers; experience in its use will no doubt suggest further refinements and applications. Three lines of research might be worthwhile in the future. One would be to combine the training program with one of the complete creative problem-solving models and assess the effects on teachers and/or pupils. The second would be to develop an instrument or technique for measuring the effects of the training program on either preservice or inservice teachers in the classroom. Finally, the program should be tested in a rigorous fashion using a larger and more varied sample of pupils and trainees. Follow-up studies of this type however, are all too rare in the realm of educational research.

References

Amidon, Edmund, Peggy Amidon, and Barak Rosenshine, *SKIT, Work Manual*. Minneapolis: Assn. for Productive Teaching, 1969.

Borg, W. R., M. L. Kelly, P. Langer, and M. Gall. *The Minicourse: A Micro-teaching Approach to Teacher Education*. Beverly Hills, California: Macmillan Educational Services, 1970.

Bottenberg, Robert A. and Joe H. Ward, Jr. *Applied Multiple Linear Regression*. U.S. Department of Commerce/National Bureau of Standards (Distributed by Clearinghouse for Federal Scientific and Technical Information. No. AD 413 128, Springfield, Virginia).

Flanders, N. A. *Analyzing Teacher Behavior*. Reading, Massachusetts: Addison-Wesley 1970.

Gordon, W. J. J. *The Metaphorical Way of Learning and Knowing* (rev. ed. by Tony Poze). Cambridge, Massachusetts: Synectics Education Systems, 1969.

Gordon, W. J. J. Synectics: *The Development of Creative Capacity*. New York: Harper and Row, 1961.

Gray, Charles E. and Richard C. Youngs. *Instructional Strategies for Creative Hypothesizing: A Training Program. Final Report*. Normal: Teacher Education Project 1971 (ERIC ED 054 040).

Guilford, J. P. *The Analysis of Intelligence*. New York: McGraw-Hill, 1971.

Guilford, J. P. *A General Summary of Twenty Years of Research on Aptitudes of High-Level Personnel*. Final Report of Project NR-150-044, Personnel and Training Branch, Psychological Sciences Division, Office of Naval Research. Washington, D.C., Office of Naval Research, 1969.

VI

IDENTIFICATION AND MEASUREMENT

19. NON-TEST WAYS OF IDENTIFYING THE CREATIVELY GIFTED

E. Paul Torrance

"How can I tell, if Mercedes or Samuel is creatively gifted?" parents and teachers frequently ask. Is he a creative genius or is he out of his mind? Is he independent and creative or is he just unruly? Is his thinking creative or is it morbid and unhealthy? Although much progress (Getzels and Jackson, 1962; Torrance, 1962) has been made in the development of testing methods to identify the creatively gifted and to help answer questions like these, there is still much need for non-test ways of assessment.

In the first place, it will be some time before existing tests of creative thinking will be in common use in school systems and psychological clinics. Furthermore, Mercedes or Samuel might live in some remote area where there are no school psychologists or other persons qualified to use tests of creative thinking. Or, they might not be motivated to perform creatively on a test. There are also a number of inherent limitations of tests of eliciting creative behavior. Tests almost always have time limits, and creativity cannot always be hurried or forced. Some highly creative children, we find, have difficulty in writing down their ideas. Others are far more successful in writing down their ideas than they are in communicating them orally. The immediate testing conditions, personality disturbances, unfavorable reactions to time pressures, and the like may prevent some highly creative individuals from revealing their creative potential through tests.

NECESSITY FOR REDEFINING
MEANING OF BEHAVIOR

Before parents or teachers can successfully identify, understand, and guide the creatively gifted individual, it may be necessary for them to redefine many kinds of behavior. Recently I asked two teachers of high achieving sixth graders to give me the names of five of the most and five of the least creative children in their classrooms. To help them in this redefinition process, we used Wallace and Ethel Maw's (1961) criteria of curiosity which are as follows:

1. Reacts positively to new, strange, incongruous, or mysterious elements in his environment by moving toward them, by exploring them, or manipulating them.
2. Exhibits a need or desire to know about himself and/or his environment.
3. Scans his surroundings, seeking new experiences, and
4. Persists in examining and exploring stimuli in order to know more about them.

Reprinted by permission from *Gifted Child Quarterly*, Vol. 6, No. 3, 1962.

After trying to apply these criteria, both of these teachers commented that they had never before thought of their pupils in this way and admitted with some discomfort that they were forced to place in the low group some of the children whom they valued most as pupils because they were so good in arithmetic computation, spelling, and the like. Incidentally, we obtained excellent differentiations on all of our measures of creativity between the two groups of children nominated as most and least curious. Almost all of those nominated among the more curious made higher scores on each of several tests of creative thinking than their equally intelligent but less curious classmates.

We first began examining the need for redefining many kinds of behavior soon after we had administered our first battery of creative thinking tests in our first school. A third grade teacher commented that the study had already helped the whole school, whether our research revealed anything or not. She said, "You have changed the entire way we look at children's behavior. For example, we no longer think of children as *being naughty* but as *creating ideas for being naughty."* As I began to think about the matter, I began to see what a difference it makes in the way teachers treat children, whether they see them as *being* naughty or as *creating ideas* for being naughty. Seeing children as *being* naughty is associated with a punitive approach to education; seeing children as *creating ideas for being naughty* is associated with a constructive, challenging approach.

What I mean by this is illustrated dramatically through the experience of one of my friends who teaches in the industrial arts field in college. He caught one of his students cheating on an examination near the middle of the course. The methods this student used in cheating were so clever and ingenious that this instructor recognized that he was dealing with an exceptionally talented individual. Suddenly the instructor realized that his assignments had called only for reproductive thinking and that he had nothing to challenge this unusual talent. Instead of giving this cheater an automatic failing grade or expelling him from the class, he began thinking of more and more difficult problems calling for creative problem-solving and imagination. At the end of the course, this student's achievement was so far ahead of everyone else's that the instructor felt compelled in all fairness to award him a grade of "A." Many parents and teachers condemn this behavior of the teacher and call it immoral. I wonder which is more immoral: the failure to punish a student or failure to develop outstanding creative talent and to correct the deficiencies of one's teaching procedures?

Lying behavior in young children may need to be redefined in much the same way, as the industrial arts teacher redefined cheating behavior and transformed the abilities involved into productive creative responses. Leuba (1958), for example, contends that lying is frequently the first clear indicator of intellectual creativity. Lying may be a child's first creativity in the manipulation of symbols. "We may have failed to realize how commonplace creativity is," Leuba suggests, "because we have given that label only to socially desirable forms and they are rare." This does not mean that we should reward lying; it simply means that there are times when we need to recognize lying as an indication of creative talent which *can* be guided in positive, constructive directions.

SOME CREATIVE CHILDREN LEAD A DOUBLE LIFE

It may be difficult for parents or teachers to identify creatively gifted children because, some of the most creative ones live double lives. They behave quite creatively at home and quite non-creatively in school. Or, they may behave quite creatively at school and non-creatively at home. The first type is illustrated in the following excerpts from the letter of a mother whose son is apparently creatively gifted:

"He is now 13 years old and has had a steadily declining academic record that ended in his being retained in the seventh grade this year. . . . He has a burning main interest in electronics and rocks and believe me, his knowledge and interest in these two subjects is great.

"His teachers, principals, and counselors . . . all agree that he is very bright, very bored (day dreams in class constantly), and very withdrawn, though not rebellious. Two teachers have told me the school has destroyed his desire to learn. One teacher told me the school cannot help him because the only 'special cases' they are informed enough to help are the 'slow' children. Another teacher said to me, 'I'll make him work if I have to break his spirit to do it—and ridiculing and shaming him is the only way with children like him. . . .' Last spring the school counselor and principal decided that flunking him was the only way to make him 'buckle down or else.' He can't join the different types of science clubs because he doesn't have a B average—to which the principal urged that he take up football.

"Now, I will tell you of the boy *I* know, my son. . . . He is an irresponsible scatterbrain—he just can't harness his brain to such unimportant things as taking out the trash when he's hot on the trail of discovering perpetual motion. He *never* daydreams, *loves* to learn, and is *always* getting books from the library. He is a hard worker; many times he almost collapses trying to work and experiment late in the night. He has enough energy for ten people. He has an outgoing, bubbling personality and a terrific sense of humor. All this he is at home and in the rest of his world *until* he gets to school. . . ."

A youngster such as this thirteen-year-old may or may not arise to the occasion when a test of creative thinking is administered. Much would depend upon the quality of the relationship established by the examiner, the adequacy of the warm-up process, and the challenge of the tasks presented.

SOME SUGGESTED REDEFINITIONS

What specific kinds of behaviors then can be used to identify the creatively gifted? I shall now present two tentative tests, one derived from descriptions by parents of children whom they have identified as creative and the other derived from the experiences of participants in a creative thinking seminar I conducted recently.

Parents' Descriptions of Creative Children. I analyzed letters from 150 parents describing the behavior of their children whom they had identified as "creative." Most of the children described were having difficulty in adjusting to school. Thus, the list derived from this source is likely to include many of the kinds of behavior which might possibly call for redefinition, not that the particular behavior is socially desirable, but that it indicates special abilities which might be

167

applied to achieve socially desirable goals. The following is a list of behaviours most frequently described in these 150 letters:

Overactive physically and/or mentally
Annoying curiosity
Forgetful and absentminded
Good sense of humor
Doesn't participate in class
Reads in room while friends (boys) roughhouse with sisters
Enjoys nature and outdoors
Won't join Scouts
Mind wanders too much
Friends think him slightly queer
Likes to work by himself
Imaginative; enjoys pretending
Sensitive
Likes color
Uncommunicative
Is a "what-if?" man
Daydreams; gets lost in thought
Feels left out of things
Spends time watching others
Loves to read
Good only in science; good only in art and music, etc.

Although these characteristics may be displayed by creative youngsters, it does not mean that such characteristics are necessary for creative behavior. Some of these characteristics are rather obviously reactions to the way in which creative children are treated. Nevertheless, a checklist of characteristics might be helpful.

Indicators Listed By Teachers, Counselors, and Administrators. Eighty-seven teachers, counselors and school administrators participating in a Creative Thinking Seminar responded to my request to draw up a set of five behavioral indicators of creative talent. Their responses were analyzed and summarized by Wilbur Kalinke, a Seminar participant. The most frequent categories of behavioral indicators are as follows:

Curiosity, inquisitiveness, investigativeness, penetrating questioning, etc. 66%
Originality in thinking and doing, unusual solutions, unusual answers, unusual approach to problem-
    solving etc. 58%
Independent in thinking and behavior, individualistic, self-sufficient, etc. 38%
Imaginative, fantasy creating, story teller, etc. 35%
Non-Conforming, not bothered by acceptance of others, etc. 28%
Sees relationships, perceptive of relationships, etc. 17%
Full of ideas, verbal or conversational fluency, etc. 14%
Experimenter, tries new ideas, new products, etc. 14%
Flexibility of ideas and thoughts 12%
Persistent, perseverant, unwilling to give up, etc. 12%
Constructs, builds, or rebuilds 12%
Irritated and bored by routine and obvious, *prefers the complex,* copes with several ideas at the
    same time 12%
Daydreamer, preoccupied, etc. 10%

The following are examples of specific kinds of behaviors suggested as indicators of creative talent:

He can occupy his time without being stimulated.
He prefers to dress differently.
He goes beyond assigned tasks.
He is able to amuse himself with simple things in imaginative ways.
He may look like he's loafing or daydreaming when he's actually thinking.
He questions beyond the single "why" or "how."
He experiments with familiar objects to see if they will become something other than what they are intended to be.
He is a window watcher during class but keeps up with what's going on in class too.
He likes to make up games on the school yard.
He enjoys telling about his discoveries and inventions.
He comes up with ways of doing things that are different from the standard directions.
He finds unusual uses of toys other than the intended uses.
He is not afraid to try something new.
He draws designs and pictures on his notebook while the teacher is giving lecture or directions.
He draws elaborate pictures.
He goes further in his play with games than the directions accompanying them.
He doesn't mind consequences if he appears to be different.
He uses all of his senses in observing.

In summary, most of the behaviors listed by Seminar participants could be conceptualized in terms of the six kinds of thinking ability which Guilford and Merrifield (1960) now consider to be involved in creativity:

1. *Sensitivity to problems:* seeing defects, needs, deficiencies; seeing the odd, the unusual; seeing what must be done.
2. *Flexibility:* ability to shift from one approach to another, one line of thinking to another, to free oneself from a previous set.
3. *Fluency:* ability to produce a large number of ideas.
4. *Originality:* ability to produce remote, unusual, or new ideas or solutions.
5. *Elaboration:* ability to work out the details of a plan, idea, or outline; to "embroider" or elaborate.
6. *Redefinition:* ability to define or perceive in a way different from the usual, established, or intended way, use, etc.

Thus, if we are looking for a systematic way of redefining behaviors in such a way as to identify potential creative talent we can examine behavior in terms of these six kinds of thinking.

Procedures and Devices for Obtaining Non-Test Indicators. A variety of procedures have been reported by teachers, counselors, and school administrators in obtaining non-test indicators of creative talent. Several of these have been mentioned in the foregoing discussion: play activities, regular school activities such as examination, the use of a set of indicators such as the Maw and Maw (1961) curiosity criteria, various crisis situations or emergencies, and the like.

A number of more formal procedures might be considered. One of the most obvious of these is the use of school and home assignments which require creative behavior. Another obvious method is through the use of creative achievements in high school, in college, or in a profession. Holland (1961), for example, has reported the use of indicators of creative achievement in high school in the program of the National Merit Scholarship Corporation. Various kinds of checklists, life experience inventories, and reading questionnaires have also been used. I would like to discuss briefly two rarely mentioned but promising techniques: self-identification and descriptions of crisis experiences.

A number of programs for gifted students use some type of self-identification process. Brandwein's (1955) description of an apparently highly successful program for students gifted in the sciences constitutes an effective argument for self-identification. Many Honors programs make use of one kind of self-identification procedure in that students must apply for admission to the program. Recently I have designed a self-identification instrument which includes a 68–item check list composed of characteristics associated with the creative personality, items concerning test and learning preferences, self-ratings on the six kinds of abilities in the Guilford-Merrifield conceptualization of creative thinking, and a checklist of creative achievements. The value of such an instrument is yet to be demonstrated and will perhaps be most useful at the college and graduate school level.

Many teachers and counselors ask students to write descriptions of their most trying, most satisfying, or most embarrassing experience. Seldom do they use these as an aid in identifying the creatively gifted. An example from my wife's use of this technique in a course on interpersonal relations for freshman nursing students will illustrate the potential usefulness of this technique. Vast individual differences in creative thinking are reflected in these materials, ranging from the extremely obvious and commonplace experiences and solutions to highly imaginative, bold, and surprising ones. One which we particularly enjoyed involved a freshman girl who was suddenly confronted with the problem of exhibiting her older brother's prized calf at a cattle show. Her brother had given the calf little training and the calf absolutely refused to respond to all of the usual training procedures. In desperation, this freshman girl hooked the calf onto a tractor and pulled him along until he decided to walk. After this, the calf responded to training and the sister exhibited the calf with the highest of success. On a battery of creative thinking tests, this girl achieved one of the highest scores in a class of 100 students.

As imaginative teachers, counselors, principals, and parents come to understand creative behavior, they will be able to redefine many behaviors which they have usually labeled as socially undesirable and see in them a reflection of abilities which give promise of highly desirable talent. The next step should be an acceptance of the challenge to help individuals who possess such talents to apply these valuable abilities in productive, socially desirable achievements.

References

Brandwein, P. F. *The Gifted Student as Future Scientist*. New York: Harcourt, Brace and World, 1955.

Getzels, J. W. and P. W. Jackson. *Creativity and Intelligence*. New York: John Wiley, 1962.

Guilford, J. P. and P. R. Merrifield. *The Structure of Intellect Model: Its Uses and Implications*. Los Angeles: Psychological Laboratory, University of Southern California, 1960.

Holland, J. L. Creative and Academic Performance among Talented Adolescents. *Journal of Educational Psychology,* 1961, *52*, 136–147.

Leuba, C. A. New Look at Curiosity and Creativity. *Journal of Higher Education,* 1958, *29*, 132–140.

Maw, W., and Ethel W. Maw. Establishing Criterion Groups for Evaluating Measures of Curiosity. *Journal of Experimental Education,* 1961, *29*, 299–305.

Torrance, E. P. *Guiding Creative Talent*. Englewood Cliffs, N.J.: Prentice-Hall, 1962.

20. THE KHATENA-TORRANCE CREATIVE PERCEPTION INVENTORY FOR IDENTIFICATION, DIAGNOSIS, FACILITATION AND RESEARCH

Joe Khatena

Considerable evidence has accumulated to support the use of autobiographical instruments as screening devices for giftedness and creativity. Instruments to measure an individual's perception of himself in the form of checklists, questionnaires, and inventories have been found to be an efficient way of identifying creative talent (e.g. Roe, 1963; Taylor, 1958). More recent studies using the biographical inventory technique to identify creative talent and to predict success in artistic, literary and scientific creativity have confirmed this view (Anastasi and Schaefer, 1969; Ellison, James, Fox and Taylor, 1971; IBRIC, 1974).

Perception can be related to creative components of personality which when operationalized will allow for measurement. An individual who perceives himself as creative, and with accuracy, is a person who can be expected to behave in creative ways. If propensity for creative behavior is to be measurable, creativity needs to be operationalized or broken down into specific behaviors, and presented to an individual who is called upon to perceive himself relative to this model.

KHATENA-TORRANCE CREATIVE PERCEPTION INVENTORY

One such model is the *Khatena-Torrance Creative Perception Inventory* (Khatena and Torrance, 1976). It comprises of two measures of creative perceptions, namely, *What Kind of Person Are You?* and *Something About Myself,* with each taking a different approach to the measurement of creative perceptions. The first measure (Torrance and Khatena, 1970) is based upon the rationale that the individual has a psychological self, whose structures have incorporated creative and non creative ways of behaving. The purpose of this measure is to present verbal stimuli to trigger those subselves that would yield an index of the individual's disposition or motivation to function in creative ways. The second measure (Khatena, 1971) is based upon the rationale that creativity is reflected in the personality characteristics of the individual, in the kind of thinking strategies he employs, and in the products that emerge as a result of his creative strivings.

Both measures present words or statements to which people are required to respond with the expectation that they will reflect the extent to which they tend to function in creative ways. Each measure is made up of 50 items which can be easily administered and interpreted, and yields a creative index obtained by counting the number of correct responses out of 50.

In addition to a creative perception index, *What Kind of Person Are You?* yields 5 factors or orientations (Bledsoe and Khatena, 1974). *Acceptance of Authority* relates to being obedient, courteous and conforming, and to accepting the judgements of authorities. *Self-Confidence* relates to being socially well-adjusted, self-confident, energetic and curious, thorough and remembering well. *Inquisitiveness* relates to always asking questions, being self-assertive, feeling strong emo-

Reprinted by permission from *Gifted Child Quarterly,* Vol. 21, No. 4, 1977.

tions, being talkative and obedient. *Awareness of Others* relates to being courteous, socially well-adjusted, popular or well-liked and considerate of others, and preferring to work in a group. *Disciplined Imagination* relates to being energetic, persistent, thorough, industrious, imaginative, adventurous, and never bored, attempting difficult tasks and preferring complex tasks.

The results of the factor analysis showed Acceptance of Authority to be a non creative orientation and Disciplined Imagination as a creative orientation. The remaining three orientations, namely Self-Confidence, Inquisitiveness, and Awareness of Others comprise of both creative and non creative elements. Creative elements in each of the orientations are as follows: Self-Confidence—curious, self-confident, remembers well; Inquisitiveness—always asking questions, self-assertive, and feels strong emotions; and Awareness of Others—receptive to ideas of others, courageous in convictions, truthful even when it gets you in trouble, and non-conforming. The more creative person would be expected to score low on Acceptance of Authority and high on Disciplined Imagination, with the reverse being true of the less creative person. Interpretation of Self-Confidence, Inquisitiveness, and Awareness of Others, since these include creative and non-creative components would seem tenuous but it is speculated that people who obtain average scores on Acceptance of Authority and Disciplined Imagination are likely to obtain above average or high scores on Self-Confidence, Inquisitiveness, and Awareness of Others. If this were found to be the case then people in the average range of the creative personality would probably have been identified, and this could very likely be verified by reference to their score on the total scale.

Something About Myself, in addition to a creative perception index yields 6 factors or creative orientations (Bledsoe and Khatena, 1973). *Environmental Sensitivity* involves openess to ideas of others; relating ideas to what can be seen, touched, or heard; interest in beautiful and humorous aspects of experiences; and sensitivity to meaningful relations. *Initiative* relates to directing, producing, and/or playing leads in dramatic and musical productions; producing new formulas or new products; and bringing about changes in procedures or organization. *Self-strength* relates to self-confidence in matching talents against others; resourcefulness; versatility; willingness to take risks; desire to excel; and organizational ability. *Intellectuality* relates to intellectual curiosity; enjoyment of challenging tasks; imagination; preference for adventure over routine; liking for reconstruction of things and ideas for form something different; and dislike for doing things in a prescribed routine. *Individuality* relates to preference for working by oneself rather than in a group; seeing oneself as a self-starter and somewhat eccentric; critical of others' work; thinking for oneself; working for long periods without getting tired. *Artistry* relates to production of objects, models, paintings, carvings; musical compositions; receiving awards or prizes or having exhibits; production of stories, plays, poems and other literary pieces.

Reliability, validity and normative data and other relevant information of the two components of the *Khatena-Torrance Creative Perception Inventory* can be found in the Manual of the measure.

IDENTIFICATION DIAGNOSIS FACILITATION MODEL

Components of the *Khatena-Torrance Creative Perception Inventory* have been used for the purpose of identification, classroom grouping and/or diagnosis and program planning. Both Dr. Torrance and the writer recognized that few teachers could have direct access to instruments that would help them appropriately identify the creative talent of their children for purposes of special grouping and educational experiences in the classroom or school. That they have had to rely solely on psychologists and psychometrists for information about their children's abilities seemed to place them in a position of definite disadvantage, an instrument that was designed for their use would allow them not only to derive the information they needed almost at once, but also to understand what the instrument was doing and so put them in a better position to utilize the information they obtained.

The conceptualization of identification of various creative behavioral and mental functioning traits for diagnosis and facilitation began with a talk given to parents (Khatena, 1974a). It developed focus from a comprehensive experimental study (Khatena, 1974b) whose conclusions were "that not all children at every stage of their lives need exposure to nurturing procedures designed to increase their productivity with similar intensity, and that it would be worthwhile exploring the effects of providing nurture where and when it is needed-nurture specific possibly being one answer to the problem of maintaining and even increasing the creative performance of children; further, that curricular and methodological change incorporating principles of creative mental functioning are conceived as necessary in an all or nothing way when it may be even more legitimate to conceive these changes as need-specific as well. This latter found expression in an address recently made at a Conference on the Talented and Gifted held in Lansing, Michigan (Khatena, 1977) where a four-step plan that would involve identification, diagnosis and construction of planned experiences relative to *Something About Myself* was suggested as follows:

(1) Administer the measure to your students. If a student needs your help to respond to statements relative to the measure, give the help needed.

(2) Score the measure to determine the student's creative perception index and indices on the six creative orientations.

(3) Identify the student's strengths and weaknesses by observing the direction of items checked individually, and within each of the six creative orientations.

(4) With this information you are now in a position to decide what to do for each child according to his special needs. As back-up to this it would be better that you have prepared activities and situations either of your own composition or the composition of others like those proposed by Renzulli (1973) or Williams (1971).

Such a model was used to identify those areas of strengths and weaknesses in the creative behavior and mental functioning of gifted students attending Project Talented and Gifted in West Virginia, for Program remodelling and refinement, details of which can be found in three Evaluation Reports (Khatena, 1974c, 1975b, 1976).

The identification-diagnosis-facilitation model is workable and effective, and can be a valuable tool particularly for the teacher who hitherto has had to depend upon psychological services for measurement and interpretation, and that the *Khatena-Torrance Creative Perception Inventory* may be used for the purpose.

RESEARCH

Both components of the *Khatena-Torrance Creative Perception Inventory* have been used to identify creative perceptions and orientations of various groups of adolescents and adults both in the United States and abroad. The main findings of these studies are given as follows:

(1) People who perceive themselves as high creatives are experimentally and power oriented, have less need for structure and possess relatively high intuition (Khatena, 1972; Torrance, 1971).

173

(2) Adults perceive themselves to be more creative relative to receptivity to ideas of others, affection, sense of humor, determination, versatility, strong emotions, competition, curiosity, unwillingness to accept things on mere say so, and sense of beauty; adults and adolescents perceive themselves to be creative relative to confidence in matching talents in competitive circumstances, playfulness and regression in the act of production, eccentricity, using the strategy of restructuring, playing lead role, directing or producing a play or musical evening, productivity recognized by exhibition or award, willingness to take risks, resourcefulness, ability to identify the source of a problem and define it, desire to excel, production of a new formula, willingness to review judgements in the event of fresh evidence, planning and executing experiments, complex task absorption, invention, sensitivity to problems, experiments in cooking and making new recipes, and insightful thinking (Khatena, 1971; 1973a; Khatena and Torrance, 1973).

(3) On the matter of past experiences, highly gifted adolescent girls who perceived themselves as creative regularly read news magazines and other non required reading materials, watched television news and special reports frequently, enjoyed courses in the sciences, music, or art and were active in dramatic and musical groups, liked their teachers and generally felt that their high school education was adequate, dated more infrequently than their less creative peers in high school and going steady at an older age, not close to mother and did not discuss intimate and/or important matters with her, did not often suffer "attacks of conscience" when they felt that they had done wrong by the standards of society, church or parent, and did not want to become more socially acceptable or better prepared as a responsible family member, daydreamed, a lot felt downcast, dejected and sensitive to criticism, brooded over the meaning of life to a greater extent, and overtly expressed anger towards friends and tried to get even when someone close hurt or upset them.

Creative adolescent boys, however, disliked school and their teachers, did fewer hours of homework, had teachers who were not very successful in arousing academic interests, disliked physical education courses and seldom engaged in team sports and physical activities, did not particularly like science, enjoyed discussion courses often questioning teachers about subject matter, were regarded as radical or unconventional often wanting to be alone to pursue their own thoughts and their own interests, had parents of high educational income and occupational levels who were less strict, critical, or punitive, generally allowing them greater freedom than parents of less creative peers, and where this was not the case creative boys would express anger, and they did participate in church, religious or charitable organizations' activities (Halpin, Payne and Ellett, 1973; Halpin, Halpin and Torrance, 1973).

(4) When adults perceived themselves as creative, they tended to be more verbally original and imaginative (Halpin, Halpin and Torrance, 1974).

(5) Teachers who perceived themselves as high creatives were low value-centered and low creatives were high value-centered, where value-centeredness was the extent to which judgement of behavior was based on subjective approval or disapproval (Kallsnick, 1973).

(6) Adolescents and adults perceived themselves as growing more creative with age from grades 9 through the senior year of college, with some rise and fall between grades 10 and 11 for both boys and girls and between the sophomore and junior years of college for women.

Adolescent boys and girls perceived themselves as less creative than college men and women, with boys and men perceiving themselves as more creative than girls and women.

Relative to the six creative orientations, generally both adolescent boys and girls, and college men and women perceived themselves as having orientations of Environmental Sensitivity, Intellectuality, Individuality, Self-Strength, Artistry, and Initiative and in that order of priority (Khatena, 1975a).

(7) The teacher perceived his students to be more creative than the students perceived themselves, and female students more creative than male students. Relative to the six creative orientations the teacher perceived his students to be creative in the order of Environmental Sensitivity, Intellectuality, Individuality, Self-Strength, Artistry and Initiative (Johnson, 1976) just as students perceived themselves in an earlier study (Khatena, 1975a).

(8) Comparing the creative perceptions of adult Hungarians and Americans, it was found that some cultural variation exits in their creative perceptions: Americans perceived themselves higher on Environmental Sensitivity, Self-Strength and Intellectuality. Individuality and Artistry (Khatena, Bledsoe and Zetenyi, 1975).

(9) Talented and Gifted students were also seen to exhibit the same pattern of creative orientations with parents, however, perceiving them as being more Intellectually oriented while the students perceived themselves as being more Intellectually oriented (Khatena, 1974c). These findings diagnosed strengths and weakness in creative perceptions and applied to program refinement (Khatena, 1975b, 1976).

(10) Both high and low creative adults benefit from training to think in creative ways (Khatena, 1973b).

(11) Creative perceptions of adults were found to relate to Vividness of Visual, Auditory and Cutaneous Imagery, and to Vividness of Imagery production in general. Further, that Vivid Imagers perceived themselves as more creative than Moderate and Weak Imagers, and Moderate Imagers more creative than Weak Imagers (Khatena, 1975c).

(12) More Autonomous Imagers perceived themselves as creative than Moderate Autonomous Imagers, and Moderate Autonomous Imagers. Autonomy of imagery is central to hypnogogic imagery where images appear to follow their course independent of the experiencer's, and will often surprise him by their highly creative or unreproductive character (Khatena, 1975d).

SUMMARY AND CONCLUSIONS

Research evidence was found to support the use of biographical measures to identify the creatively gifted. One such biographical measure, the *Khatena-Torrance Creative Perception Inventory* comprising of *What Kind of Person Are You?* and *Something About Myself,* required people to decide the extent to which they perceived themselves as creative. The main features of the instruments were described. The accessibility of The *Khatena-Torrance Creative Perception Inventory* to teachers, and an identification-diagnosis-facilitation model using it were presented. Further, research done with the instrument and their major findings were listed.

In conclusion, the writer reiterates the value of the *Khatena-Torrance Creative Perception Inventory* as an instrument that can be used to measure creative perceptions and identify creative adults and adolescents, that it can be used with adult help to identify creative children in upper elementary grades, and further that it can be used by parents, teachers and anyone else like the counsellor, psychologist, manager, and business executive interested to identify creative people. In addition the instrument can be used for purposes such as educational placement, creative education programming, and research.

Relative to research, so many variables may be explored with the *Khatena-Torrance Creative Perception Inventory* some instances of which have been cited earlier in the paper. The creative pereptions of various ethnic groups in and out of the United States, of people with special difficulties or disabilities, of flexibility and rigidity and related personality variables, offer some viable directions for research. To these may be added explorations of developmental patterns of creative perceptions, effects of educational intervention upon creative perceptions, pressures that may cause distortion to creative perceptions, and creative perceptions by self and others.

References

Anastasi, A., and Schaefer, C. E. Biographical correlates of artistic and literary creativity in adolescent girls. *Journal of Applied Psychology,* 1969, 53, 267–273.

Bledsoe, J. C., and Khatena, J. A factor analytic study of Something About Myself. *Psychological Reports,* 1974, 34, 647–650.

Bledsoe, J. C., and Khatena, J. Factor analytic study of the test, What Kind of Person Are You? *Perceptual and Motor Skills,* 1974, 39, 143–146.

Ellison, R. L., James, L. R., Fox D. G., and Taylor, C. W. The identification and selection of creative artistic talent by means of biographical information. Report submitted to the United States Office of Education, Department of Health, Education and Welfare. Grant No. OEG–8–9–540215–4004(010). Project No. 9–0215, 1971.

Halpin, G., Payne, D. A., and Ellet, C. D. Biographical correlates of the creative personality: gifted adolescents. *Exceptional Children,* 1973, 39, 18, 31–33.

Halpin, G., Halpin G., and Torrance, E. P. High school experiences related to the creative personality. *High School Journal,* 1973, 39, 18, 31–33.

Halpin G., Halpin, G., and Torrance, E. P. Relationships between creative thinking abilities and a measure of the creative personality. *Educational Measurement,* 1974, 34, 75–82.

Institute for Behavioral Research in Creativity (IBRIC). The identification of academic, creative and leadership talent from biographical data. Unpublished manuscript. Salt Lake City, Utah: IBRIC, 1974.

Johnson, R. A., Teacher and student perceptions of student creativity. GIFTED CHILD QUARTERLY, 1976, 20(2), 164–167.

Kallsnick, L. R. Values and the creative personality. Unpublished masters thesis, University of Georgia, 1973.

Khatena, J. Something About Myself: a brief screening device for identifying creatively gifted children and adults. GIFTED CHILD QUARTERLY, 1971, 15, 262–266.

Khatena, J. Attitude patterns as providing validty evidence on Something About Myself. *Psychological Reports,* 1972, 34, 563–564.

Khatena, J. A profile of adolescent and adult creative self-perceptions. Unpublished manuscript, Marshall University, 1973 (a)

Khatena, J. Creative level and its effects on training college adults to think creatively with words. *Psychological Reports,* 1973, 32, 336. (b)

Khatena, J. Parents and the creatively gifted. GIFTED CHILD QUARTERLY, 1974, 18(3), 202–209.

Khatena, J. Developmental patterns in training children between the ages 5 and 11 to think creatively with pictures. *The Educational Trends,* 1974, 8, 138–149. (b)

Khatena, J. Project talented and gifted first evaluation report (ESEA Title III, Region II). Prepared for the West Virginia State Department of Education, Charleston, West Virginia. Unpublished manuscript, 1974. (c)

Khatena, J. Development patterns and creative orientations on Something About Myself. *Talents and Gifts,* 1975, 17(3), 23–26.

Khatena, J. Project talented and gifted second evaluation report (ESEA Title III, Region II). Prepared for the West Virginia State Department of Education, Charleston, West Virginia. Unpublished manuscript, 1975 (b)

Khatena, J. Vividiness of imagery and creative self-perceptions. GIFTED CHILD QUARTERLY, 1975, 19(1), 33–37.

Khatena, J. Relationship of autonomous imagery and creative self-perceptions. *Perceptual and Motor Skills,* 40, 357–358. (d)

Khatena, J. Project talented and gifted final evaluation report (ESEA Title III, Region II). Prepared for the West Virginia State Department of Education, Charleston, West Virginia. Unpublished manuscript., 1976.

Khatena, J. Facilitating the creative functioning of the gifted. GIFTED CHILD QUARTERLY, 1977, 21(3), in press.

Khatena, J., and Torrance, E. P. *Thinking Creatively with Sounds and Words: Normstechnical manual* (rsch. ed.). Lexington, Mass.: Personnel Press, 1973.

Khatena, J., and Torrance E. P. *Manual for Khatena-Torrance Creative Perception Inventory.* Chicago, Ill.: Stoelting, 1976.

Khatena, J., Bledsoe, J. C. and Zetenyi, T. Creative perceptions of Hungarian and American students. *Perceptual and Motor Skills,* 1975, 41, 901–902.

Renzulli, J. S. *New directions in creativity.* New York: Harper & Row, 1973.

Roe, A. Personal problems and science. In C. W. Taylor & F. Barron (Eds.) *Scientific creativity: Its recognition and development.* New York: Wiley, 1963, pp. 132–138.

Taylor, C. W. (Ed) *The 1957 University of Utah Research Conference on the Identification of Creative Scientific Talent.* Salt Lake City: University of Utah Press, 1958.

Torrance, E. P. Some validity studies of two brief screening devices for studying the creative personality. Journal of *Creative Behavior,* 1971, 5, 94–103.

Torrance, E. P., and Khatena, J. What Kind of Person Are You?: A brief screening device for identifying creatively gifted adolescents and adults. GIFTED CHILD QUARTERLY, 1970, 14, 71–75.

Williams, F. E. *Total creativity program for individualizing and humanizing the learning process.* Englewood Cliffs, N.J.: Educational Technology Publications, 1971.

21. A CHILDREN'S FORM OF YOUR STYLE OF LEARNING AND THINKING: PRELIMINARY NORMS AND TECHNICAL DATA

Bill Kaltsounis
Cecil R. Reynolds
E. Paul Torrance

Note:

Requests for reprints should be addressed to Cecil R. Reynolds, Department of Educational Psychology and Measurements, 130 Bancroft Hall, Lincoln, Nebraska 68588.

Abstract

The development of a children's form of your style of learning and thinking is briefly described. Equivalent forms, reliability coefficients from several samples generally proved satisfactory. Normative data for several reference groups are reported. Cautions concerning use of the scale in its present, preliminary form are provided and the scale itself presented.

Torrance, Reynolds, Riegal, and Ball (1977) recently reported in this journal on the research edition of a self-report inventory designed to estimate the relative psychological dependence of an individual on the right or left hemisphere of the brain (hemisphericity). The instrument, *Your Style of Learning and Thinking,* is based upon research findings of the last decade pertaining to the information processing preferences of the two cerebral hemispheres. These findings, briefly, tend to implicate the left hemisphere in propositional, linear sequential, verbal functions and the right hemisphere for nonverbal, appositional, simultaneous processing functions (e.g., Bogen, 1969; Gazzaniga, 1970; Kinsbourne and Smith, 1974; also see Reynolds, Riegel, and Torrance, 1977). The inventory contains questions regarding primarily right and left hemisphere functions as well as the integrative capacity of the two hemispheres. Substantial validity data have been reported on the high school and adult forms in the recently revised manual (Torrance, Reynolds, Ball, and Riegel, 1978) and elsewhere (Kaltsounis, 1979; Reynolds and Torrance, 1978; Torrance and Reynolds, 1978).

Since hemisphericity seems well established rather early in life (Kinsbourne, 1975; Reynolds and Kaufman, 1978), the next logical step is the development of a children's form of the instrument. Even though the use and interpretation of the scale has been misunderstood by some writers (Kraft, 1979), a presentation of the children's form at this year's Creative Problem Solving Institute (CPSI) (Reynolds, 1979) was greeted with considerable interest and enthusiasm. It is because of the interest expressed at CPSI and to several of the authors in numerous pieces of correspondence that the children's form is being presented here in its present form.

Potential users are cautioned that the children's form is considered to be in a research edition form and should be interpreted accordingly. Validity data are lacking and reliability data, while presented, need confirmation with larger samples. Anyone using the scale is encouraged to report

Reprinted by permission from *Gifted Child Quarterly,* Vol. 23, No. 4, 1979.

their data to the authors for inclusion in the next revision of the *Manual* (Torrance, Reynolds, Ball, and Riegel, 1978), which will incorporate the children's version of the scale.

In producing the children's form, items were rewritten to lower the reading level as much as possible without forfeiting the item's concept. This process yielded two scales (forms A and B) read with little difficulty by most fourth graders. Younger children in gifted programs have also successfully completed the scale.

TECHNICAL INFORMATION

Table 1 presents the Pearson product-moment coefficients of correlation between the Right, Left, and Integrated scales between Forms A and B of the Children's SOLAT. An interesting pattern of equivalent form reliability coefficients developed that will need further exploration. For males, the Integrated scale was clearly the most reliable of the three scales, while for females the Integrated scale was the least reliable. Good reliability is apparent for females with the Right and Left scales with mixed results for males. The differing results for males and females are conceivably due to the relatively small subsamples though the consistent pattern suggests another interpretation. That is, gender differences in reliability may be due to differences in the neuropsychological organization of the grain as suggested by several recent researchers (e.g., Buffery, 1971; Witelson, 1976, 1977). The above reliabilities are considered sufficient for group comparisons in experimental or evaluative studies, however further explanation of the gender differences is necessary prior to making interpretations of individual scores.

SCORING

Items in the children's form are keyed the same as the corresponding choice of the adult and high school forms. To preserve space, the key is not reproduced here. The reader is referred instead to Torrance, Reynolds, Riegel, and Ball (1977) and Torrance, Reynolds, Ball, and Riegel (1978).

Table 1
Reliability
Equivalent Forms Reliability Coefficients for the Children's Form of Your Style of Learning and Thinking for Several Samples.

Group[a]	Reliability Coefficients		
	Right	Left	Integrated
Problem Solving Bowl Finalists			
Young Males	.86	.65	.87
Young Females	.97	.92	.58
Older Males	.57	.71	.82
Older Females	.82	.95	.54
Challenge Program Males	.56	.66	.74
Challenge Program Females	.73	.89	.66

[a] Sample size and ages are presented in Table 2.

REFERENCE GROUP DATA

Preliminary reference group, or normative data, are reported in Table 2. Interpretation of the two scales is consistent with the high school/adult forms (See Torrance, Reynolds, Ball and Riegel, 1978) though considerably more caution is necessary.

The interpretive forms for the high school/adult edition may also be used with the children's form. The various group means in Table 2 appear relatively stable across the individuals polled and should provide useful comparisons with other samples. Validity data will be reported as they are developed by the present authors and other users.

Table 2
Reference Group Data for the Children's Forms of Your Style of Learning and Thinking.

Group Description 1978–79 National Future		Form A			Form B		
		Right	Left	Integrated	Right	Left	Integrated
Problem Solving Bowl Finalists[a]							
Males Age 9–12	X̄	9.84	10.18	15.18	11.00	12.74	16.16
N = 41	SD	3.92	4.00	6.10	4.15	4.58	6.39
Females Age 9–12	X̄	10.00	8.73	16.54	11.67	10.27	17.94
N = 31	SD	5.35	4.06	6.50	5.27	4.13	6.98
Males Age 13–18	X̄	10.85	8.05	16.97	11.90	8.93	18.63
N = 41	SD	4.26	3.67	6.08	5.03	3.93	6.67
Females Age 13–18	X̄	12.09	7.78	16.00	12.59	10.06	17.40
N = 32	SD	4.28	2.76	4.85	4.25	3.33	5.66
Summer Challenge							
Program Participants							
Males Age 9–14	X̄	10.85	9.40	16.01	11.01	12.09	16.91
N = 80	SD	9.63	3.50	9.63	6.11	6.21	9.51
Females Age 9–14	X̄	10.64	10.05	15.38	12.32	11.49	16.53
N = 89	SD	9.47	3.92	9.41	6.25	6.35	9.92
Grades 10–12 Inner City Students							
Whites[b]	X̄	9.49	9.95	16.78	12.28	11.84	15.81
	SD	4.20	3.05	4.79	3.93	3.59	5.31
Blacks	X̄	9.23	9.17	17.50			
	SD	3.09	3.10	4.91			
Mixed Group[c]	X̄	9.21	8.72	17.19			
	SD	3.97	3.00	5.04			

[a] Samples exceed 98% white
[b] Different samples were employed for each form. Whites Form A N=49; Whites Form B N=47; Blacks Form A N=53.
[c] Racial composition of this group was not known. Sexual makeup was 13 males and 19 females.

References

Bogen, J. E. The Other side of the brain: Parts I, II, and III. *Bulletin of the Los Angeles Neurological Society*, 1969, *34*, 73–105, 135–162, 191–203.

Buffery, A. W. H. Sex differences in the development of hemispheric asymmetry of function in the human brain. *Brain Research*, 1971, *31*, 364–365.

Gazzaniga, M. S. *The bisected brain*, NYC: Appleton-Century-Croft, 1970.

Kaltsounis, B. Evidence for the validity of the scale "Your style of learning and thinking." *Perceptual and Motor Skills*, 1979, *48*, 177–178.

Kinsbourne, M. The ontogeny of cerebral dominance. In D. Aaronson and R. Reiber (Eds.), *Developmental Psycholinguistics and Communication Disorders*, NYC: New York Academy of Sciences, 1975.

Kinsbourne, M. & Smith, W. L. (Eds.) *Hemispheric disconnection and cerebral function*. Springfield, IL: Charles Thomas, 1974.

Kraft, R. H. Review of "The human brain." *American Educational Research Journal*, 1979, *16*, 89–90.

Reynolds, C. R. *A children's form of "Your Style of Learning and Thinking."* Paper presented to the 25th annual Creative Problem Solving Institute, Buffalo: June, 1979.

Reynolds, C. R. and Kaufman, A. S. *Lateral eye movement behavior in children*. Paper presented to the annual meeting of the Southeastern Psychological Association, Atlanta: March, 1978.

Reynolds, C. R., Riegel, T., and Torrance, E. P. A bibliography for interdisciplinary research on lateral cerebral specialization and interhemispheric integration and processing of information. *Gifted Child Quarterly*, 1977, *21*, 574–585.

Reynolds, C. R. and Torrance, E. P. Perceived changes in styles of learning and thinking (hemisphericity) through direct and indirect training. *Journal of Creative Behavior*, 1978, *12*, 247–252.

Torrance, E. P. and Reynolds, C. R. Images of the future of gifted adolescents: Effects of alienation and specialized cerebral functioning. *Gifted Child Quarterly*, 1978, *22*, 40–54.

Torrance, E. P., Reynolds, C. R., Ball, O., and Riegal, T. *Revised norms technical manual for Your Style of Learning and Thinking*. Athens, GA: Department of Educational Psychology, University of Georgia, 1978.

Torrance, E. P., Reynolds, C. R., Riegel, T., and Ball, O. Your Style of Learning and Thinking: Preliminary norms, abbreviated technical notes, scoring keys, and selected references. *Gifted Child Quarterly*, 1977, *21*, 563–573.

Witelson, S. W. Early hemisphere specialization and interhemispheric plasticity: An empirical and theoretical review in S. Segalowitz and F. Gruber (Eds.), *Language Development and Neurological Theory*, NYC: Academic Press, 1977.

Witelson, S. W. Sex and the single hemisphere: Right hemisphere specialization for spatial processing. *Science*, 1976, *193*, 425–427.

Appendix A
Form A of the Children's Form of "Your Style of Learning and Thinking"
(Form C–A)

DIRECTIONS: CHILDREN THINK AND LEARN ABOUT THINGS IN MANY DIFFERENT WAYS. EACH QUESTION BELOW TALKS ABOUT THREE DIFFERENT WAYS THAT CHILDREN USE TO THINK AND LEARN ABOUT THINGS. OF THE THREE, PICK THE ONE THAT BEST TELLS HOW YOU THINK AND LEARN ABOUT THINGS. COLOR IN (a) (b) or (c) ON YOUR ANSWER SHEET. *DO NOT WRITE ON THIS BOOKLET.*

1. (a) I am good at remembering faces.
   (b) I am good at remembering names.
   (c) I am just as good at remembering names as I am at remembering faces.

2. (a) I answer best to directions which are told to me or written for me.
   (b) I answer best to directions when I have someone to show me how.
   (c) I follow directions just as good either way.

3. (a) I like to let people know how I feel.
   (b) I show my feelings only with good friends.
   (c) I keep my feelings to myself.

4. (a) I like to try things that I have not tried before.
   (b) When I try something new, I always like to think up different ways to do it before I try it.
   (c) I like to try new things just as good as I like trying things that I have seen and thought about.

5. (a) I like to do things one at a time.
   (b) I like to do more than one thing at a time.
   (c) Doing one thing at a time or more than one thing at a time, does not matter to me.

6. (a) I like tests where the answers are given to me and I pick the best one.
   (b) I like tests where I write the answer out myself.
   (c) I like both kinds of tests just as well.

7. (a) I can tell when a person is happy or not without the person telling me.
   (b) People have to tell me when they are happy or sad.
   (c) I can do both just as well.

8. (a) I am good at thinking up funny things to say and do.
   (b) I am not good at thinking up funny things to say and do.
   (c) Sometimes I am good at thinking up funny things to do.

9. (a) I like teachers who show me how to do things.
   (b) I like teachers who tell me how to do things.
   (c) I like both ways of learning just the same.

10. (a) I like to know everything about a question before I answer it.
    (b) I answer questions according to the way I feel.
    (c) I like to answer questions just as well both ways.

11. (a) I like to have fun when I try to figure things out.
    (b) I like to have quiet when I try to figure things out.
    (c) Sometimes I like to have fun when I figure things out and sometimes I like to have quiet.

12. (a) I like to make up my own games when I play.
    (b) I always like to play by the rules with no changes.
    (c) I like to do both just as well.

13. (a) I am willing most of the time to use anything around to get things done.
    (b) I am not always willing to use anything around just to get things done.
    (c) I like to use the right tools for the right job.

14. (a) I like teachers who tell ne what to learn and how to learn it.
    (b) I do not like teachers who tell me what to learn and how to learn it.
    (c) I like both kind of teachers just as well.

15. (a) I always come up with new things and ideas.
    (b) Sometimes I come up with new things and ideas.
    (c) I never come up with new things and ideas.

16. (a) I come up with ideas best when I lie flat on my back.
    (b) I come up with ideas best when I stay in my seat.
    (c) I come up with ideas best when I walk.

17. (a) I like to learn about things that I can use.
    (b) I like to think about the other places and new things.
    (c) I like both just the same.

18. (a) I always seem to know what other people are thinking.
    (b) Sometimes I know what other people are thinking.
    (c) I never know what someone is thinking until they tell me.

19. (a) I often use examples when I talk.
    (b) I occasionally use examples when I talk.
    (c) I hardly use any examples when I talk.

20. (a) I often get many ideas from examples.
    (b) I occasionally get ideas from examples.
    (c) I hardly get any ideas from examples.

21. (a) I like to answer easy questions.
    (b) I like to answer hard questions.
    (c) I like to answer both kinds of questions just the same.

22. (a) I always like to answer to people who excite me.
    (b) I always like to answer to people who can show me that they are right.
    (c) I like to answer to both kinds of people just the same.

23. (a) I like to work on one problem at a time.
    (b) I like to work on many problems at the same time.
    (c) I can do just as well both ways.

24. (a) I like to learn facts like names and dates.
    (b) I like to learn about what people think might happen someday.
    (c) I like to learn facts like names and dates just as well as learning about what people think might happen someday.

25. (a) I like to make sense out of everything I read.
    (b) I like to use the things I read about.
    (c) I like to do both.

26. (a) The way I answer a problem depends on how I feel inside.
    (b) I answer a problem by carefully picking the best answer.
    (c) I answer problems both ways.

27. (a) I like to picture the answer to a problem in my head.
    (b) I do not like to picture the answer to a problem in my head.
    (c) It does not make any difference to me.

28. (a) I like to answer questions by carefully picking out the best answer.
    (b) I like to answer questions by guessing.
    (c) I like to answer questions either way.

29. (a) I can explain myself better by talking.
    (b) I can explain myself better by moving my hands while I talk.
    (c) I can explain myself either by talking or by showing with my hands.

30. (a) I learn best when the teacher explains the lesson to me.
    (b) I learn better when the teacher shows me a picture of what she/he wants me to do.
    (c) I can learn either way.

31. (a) I remember better when the teacher explains things to me.
    (b) I remember answers better to problems I picture in my head.
    (c) I can remember things just as well either way.

32. (a) I like to figure out all the steps in the answer to a problem.
    (b) I like to write out everything about the answer to a problem.
    (c) I like answering problems either way.

33. (a) I like to tell a story by talking or writing it down.
    (b) I like to tell a story by drawing or giving a puppet show.
    (c) I like to tell a story either way.

34. (a) I get lost very easily.
    (b) I can find my way around even in strange places.
    (c) Sometimes I find my way around sometimes I get lost.

35. (a) I like to do things.
    (b) I like to explain things.
    (c) I like both just as well.

36. (a) In school, I like to read best of all.
    (b) In school, I like to draw things.
    (c) I like drawing and reading about the same.

Appendix B

Form B of the Children's Form of "Your Style of Learning and Thinking" (Form C–B)

(Directions have been excluded but are identical to Form A.)

1. (a) I am good at remembering faces.
   (b) I am good at remembering names.
   (c) I am just as good at remembering names as I am at remembering faces.

2. (a) I answer best to directions which are told to me or written for me.
   (b) I answer best to directions when someone gives me an example.
   (c) I follow directions just as well in both ways.

3. (a) I like to let people know how I feel.
   (b) I show my feelings only with good friends.
   (c) I keep my feelings to myself.

4. (a) I like to try things that I have not tried before.
   (b) When I try something new, I always like to think up different ways to do it before I try it.
   (c) I like to try new things just as good as I like trying things that I have seen and thought about.

5. (a) I like teachers who give one homework assignment at a time.
   (b) I like teachers who ask me to study or work on many things at the same time.
   (c) I like either kind of teacher.

6. (a) I like tests where the answers are given to me and I am asked to pick the best one.
   (b) I like tests where I write out the answer myself.
   (c) I like both kinds of tests just as well.

7. (a) I can tell when a person is happy or not by watching him or by listening to him talking.
   (b) I cannot tell when a person is happy or not by watching him but I can tell by listening to him talking.
   (c) I can do both just as well.

8. (a) I am good at thinking up amusing things to say and do.
   (b) I am not good at thinking up amusing things to say and do.
   (c) Sometimes I am good at thinking up amusing things to say and do.

9. (a) I like to be in classes where teachers let me move around and do things.
   (b) I like to be in classes where the teacher asks me to sit and listen.
   (c) I like both kinds of classes just as well.

10. (a) Before I do something I like to know as much as I can about it.
    (b) I can do something better if I like it or I am used to it.
    (c) Before I do something I like to know a lot about it as well as to like it and be used to it.

11. (a) I like to have fun when I try to figure things out.
    (b) I like to have quiet when I try to figure things out.
    (c) I like to have fun when I figure things out as well as quiet.

12. (a) I like to play out things that I hear and see but not things that people tell me about.
    (b) I always like to make believe that I am playing with other people.
    (c) I can do things just as well both ways.

13. (a) I am able most of the time to use anything around to get things done.
    (b) I am not always able to use anything around to get things done.
    (c) I like to use the right tools for the right job.

14. (a) I like teachers who tell me what to learn and how to learn it.
    (b) I like teachers who tell me what to learn but allow me to decide how to learn it.
    (c) I can do just as well with both kinds of teachers.

15. (a) I always come up with new things.
    (b) Sometimes I come up with new things.
    (c) I never come up with new things.

16. (a) I think best when I lie flat on my back.
    (b) I think best when I sit.
    (c) I think best when I walk or move around.

17. (a) I like to learn about things that I can use right away.
    (b) I like to learn about things even if I cannot use them right away.
    (c) I like to learn about things that I can use right away just as well as I like to learn about things that I cannot use right away.

18. (a) When I do not know the answer to a question, I like to take a guess at it.
    (b) When I do not know the answer to a question, I do not like to take a guess at it.
    (c) Sometimes I like to guess at things when I do not know the answer.

19. (a) I like to tell people just how I feel.
    (b) I like to show people how I feel with a poem, a song or a dance.
    (c) Sometimes I like to tell people how I feel and sometimes I like to show people how I feel with a poem, song, or a dance.

20. (a) Many times I get ideas from reading poems or looking at posters.
    (b) Once in a while I get ideas from reading poems or looking at posters.
    (c) I hardly get any ideas from reading poems or looking at posters.

21. (a) I like to answer simple questions.
    (b) I like to try hard questions.
    (c) I like to answer simple questions just as well as I like to try hard questions.

22. (a) I like to follow people who excite me.
    (b) I like to follow people who make sense to me.
    (c) I like to follow people who excite me just as well as I like to follow people who make sense to me.

23. (a) I like to work on one problem at a time.
    (b) I like to work on many problems at once.
    (c) I like to work on one problem at a time just as well as I can work on many problems.

24. (a) I like to learn about things that have been proven to be right.
    (b) I like to learn about what people think might happen someday.
    (c) I like to learn about things that have taken place as well as about things that might happen someday.

25. (a) I like to make sense out of everything I read.
    (b) I like to put into use everything I read and learn.
    (c) I like to make sense out of everything I read as well as put it into use.

26. (a) I like to use the way I feel in answering a problem.
    (b) I answer a problem by thinking out the best answer.
    (c) I like to solve problems both ways.

27. (a) I like to picture in my head the answer to a problem.
    (b) I like to answer a question by using things that I have learned.
    (c) I do not care which way I answer a problem.

28. (a) I like to answer a question by carefully picking out the best answer.
    (b) I like to answer a question by using things that I have learned.
    (c) I can answer a question by carefully picking out the best answer or by using things that I have learned.

29. (a) I can explain things best by talking about them.
    (b) I can explain things best by using my body or hands than by talking about them.
    (c) I can explain things by talking about them or by using my body to act them out.

30. (a) I learn best from a teacher who explains the lesson to me.
    (b) I learn best from a teacher who shows me pictures of what to learn.
    (c) I can learn just as well from either kind of teacher.

31. (a) I remember better when the teacher explains things to me.
    (b) I learn better when the teacher uses pictures to explain things.
    (c) I remember things just as well both ways.

32. (a) I like to look back at things that I have done and try to figure them out.
    (b) I like to figure out my own way of doing things that I am trying for the first time.
    (c) I do not really care how I go about doing things.

33. (a) I like to talk and write about things.
    (b) I like to draw and make things.
    (c) I like to do both.

34. (a) I get lost easily even in places that I have visited.
    (b) I can find my way even in strange places.
    (c) Sometimes I find my way in places.

35. (a) I rather do something than explain it.
    (b) I rather explain something than do it.
    (c) I do just as well either way.

36. (a) I like to be in noisy and crowded places where people do many things at the same time.
    (b) I like to be in quiet places where I am able to think carefully.
    (c) I can do just as well in both places.

37. (a) I like best to draw and listen to music.
    (b) I like to do things with other people.
    (c) I like to draw and listen to music as well as work with other people.

38. (a) When I grow up I would like to be a business man or a scientist.
    (b) When I grow up I would like to be a teacher or a minister.
    (c) I really do not care what I will be when I grow up.

39. (a) I learn only what I read and what people tell me.
    (b) I learn lots of things that people don't teach me.
    (c) Sometimes I like to learn everything about things and sometimes I like to learn only the important parts.

40. (a) I like to use the things I hear and read.
    (b) I like to think out the things I hear and read before I use them.
    (c) I can go both ways.

22. PERSONALITY INVENTORIES AS TESTS OF CREATIVE POTENTIAL AND THEIR USE AS MEASUREMENTS IN PROGRAMS FOR THE GIFTED

C. K. Rekdal

INTRODUCTION

Theobald and White (1974) share a famous story once told by Danish philosopher Soren Kierkegaard about a man who liked to watch the wild ducks fly south in great flocks each fall. However, when habituated to being fed by him, the ducks no longer bothered to fly the great distance south, content instead to feed safely in familiar ponds. After several seasons, the ducks found it difficult to fly at all. They spent the rest of their lives swimming and feeding in the same pond.

Kierkegaard's point was—you can make wild ducks tame, but you can never make tame ducks wild again, the implication being that a tamed duck would never again go anywhere.

At IBM, according to Theobald, et al. (1974), the term wild duck refers to "innovators and creators, probers and eccentrics—those people needed to drive, stimulate and challenge large organizations" (p. 12).

In Education, the survival of the "wild ducks" should be a top priority. These students will be the ones capable of inventive, curious, energetic, original and productive actions, those able to use their intelligence in creative, ingenious ways to examine and explore the world of learning, who in all probability will not be content to merely seek solutions, but imaginative enough to formulate the questions.

ANALYSIS

Programs for gifted children traditionally focus on the academically or intellectually talented student, as these qualities appear in IQ scores achieved on tests such as the Stanford-Binet (Guilford, 1975). High intelligence is usually defined in gifted programs as an IQ score of 130 or more.

This practice has come under attack from many quarters in recent years, particularly by those who consider creativity a function of intelligence, and who believe they can demonstrate that IQ tests do not measure it. IQ tests have continually stressed convergent or singular correct responses. Creativity measures, by contrast, evaluate divergent abilities reflected in major areas of fluency (the ability to think of the most number of relevant responses), flexibility (the ability to take different approaches in generating ideas) and originality (the ability to think in novel or unique ways). These abilities, according to DeHaan and Havighurst (1961), Jackson and Messnick (1965), Roslansky (1970), Shouksmith (1970), Gowan (1971), Lesher (1973) and Taylor and Getzels (1975) are necessarily connected with the production of useful ideas, institutions or products.

Reprinted by permission from *Gifted Child Quarterly*, Vol. 21, No. 4, 1977.

The shift in gifted child research from studies involving children with high IQ to creative processes began in 1950. Since then, inclusion of the creatively gifted in program definitions for gifted education has been widespread. Research has moved creativity beyond definitions limiting the "creatively gifted" to those who are talented in one or more of the performing arts. And it now places greater stress on areas of cognition, motivation, personality; and environment associated with originality in problem solving (Jackson et al., 1962; Guilford, 1968; Gowan, 1971; Lesher, 1973).

In an attempt to locate the creatively gifted, much research on the nature of the relationship between creativity and intelligence has been done. Most of the scholarly literature concentrates on several inconsistent, but not entirely contradictory themes: 1) that there is no correlation between them; 2) that there is an ambiguous, somewhat overlapping correlation; and 3) that there is a definite, but low correlation. Those in support of the latter view are currently more numerous.

According to Rossiman and Horn (1972), and many others, intelligence is a necessary but not a sufficient condition for creativity. Schubert (1973), e.g., states that intelligence allows for the development of creativity, but does not necessarily insure it. Shouksmith (1962) points to factor studies indicating that creativity makes up only one-third of what we call general intelligence. Yamamoto (1965) contends that creativity is neither independent from nor exclusive of the general factor of intelligence. Thurstone (in Getzels and Jackson, 1962) supports what he terms a common observation in universities, i.e., that those of high intelligence are not necessarily the ones who produce the most original ideas. Although intelligence is seen as an essential component or prerequisite of creativity, Shouksmith (1970) finds that only a minimal level is necessary in order to engaged in creative activities, and Barron (1969) sees little correlation between scores on IQ tests and creative acts.

Most evidence of the relationship between degrees of creativity and intelligence support the notion of an average IQ as more highly correlated with creative achievement that any other group. Guilford (in Gowan and Torrance, 1967) suggests that 120 is the IQ level above which creativity and intelligence are least likely to be correlated. Torrance (in Gowan, et al. 1967) holds that intelligence tests miss 70% of those who score in the top 20% on creative thinking measures, a fact, he says, which is constant in hundreds of studies. The relationship of either creative potential or creative production to traditional IQ is, according to Getzels et al. (1962) close to zero with groups of superior IQ. Correlation, he finds, is stronger in the lower IQ ranges. Anastasi and Schaefer (1971) state that many investigators believe that high IQ not only does not imply high creativity, but may, indeed, hinder creative achievement. These findings are substantiated by many others, including Hasen and Butcher (1966), Wallach (in Rosner and Abt, 1974) and Gowan (1971), who suggests that in the future we may wish to move to an operational definition of giftedness identifying the gifted child as one who has the potential to become creative. He appears more optimistic than Barbe and Renzullia (1975) who complain that twenty years of investigation have produced few advances in the controversy over the definition and measurement of creativity. The critical questions of identification and evaluation still remain unanswered (Stein and Heinze, 1960; Khatena, 1971; Treffinger, Renzulli and Feldhusen, 1971).

Recently, concern has mounted over evidence that neither the broadened definition of the gifted, nor an awareness of the limitations of the IQ score in identification have helped to locate or place the creatively able into gifted programs. Screening devices not related to IQ were needed in the selection process (Khatena, 1976). The use of peer, teacher or supervisor nominations as criteria rating for creativity indicators was once thought to be a method of alleviating this problem. However, teachers and peers have not been effective in nominating creatives beyond those who are either high achievers or have high IQs (Treffinger, et al. 1971). These nominations as criteria ratings for creativity produce minimal or negative correlations with tests of ingenuity and performance (Yamamoto, 1965). With teacher training, however, correlations do raise to the .05 significance level (Ogletree, 1971).

Those involved in creativity research have attempted to locate measures that solve this problem. Guilford (1975) suggests that IQ tests could be replaced by divergent production tests, since individuals who are high in these abilities are usually high in IQ, while the reverse is not true. Khatena (1976) argues that *either* IQ or creative thinking tests will locate the intellectually creative, since they will be two standard deviations above either mean.

Tests for creativity abound; there may in fact be too many according to Davis (1975). But they have all come under some type of criticism. Torrance (in Ogletree, 1971) acknowledges that creativity tests do not sample any kind of universal creative thinking abilities, or guarantee that the high scorer has an increased chance of behaving creatively. Maddi (in Taylor et al., 1972), Nicholls (in Rosner et al., 1974) and Crockenburg (1972) emphasize the distinction between techniques of problem solving and creativity itself, questioning whether tests for originality (e.g., how many ways you can use a paper clip) express creativity of the same kind as that which is displayed in the actual creation of things and ideas in the real world. Mednick (in Lesher, 1973), Mackworth (in Shouksmith, 1970) and Duckworth (1972) suggest that the creative act culminates not in fluency and divergence, but in a new synthesis or convergence reached after divergent behavior has occured. Guilford (1976) suggests that creative aptitude may in fact move beyond the categories of divergent production. He sees transformational ability as equal in importance to that of divergence. Treffinger, et al (1971) state that if creativity is viewed as a complex kind of human problem solving, divergent thinking may be a necessary, even though not a sufficient component. Nuttall (in Zegas, 1976) states that few studies attempt empirical validation against creative criteria, and those that do rarely meet with any success. Others have criticized tests of creative ability on the grounds that they more often correlate with IQ measures than they do with each other (Treffinger and Poggio, 1972).

Of the major tests of creative thinking available (those most widely used) the greater number focus on divergence. It is instructive here to examine and review some of the criticisms which have been leveled against them.

One of the major problems centers around the difficulty of formulating objective measurements. For example, the Wallach-Kogan Association Test measures the number and uniqueness of ideas which the subject can give for a problem, e.g., list the uses for a shoe. Although studies have shown it to indicate creative ability (Wallbrown and Huelsman in Dice, 1976), and at the same time maintain independence from IQ (Davis, 1975), it is difficult to score large numbers of tests due to subjectivity and emphasis on response volume.

Another frequent problem is that of validity. Mednick's Remote Associations Test (RAT) is a 30 item covergent test which is easily administered and scored. Given three words, a subject is asked to find a fourth which is related, e.g., surprise, birthday, line are all related to the word party. However, criticism ranges from punishing more imaginative response (Davis 1975) to being too highly correlated with IQ and achievement award, 1975; Davis and Belcher, 1975; Dice, 1976).

190

Reliability is also an important measure of a test's worth. The Torrance Test of Creative Thinking is a divergent measure. The subject is asked to list, for example, many possible uses of a tin can. Although it has received satisfactory validity results, critics find scoring time consuming (Davis, 1975), long range predictibility lacking in actual life situation performance (Ogletree, 1971) and an inherent bias against young or verbally underdeveloped children (McCormack in Dice, 1976).

Guilford's Divergent Thinking Battery is similar in form to both the Wallach-Kogan and Torrance Tests. Although it has been shown able to measure divergent thinking abilities (Zegas, 1976), there is zero correlation to real world creative productivity (Davis, 1975).

Because of continuing controversies involved with creative assessment measures, researchers have maintained a steady search, attempting to develop and locate tests which move beyond the divergent production criterion, and yet are separate from IQ. Particular importance attaches to the need for tests that are easy to administer, score and reliably predict creative behavior (Dice, 1976). Based on the rationale that creativity is reflected in the personality characteristics of an individual, the kind of thinking strategies he employs and the products that emerge, many current psychologists and psychometrists in the field have turned to personality inventories and biographical checklists as a screening device in locating the creatively gifted (Klausmeier, 1971; Khatena, 1971a; Payne, Halpin, Ellet and Dale, 1975; Davis, 1975). The use of personality inventories in students (Rimm and Davis, 1976). The use of personality inventories is not new, biographical data have been employed with significant success in many business and scientific fields as a means of screening in potentially creative employees (Whiting, 1973). Inventories also have been used in a number of tests which provide personality profiles, such as the Allport-Vernon Lindzey Study of Values (1951), the California Personality Inventory Type Indicator (1962) and the Runner Studies of Attitude Patterns (1965). However, none of these attempts yield a single index of creative personality (Torrance, 971).

It is not yet clear that bio-data tests can be used as screens for gifted programs. Treffinger, et al., 1971, are concerned that profiles of creative adults may be very different from profiles of creative youngsters. But as bio-inventories in creativity research become more common, further information will surface on their effectiveness, allowing more precise evaluations of their future potential in programs for the intellectually creative student.

In attempting to assess which bio-inventory tests project possible usefulness as screening devices for gifted programs, a research of current inventory studies was made. The four selected were chosen from the field based on two or more of these criteria: 1) the inventory is useable—it is easily administered, scoring is objective; 2) the inventory is a valid (real) measure of creative potential; 3) the inventory is a reliable (consistent or stable) measure of creative potential. Additional consideration was given to studies related to teaching models used in programs for the gifted, e.g., Williams' study.

Each study is briefly summarized in general terms as to the research problem, samples and procedures used in the research and results or conclusions given. More specific information from the studies is arranged in chart form, supplying detail and simplifying comparisons between them.

A discussion evaluating both weaknesses and strengths follows each summary. The Khatena, Torrance and Williams studies are not discussed in great length. The first two deal with adolescents and adults, the last with upper elementary and beginning Jr. High subjects in a limited manner. My area of interest is that of k–6, a population which has been neglected in this type of research in comparison to other age groups. For those who believe in the importance of early educational nurturing, the identification of creatively gifted students in order to place them into programs to develop and increase their potential is a high priority item. Torrance (Johnson, 1976) sees these screening inventories as an aid in helping them to use and fulfill their creative talents. The work of many, including Parnes and Osborn have shown that creativity can be increased and developed with special instruction. It is not the intent of this paper to argue whether or not programs to enhance creativity should be offered to all students. The purpose is to underscore the fact that we have students who are high in their ability to be creative and that they need to be identified as early as possible in order to offer them programs which will encourage and stimulate their talent.

Based on the evaluations of the studies, conclusions are drawn as to the possible use of personality inventories as tests of creative potential, and their use as screening measures in programs for the creatively gifted.

INVENTORY	ADMINISTRATION	SCORING AND ITEMS	AGE	COST
KHATENA Something About Myself (SAM)	-Easy for groups or individuals -No time limit: time required is usually 10-15 minutes	-Objective: 50 items; yes/no answers -Item categories: -personality traits -use of creative thinking strategies -creative products/productions *Bledsoe & Khatena (1973) gives further factor analysis of inventory items -Sample items: -I am an imaginative person, a dreamer or visionary. -I have improvised in dance, song or instrumental music. -When I think of an idea I like adding to it to make it more interesting.	-Adolescents -Adults	-Minimal
RIMM & DAVIS Group Inventory for Finding Creative Talents (GIFT)	-Easy for groups or individuals	-Objectives: 35-36 items: yes/no answers -Item categories: -interests -biographical information -independence and perseverance -peripheral item -Sample items: -I like to make up my own songs. -I have some really good ideas. -Easy puzzles are the most fun.	-Primary, gr. 1-2 -Elementary, gr. 3-4 -Upper Elem., gr. 5-6	-Minimal

INVENTORY	ADMINISTRATION	SCORING AND ITEMS	AGE	COST

TORRANCE: What Kind of Person Are You (WKOPAY)	-Easy for groups or individuals
	-Immediate feedback available
		-Objective: 50 items: forced choice selection
		-Item categories:
		  -creative/uncreative
		  -socially desireable characteristics
		  -socially undesireable characteristics
		-Sample items: (choose one)
		  -industrious or neat
		  -persistent or does work on time
		  -considerate of others or courageous in convictions
			-Adolescents
			-Adults
				-Minimal

WILLIAMS: How Do You Really Feel About Yourself	-Easy for groups or individuals	-Objectives: 50 items: true/false answers
		-Item categories:
		  -curiosity
		  -imagination
		  -complexity
		  -risk-taking
		-Sample items:
		  -I like to daydream about things that have never happened.
		  -I never suggest playing a game no one else has thought of.
			-Grades 5-7	-Minimal

INVENTORY	VALIDITY: An instrument is valid if it accomplishes the purposes for which it is designed.	RELIABILITY: An instrument is reliable if it is consistent.
KHATENA: Something About Myself (SAM)	Criterion tests of validity: -Form I Adult Version of the Cunningham/Torrance Sounds and Images Test -Khatena's Onomatopoeia and Images Test Coefficients ranged from .15 to .40 with over 1,000 adolescent and college students	Interscorer reliability of 100 adult and adolescent subjects was .99 (p .01). Internal consistency scores for adults and adolescents was .94. Test-retest coefficient for a 4 week interval with 43 adults was .77.

INVENTORY	VALIDITY: An instrument is valid if it accomplishes the purposes for which it is designed.	RELIABILITY: An instrument is reliable if it is consistent.

RIMM & DAVIS Group Inventory for Finding Creative Talent (GIFT)	Criterion tests of validity: (composite score)
	-teacher nominations
	-short stories
	-pictures/art work
	-art teacher nomination
	-Torrance Circles and Squares Test
	-Torrance Uses Test
	Coefficients ranged from .03 to .42 with 365 students in grades 1-6; correlation increased with increase in grade level
		Hoyt r for primary—.55
		   elementary—.69
		   upper elementary—.61
		Test-retest coefficient for a 6 month interval with 126 students was .56.

TORRANCE: What Kind of Person Are You (WKOPAY)	Criterion tests of validity: -Cunningham/Torrance Sounds and Images Test -Khatena Onomatopoeia and Images Test -Torrance Provocative Questions Test -Runner Studies of Attitude Patterns -Torrance original story scale -Creative Mental Checklist Coefficients ranged from .37 to .75 with groups of students and teachers enrolled in a university. These grouped varied from 27-123 in number.	Test-retest coefficient for a 1 week interval with 18 subjects was .91. Test-retest coefficient for same day interval with 26 subjects was .97. Test-retest coefficient for a 1 week interval with 47 subjects was .71. Test-retest coefficient for 1 month with 27 subjects was .73.
WILLIAMS: How Do Your You Really Feel About Yourself	Criterion tests of validity: -Torrance Tests of Creative Thinking, Figural and Verbal Only report of a positive correlation with ninety-four 5th, 6th and 7th graders.	No information cited

Study No. 1: "Something About Myself: A Brief Screening Device for Identifying Creatively Gifted Children and Adults" (Khatena, 1971) gives preliminary reliability, validity and normative data on the use of the Something About Myself (SAM) inventory.

The subjects, 544 adolescents in three schools in West Virginia and 814 college adults from five different colleges were given the checklist and, according to the scores, placed in a high or low creative group. The predictive ability of this procedure was validated by two tests of verbal originality. The results showed that the mean original scores of high creative groups were found to be significantly above those of low creative groups.

The author views the results as promising, indicating that SAM may be useful as a screening device in locating creative individuals. *Discussion:* Although all of the correlations of validity are significant, they are not highly significant. The author's conservative judgement of the inventory's promise is well made. Kaltsounis (1975) in another validation study of SAM, using the Torrance Tests of Creative Thinking as the validating criterion, had similar results. He was also guarded in his concluding statements, admitting that the instrument showed promise, but additional research was needed.

Johnson (1976) reports some interesting findings after using the SAM with 81 black and white males and females of low income and general below average IQ. He found that males and females of low income and general below average IQ. He found that males perceived themselves as less creative than females and that their teacher viewed them as more creative than they viewed themselves. Both of these findings are not surprising in light of comments made by other researchers. What is of interest in pointing them out here, is that a growing need is shown in the area of making what have been peripheral finds in bio-inventory research a major investigatory need. Although teacher nomination has been fairly well researched in the general area of measurements, the male/female personality in bio-inventory studies has not been. Davis and Belcher (1971) in an interesting aside relative to their Alpha Biographical Inventory (ABI) study noted that males' creativity and intelligence test scores were not correlated whereas female scores on intelligence and creativity tests correlated significantly. Whether or not this may point to a need for developing creativity inventories based on sexual identification has been one recurring thought since reading these studies, however more investigation into this particular aspect of the literature must be made before these conclusions can be drawn.

Bledsoe and Khatena (1973) factor analyzed SAM and found the inventory yielded 6 orthogonal factors identifying creative students in terms of total or separate scores on Environmental Sensitivity, Initiative, Self-strength, Intellectuality, Individuality and Artistry. Johnson (1976) commented that the SAM's use could well be extended beyond its original purpose to include that of diagnosis of all populations in terms of one or more of these factors. I wonder if this might not be a very limited proposal. The SAM inventory is only 50 items. How much strength would an eight-item test on intellectuality have? It might give as a tentative feeling for the student's potential, but I would hazard to estimate what that might be. If Johnson wishes to diagnose any of the above areas, he would be better off using a personality inventory which is specifically designed for that factor or function, and would reflect greater depth and breadth in that area.

Study No. 2: "GIFT An Instrument for the Identification of Creativity" (Rimm and Davis, 1976) is a study which describes the reliability and validity of the GIFT, based on Davis's How Do You Think Inventory.

The results of two studies are given—a pilot version involving 175 K–6 grade students in a middle class suburban elementary school, and one involving 365 1–6 grade students in the same school. Students were assigned creativity ratings based on a combined criterion score. Their score on the GIFT and their combined criterion score indicated significant positive correlations in all grades with a tendency for increased correlations in higher grades.

Rimm and Davis suggest with this study that the possibilities exist for constructing an elementary school level inventory which *can* predict creative behavior.

Discussion: This study, as previously mentioned, is a particularly interesting one because it focuses on elementary students, whereas most inventories are designed for older subjects. The stronger correlation between validating criteria and GIFT scores as age levels increase serves to underscore problems in assessing young subjects. It also serves to emphasize the need for further research in this area.

The validation criteria procedures in this study are more involved and time consuming than in the other studies. There are, however more painfully these validations were arrived at, some serious criticisms I wish to make.

First-graders were excluded from the story writing criterion because "first-graders are not able to write stories." I protest against this notion. It is implicit in the study that the validation criteria are to pursue creative/original ideas. It is not the physical act of spelling, punctuating, sentence and paragraph formation which is being evaluated. Therefore, first-graders *can* write stories. By having them tell or dictate their stories to secretary-recorders, we can get a very accurate picture of the creative/original stories which they carry inside them. Since the story writing was a main validating criterion, by including a score based on this method, perhaps there may have been more significance in assessing their scores. Also, this may have altered the statement that a pattern of increased correlations based on rise in grade level was seen.

Authors also state that questions/items in the GIFT are to be read to first-graders only. This assumes that only first graders cannot read. Elementary teachers are well aware of the fallacy in this reasoning. I have had first graders who have read as well as some sixth graders, and sixth graders who were able to read only at a first grade level. This also points out the dependence of the test on reading ability. In order to complete the GIFT one must know how to read, at least in grades 2–6. The question then arises—"How valid is GIFT?" Not very for low or nonreaders. I suggest since GIFT is short, that all items be read to all students in every grade level.

For very young students, k–1, Jay (1952) uses pictures in evaluating pupil personality. Although the *Book About Me* test is blatant in sex role stereotyping and severely biased culturally, not mention being quaintly dated pictorially/stylistically, its use of pictures may offer some suggestions to Rimm and Davis. Adkins and Ballif (1973) k–1 motivation test, *Animal Crackers,* resolves some of Jay's problems by using animal pictures. The subject sees two identical animal pictures and is asked to identify the one most like himself. A description is read about each, e.g., This penguin likes to sing. This penguin likes to dance. The student marks the one most like himself.

Although Rimm and Davis made an obvious attempt at helping teachers distinguish between creative and intelligent students in order to insure greater validity in their teacher nomination process, I question whether they might not have done more towards training teachers in identifying creative behavior than to just ask them to rate each child on an intelligence scale and then on a creative one. As previously discussed, teachers do not have high success in nominating creatives without training. Interrater reliability for the study in judging stories and pictures was only established after raters practiced joint rating and their agreement was judged acceptable. It seems only sensible that teachers should have gone through the same type of training process.

With at least two other creativity inventories available—The Children's Reactive Curiosity Scale (Penny and McCann, 1964) and the Pennsylvania Assessment of Creative Tendency (Rookey, 1974) it is curious that Rimm and Davis chose such cumbersome methods to validate their inventory. All other studies used prevalidated tests in order to validate their own. As these tests were not available to me, I can only guess as to the authors' reasons. One factor considered might have hinged on the fact that the inventories mentioned have been validated with students from only grades 3–6, not the population the GIFT inventory measures, grades 1–6.

As with the Khatena study, the correlations are significant, but low. It is probably advisable for the authors to revise their instrument further. The areas pointed out in the preceding paragraphs provide possible starting points.

Study No. 3: "Some Validity Studies of Two Brief Screening Devices for Studying the Creative Personality" (Torrance, 1971) presents information and research on the Creative Motivation Checklist (CMC) and an inventory which the author has designed, the What Kind of Person Are You (WKOPAY).

Torrance recounts the validation studies of researchers who have used the WKOPAY, and they are many. Criterion tests and test-retest results have produced several high positive correlations supporting the predictive ability of the WKOPAY.

Torrance concludes that the WKOPAY, based on the validation evidence, is useful as a brief screening device in identifying creative adolescents and adults.

Discussion: correlational validity is more highly significant (above .50) on the WKOPAY than on any other of the studies represented in this paper. However, there appears to be a pattern as to *when* correlations occur. When the WKOPAY is validated using tests also authored by the WKOPAY, correlations are high: .75 between the Cunningham/Torrance and WKOPAY, .60 between the Torrance Provocative Questions Test and the WKOPAY. When validated against other tests, the correlations are substantially different: .37 and .48 between two studies using the Khatena Onomatopoeia and Images Test and the WKOPAY. Granted, there might be other reasons why there is a low correlation, e.g., the Khatena may not correlate well with the WKOPAY for reasons beyond just the creativity factor.

Since the many studies gathered by Torrance have indicated more highly significant correlations than the other studies reported on in this paper, it may be instructive to look at his test items closely. Of the four studies, the WKOPAY is the only one which differs from the rest in method of arriving at a subject's personality index. While the others require only a yes/no, true/false response to each item, the WKOPAY forces difficult choices between items which are purposely either both desireable or both undesireable items. If this same psychology is not used, only more subtly in the other tests, it may be important to investigate this technique more carefully.

Study No. 4: "Assessing Pupil-Teacher Behaviors Related to A Cognitive-Affective Teaching Model" (Williams, 1971) includes a very brief study of the How Do You Really Feel About Yourself Inventory. In attempting to develop an instrument which tests the four affective pupil behaviors delineated in his model, Williams has constructed a self-concept scale which measures imagination, curiosity, risk-taking and complexity.

His study involved 94 fifth, sixth and seventh grade students from an experimental school in the National Schools Project for Encouraging Creativity. The validating criterion used was the Torrance Test of Creative Thinking, Figural and Verbal. The results of the study show that those who perform high on the Torrance Tests also score high on the Williams inventory and vice versa in the case of low scores.

The author concludes that the validated inventory is a workable instrument for measuring the effective behaviors of creative personalities as outlined in his model.

Discussion: Williams states that the number of subjects in the study is 94; the table to which he refers accounts for only 35. No explanation is given for the difference.

Sample items of the Williams inventory are quite different in a restrictive sense. For example, in the question—"I am inquisitive about things, like looking into a mirror"—his attempt at providing an example of inquisitiveness seems instead to bring about closure, inhibiting more than eliciting a response. Looking into a mirror may be less interesting and more vanity-laden than attempting to find out how one works. All of his sample items seem to "close inward" like this.

Compared to Khatena (I am an imaginative person, a dreamer or visionary), Rimm and Davis (I like to make up my own songs) and Torrance (Becomes absorbed in tasks), the Williams items may be too confining in their structure.

There is some question in my mind as to whether or not Williams has really separated cognitive from affective behavior and is indeed really measuring the same thing under different labels, but this is a question which is not pertinent to the direction of this paper.

CONCLUSION

The use of personality inventories as tests of creative potential has been well established by many fields not directly related to education (Whiting, 1973). Based on the four representative studies presented here, screening devices in programs for the gifted based on personality inventories, offer a possible solution in helping to locate creative populations.

Most current inventories have had significant but low validation scores when tested against other criteria of creative ability. They have very high reliability scores which indicate consistency in their ability to measure creative potential. They are simple to administer, score, costs are minimal. These are all important indicators of a useful test. However, there are several problems which must be considered in the overall research of these inventories.

The most successful tests so far have dealt with adolescents and adults. Tests at the elementary level are minimal; at the early elementary level several difficulties are apparent. These difficulties involve test construction and validation.

Studies generally, with exceptions noted, have all dealt with a relatively honogeneous population based on combinations of the middle class, college student, teacher, adolescent and adult. These inventories have not addressed to any great extent the variables of sex, age, environment, socio-economic, cultural or ethnic differences.

But even with consideration given to all of the difficulties in developing a useable, valid and reliable screening inventory for the creatively gifted, the results so far have been encouraging. We may, in the not too distant future, be close to insuring a better means of locating our "wild ducks."

References

Adkins and Ballif *Animal Crackers Motivation Test* K–1(1973) Monterey, Calif.: CTB/McGraw-Hill.

Anastasi A., and Schaefer, C. Note on the concepts of creativity and intelligence. *Journal of Creative Behavior,* 1971, *5,* 113–116.

Barbe, W. B., and Renzulli, J. S. *The psychology and education of the gifted.* New York: Irvington Pub., 1975.

Barron, F. The dream of art and poetry. *Psychology Today,* 1968, *2,* 18–23.

Bledsoe, J. C., and Khatena, J. Factor analytic study of something about myself. *Psychological Reports,* 1973, *32,* 1176–1178.

Crockenburg, S., Creativity tests—boon or boondoggle for education? *Review of educational research,* 1972, *43,* 27–45.

Davis, G. A. In frumious pursuit of the creative person. *The journal of creative behavior,* 1975, *9,* 75–87.

Davis, G. A., and Belcher, T. L. How shall creativity tests be measured? Torrance tests, RAT, alpha biographical, IQ. *Journal of Creative Behavior,* 1971, *5,* 153–161.

DeHaan and Havighurst, *Educating gifted children.* Chicago: University of Chicago Press, 1972.

Dice, M. In search of creativity: some current literature. *Gifted Child Quarterly,* 1976, *XX,* 196–204.

Duckworth, E. The having of wonderful ideas. *Harvard educational review,* 1972, *42,* 217–231.

Getzels and Jackson, *Creativity and intelligence*. New York: Wiley, 1962.

Guilford, J. P. *Intelligence, creativity and their educational implications*. San Diego: Knapp, 1968.

Guilford, J. P. Varieties of creative giftedness, their measurement and development. *Gifted Child Quarterly*, 1975, *XIX*, 107–121.

Guilford, J. P. Aptitude for creative thinking: one or many? *Journal of Creative Behavior*, 1976, *10*, 165–169.

Gowan, J. The relationship between creativity and giftedness. *Gifted Child Quarterly*, 1971, *15*, 239–243.

Gowan, J. and Torrance, P. *Educating the ablest*. Itaska, Illinois: Peacock Pub., 1975.

Hasen and Butcher, Creativity and Intelligence. *British Journal of Psychology*, 1966, *57*, 120–135.

Jackson and Messnick The person, the product and the response: conceptual problems in the assessment of creativity. *Journal of Personality and Social Psychology*, 1965, *33*, 309–329.

Jay, E. S. *A Book About Me Personality Test K–1* (1952) Chicago: Science Research Associates.

Johnson, R. A. Teacher and student perception of student creativity. *Gifted Child Quarterly*, 1976, *XX*, 164–168.

Kaltsounis, B. Further validity on something about myself. *Perceptual and motor skills*, 1975, *40*, 94.

Khatena, J. Some problems in the measurement of creative behavior. *Journal of Research and Development in Education*, 1971a, *4*, 74–80.

Khatena, J. Something about myself: a brief screening device for identifying creatively gifted children and adults. *Gifted Child Quarterly*, 1971b, *15*, 262–266.

Khatena, J. Educating the gifted child: challenge and response in the USA. *Gifted Child Quarterly*, 1976. *XX*, 76–87.

Klausmeier, H. J. *Learning and human abilities*. New York: Harper & Row, 1971.

Lesher, R. *Assessment of creativity*. Trenton, New Jersey: New Jersey Department of Education, 1973.

Ogletree, E. J. Are creativity tests valid in cultures outside the United States? *Journal of Research and Development in Education*, 1971, *4*, 129–130.

Payne, D. A., Halpin, W. G. Ellet, C. D., Dale, J. B. General personality correlates of creative personality in academically and artistically gifted youth. *Journal of Special Education*, 1975, *9*, 105–108.

Rimm, S. and Davis, G. A. GIFT an instrument for the identification of creativity. *Journal of Creative Behavior*, 1976, *10*, 178–182.

Roslansky, *Creativity at the nobel conference*. Amsterdam: North Holland Press, 1970.

Rosner, and Abt *Essays in creativity*. Croton-on-Hudson, New York: North Riverside, Press, 1974.

Rossiman and Horn, Cognitive, motivational and temperamental indicants of creativity and intelligence. *Journal of educational measurement*, 1971, *9*, 265–286.

Schubert, Intelligence as necessary but not sufficient for creativity. *Journal of Genetic Psychology*, 1973, *122*, 45–47.

Shouksmith, *Intelligence, creativity and cognitive style*. London: Batsford, 1970.

Stein and Heinze, *Creativity and the individual*. Illinois: Free Press of Glencoe, 1960.

Taylor and Getzels, *Perspectives in creativity*. Chicago: Aldine Press, 1972.

Theobald, T. and White, K. How to unstuff a wild duck. *Journal of Creative Behavior*, 1974, *8*, 78–80.

Torrance, P. Some validity studies of two brief screening devices for studying the creative personality. *Journal of Creative Behavior*, 1971, *5*, 94–103.

Treffinger, D. J., Renzulli, J. S., and Feldhusen, J. F. Problems in the assessment of creative thinking. *Journal of Creative Behavior*, 1971, *5*, 104–112.

Treffinger, D. J., and Poggio, J. P. Needed research on the measurement of creativity. *Journal of Creative Behavior*, 1972, *6*, 253–267.

Ward, W. C. Convergent and divergent measurement of creativity in children. *Educational and Psychological Measurement*, 1975, *35*, 87–95.

Whiting, B. G. How to predict creativity from biographical data. *Journal of Creative Behavior*, 1973, *7*, 201–207.

Williams, F. E. Assessing pupil-Teacher behaviors related to a cognitive-affective teaching model. *Journal of Research and Development in Education*, 1971, *4*, 14–21.

Yamamoto, K. Validation of tests of creative thinking; a review of some studies. *Exceptional Children*, 1965, *31*, 281–290.

Zegas, J. A validation study of tests from the divergent production plans of the Guilford structure-of-intellect model. *Journal of Creative Behavior*, 1976, *10*, 170–177.

VII

GUIDANCE

23. THE COUNSELOR AND THE CREATIVE CHILD

John C. Gowan and George D. Demos

What can a counselor do to help a child become more creative? As educators have grown more cognizant of and interested in creativity, this question has become more important. It has also become more obvious that creativity development and preservation is not purely a curriculum matter, but depends upon interpersonal relationships, and guidance can be a factor in promoting these. Although there has been little written upon the subject, we can learn a good deal by looking at the personality of the creative child, and then discovering what aspects can best be promoted by guidance.

The first point to note about the creative child is that he is usually well-adjusted, mature for his age, fully-functioning, and responsible. He is in this respect opposite of the delinquent. Dr. Paul Torrance, of the University of Minnesota, upon being asked, "What makes a child creative?" replied: "Anything that makes him *more* alive." This zest for living and acme of mental and physical health is often evident in bright, creative children. Whatever guidance can do to help a child to better mental health and maturity will aid what creativity he may possess.

It should, perhaps, be noted that in advocating guidance for children, we do not imply that guidance will produce creativity, but only that it will bring it out and make it manifest. It is probable that most of our educational aids to children merely *preserve* rather than *produce* their creative functions. Children are naturally creative and only require the right atmosphere to manifest it.

A second point for the counselor is to help the child to value. A child needs to value himself and to have his ideas valued before he can value others or their ideas. Counselors should therefore help children build a consistent value system—the children's not the counselors. The values a creative child builds may flow from his divergent thinking, and hence he may not wish to emulate grown-up models. This includes the counselors' values, and as a result may cause problems, but it is important to remember that it is *his* values and *not ours* which are being built.

A third point that counselors need to remember is that creative thinking takes place only when other higher-priority systems have been satisfied. A child's basic needs come *before* the luxury of cognitive actualization. Body needs, safety, love, social-ego needs, and others in the Maslow hierarchy cannot be paramount in a child who is willing to risk "ego-capital" on creative effort. A child who is thinking about what others may think about him, or if his place with them is insecure enough to be of concern to him, cannot be expected to be creative. This implies that counselors need to help children "be themselves" (congruent) enough so that they can shut out their social anxieties long enough to be creative. Only a counselor who *values differences* rather

Reprinted by permission of the authors and *Gifted Child Quarterly*, Vol. 9, No. 3, 1965.

than conformity in children can be supportive enough of these differences he finds to foster creativity.

Being creative is similar to "mining ore" from the subconscious. Yet many of us, children included, are afraid to "mine this lode" systematically for fear of some of the frightening or unpleasant things that may emerge. Counselors should give children, (1) the confidence to pull latent ideas from their preconscious minds, (2) the patience to examine each idea carefully, and (3) the ability to make the mind tranquil enough so that this kind of inner exploration can take place. Often the "ore comes out in an unpolished form," and the child may easily reject something, which with development and polishing could represent real value. Calm acceptance, understanding and positive reinforcement with the suspension of harsh evaluative processes at this time is exceedingly important for the successful experience and continuation of being creative. The child needs this experience, and he can best effect suspension of evaluation himself, when he is in the presence of a supportive, non-directive, non-evaluative person such as the effective counselor.

The fourth point for counselors to promote is the process of helping children channel their creative thrust and aggressiveness into constructive and not destructive channels. Creative children are going to be *nonconformists*. We can help them become constructive rather than nonconstructive noncomformists. The difference is often so subtle as to be imperceptible to many adult eyes, but whereas the constructive noncomformist is *situational* and *selective* in his aggressive attack on society and its ills, the nonconstructive, nonconformist is *compulsive* and *nondiscriminative* in attacking everybody and everything. As Sylvia Ashton Warner so well stated: "A child's mind is a twin fountain of creativeness and destructiveness, and the more open we keep the creative fountain, the more we help to close the destructive one." We need therefore to watch the ambivalence creative children have toward creativeness-destructiveness, and to help them channel their energy in the positive diastole into constructive action, and in the negative diastole into harmless outlets—like thrashing around and making splashes in a swimming pool. In the beginning, even creative children do not distinguish much between being creative and being destructive—both are an expression of sheer energy and libido. If the creative actions are not more rewarded than the destructive ones, it will be difficult for a wise counselor to untangle the child.

A fifth point for the counselor is to provide the emotional support for the child to become able to participate in peak experiences in the Maslovian sense. Peak experiences are often found in creative people, and they require a narrowing and constricting of attention so that a new perspective emerges. Such experiences also require psychological courage to give of oneself. They also produce a sense of strangeness, awe, and even a sense of the mystic in some people. These conditions require counseling support for many children. Just as oxygen may be required by the extended, perspiring athlete as well as the expiring invalid, so generous amounts of counseling may be necessary at the time of peak experiences as well as the removal of psychopathology.

The sixth point is there will be many times when the creative child finds himself either alone, neglected, ignored, or unrewarded as a result of a creative response on his part. Both his peers and his adult acquaintances will on occasion fail to appreciate or even notice some of his creative actions, and at other times they may vociferously oppose them. In fact, many creative children have the experience of having their ideas turned down before examination, because the creative child in enunciating the idea sometimes engenders opposition to it by his manner or approach; whereas, the same idea may later be advocated by some more popular or high status member of the group and it will be readily adopted or rewarded. Thus, it is only natural that creative children may become somewhat embittered under these circumstances. They may wish to withdraw from the group, engage in passive resistance, or "reform" and conform for the sake of external reward. The counselor should talk with such children, and try to point out that to take any of these steps is to deny their gift. He can help them to reward themselves, to intrinsically value their own efforts, and learn to "market their different ideas." *Benjamin Franklin's Autobiography* contains a famous and helpful recital of his early difficulties in this regard. The counselor may not be able to improve the *external situation,* but he can aid the child in understanding the *internal* one; namely, his own feelings. This may be sufficient.

Finally, the seventh point, guidance for the creative involves the realization that counseling is not just the solving of problems, but a positive process promoting mental health. This is important for all students, but it is vital for creative children. We have found, in an institute for promoting creativity in children, that gifted children willingly sought and absorbed the counselor's efforts when on a 1/25 counselor-client ratio, which is twelve times the concentration of guidance, (1/300 ratio), recommended by Dr. James Conant and others. In order to deal with more complex problems, to bring into concert and focus more kinds of abilities, in longer process sequences, for more constructive endeavors under conditions of less external reward, *the creative youth needs a higher level of mental health than the average youngster.* He needs it so that he can handle without disabling stress, keep in tension longer the problems which he can cope with, and the solutions which he alone can find. Like the diver whose oxygen supply enables him to stay under water longer, he is better equipped for the strange conditions under which he must labor. Thus, we *can* enhance the creativity of those who are highly able cognitively and highly sound emotionally—May we be more successful at this most important task.

References

Conant, J. B. *The American High School Today.* New York: McGraw-Hill Co., 1959.

Damos, G. D. "Guidance and Counseling with the Ablest" (pp. 75–8) in Gowan, J. C. and Demos, G. D. Editors *The Guidance of Exceptional Children.* New York: David McKay Co., 1965.

Gowan, J. C. "The Organization of Guidance for Gifted Children" *Personnel and Guidance Journal* 39:275–279, Dec. 1960.

Gowan, J. C. and Demos, G. D. *The Education and Guidance of the Ablest.* Springfield, Ill.: Charles C. Thomas, 1965.

Maslow, A. H. *Religious, Values and Peak Experiences.* Columbus: Ohio State University Press, 1964.

24. MANAGING THE "POST PARTUM" DEPRESSION IN CREATIVE INDIVIDUALS

John C. Gowan and George D. Demos

The phenomenon of "post-partum depression" in biological creativity is well-known, but little understood, and with less knowledge regarding its psychodynamics. A depressed period after childbirth is not rare in women. To be sure, this phenomenon is not always found, particularly in those in robust physical or mental health, but is more usually seen in cases where energies are lowered. Because an analogous situation seems to exist in persons who are mentally rather than "physically creative," we have called attention to this "post-partum" phenomenon together with some suggestions for its management. Numerous, similar reports in cases of artists, writers, musicians, actors, composers, and other creatives indicate that this problem is a general one. It has also been noted to occur after creative but more mundane occurrences such as giving a public address, cooking a meal successfully, helping a client in psychotherapy, hosting a party, teaching a class, etc., and has also been found in adolescent students.

There is often a feeling at such a time that "the best has gone out of one." The word "spent" which also applies to the physical situation is apposite here; one feels "used up"; muscle tonus is flaccid and slack; one doubts that one can ever do anything else; there may even be a death wish, or a desire to punish oneself. Let us examine why this is so, and what may be done about it:

In the first place it should be pointed out that creativity is a gift from what Erikson (1950) calls the narcissistic or initiative period of life which occupies the child from age four to about seven. The positive side of this period is a thrusting initiative which carries the child into various dimensions of discovery; the negative side is the immobilization of inner fear and outside prohibitions. Because the child at this stage discovers choice, he also discovers what Skinner (1965) refers to as aversive consequences. In the previous autonomy stage the child's failure to perform as society demands is a vice, for it is something (such as bladder accidents) which he cannot control—but now the child discovers that there are sins of commission, engendered by making the wrong choices, and this invests choice-making with special dangers. The joy and sheer delight (the German *Lust* is comparable) which the child finds in all kinds of new and creative discoveries is balanced by the guilt which society's sanctions against some of these efforts bring home to him in the form of myriad reinforcements (Skinner, 1965). Thus we have a balance of initiative and joy on one side and immobilization and guilt on the other.

All children go through this state, but the creative child appears to get more out of it. Perhaps this is due to the affectional approach of the opposite sexed parent at this time, whose warmth puts a higher valence on creative activities, making available more preconscious areas in the reach of the ego. But at any rate, the *fantasy* of this period for most children is more of a *reality* for creative children. Whereas some children seen almost to have aborted this stage of development, the creative child seems to have "overstayed his leave in this kingdom," and its doors to fantasy are always "left slightly ajar." In a sense this is the opposite of regression, but it tends to throw the psychic energies slightly out of line. In particular the creative individual is

Reprinted by permission of the authors.

apt to retain a super-abundance of initiative and joy in activity and discovery, only later to pay for this outburst of energy, by a slack time characterized by guilt and immobilization.

What can the counselor, teacher, psychologist or friend do to help the creative person who is in this depressed phase of such a cycle? A number of suggestions seem to be pertinent that can be ameliorative and therapeutic if not wholly regenerative:

1. An understanding and empathic discussion of the previous rationale may in itself be enough to help the client, who may come to see that this is part of a *normal not an abnormal process and does not signify a pathological condition.* A characteristic of cyclic or periodic processes is that conditions are certain to change. Frequently just being available for help is very therapeutic.

2. It is important for all to realize that descents from peak experiences (and creativity in any form is a peak experience) are apt to be disappointing. The frustration at the loss of pleasure is frequently associated with the appearance of certain types of brain waves on the electro-encephalogram (EEG) as the individual vainly tries to maintain the pleasurable level. Whenever one's schedule of positive reinforcement or reward has been disturbed, it is apt to be somewhat distasteful. Moodiness is an interim method the ego utilizes in solving this loss of pleasure without an outburst of hostility.

3. The creative client needs to be made cognizant of the fact that *there is no evidence that creativity is limited or completely spent—once used;* on the contrary, all evidence points to the fact that it is like a well which soon refills when we dip water out of it; and that like most other powers, *it improves when fully functioning and actualized.*

4. The creative individual should know that while a pause and rest after a creative effort is natural and normal, *there is no evidence that it must be a depressive pause;* as a part of the natural rhythm it can be as refreshing as sleep after physical love.

5. *It can help to make the creative person aware that depression may be felt in part because the creative gift is not at first valued by others.* The creator may have been conditioned too much to expect his rewards extrinsically from society, and not enough to enjoy the intrinsic rewards of the creative act itself. *It is in action not accolade where we come to terms with our identity in full functioning* (This is, however, a high level form of functioning and may not be achieved but by a small number of self-actualized individuals).

6. *Creative people have need to be valued.* As a mother wishes her child to be appreciated, so creative people need valuation and love after their exertions. Those who are close to creative children, adolescents, and adults should remember to give them such valuing (unconditional positive regard—Rogers, 1961), during and following the time of creative activity. Otherwise the ego is thrown back on self reward and this may tend to make it a prey of depression on the down cycle.

Therapeutic aids of these sorts to creative people during and after creative performance may prevent them from developing neurotic symptoms which tend to represent a "dark valley" for some creative individuals. It is not necessary for creative youth to develop these patterns any more than it is a rule for all mothers to suffer "post-patrum" depression. Some persons who *might otherwise be creative,* learn to control, permit to lie dormant or block it because of their fear of the guilt they experience afterward; others become too inhibited to use their full initiative in a joyful venturing forth. In any case, the world as well as the individual loses.

Thus, guidance which is important for all persons during their formative years is absolutely vital for the creatives (Gowan and Demos, 1964–65). For in order to deal with more complex aspects of problems and to bring into focus more kinds of abilities in longer process sequences, for more creative endeavors, under conditions of less external reward, the creative youth needs a higher level of mental health than the average. He needs this so that he can handle without disabling stress the problems he alone can cope with. *We can enhance creative performance in those who in addition to being highly able cognitively are highly sound emotionally.*

References

Erikson, E. H. *Childhood and Society,* W. W. Norton & Co., New York, 1950.

Gowan, J. C. and Demos, G. D. *The Education and Guidance of the Ablest,* Charles C Thomas, Publisher, Springfield, Illinois, 1964.

Gowan, J. C. and Demos, G. D. "Counselor and the Creative Child," Mimeograph, California State College at Long Beach, Fall, 1965.

Rioch, M. J. in Farnsworth, P. R., Editor, *Annual Review of Psychology,* Annual Review, Inc. Palo Alto, California, 1965, pp. 193–96.

Rogers, C. R. *On Becoming a Person: A Therapist's View of Psychotherapy,* Houghton Mifflin Co., Boston, 1961.

Skinner, B. F. "Why Teachers Fail," *Saturday Review,* October 16, 1965, p. 80.

25. UNDERSTANDING CREATIVITY IN TALENTED STUDENTS

E. Paul Torrance

COUNSELING PROBLEMS OF HIGHLY CREATIVE INDIVIDUALS

Isolation and Estrangement from Peers and Teachers. On the basis of information developed through our research with children in the early school years and by Getzels and Jackson in the high school years, I would suspect that a large share of the highly creative individual's personal problems are likely to be centered in his psychological isolation and estrangement from his peers and teachers. It will be no news to counselors that peer groups exercise rather severe sanctions against their most creative members. In no group thus far studied has the author failed to find relatively clear evidence of the operation of these pressures. Both sociometric studies and small-group experiments have thus far been used. Both types of study have yielded many clues for helping youngsters avoid some of the severity of peer sanctions without sacrificing their creativity. Since the results of the experimental study are simpler and more straightforward, only this study will be described.

In this study (Torrance, 1959) we formed groups of five children, and in each we placed one of the most creative children in the class, as identified by tests administered earlier. We then placed each group in a situation requiring creative thinking and involving competition among groups. This situation permitted the group to experiment for 25 minutes trying to discover all the things which could be done with a box of science toys and the principles whereby they worked. After a period of 5 minutes for planning demonstrations and explanations, each group was given 25 minutes in which to present their demonstrations and explanations. The focus of observation was upon the techniques used by the groups to control the most creative member and the strategies of the most creative member in coping with these pressures. Much of the behavior observed suggests that in many cases the highly creative individual may be responsible for his own woes.

At the second-grade level, the most highly creative individuals were generally quite unpleasant, showing little consideration for the group, little or no goal orientation, little or no identification with the group, and little or no heed to the leadership attempts of their less creative peers. In the third grade, the most creative subjects tended to work independently and were ignored for the most part. This tendency persisted into the fourth grade, where the most creative members assumed little responsibility for leadership and were given little credit in the final ratings for the important contributions which they actually made to the group's success. The highly creative subjects in the fifth grade manifested more leadership attempts and were more dominant than in the fourth grade but brought upon themselves open criticism and attack for "being too scientific," "being too greedy," and the like. These tendencies became more pronounced in the sixth-grade groups.

An examination of almost any of the many lists of personality characteristics of highly creative individuals suggests a number of quite valid reasons why such individuals alienate their peers and elders. In our studies it has certainly become quite obvious that many of the highly creative individuals are disturbing elements in classroom groups in elementary schools. The prob-

Reprinted by permission from *The Guidance of Exceptional Children*, May 1965.

lem of teachers and guidance workers resolves itself into one of helping highly creative individuals maintain those characteristics which seem essential to the development of creative talent and at the same time helping them acquire skills for avoiding or reducing to a tolerable level the peer sanctions.

Stein (1956) has offered a set of interesting suggestions concerning the social role of the creative industrial researcher. If we translate Stein's principles to teachers and guidance workers, the objective in helping highly creative youngsters would run something like the following: Help the highly creative child to maintain his assertiveness without being hostile and aggressive. He must be aware of his superiors, peers, and subordinates as persons. He may work alone, but he must not be isolated, withdrawn, or uncommunicative. He must "know his place" without being timid, submissive, or acquiescent and must "speak his mind" without being domineering. As he tries to gain a point, he can be subtle but not cunning or manipulative. In all relationships, he must be sincere, honest, purposeful, and diplomatic but not unwilling to accept "short cuts." In the intellectual area, he must learn to be broad without spreading himself too thin, deep without being "bookish" or "too scientific," and "sharp" without being overcritical.

The model above obviously asks much of the child, but at least it provides a model which the highly creative child apparently needs to achieve, and it should challenge the imaginative counselor.

"Unrealistic" Career Choices. The career aspirations of highly creative students are sure to puzzle the counselor and to seem unrealistic. Getzels and Jackson's data throw some light upon this problem. When their highly intelligent and highly creative subjects were asked (Getzels and Jackson, 1959), on sentence-completion type questionnaires, to state the kinds of occupations they would like to have, the Creatives gave a significantly greater variety of occupations than did the highly intelligent group. When the occupations reported were divided into conventional and unconventional categories (e.g., doctor, engineer, businessman, etc., were classified as conventional; inventor, artist, spaceman, disk jockey, as unconventional), 18 per cent of the highly intelligent group gave unconventional career aspirations; 67 per cent of the high Creatives gave such aspirations.

I would also like to mention another problem regarding career choice, which has been discussed in detail by Anne Roe (1959). This problem concerns the highly creative and talented individual from the lower socioeconomic class. Even in the grade school, such an individual is likely to suffer as a consequence of the differences in the value structure of the home and those built into the educational career required for a full-fledged career as a creative scientist. Roe particularly emphasizes some of the hazards inherent in current national testing programs and efforts to urge talented youngsters to go to college and to prepare for careers in science. Counselors should be aware of the conflicts such youngsters are likely to experience. Both the lower and higher socioeconomic classes tend to devaluate scientific careers. She maintains that many scholarship students are likely to drop out in college because they do not become members of any in-group in college. She suggests that personnel workers give consideration to establishing the kinds of in-groups in which such individuals can obtain support.

Another career choice problem quite likely to exist among highly creative individuals concerns the choice made because it provides a technique for handling a particular personal problem. Their curiosity and their searching is for a solution to a personality problem. Roe (1959) maintains that in such cases all may go well as long as the individual is still climbing in his career and still has hopes of solving his problem. When the apex is reached, however, he may experience depression and become unproductive. Individuals so motivated in their career choices may be blocked in finding the solution to problems; they "just can't see the answer." Some such individuals are noted for their compulsive repetitions of experiments and inability to complete a task. Counselors could probably assist here by helping them to understand the nature of their creative processes and to seek psychotherapy. Successful psychotherapy is more likely to unlock greater powers of creativity than to destroy creative genius.

Values and Attitudes. The counselor should also recognize that the values and attitudes of the highly creative student are likely to be different from those of other students. The very fact that he is capable of divergent thinking, has unusual ideas, and is independent in his thinking in itself is likely to make his values and attitudes different from the norms of his group. Some of these differences are highlighted in the Getzels and Jackson (1959) study. They found that for the high IQ group, the rank-order correlation between the qualities they would like for themselves and the qualities making for adult success was .81; for the high Creativity group it was .10. Among the highly intelligent, the correlation between the qualities they desire and the qualities they believe teachers favor was .67; for the highly creative group, it was minus .25. In other words, the highly creative student desires personal qualities having little relationship to those which he believes make for adult success and which are in some ways the opposite of those he believes his teachers favor. Thus, counselors should recognize that the desire to emulate the teacher is absent or weak among creative students.

Getzels and Jackson (1959) also found a certain mocking attitude on the part of the Creatives toward what they call the "All-American Boy"—a theme almost totally lacking in the stories of the highly intelligent group. Again, this highlights the counselor's problem in helping the highly creative student to learn to be independent without being obnoxious.

HELPING TEACHERS UNDERSTAND THE CREATIVE STUDENT

In closing, I would like to discuss briefly the problem of the counselor in helping teachers understand the highly creative student. In attempting to do this, the counselor should recognize that highly creative students think up many things which are difficult for teachers to cope with. Many of the most highly creative subjects in our studies in the early school years are almost famous for their skill in thinking up ideas for being naughty as well as for their wild or silly ideas. Few teachers are likely to respond as did one of the third-grade teachers in our study, who commented to me: "Even if you do not learn anything from the data you have collected, the study has changed the school and the way we teachers look at our students. For example, we no longer look upon them as being naughty but as creating ideas for being naughty." This difference at first glance might seem too subtle, but I think it is an important one.

As I have discussed the matter at length in another paper (1959), I shall only list what I think the counselor can do to help the teacher to understand the highly creative student and help him develop his creative thinking to its fullest degree. I believe that the counselor can help the teacher to:

1. Learn to value creative thinking and to forge an environment which places value on creative activity so that the highly creative student will not have to exist as a miserable deviate in the shadow of his more socially successful peers.

2. Find ways of assisting children to be more sensitive to environmental stimuli and to trust their own perception of reality.
3. Permit and encourage manipulation of objects and ideas.
4. Lead students to test systematically each new idea.
5. Develop tolerance of new ideas.
6. Beware of forcing a set pattern.
7. Develop a creative classroom atmosphere.
8. Teach the child to value his own creative thinking.
9. Teach skills for avoiding peer sanctions.
10. Understand the creative process and share this understanding with pupils.
11. Dispel the sense of awe of masterpieces.
12. Encourage and evaluate self-initiated learning.
13. Create "thorns in the flesh," to be sensitive to defects, to recognize the disturbing element.
14. Create necessities for creative thinking.
15. Provide for both active and quiet times for the production of ideas.
16. Make available resources for working out ideas.
17. Encourage the habit of working out the full implication of ideas.
18. Develop constructive criticism—not just criticism.
19. Encourage acquisition of knowledge in a variety of fields.
20. Become more adventurous-spirited.

SUMMARY

In summary, I would maintain that counselors and guidance workers should be concerned about understanding creativity in talented students. Such an understanding is important from the standpoint of personality development and mental health, the acquisition of knowledge and understanding, vocational success, and social welfare. A variety of materials are being developed and tested for identifying creative thinking at all educational levels and for guiding its fuller development. New directions have been toward the development of procedures for identifying creative talent at an early age and for understanding its development during the important early school years. The direction has been toward materials which can be manipulated and which yield such measures as Inventivlevel, Spontaneous Flexibility, and Constructiveness; materials which permit exploration through "asking" and "guessing" (formulating hypotheses) concerning the causes and consequences of behavior; and the like.

Both measures of IQ and measures of creativity appear to be essential in identifying giftedness. In spite of large differences in mean IQ (23 to 26 IQ points), elementary and secondary school pupils high on creativity but not high on IQ achieve as well as those high on IQ but not on creativity, as measured by standardized achievement tests. Children high on measures of creativity appear to become alienated from peers and teachers and manifest behaviors which elicit pressures from their peers.

Counselors need to understand the special blockages to the development of creative thinking. Among those which appear most prominent and obvious are the following: premature attempts on the part of parents and teachers to eliminate fantasy, restrictions on manipulativeness and curiosity, overemphasis on prevention, overemphasis on sex roles, fear and timidity, emphasis in education on verbal skills, and limitations of resources for working out ideas.

Major counseling problems presented by the highly creative student are likely to center around his isolation and estrangement from his peers and teachers, what appear to be "unrealistic" career choices, divergent values and attitudes, and the like. Counselors can possibly do much by working with teachers to help them understand the creativity in talented students and to use procedures which will implement the greater development of creative thinking in all students.

26. GUIDING THE CREATIVE DEVELOPMENT OF THE GIFTED AND TALENTED

John Curtis Gowan

Our title carries five key words which need explication before they can be put together for discussion. *Development* assumes that our subject is part of developmental life process, similar to growth but differing from it in being discontinuous and qualitative whereas growth is continuous and quantative. *Creative* assumes that creativity is the actuality of which giftedness is the potentiality, and that it can be enhanced as part of the developmental process. *Gifted* and *talented* can be defined as the potential for verbal and non-verbal creativity respectively. And *guidance* can be assumed as necessary to facilitate the process of creative development across developmental stage discontinuities. Admittedly, these are brief and incomplete definitions and assumptions but they show the course of our discussion.

We are interested in the gifted because they form the easiest identifiable pool of potentially verbally creative adults. (For Talented we may substitute "non-verbally creative"). The maximization of the creative abilities of its members is an imperative for the future welfare of our society. We are just beginning to realize (Simonton 1978) that renaissances depend upon the bunching of creative persons in societies, and that since we now have the technology to control and augment this factor, we have the power to produce a *permanent* renaissance in culture. This fact alone gives this essay its import.

Differentiated guidance for the gifted in order to make them creative rests on the following assumptions:

1. We want to increase the percent of creative adults in society.
2. The gifted offer the most likely pool of such identifiable talent.
3. We want to facilitate the on schedule accomplishment of cognitive and affective developmental tasks, according to the developmental stage theory.
4. Since the theory assumes discontinuities between stages, guidance is the best method for facilitating escalation over the discontinuities.
5. Guidance is also concerned with individual problems associated with acceleration of the individual in some cognitive stages.
6. Since this guidance is pointed toward creativity, it will be preventative, developmental and maintenance in form rather than crisis oriented. While all children will need developmental guidance, gifted children must have it if an enriched proportion of them are to become creative adults. Hence the developmental guidance for the gifted must be differentiated.

The concept of differentiated guidance for the gifted in order to make them creative is a very new idea. In order to introduce it properly, it is perhaps best to take a look at history. The concept of guidance itself is less old than the century. First it was assumed that the only kind of guidance needed was vocational guidance. Truman Kelley did the first dissertation on educational

This article contains material from Gowan 1960, 1964, 1965, 1971, 1977, and from an editorial in *Gifted Child Quarterly,* Vol. 21, 1977.

guidance in 1915, and John Brewer wrote the first book on educational guidance in the 1920's, but these ideas were considered radical before World War II. Indeed the APGA's *Personal and Guidance Journal* was called *Occupations* until 1952. After the G.I. Bill of the 1940's and NDEA in the 1950's educational guidance came of age and was accepted in American education. At that time some nonconformists, such as the writer, suggested that special guidance might be needed for gifted underachievers (1955), and later (1964) that all gifted children needed differentiated guidance. This was a part of the dawning conception that special guidance was needed by exceptional and disadvantaged children also. It took time for these new ideas to sink in, and further time for differentiated techniques to be discovered and accepted. Much depended on the concept of developmental guidance developed by Blocher in 1966. Those who didn't see why the gifted needed guidance in the sixties had their counterparts in the twenties in those who didn't see that anyone needed guidance. So it is not surprising that the concept of differentiated guidance for the gifted (in order to facilitate their creativity) is a difficult idea to get across.

In the *Development of the Creative Individual*, (Gowan: 1972:73–4) the central argument regarding the creative development of gifted persons was laid out as follows:

In particular, it has not been realized that the more complex developmental processes reached by a few through their intense reactions to enriched environmental stimulation offer a promise of future development for the many.

Two developmental principles have been indicated heretofore as in operation:

(1) Functions which emerge spasmodically or periodically at earlier stages may be performed more regularly or continuously at higher stages.
(2) An accomplishment held tenuously only in conditions of peak experience or great mental health will in later development persevere and be present under conditions of more stress.
(3) Performance reached first by a few superior individuals in a culture will later be reached by more, and, eventually, by the representative members of the culture.
(4) What first appears as a phenomenon gradually becomes a norm.

This is certainly the time for some thoughtful reader to ask why it is necessary to talk about superior individuals at all if one is discussing a developmental problem. This question deserves a careful answer.

(1) By superior individual we mean an individual of superior intelligence which would place him in the top two stanines or the upper 11 percent. (It is indeed possible that the future will go to an operational definition of giftedness which is that a "gifted" child is one that has the potentiality to become creative. If this is true, the definition of giftedness on the IQ scale will need to be dropped to about 120, or top 10 to 11 percent). The basis of experience indicates that these individuals are more likely to become self-actualized than others. Maslow (1954, pp. 202–03), in his famous study, picked no historical figures who were not in this category; indeed, it would be difficult to describe a self-actualized cretin. Let the reader pick his own candidate for self-actualization and then discover if he is not of this level of intelligence.
(2) Such individuals appear to have a longer mental growth span than others. They appear to continue growing in mental age even into their seniority (whereas others decline) according to the Terman study (1954) followup, which found mental age still increasing at age 50.

(3) Superior individuals seem to have a "higher ceiling," permitting them access into higher developmental stages which ordinary people seldom attain. This is like "overdrive" on an expensive car.

(4) Superior individuals accomplish cognitive tasks more quickly and hence go through stages more thoroughly. They, therefore, develop more fully during their life span than do others.

(5) The mental capacities of the superior individual help him with cognitive tasks, just as improved mental health helps him with affective tasks; both are needed to meet the dual nature of developmental stages.

(6) Superior individuals first reach new levels of performance and exhibit them only spasmodically or tenuously. Later in evolutionary progress, such attainment will be reached by more individuals and eventually by representative individuals in a culture. It is to the development of the superior individual, therefore, that we must look for a clue to the future developmental potential of the species.

DEVELOPMENTAL STAGE THEORY AND GUIDANCE IMPLICATIONS

Maslow (1954), Piaget (1950) and Sullivan (1953) have all stated that there are qualitatively different developmental stages, each with different specific emphases. If such discontinuous stages exist, then a prime task of guidance is to facilitate transfer from one stage to another smoothing over the break. Piaget (1950) identified cognitive developmental stages, and Erikson affective developmental stages (1950). Kohlberg (1972) similarly identified moral growth stages, and Simpson did the same for the psychomotor (1966). Indeed, the concept of developmental stages seems to be one whose time has come. Says Dr. Stephen Bailey (1971):

> It seems to me that the most liberating and viable educational reforms of the next several years will come through the building of curricular and other educative activities around some of the developmental insights of men like Piaget, Bruner, Erikson, Bloom, and Maslow. Although much separates these scholars in terms of analytic style and specific fields of concentration, they all seem to hold to the idea that human beings go through fairly discrete stages of development and that each stage calls for rather special educational treatment. And all of these men seem to be united in their belief that the maximization of human potential within the constraints of each life stage is the best way of preparing for succeeding stages.

In *The Development of the Creative Individual* (1972) the writer stated the new hypotheses as a set of theorems:

1. Developmental process is best understood by conceptualization of the Erikson-Piaget-Gowan periodic table of developmental stages, consisting of triads, thus:

Latency	Identity	Creativity
1. Trust-Sensori-Motor	2. Autonomy-Prooperational	3. Initiative-Intuitive
4. Industry-Concrete Operations	5. Identify-Formal Operations	6. Intimacy-Creativity
7. Generativity-Psychedella	8. Ego-Integrity-Illumination	

In which each stage has a cognitive and an affective characteristic.

2. Each stage has a special affinity for another three removed from it. Stages 1, 4, 7 are noticeable for a thing-oriented, sexually latent aspect, dealing with the world of experience. Stages 2, 5, 8 are ego-bound, ego-oriented, and ego-circumscribed. Stages 3 and 6 are times for love and creativity.

3. Within each stage, development occurs through cycles of escalation. Escalation is described as an aspect of developmental process which involves increasing complexity and embraces five attributes: succession, discontinuity, emergence, differentiation, and integration. Succession implies a fixed order within a hierarchy of developmental stages. Discontinuity involves an ordered and discrete sequence of equilibriums like a series of stairs. Emergence involves budding and the making of the implicit, explicit in the flowering of characteristics unseen before. Differentiation refers to the attribute which clarifies, fixates and metamorphosizes the emphasis in successive developments. Integration summates the other attributes into a higher synthesis with greater complexity.

As a result of this process the environment may have maximum or minimum effect on the individual, depending on his position in the cycle. Continual environmental stimulation, however, is required for escalation into the higher (self-actualizing) levels.

4. There are three higher cognitive stages than those named by Piaget, (Flavell 1963). They go with the intimacy, generativity and ego-integrity periods respectively, and are called: *creativity, psychedella,* and *illumination.* These stages involve increasing mind expansion beyond formal operations (convergent thinking), and hence, are increasingly rare, even in intelligent, healthy adults. Facilitation of escalation into them by various kinds of educational, therapeutic, sensitivity-training, meditational, and allied techniques is in the process of becoming a major movement for superior adults.

Although time and space are not available to offer proof of the validity of these hypotheses, some explanatory discussion may be useful to the reader. One immediate question is: "Why should there be developmental stages at all; why cannot development, like growth be one smooth accretion?" The answer lies in the critical aspect of energy transformations in the individual. The transformation and focusing of energy is the essence of both the developmental and the creative process. Since the amount of energy available for use is not enough to be expended upon the three areas of "the *world,* the *I,* and the *thou*" simultaneously, it must be focused through attention and expended on first one and then another of these three aspects; this process is what leads to the three-phase periodicity of the developmental stages.

Since divergent thinking follows convergent in the SOI model, the author (1972) also hypothesized that creativity was the next cognitive stage above formal operations. For fuller discussion of these theories, the reader is referred to the bibliography. It is necessary, however, to examine the concepts of escalation and dysplasia which follow directly on developmental stage theory.

Escalation and Dysplasia

The theory of developmental stages can be regarded as the carrying over of the discontinuity of the quantum theory to behavioral science. Escalation is the name of the jump from one riser to the next on the developmental staircase; it takes energy from the organism to make them; guidance is needed to enable the individual to surmount this developmental discontinuity. Escalation consists of five interrelated aspects: discontinuity, succession, emergence, (the debut of new powers), differentiation, and integration. Each of these has specific guidance implications.

Dysplasia, the writer has theorized (1974), means malformation of development, and occurs when one aspect of the psyche (e.g. affective) continues to escalate, although another (e.g. cognitive) becomes arrested. This irregularity produces block, anomie and eventually neurosis. Since the most common dysplasia is the one that prevents cognitive escalation to creativity in young adults, this problem becomes a prime focus for guidance of the gifted. Elsewhere we have pointed out that most counseling problems can be ordered in terms of maladaptations of development. The real function of guidance for the gifted is hence the escalation of all parts of the psyche beyond the fifth developmental stage of formal operations, so that the individual can become fully creative and self-actualizing. The importance, of understanding of escalation and dysplasia becomes more apparent when we consider the benefits of full synergestic function.

Obviously what has just been said about developmental stage theory applies to all children, as do the guidance implications. But the guidance implications for gifted children are particularly important because upon them probably depends the issue of whether the gifted child will become the creative adult.

There is first the issue of accelerated development in both cognitive and affective processes. The discontinuous escalations from one stage to another require energy, and if they are to be accelerated more energy is required. Part of this energy comes from the child's own physical health, but part of it comes from his mental health, and especially essential freedom from the lower demands of the Maslovian hierarchy so that he can be at liberty to devote himself to full cognitive and affective development. Preventative and maintenance group guidance can help here.

An even more important aspect comes into play in the issue of whether guidance can facilitate escalation in the gifted from formal operations to true creativity, (from convergent production to divergent production), in adolescence. Both biology and society encourage development up to the fifth stage of formal operations, but neither of them help afterwards. If the young person is to escalate further, he must do it on his own or as a result of guidance or mentoring. It is in the social sanctions by peers against adolescent creativity that most gifted children lose their creative potential, and it is here that guidance for the gifted pays its biggest dividends.

Guidance in the Synergestic Development of the Person

If one compares a solo pianist with the effect of an orchestra in concert, it is evident that the synergestic effect *tout ensemble* is more than additive: interaction between the instruments produces a new level of musical sound. In a similar manner, when the various modes into which we have analyzed the psyche are all operating harmoniously, there is an indescribably enhanced effect, and this is the necessary basis for higher levels of creativity and self-actualization. Guidance for positive mental health is indeed an object for all, but for the gifted such guidance may release high level functioning which is the necessary condition for major creative work, as well as continued personal development after sexual maturity.

We know little from a psychological point of view about the higher reaches of such personal development, formerly described as "theophanies" although both Maslow and Erikson have given us hints. They were first described and attributed to high intelligence by Bucke (1901). That such conditions which occur spontaneously in genius, can be domesticated and induced in more ordinary gifted persons by guidance was the theme of the editor's *Development of the Creative Individual* (1972), and it points to the importance of differential guidance. Since there are probably more domains than the cognitive and the affective (e.g. psychomotor, conative, and moral), it is probable that the full effect of guidance will not be felt until all these modes are affected by it.

Finally it may be that this synergetic effect reduces stress and internal resistance. Analogous to a radio receiver when this type of static is cleared away, the instrument can be more finely tuned, and what was a howl now becomes an intelligent signal. The resonance or sympathetic vibration which accomplishes this right-hemisphere reception of creative influx from the *Zeitgeist* and allows it to be amplified without distortion is at the same time creative actualization in society, and mental health in the individual.

A MODEL GUIDANCE PROGRAM FOR THE GIFTED

At the San Fernando State College Workshops for the Gifted Children we invested very large amounts of guidance, not for the curing of psychopathology, but in order to help children become creative. If we are to ask children to step off the dime of psychological safety which they have built for themselves, and risk status in creative effort, we need to give them supportive approbation, and to help them gain the ego strength and self-confidence to hold in tension longer the stress occasioned by complexity and disorder out of which creative innovation is born. Our guidance program differed from that in a good modern school in several ways:

1. There is a grade counselor for every class of 25 children, plus two head counselors.

2. The counselor and the teacher are a unified team; the counselor frees the teacher of all classroom activities except the development of curriculum and direction of learning.

3. Since the counselor is in class with the children, she sees behavior (it is not just reported to her); moreover when abnormal behavior occurs, she has a baseline of previous observations with which to observe it.

4. The counselor concentrates on improving the mental health of the children, not just on treating symptoms in crisis situations. She has time and opportunity to treat directly with children, to know all of them and their parents on an intimate basis, and to establish friendship with them.

5. The counselor is taught to recognize the two prime tasks of guidance: a) helping the normal developmental tasks of the child. b) helping with the special problems occasioned by the giftedness of the child.

6. Since there are several counselors in adjacent classrooms, there is much opportunity for professional consultation, discussion and support. The almost instant availability of the head counselor is also helpful in this regard. Such back-ups helps the counselor's own mental health and is reflected in the classroom atmosphere.

7. The counselor is accessible before class begins in the morning. Many children come to her and relieve tensions by talking briefly. Some get a little extra attention and love; others get desired valuing on a creative thought, a new poem, or a new possession. This all just naturally happens if the counselor is around,—ready to receive, respond, and value. Such psychological "grooming" helps the child channel his thoughts and energies onto the class curriculum. Obviously children could get by without this, but they are the more creative for having it.

8. The counselor is in an ideal situation to use both individual and selected group counseling toward accomplishing an objective in whatever manner is most appropriate. Individual and group dynamics can be used to reinforce each other.

9. There is opportunity to contact parents on a positive note, just to let them know that all is going well. Many parents report they have never before been contacted by a counselor except for negative information. Students quietly singled out and praised have the same surprised reaction.

SOME SPECIFIC COUNSELING PROBLEMS

In carrying the affective developmental curriculum for the individual student, the counselor has the function of helping to bridge the developmental discontinuities, so that the gifted youth may escalate into verbal creativity, and so that the talented youth may escalate into non-verbal creativity. We say youth rather than child because the critical period lies between the period of formal operations in the early teens and creativity new to the culture in the late teens and early twenties. This is where most failure to escalate takes place. This failure is due to lack of preservation of right-hemisphere functioning, lack of training in left-hemisphere verbal processing of right-hemisphere images, and lack of a degree of mental health in adolescence which allows the ego to attend to these high level functions rather than the more basic aspects of the Maslovian hierarchy. This is the spot where counseling for creativity really makes a difference.

Once this central idea is grasped a whole host of specifics at once suggest themselves. The sheltering of adolescents from peer sanctions, through group segregation, or group guidance are viable possibilities. The use of mentors, and model adult figures also comes at once to mind. Stimulation and "predisposition" in the manner advocated by Brandwein (1953) is also helpful. Some other specific suggestions follow.

In the first place developmental guidance for gifted youth differs markedly from clinical therapy for adults. The former treats normal developmental tasks, the latter abnormal states: the former is preventative, the latter therapeutic; the former deals with youth in flux and development, the latter with adults in block and stasis. Finally, whereas a psychotherapist is attempting to remove stress from his patient, the guidance counselor is more interested in getting the student to accommodate to a reasonable amount of stress, modified to fit his individual tolerance level so as not to block out potential creativity.

In the case of guidance for gifted adolescents, the counselor's job is less to adjust the student to society than it is to help him with the Havighurst adolescent developmental tasks, so that he may become creative. These tasks as you remember are 1) the breakaway from home, 2) social adjustment, 3) sexual adjustment, 4) vocational adjustment, and 5) intellectual/moral adjustment. In this large endeavor the counselor's curriculum is the Krathwohl taxonomy of the affective domain: receiving, responding, valuing, conceptualization, and value complex,—in other words the cultivation of mature emotional attitudes and moral integrity. By and large counselors do a miserable job in this, and that is one reason why there are so many alienated gifted adolescents. If the counselor does not do the job right, the end product is a delinquent one.

Very often the physical education coach does a better job in this area than the counselor. First, the coach teaches and practices what Paul Brandwein (1953) called "the predisposing factor" and what Joe Renzulli (1976) refers to as "task commitment." It involves the development of strong and whole-hearted will to excel at the task so that most of one's attention and waking hours are devoted to it. This involvement gives idealistic youth what William James called "the moral equivalent of war," and is necessary to preserve creativity and avoid alienation.

218

Secondly, the coach also knows that one cannot get superior performance out of youth without group solidarity, and he uses group cohesiveness constantly in the segregation of his charges, for practice, games, and sometimes even meals and lodging. Yet most counselors oppose the grouping of gifted adolescents, seemingly unconscious of the well known fact that the herd instinct at this period is so strong that peer sanctions will prevent most boys from creativity, and most girls from even showing their superior intelligence.

In carrying out these objectives, there are some special guidance problems which gifted children face, which need specialized attention from counselors who themselves have received specialized training. Here are some of them: (Gowan, 1960)

1. They may be faced with an embarrassment of riches in trying to make wise occupational and educational choices.
2. There may be problems attendant upon upward social mobility.
3. They may become aware of developmental tasks before they have the physical resources to solve them.
4. They may have more need than usual to develop the specialized interests which go with certain professional occupations.
5. There may be problems connected with the lack of adult model figures.

One of the problems which many gifted youngsters face in connection with guidance has been expressed with some humor by a gifted student as the perennial question of "How far out beyond the safety railing can I lean without going over the cliff?" Gifted students are bright enough to know that they deviate in characteristics considerably from the norms and to see that, in consequence, many generalizations that apply to the average student do not apply to them. The problem for them is to discriminate between those situations which apply equally to all persons, regardless of ability, and those which apply to them only with diminished force. For example, the gifted student frequently finds that he can take one or two courses in excess of the requirements and that he does not need this or that prerequisite. It takes a wise counselor to help him discriminate between those experiences he can safely telescope and those that he should undertake in as full measure as the next student.

The function of guidance workers at the different grade levels will differ somewhat as being more concerned with identification in the grades and more concerned with placement in the senior high school. What is not sufficiently appreciated at present is that guidance must be integrated throughout the system and that guidance in the grades is as valuable as guidance in the high school. No elementary school should be without the services of a full-time counselor. The gifted in elementary school face special problems in not being challenged by the curriculum and in failing to find friends who are agemates. Thus twin developmental tasks of industry and socialization, plus problems of identification, home, and environmental difficulties, can be cleared away with minimal difficulty if counseling help is available. But if allowed to run unchecked, another gifted underachiever is too likely to be delivered to the high school.

The major function of the guidance person working with the able youth is twofold: first, to assist in personality development and the removal of emotional or environmental handicaps; and second, to aid and advise in the maximizing of achievement and college placement which will facilitate his progress to a professional career. Both of these matters are complex enough to require separate analysis and hence will not be developed here. It should be emphasized, however, that these tasks should be prosecuted with positive, aggressive action in place of the all too current passivity about able youth which infects many guidance offices. It is not enough to measure the function of the guidance office against the comparison of the mental health and scholastic achievement of these able youngsters with the norms; instead, we should strive to prepare these outstanding representatives for the really grueling task ahead of them. If our intellectual leaders are to keep pace and be found in the frequencies demanded by modern conditions, we need not only to deliver a much higher percentage of our able youth to the door of the university but to ensure that they have the motivation and mental health to graduate. This means a program of college-going for able youth involving the encouragement, the motivation, the strengthening of curriculum, and the upbuilding of achievement on a level not approached by our high schools at present. It means a change of attitudes in students, teachers, parents, and the public regarding the importance of high school scholarship, the desirability of taking more than four "solids" per year, the need for new prestige symbols in adolescent groups, the decrease of community anti-intellectualism, the fostering of the conservation principle in young human talent—all matters of social values with which the guidance worker is concerned. While these issues are matters of community concern, they can be raised and fought for if professional educators are truly social leaders. A program for scholarship in the senior high school extending through the three years—not just the senior year— with prestige and other rewards for the participants and with good publicity regarding effective college placement and the various scholarships and awards which come to students is one way of starting such a program. Needless to say, such a job is a full-time task in the average high school and can scarcely be accomplished if the counselor is so burdened with the problems of the lower 10 percent that he has no time for the able.

Another problem which needs much more attention than it is presently receiving has to do with special efforts and techniques to be developed for use with gifted girls to preserve their creativity, and sense of personhood as against sexual and social stereotype roles enjoined upon them.

Effective guidance is essential in providing girls with the information and help they need in order to complete college and secure a career commensurate with their abilities. Occupational information outlining the advantages and attractions of various careers for gifted women needs wide circulation. This is an area where male counselors may not do a good job because of their implicit concept that it must either be marriage *or* a career, when in actuality it may be both. For even if the career is to be temporarily interrupted by motherhood, it is better to prepare for a career that can be resumed, than to have to accept substandard employment or start in preparing for a career after the nest is empty. Individual counseling by trained counselors from elementary to graduate school will not only help gifted girls to continued academic achievement, but also to plan for some type of career commensurate with their particular aptitudes and interests.

Of particular importance in this effort is group maintenance counseling to support gifted female adolescents against cultural social and male sanctions against creativity, and individual divergence. Girls at this period are under enormous pressures to conform, look pretty and act in an acquiescent manner. If they are not to "cop out" they need group reinforcements, female adult model figures, and probably a segregated havens where they can get support, comfort, and advice.

A final, and in the view of the writer, a most important problem, has to do with the role of counselors in the development of right-hemisphere stimulation and other incubational techniques.

It is becoming clearer that whereas the curriculum of the teacher is the cognitive aspects of the left hemisphere, the curriculum of the counselor is more concerned with the affective aspects of the right hemisphere. Research on the differentiated functions of the left and right cerebral hemispheres has been so rapid of late, that it is difficult for anyone to keep up with the developments. It does seem very possible that guidance, particularly for gifted students who wish to become creative will develop incubational techniques in group guidance sessions. These techniques relax the overriding hold of the usually dominant left hemisphere through fantasy, meditation, guided reveries, etc. Left hemisphere cognitive function appears to require two conditions: a) continual sensory input, and b) continual internal discourse. Any of the previous techniques appear to allay left hemisphere function through cutting down one or the other of these dual inputs. While researchers have known about such techniques for a few years, their widespread use in schools had been handicapped because of the religious, moral, legal or social sanctions against some of them.

The previous approach has been mainly a negative one: cut out the activity of the dominant left hemisphere, and imagery will automatically appear in the right hemisphere (since it goes on there all the time, but is ordinarily not paid attention to). But the new approach is more positive: Find positive activities (i.e. art and music) which stimulate the right hemisphere directly, despite activity in the left.

What research has now discovered is that imagery is the precursor of creativity in both the arts and sciences, that right hemisphere activity is the precursor of imagery, and that positive means of right hemisphere stimulation through art and music is equally as effective as other incubatory techniques for allaying left hemisphere function. Education is thus presented with a new and powerful tool in its efforts to make gifted children creative, and art and music education has received a research rationale of immense importance.

THE COUNSELOR'S ROLE

Characteristics of the counselor for the gifted youngster have never been better summarized than by Dr. Sidney Parnes, Director of the Buffalo Creative Education Foundation (1978) in describing what he seeks in the temperamental qualities of a strong facilitator:

> The effective facilitator needs to be open to ideas, to viewpoints, and prone to question rather than tell. Enthusiasm is very helpful in a facilitator, but this need not be the "bubbly" type; it can be a kind of self-evident sincerity. Some of the other qualities that come especially to mind are the following: a fondness or acceptance of all kinds of people; quick thinking; ability to live happily in ambiguity—not just tolerate it; perhaps the tendency to invite ambiguity—yet maintain the balance necessary for bringing about an ultimate greater order from the disorder (via the creative process); always *looking* for something good or positive in a circumstance, an idea, a person, a thing; tactful; hard working—self-motivated; flexible; has "group-building" ability and a sense of humor.

Wide cultural background with superior scholarship may be taken for granted. In addition to successful teaching experience and an absorbing interest in children, the counselor should have professional training, being well grounded in testing, statistics, education of the able, psychology, and interviewing techniques. The counselor, compared to the teacher of the gifted, should be even more permissive, intraceptive, nondirective, and nonauthoritarian and should be eminently capable of playing the adult model role for these bright charges.

What kind of counseling works best with the gifted? Obviously, not the directive variety. The able are independent-minded and want to figure out problems for themselves. This is not to say that they will not need and even demand information. They are usually more effective than the average in evaluation of their own position. The counselor, therefore, should distinguish between providing information and providing decisions. It is not directive to provide the former, but it is directive to provide the latter.

The able student is often more able to profit much more from the inspection of his own test results than the average youth, and the counselor need feel few qualms about giving him considerable test information. It will come as no shock to the bright child to find that he is able, nor is it likely to make him boastful or vainglorious. The counselor can do the youth a valuable service by pointing out specific, relative weaknesses as clues either for remedial work or for college or career planning. A gifted child who is at the 75th percentile of his grade in reading skill needs remediation; another who has A's in all senior subjects, but with an ACE score on the 99th percentile in linguistic areas and the 88th percentile in numerical areas, needs to be apprized of his problem before he elects M.I.T. or C.I.T.

Counselors working with the able will need to take special precautions against counselors involvement. It is very easy to identify with these youngsters, and resultant countertransference phenomena may obscure detailed consideration on the youngster's real problems. In such a situation the counselor is very apt to push the youth toward his occupational or educational bias, forgetting that a counselor, unlike a teacher, is not looking for disciples. Another easy mistake to make in counseling with the gifted is to be misled by the general halo effect of good grades, sound attitude and other positive aspects. It is important to remember that these youngsters are preparing for top-level competition against far more difficult college and graduate standards than they are ever likely to meet in high school. The counselor who does not provide the gifted student with some prognosis of the problems which he may face in the future is doing him no service. Another special difficulty often encountered with the able is that of keeping grades and morale up until the gifted and sometimes temperamental youth can get away to college. With some of these talented underachievers, it is almost a race to see if they can make college before their environmental frustrations sidetrack them completely. Sometimes, the form book of grades and deportment needs to be thrown away and a college encouraged to take a chance on the wild talents of some fiery nonconformist.

While guidance should be a continuous process throughout school, there are some critical junction points where lack of guidance may shunt the gifted onto the wrong track. Especially at the ninth and twelfth grades, the efforts (or lack of them) of the guidance worker to locate all the able youths, despite poor grades and lower socioeconomic status, is crucial. In the ninth grade all these youngsters should be strongly encouraged to take an academic college preparatory program, and at the twelfth grade all of them should be encouraged to go on to college.

While the counselor for the able has the major responsibility for their guidance, he cannot be expected to function alone. He needs co-operation from the principal, staff members, and teachers. On the part of the teachers, this co-operation includes, besides consultation with counselors, the ability, skill, and presence of mind to make referrals promptly when able students are not performing properly. On the part of other staff members, such co-operation includes communication, so that the co-ordination of the special program may blend harmoniously with that of general education. Co-operation with curriculum personnel is especially important. The prin-

222

cipal can help by understanding and supporting the guidance role and by not confusing this function with that of errand boy, disciplinary assistant, stool pigeon, or substitute teacher. The proper relationship between administrator and personnel worker is somewhat like that between the commander of a military unit and its chaplain. The counselor should have "non-combatant" status. Other needs which the administrator can help supply include office space with privacy for interviewing, a budget and work load which are realistic, tests and supplies, an information library, and the appreciation that pupil personnel work embraces something more than programming.

It goes without saying that every guidance program should have the funds and staff to conduct a continuous follow-up of its able students. In the first place, no other group can acquaint the administration so well with the benefits and weaknesses of the program. Second, the community deserves and needs to have an accounting of how well its able graduates are doing in college. Proper publicity on this score will do much to ensure that public support for guidance will be forthcoming. Finally, no other group is so likely in later years to bring credit to the school and the community, and these youngsters should not be lost.

The feed-back process from able students constitutes probably the most important and intelligent evaluation a school can make of its services. The administrator who is able to employ this procedure will find that the feed-back from these youngsters even while in school will be helpful. The administrator who makes it a policy to find out "how guidance feels" about a school problem can save himself many headaches and gain a reputation for ideas which are likely to make his administration highly successful.

Proper guidance for the able is not a luxury but a necessity of American cultural life. The organization of adequate programs of guidance for the academically talented awaits only the demands of the districts and the efforts of educational personnel. It is time for us all to come to a realistic appraisal of the importance of guidance programs for all youth in the procedures of general education and in the specific problems of the able. In no other way shall we meet the problem of achievement and productivity which appears to be in the process of becoming the central educational issue of the mid-twentieth century.

Let us try to recapitulate the arguments of this paper in very short and simple sentences:

1. Renaissances in culture occur as a result of a "critical mass" or bunching of creative adults.
2. Renaissances in the past were ephemeral because they were accidentally produced; we now have the technology to produce them by design, and hence to create a permanent super-renaissance.
3. The technology includes an understanding of the dynamics of creativity and how to develop it.
4. The best potential creative adults are gifted children, but only a small fraction of them will become creative accidentally. Education, however, can vastly increase the percent of such creatives by proper development, curriculum and guidance.
5. Such guidance involves an understanding of the principles of development and developmental stage theory with special applications to gifted children.
6. Such guidance involves an understanding of the principles of creativity, and the teaching of those principles to gifted children.

If one asks why in view of the possibilities laid out in this paper, there has been so little accomplished, the answers are several. IN the first place much of the research is new, and not well disseminated. Secondly, there has been only recent attention to the guidance of the gifted: in fact this book is the first book of readings on the subject. There are very few persons or places in the United States where such specialized guidance for the gifted is known or available. Besides the writer's *The Education and Guidance of the Ablest* (with George Demos) 1964, and *The Academically Talented and Guidance* (with Kay Bruch 1971), there have been no books in the area until now. *The Gifted Child Quarterly* for Fall 1977, 21:3 (a special issue devoted to guidance) is the other prime source in print. As is often true in the intersection of several disciplines (here gifted children, guidance, and creativity) there are many who have expertise in one area, almost no one who has expertise in all.

An important exception to this dearth, has been the Wisconsin University Research and Guidance Laboratory for Gifted Students, started under the aegis of Professor John Rothney (a classmate of the writer at Harvard Graduate School of Education in the early Thirties where we both studied under Professors Truman Kelly, and John Brewer, early exponents of guidance). The laboratory under Rothney, Marshall Sanborn and others is unique in many ways, and has made major contributions to this area, as is noted elsewhere in this volume. It is notable that the two editors of this volume received their training there.

The limitations of the past, however, are only background for the opportunities of the future, as the public and the profession acquire larger understanding of the importance of guidance for the gifted. We may expect conditions to change rapidly with the increasing urgency of the times. And we may therefore expect that differentiated guidance for the gifted will take its rightful place in the educational establishment. Pressures of this sort will gradually force teacher and counselor training programs in schools of Education to take more cognizance of the importance and need of such guidance. Concern for the qualities of exceptional human beings comes out of an exceptional concern for the qualities of all human beings. The history of the last quarter century in the guidance area has been a growing realization of the needs of various subgroups for specialized guidance. We may expect this trend to continue and to have its culmination in the production of more creative adults in our society.

CONCLUSION

These ideas are so new that all we can do in turning from theory to practice is to sketch some ways in which such views may affect the classroom in the future. It would be a grave error to conclude that we should abandon all that has gone before and delve into divination and the occult; indeed, such a procedure would be disastrous. The Wallas paradigm still holds true and useful. Mental discipline and scholarship are still required for the preparation phase. What we are talking about is more conscious attention to the incubation phase.

Moreover, to look at the end product in highly creative geniuses at their best hardly tells us much about how to induce creativity consciously through educational procedures. What they gained in flashes of creative intuition may come to lesser lights through longer and more painstaking efforts. Inducing creativity in the classroom may not be the same as observing it in the field.

There are, however, some procedures we can begin to make use of. I should like to list a few for you now:

1. We should study creativity directly in high school and university classes. Almost no schools at the present time have courses on this subject. The 21st century will find this lack incomprehensible.
2. We can help young children learn techniques of relaxation and incubation. This does not mean that we should teach them any particular form of meditation, but it might be useful for all children to know what meditation, relaxation, and other types of unstressing are.
3. We should help children practice imagination and imagery during such relaxed periods. The Torrance and Khatena record, *Sounds and Images,* is only one of several devices on the market for this purpose. As a consequence of such periods we should encourage the production of poetry, art, music, etc.
4. As long as the child is in the concrete operations phase, the images will tend to be static and not particularly creative; but when he enters the formal operations phase one can expect and should push for more finished artistic creations, especially in poetic form. Children at this stage should be strongly encouraged to keep a journal and put their poetry and other thoughts into it. The development of the easy ability at this level helps the child to become truly creative in the next stage, and this is where (in upper high school and in lower division college) most gifted children do not make the transition to creative production. I think the most important facilitation which can take place at this time is a seminar type home room where the adolescent can be with others of the same persuasion, for (because of the strong gregarious needs at this stage) nothing does more to inhibit creativity than group sanctions against it in other adolescents.

It might be prudent of us to listen to the last testament of a prophet and sage on educational objectives in a utopia:

> How does he do his thinking, perceiving, and remembering? Is he a visualizer or a non-visualizer? Does his mind work with images or with words, with both at once or with neither? How close to the surface is his story-telling faculty? Does he see the world as Wordsworth and Traherne saw it when they were children? And if so, what can be done to prevent the glory and freshness from fading into the light of common day? Or in more general terms, can we educate children on the conceptual level without killing their capacity for intense non-verbal experience? How can we reconcile analysis with vision? (Huxley, 1962).

Few orthodox teachers will agree with Huxley's tripartite prescription for accomplishing this educational miracle, which consisted of *maithuna* for the psychomotor level, *moksha*-medicine (drugs) for the affective level, and meditation for the cognitive level. But let us remember that Huxley was a visionary, and that many of the predictions in *Brave New World* have come true. Certainly his ideas are worth thinking about, if only to trigger our own.

About 9,000 years ago, prehistoric man was suddenly catapulted into history as the result of an astonishing social discovery. Previous to this, small bands of nomadic tribes had roamed a large hunting area looking for game and gathering live fruits and vegetables wild. Then someone found out that if one domesticated animals and plants, one could have a ready supply of food always at hand in a confined space. Thus was agriculture and civilization born, and man escalated into history, and to the possibility of a far greater population on a given land mass. We are still reaping the benefits of that change, but our continuing ecological crises show us that we are nearing the end of that period. Fortunately we are on the brink of another momentous discovery which will have even greater impact on cultural and personal escalation.

Heretofore we have harvested creativity wild. We have used as creative only those persons who stubbornly remained so despite all efforts of the family, religion, education, and politics to grind it out of them. In the prosecution of this campaign, men and women have been punished, flogged, silenced, imprisoned, tortured, ostracized, and killed. Jesus, Socrates, Huss, Lavosier, Lincoln, Gandhi, Kennedy, and King are good examples. As a result of this misguided efforts, our society produces only a small percentage of its potential of creative individuals (the ones with the most uncooperative dispositions).

If we learn to domesticate creativity—that is, to enhance rather than deny it in our culture—we can increase the number of creative persons in our midst by about fourfold. That would put the number and percent of such individuals over the "critical mass" point. When this level is reached in a culture, as it was in Periclean Athens, the Renaissance, the Aufklarung, the Court of the Sun King, Elizabethan England, and our own Federalist period, there is an escalation of creativity resulting and civilization makes a great leap forward. We can have a golden age of this type such as the world has never seen, and I am convinced that it will occur early in the 21st century. But we must make preparations now, and the society we save will be our own. The alternative is either nuclear war or learning to speak Arabic and bow down four times a day toward Mecca.

In conclusion, if we may be permitted a peep at the future, we see an integrated science of human development and talent. The gestalt we are talking about there is at present at best a shore dimly seen, but it is the coming science of man of the 21st century. A genius is always a forerunner; and the best minds of this age foresee the dawn of that one. All of these branches of humanistic psychology will be welded together in a *structure d'ensemble,* greater than interest in the gifted, greater than interest in creativity, greater, in fact, than anything except the potential of man himself. We may come from dust, but our destiny is in the stars. Throeau, that rustic seer, prophesized in the last sentence of *Walden*: "That day is yet to dawn, for the sun is only a morning star."

References

Bailey, S. K. "Education and the Pursuit of Happiness" *UCLA Educator* 14:1, 1971

Blocher, D. *Developmental Counseling.* New York: Ronald Press, 1966

Brandwein, P. *The Gifted Child as a Future Scientist.* New York: Harcourt-Brace, 1953

Bucke, R. M. *Cosmic Consciousness,* New York: E. P. Dutton, 1901

Erikson, E. H. *Childhood and Society* New York: W. W. Norton, 1950

Ferguson, E. S. "The Mind's Eye: Non-Verbal Thought in Technology" *Science* 197:827–36, Aug 26, 1977

Flavell, J. H. *The Devlopmental Psychology of Jean Piaget.* New York: Van Nostrand 1963

Galton, F. *Inquiries Into the Human Faculty and its Development.* London: Dent & Co, 1870, (reprint, N.Y.: Dutton, 1927).

Ghiselin, B. (Ed.) *The Creative Process.* Berkeley: Univ. of Calif. Press, 1952.

Gowan, J. C. "The Gifted Underachiever: A Problem for Everyone" *Exceptional Children* 21:7:247–9, 270, 1955

Gowan, J. C. "The Organization of Guidance for the Able" *Personnel and Guidance Journal* 39:4:275;79, Dec. 1960

Gowan, J.C. *Development of the Creative Individual.* San Diego: Knapp, 1972

Gowan, J. C. *Development of the Psychedelic Individual.* Buffalo: Creative Education Foundation, 1974.

Gowan, J. C. *The Development of the Psychedelic Individual.* Buffalo: The Creative Education Foundation, 1974.

Gowan, J. C. *Trance, Art and Creativity.*Buffalo: Creative Education Foundation, 1975.

Gowan, J. C. "Some New Thoughts on Creativity" *Journal of Creative Behavior* 11:2:77–90, 1977

Gowan, J. C. "Incubation, Imagery and Creativity" *Journal of Altered States of Consciousness*, (in press), 1978.

Gowan, J. C. and Demos, G. D. *The Education and Guidance of the Ablest.* Springfield, Ill: C. C. Thomas, 1964

Gowan, J. C. and Bruch, C. B. *The Academically Talented and Guidance* Boston: Houghton-Mifflin Co. 1971.

Gowan, J. C. and Demos, G. D. *The Guidance of Exceptional Children* New York: McKay, 1965, 1972

Huxley, A. *Island.* New York: Harper & Row, 1962

Jaynes, J. *The Origin of Consciousness in the Breakdown of the Bicameral Mind.* Boston: Houghton-Mifflin Press, 1976.

Khatena, J. and Torrance, E. P. *Thinking Creatively with Sounds and Images.* Lexington Mass.: Personnel Press, 1973.

Kohlberg, L. and Mayer, R. "Development as the Aim of Education" *Harvard Educational Review* 42:449–96, 1972

Maslow, A. H. *Motivation and Personality.* New York: Harper, 1954

Meeker, M. *The Structure of Intellect: Its Interpretation and Uses.* Columbus, OH: Merrill, 1969

Parnes, S. J. Brochure of the Creative Education Foundation, State University College, Buffalo, New York, Jan. 1978

Piaget, J. *The Psychology of Intelligence.* London: Routledge & Kegan Paul, 1950

Renzulli, J. "The Enrichment Triad Model" *Gifted Child Quarterly* 20:3:303–27, 1976, and 21:2:227–233, 1977

Simonton, D. K. "The Eminent Genius in History: The Critical Role of Creative Development" *Gifted Child Quarterly* 22:2 1978

Simpson, E. J. *The/ Classification of Educational Objectives: Psychomotor Domain.* Urbana, Ill: University of Illinois Press, 1966

Sullivan, H. S. *The Interpersonal Theory of Psychiatry.* New York: W. W. Norton, 1953

Terman, L. M. "The Discovery and Encouragement of Exceptional Talent" *American Psychologist* 9:221–230, 1954

Wallas, G. *The Art of Thought.* London, C. A. Watts, 1926

Williams, F. *Classroom Ideas for Encouraging Thinking and Feeling* Buffalo: Dissemination of Knowledge Pub. 1970

Williams, R. "Why Children Should Draw" *Saturday Review,* (9/3/77):11-16

VIII

TEACHERS AND PARENTS

27. INCREASING CHILDREN'S CREATIVITY THROUGH A COMBINATION OF TEACHER TRAINING APPROACHES

Catherine B. Bruch

With current educational emphasis on releasing children's creativity as a national concern, a summer institute of four weeks was designed for this specific purpose. This institute was held in August of 1964 on the campus of San Fernando State College in Northridge, California. The primary objective was that of training teachers for encouraging children's creativity. An associated objective was the release of creativity within gifted children.

A combination of multiple approaches to training teachers was the unique feature of this program. Student trainees enrolled in the program were exposed not only to lectures concerned with theories of creativity, but also to panel discussions by master teachers, observation and participation in classroom with gifted children, daily discussion groups, weekly seminars and informal meetings with staff members. Approximately forty trainees were programmed for observations at their own choices of grade levels. They were also permitted freedom as to the degree of observation or participation preferred, according to their current experiences in teaching. Trainees ranged from upper-classmen to graduate students with several years of teaching experience.

Master teachers were free to concentrate upon teaching because of the additional features of the total program. These included the volunteer aides from the local San Fernando Valley Association for Gifted Children, and counselor trainees who facilitated communication between the special summer school, children and parents. Many clerical and routine tasks were performed by the volunteer aides, while the counselor trainees functioned in conferences with children and parents, and in leadership of the daily discussions with teacher trainees. The entire institute was a well-coordinated effort of cooperative staff, trainees, counselors and parent volunteers.

PROGRAM ORGANIZATION

Before the actual school program for gifted children, teacher trainees enrolled in the institute attended an hour of lectures by the institute director, Dr. John C. Gowan, or the assistant directors. Master teachers and counselors appeared as panel members at some of the later meetings to discuss practical applications of creativity from their own classrooms or counseling perspectives.

During the nine-to-twelve school morning, institute members observed and/or participated in two separate classroom settings, with their third hour scheduled for group discussions. Three groups of institute members were rotated so that the number of observers would not be too great

Reprinted by permission of the author and *Gifted Child Quarterly*, Vol. 9, No. 1, 1965.

in any classroom at a given hour. In the daily discussions these same group sections met, one group each hour. One counselor was assigned on a rotating basis to attend each discussion hour. Although the discussions were to some extent "leaderless," the counselor assigned could assume whatever leadership role seemed appropriate to the group process.

Organization of classrooms varied with different grade levels. Self-contained classrooms were maintained at the third and fourth grade levels. The fifth grade and the younger sixth grade classes were taught by an alternating team of two teachers, one specializing in mathematics and science, the other in language arts and social studies. Flexible scheduling was planned as needed between the two teachers. In the older sixth, the seventh and the eighth grades, teaching was departmentalized with language arts, mathematics and science as content areas.

Approximately 180 gifted children attended school only four mornings of the week, with Wednesday mornings between nine and twelve devoted to seminars for trainees. Each sectioned group of institute members rotated among seminars led by the director and the assistant directors, spending an hour with each. In addition to seminar emphases that varied between the directors, teacher trainees also experienced opportunities for taking and discussing results of creativity tests.

Informal meetings with staff were held, one group each week, after the seminars. Weekly informal staff meetings for constant evaluation and planning facilitated staff cooperation. Counselors, and sometimes parent group volunteers, also participated in these meetings.

STAFF

Master teachers were especially selected by the director on the basis of experience and concern with gifted children's creativity. The institute director, Dr. John C. Gowan, is a recognized authority on the gifted. He had led several previous special summer sessions for gifted children on the campus of Valley State College.

Assistant directors, both of whom taught as master teachers in the institute, were experienced in the areas of gifted and creativity. Dr. Juliana Gensley, Assistant Professor of Education at Long Beach State College, had also directed a special summer session for gifted children at Valley State College and courses for teachers of the gifted. The writer, a school psychologist, had been coordinator of the gifted program in the Lancaster Elementary School District, and had studied creativity intensively in preparation for a U.C.L.A. thesis.

FACILITIES

On the Valley State College campus, departmentalized classes were held in the Science Building, where some laboratory facilities were available for the science program. Other classes were held in bungalow classrooms on the original campus, where one classroom was equipped for observation. Surrounding lawns and areas under shade trees became locales for small group projects. College library cards for each gifted child were considered by the children as special privileges, as were visits to the data processing center, or other campus explorations. Some field trips were made off campus.

EVALUATION OF EFFECTS OF TEACHER TRAINING

As a means of continuous evaluation the director requested weekly that institute members complete brief evaluation questions. Tape recordings of the weekly seminars with the writer were made for future analysis, and for insights as to current program needs. Weekly staff meetings made possible flexible adaptation to the needs of the on-going program. Counselor trainees also provided in these meetings valuable feed-back for such adaptations. Although time has not permitted full analysis of the evaluation data collected, Table I would seem to represent synthesis of the effects of the institute upon the teacher trainees.

On the last weekly evaluation form institute members were asked to "Name three ideas you received from the institute." An initial frequency tabulation of these ideas was made. The ideas were then regrouped into areas of major concepts. This analysis is represented in Table I, with examples of categorized comments following.

Table I.

Responses to Question Three—Ideas Received from the Institute
Grouped into Areas of Major Concepts

I. Self-perceptions of institute member and interpersonal relationships in creativity		Creative writing, language arts methods	4
		Asking divergent thinking questions	2
Self-evaluation	8	Re-evaluation of classroom control as learning	1
Interpersonal relationships	5		18
Affective domain	4		
Teaching enthusiasm	4	*IV. Children's needs and interests*	
Values of guidance and counseling	3	Individualized learning	6
Classroom creativity as gradual (with "comfort")	3	Children's needs and interests	4
		Self-worth feelings of children	2
Creativity as non-neurotic	3	Group and committee work	2
Value of seminar, group discussions	2	Achievement	2
Characteristics of creative teacher	1	Responsibility of "Gifted" to society	1
Creative attitude as source of untapped energy	1		17
	34	*V. Degree of classroom structure and creativity*	
II. Creative classroom climate		Structure	7
Incubation period	6	Classroom control	4
Respect for children's divergent thinking	5	Absence of authoritarianism	2
Delayed evaluation	5		13
Creative climate	4		
Productive thinking	4	*VI. Knowledge of creativity*	
Motivation of creativity	4	Various aspects of creativity	6
Flexible classroom procedures	2	I.Q. and creativity relationships	3
Freedom to explore ideas	2	"Constructive" creativity	2
Brainstorming	2		11
	34		
		VII. Summary statement	
III. Methods and materials for classroom creativity		"Education courses can be interesting and informative"	1
Various methods and materials	6	Total ideas	128
Discovery, inquiry, logic, problem solving	5		

EXAMPLES OF SPECIFIC COMMENTS OF INSTITUTE MEMBERS

Self-Evaluation:

". . . to evaluate and re-evaluate as necessary and bounce back."

"Self-confidence—self-evaluation."

"A new self-satisfaction of using my own ideas by being more secure in what I am doing."

"Just a beginning of a new self-evaluation which will help me to be more relaxed in my teaching."

Interpersonal Relationships:

"Tremendous importance of inter-relationship between counselor and teacher in the approach and teaching of the gifted."

"Importance of sensitivity of teacher to students' responses and actions. . . ."

"That a creative attitude in teaching, learning, and in all relationships is essential. . . ."

"Real empathy between child and teacher."

"Idea of the creative relationship—it's gorgeous."

Affective Domain:

". . . most helpful to focus on the effective side of learning . . . I find it challenging and inspiring."

". . . affective domain—how enlightening."

Teaching Enthusiasm:

"Inspiration!"

"A new enthusiasm for teaching the gifted. . . ."

Guidance and Counseling:

"Importance of individual guidance and counseling."

Gradual Classroom Creativity:

"To go slowly when you try out new methods to 'induce' creativity in our classrooms. . . ."

"A learning as growth process . . . 'comfort.' "

"Importance of slow steady progress in initiating creative thinking."

Creativity as Non-neurotic:

"That it is easier, better and more fun to use all of one's powers positively than to wallow in one's neuroses."

"Clarification of the personality difference between far-out constructive creativity vs. plain 'far-out.' "

Incubation Period:

"The necessity of solitude in order to carry out the creative process."

"At last a sound reason why all children do not need to participate at all times. (Incubation period)"

"Give creative child time to develop."

"Give ideas a chance to grow."

"Results may not be immediately obvious."

Respect for Children's Divergent Thinking:

"A child needs to feel worthy—that his ideas . . . should be respected."

"Value of each person's ideas and need to encourage development of his own creative characteristics."

"Importance of accepting unusual answers from students."

Delayed Evaluation:

"Value of evaluation without final judgment."

". . . creative in a very structured and strict situation: example—creative writing . . . free from . . . evaluation of spelling, punctuation, etc."

"Idea of withholding evaluation, of postponing . . . allow children to contribute without fear of being immediately judged."

Creative Climate:

". . . sensitivity of teacher . . . in order to implement the creation of a creative atmosphere."

"That a great deal more learning takes place by the children when they are given the opportunity and climate to participate at their interest and ability level."

Additional observations of the effectiveness of the institute program may be inferred from these informal examples. During the institute many trainees became involved to the extent of volunteering for self-initiated responsibilities. They seemed to view themselves as part of the total institute "team." They expressed personal concerns that others should be permitted to benefit, as they felt they did, from such an experience. One institute member described the total institute month as a "mountain-top experience." Another unpredicted result was the volunteer continuation of one of the institute groups in holding monthly meetings during the fall and winter for the purpose of discussing creativity.

EVALUATION AND EFFECTS ON CHILDREN'S CREATIVITY

No organized data collection was attempted during this session as to specific effects of the school on children's creativity. It could be generalized, however, that parent comments were primarily favorable. In some instances parents made specific efforts to convey to school staff the increased motivation of their children for school. The degree of satisfaction on the part of parents and children may be reflected by the quantity of early enrollments already received for the summer school to be held in 1965, 175 by February, 1965.

The changes which may have taken place in the creativity of the children may only be evaluated in the next session in 1965, when creativity tests and observational data collected in 1964 can be compared. However, as an example of the interest of one sixth grade boy, when asked his ideas for the next summer school, he initiated and circulated a petition among his classmates to extend the length of the summer session program.

DISCUSSION OF PARTIAL EVALUATIONS

In reviewing Table I, the predominance of values perceived by institute members lie in their own self-perceptions in relationship to creativity, and in the understandings of characteristics of a creative classroom climate. Both of these areas would suggest implications that the teacher trainees were personally assimilating well the role of the teacher in facilitating a classroom climate conducive to children's creativity. It might be expected that this summer institute could have more than a temporary effect upon teachers' learning about creativity. The institute also may have modified attitudes so that teachers will apply in the future more creative classroom practices. That an understanding of what constitutes a creative classroom climate was more frequently acknowledged than the other conceptual categories would seem significantly related to the practical demonstrations institute members witnessed of creative characteristics and classroom conditions, as given by Torrance (1963), Parnes (1962), and Barron (1963).

Teacher trainees were exposed to a variety of examples of creative teaching, and creative and gifted children. The knowledges presented through lectures and readings were directly applied through observations, discussions, seminars, and some participation. Principles of creative teaching were applied in the organization and practices of the institute: freedom for each master teacher to plan and effect his own program; freedom for trainees to participate to the degree which was for them appropriate; freedom from the usual grading methods, such as tests upon content; highly satisfactory inter-personal group and staff relationships wherein each individual was respected as of worth; a composite of practices which represented both a complexity of inter-relationships and a vitally integrated total perspective (Barron, 1963).

SUMMARY

In that this attempt to improve the creativity of gifted children and to train teachers to do so was a beginning of an analysis of pertinent variables, no conclusive evidence can be offered as to the precise effectiveness of this experience. The total effect, from the majority of viewpoints which might be taken, was one of promise, of resourceful leads for continuing research. Tentatively, it could be said that a combination of the described methods of teacher training seems effective.

Further analyses of existing data from evaluation questionnaires, tape-recorded seminars, and creativity tests are anticipated. Follow-up procedures are being planned to determine whether there may be continued effects of the institute in actual teaching situations, and perhaps delayed effects in long-run attitudinal changes.

Continuing research in refining the variables present may lead to more effective means of training teachers for becoming more acceptant and encouraging of children's creativity. Specifically, the role of discussion and seminar groups in facilitating the understanding and application of creativity theories is apparently important, as are actual observations and experiences with gifted children. Whether the effect of such an integrated combination of training methods is superior to other single methods of presenting course content, or other combinations of methods, is yet to be investigated.

References

Barron, Frank. *Creativity and Psychological Health.* Princeton, N.J.: D. Van Nostrand Co., Inc., 1963.

Bloom, B. S. *Taxonomy of Educational Objectives:* Cognitive Domain. New York: David McKay Co., 1956.

Bloom, B. S. *Taxonomy of Educational Objectives:* Affective Domain. New York: David McKay Co., 1964.

Gallagher, James J. *Teaching the Gifted Child.* Boston: Allyn & Bacon, 1964.

Guilford, J. P., and Merrifield, P. R. "The Structure of Intellect Model: Its Uses and Implications." *Reports from the Psychological Laboratory,* No. 24. Los Angeles: University of Southern California, 1960.

Maslow, A. H. "Cognition of Being in the Peak Experiences." *Journal of Genetic Psychology,* 94:43–66, 1959.

Parnes, Sidney J., and Harding, Harold F. *A Source Book for Creative Thinking.* New York: Charles Scribner's Sons, 1962

Torrance, E. Paul. *Education and the Creative Potential.* Minneapolis: University of Minnesota Press, 1963.

Torrance, E. Paul. *Guiding Creative Talent.* Englewood Cliffs, N.J.: Prentice-Hall, Inc., 1962.

28. SUGGESTIONS FOR MOTHERING THE GIFTED TO ENCOURAGE CURIOSITY, LEARNING, AND CREATIVITY

Alison Thorne

To put it mildly, my husband and I were startled when our two oldest children became National Merit finalists.

I am a non-working mother—odd phrase, that denotes the fact that I don't earn money. For years in what spare time I could muster I have been studying housewives' values, a little explored field. Our civilization has spent more effort on improving kitchen efficiency than in scrutinizing philosophy of homemaking. Middle-class values for years judged as excellent the woman who was a good cook and perfect housekeeper, but times are changing fast and in discussing values with other mothers I can see this cake of custom crumbling.

Neither Perfect Housekeeping nor House Beautiful dominates our home. We live in a university town in a high, square, old-fashioned house. The upstairs bathroom contains an immense closet with wide shelves for quilts and blankets, but we don't keep our extra bedding there. Instead we keep stacks of *National Georgraphics,* all the art work and notebooks which our five children have lugged home from school and wanted saved, lots of maps, and a stack of very large envelopes containing pictures and clippings about American history, English history, Renaissance art, religion, plants, animals, etc.

A child comes home from school and says, "We're studying Abraham Lincoln. What've we got?" So we retire to the bathroom to emerge presently with one magazine article, several pictures, and a yellowed replica of the newspaper telling of Lincoln's assassination, this latter a souvenir saved from a trip to Washington, D.C. The shelves also hold scrapbooks on art, space, elementary French, a year spent in Tennessee, a collection of bookmarks, etc.

Precariously stacked on the very top shelf are rolled-up homemade charts, mostly on shelf paper. One chart shows the relative size of the planets. Another lists famous persons of history, arranged by civilization and chronology. Another is a rough drawing of the world with small pictures of fruits, vegetables, and flowers pasted onto the area of origin. There is also a chart showing routes our great-great-grandparents took from Europe to America and on across to the far West. These and others have each at some time been pinned to the dining room or kitchen wallpaper. We live with pin-pricked wallpaper, just as we live with shredded upholstery where the cat sharpens her claws.

By the way of further inventory let us consider the kitchen cupboards. The glassed-in shelves intended for lovely china and glassware are filled instead with games, puzzles, stamp collections, two decorated cans which contain embroidery floss and half-completed dishtowels, two sets of knitting progress—I think they are to be bedroom slippers. My silverware box does not contain silverware; it has been subdivided for a sea shell collection which has overflowed into Christmas card boxes. There are tennis and badminton rackets and three cameras.

Scattered in various other places are scratch paper, type paper, pencils crayons, scissors, water colors in small jars, three kinds of glue, chalk, compass, rulers, three kinds of tape, balls

Reprinted by permission of the author and *Gifted Child Quarterly,* Vol. 7, No. 1, 1963.

of string, and ink. At this very moment two children are at the kitchen table writing with a pheasant feather and ink, just to see how it might have felt to be a scribe in colonial days.

As for books, we have them on stars, birds, trees, flowers, shells, history, and the usual childhood classics. Our history books include one of our local valley, telling of ancient Lake Bonneville which once covered the entire valley floor and reached into the canyons of our mountains. The two older children brought home their geology texts from Cal Tech and Stanford, and the local geology professor gave us an excellent sourcebook written for elementary and secondary schools. Our nearby canyons are Paleozoic and we find such books valuable.

We also own, as a traveling companion, the WPA guidebook for our state. We studied about the fallen ghost town of Silver Reef as we walked over its rocks and picked up rusty square nails and bits of bottles turned voilet in the desert sun. Nails and glass now lie in the drawer of my dressing table after several excursions to school to be "shared."

We take the *Scientific American*. Its advertising has magnificent pictures of rockets, satellites and other matters dear to the heart of the young devotee of space. Its articles need translation for the small fry but often the puzzle pages are entrancing. We did the Chinese tangrams and wrestled with the Japanese art of paper folding.

My theory is this: Helping children to love learning involves first, creative materials. I have named some, but the last thing on earth that we ever call them is creative materials. They are "stuff."

Second: Love of learning requires enthusiasm. If parents are enthusiastic their offspring will pick it up by contagion. In fact the offspring will spring off in directions where their parents can only stumble, music, in our case. Four-dimensional geometry, another case, and thereby hangs a tale. The tale I am about to tell concerns a third requisite, sustained attention, and how four-dimensional geometry was its climax.

When our oldest son was about four years old, he brought into the kitchen a brown paper sack of clods. He had seen his father collect soil samples in brown paper sacks, so he had invaded a vacant lot and gathered his own sample. Then he asked me to get out our food chopper, an affair of cast metal, and he began to grind up the clods. It was hard work but he stayed with it to the end. Our kitchen looked like the Oklahoma dust bowl and the blade of my chopper was ruined forever.

The years went by and he reached age seventeen. I had tried to teach him and his sisters and brother that when you are pursuing an interest, throw everything you have into it and let the chips fall where they may. You can pick up the chips after the project is complete. (Here I must confess sadly that I never adequately trained them to pick up their chips because by then I was in the midst of some private project of my own, or helping someone else on a project, and couldn't stop to supervise a thorough chip-picking-up. Consequently we seem to dwell perpetually in chips.)

The Science Talent search was on. Our high school senior chose four-dimensional geometry as a project. He cut coat hangers into short strips and hung the corners together with modeling clay. The device which he created was large, angular, and occupied all the top of his desk. This meant his books moved to the floor. Scraps of paper with penciled mathematics lay scattered everywhere in the room. His clothes hung on the floor; his bed was perpetually unmade. Any real tidying-up was impossible for work was in progress, let the chips fall where they may. Just as he completed his paper two days before the deadline, he rushed downstairs, gave it to me and said, "Type this for me, will you Mom?" and hurried out the door to join his friends on an overnight hike. Well, I typed it. He can type—all our children can type—but I make the fewest mistakes. There were seven pages. I understood the first two; his father understood the first four; I still wonder if the judges understood all seven. Anyway it won a placing.

Our household usually looks chaotic because of works in progress and it was a real pleasure for me to read Frank Barron's statement that creative people can stand more chaos than ordinary people. Barron was not speaking of housekeeping but I think the principle applies.

Barron also states that creative persons are more independent in judgment than other people. Years before we ever read Frank Barron or Solomon Asch we had been trying to teach our children to think for themselves and not to conform blindly to groups.

"But all my friends are going to this movie," wails a youngster bent on attending a horror film.

"We don't live like everyone else. We have our own ideas about how to live, and that's a lousy movie," I reply firmly.

But judgment about when to conform and when to rebel comes slowly. In his enthusiasm for individuality, our oldest wore a beard for weeks and a pair of bilious yellow trousers. At the time I could not make him understand that rebellion in dress is a waste of time and energy; one should save one's rebellion for more worthwhile causes. I think he understands this now.

In contrast to the episode of the bilious pants we have a daughter who at five years insisted on more and prettier Sunday school dresses.

"But clothes are not the most important thing in life," I said.

"What is then?" she asked.

"Well," I said slowly as my mind went into high gear, "Knowing things and loving people."

Thousands of pages have been written on philosophy of values and I have struggled with a good many of them. But when you tell a five-year-old about values you do not invoke Kant's categorical imperative.

Knowing things and loving people imply the Truth and Goodness of the ancient Greeks. Beauty; the third of the famous trio, might possibly refer to more beautiful Sunday school dresses, but I think not.

Loving people is a tremendous ideal. We taught the children not to hurt the feelings of others. Their own tears over personal hurt feelings always exceeded the quantity of tears shed from physical pain, and they early learned that other people have feelings too. We taught them that teachers are people and that teachers can get tired and cross just as parents do. It is hard work to be a teacher and they should help her where possible.

Then pride reared its ugly head. "I'm the best in the room," a child would boast.

"Yes but you don't boast about it," we said. "You are fortunate to have good ability, but he who receives much must give much. It is your obligation to help smooth the way for other people. There are many things that need doing in this world and you must help do them."

Humility about one's gifts combined with the ideal of service to others will prevent snobbery, and it is the home which must take first responsibility in teaching these matters.

Because there is so much talk of giftedness these days, children of ability are likely to become self conscious and feel set apart from their friends. I say that all children are gifted; each child must be able to excel at something for his own satisfaction.

But what of the child who is superb at everything? If he is truly a member of his own neighborhood, the other children are not going to judge him as being apart. Around here our children and the neighbor children play marbles together in the living room, make popcorn in the kitchen, and roller skate in the basement. Nobody pays any attention to who is bright in school and who isn't.

I am a cub scout den mother to my young son and seven of his contemporaries. I am a 4-H leader to my young daughters and their crowd. For some reason my relatives chortle at the idea of my teaching girls how to cook, but I can follow directions as well as anyone and our club did win a blue ribbon at the county fair. We can turn out perfect products when we want to but we have flexible standards. When other matters are more important it doesn't hurt our conscience to let housekeeping and cooking go to pot.

Actually, I'm no professional at teaching children. I'm a mother struggling along, trying to strew creative materials and enthusiasm and affection as I go.

Has it occurred to anyone that it might be possible to evolve some suggestions for mothering that would encourage curiosity and learning and creativity among youngsters at home? Homemakers have been deluged for years with recipes, budgeting suggestions, and sewing patterns. But this is something else entirely.

And furthermore, has it occurred to anyone that many of today's gifted girls will be mothers of a good many of tomorrow's gifted children? If heredity causes giftedness, they have the genes. If climate of the home causes giftedness, they will have the opportunity. From the curriculum chosen by today's gifted girls, what can they adapt for use in their future mothering of the gifted? Or will they play it by ear, as mothers have been doing for generations.

29. SOME SUGGESTIONS FOR PARENTS AND EDUCATORS ON HANDLING THE CREATIVE CHILD

Joe Khatena

In view of the thrust of this issue on social and family influences affecting the gifted child, under the able guest editorship of our first vice-president, Prof. Juliana Gensley, I want to take this opportunity to present a substantive message on how parents should handle such a child in order to maximize his potential creativity.

CHARACTERISTICS OF THE CREATIVE CHILD

In a paper presented at a dinner meeting to parents of gifted and talented children at West Carolina University, Joseph Bledsoe (1973) pointed out an important aspect about the gifted and talented child which can quite easily miss us—that first and foremost he is a child, and as a child has needs that motivate him to have them met towards self-actualization and intellectual fulfillment (Maslow, 1954). However, the highly creative child is by nature more intensely affected by need pressures and generally more sensitive to resolve them for self-fulfillment. That is why besides knowing him as a child in the usual sense we must also try to know him as a person sensitized in a more than ordinary way by the energizing forces of creativity.

According to MacKinnon (1965), he may be one of three kinds of creative persons: the kind that creates a product or form made up of elements which did not exist before himself, the kind that produces a novel and appropriate product from some aspect of his environment, or the kind that expresses himself in the product and at the same time meets the demands of some external problem.

Torrance (1969) writing about the creative characteristics of young children observed that the creative child shows intense absorption in listening or doing, intense animation and physical involvement, use of analogies in speech, bodily involvement of an intense nature in writing, drawing and so on, tendency to challenge ideas of authority, the habit of checking many sources and looking closely at things, eagerness to tell others about discoveries, the desire to continue in creative activities after the scheduled time for quitting, relationships among apparently unrelated ideas, the tendency to follow-through ideas set in motion, various manifestations of curiosity, of wanting to know, and of digging deeper, spontaneous use of discovery or the experimental approach, excitement in voice about discoveries, the habit of guessing and testing outcomes, honesty and intense search for truth, independent action, boldness of ideas, low distractability, the manipulation of ideas and objects to obtain new combinations, the tendency to lose awareness of time, penetrating observations and questions, self-initiated learning, tendency to seek alternatives and explore new possibilities, and willingness to consider or toy with a strange ideas.

In a recent study using a creativity checklist entitled *Something About Myself* (Khatena, 1971, 1972). Joseph Bledsoe and I (1973) found that a person may be creative on one or more of six dimensions or factors: *environmental sensitivity* (openness to ideas of others; relating ideas

Reprinted by permission from *Gifted Child Quarterly*, Vol. 22, No. 2, 1978.

to what can be seen touched, or heard; interest in beautiful and humorous aspects of experiences; and sensitivity to meaningful relations, *initiative* (directing, producing, and/or playing leads in dramatic and musical productions; producing new formulas or new products; and bringing about changes in procedures or organization), *self-strength* (self-confidence in matching talents against others; resourcefulness; versatility; willingness to take risks; desire to excel; and organizational ability), *intellectuality* (intellectual curiosity; enjoyment of challenging tasks; imagination; preference for adventure over routine; liking for reconstruction of things and ideas to form something different; and dislike for doing things in a prescribed routine way), *individuality* (preference for working by oneself rather than in a group; seeing oneself as a self-starter and somewhat eccentric; critical of others' work; thinking for oneself; working for long periods without getting tired), and *artistry* (production of objects, models, paintings, carvings; musical compositions; awarding of prizes or having exhibits; production of stories, plays, poems and other literary pieces).

SOME PROBLEMS OF THE HIGHLY CREATIVE CHILD

Problems of highly creative children stem from the environment and their conflicting interaction with it (Torrance, 1962). The creative energizing forces that dominate the life of the highly creative child, set him up in a position of independence and nonconformity in relation to the group of which he is a part often leading to confrontations of one kind or another which constantly call for adjustment: he may either learn to cope with arising tensions or he may repress his creative needs with the one leading to productive behavior and mental health and the other to actual personality disturbances and breakdown.

Torrance further eloquently categorizes and describes the problems of the highly creative child who as a "minority of one" must learn to cope with the sanctions of society against his divergency, to learn to express his talents without alienating his friends, to cope with the demands of our system to be well-rounded to the extent of giving up productive ways of expressing himself to do what he is most interested and best able to do rather than to do what is expected of him because of his sex identity, to learn in his own way rather than in ways prescribed by others, and to continue to attempt the difficult and test the limits in risk taking behavior in spite of discouragement and control, and to find direction and purpose in what he is doing. Further, Torrance would have us recognize that the creative child has a set of values which may be quite different from the group to which he belongs so that we may help him maintain his creativity without being obnoxious; and that he is the kind person who often cannot stop working because his creative energies do not allow him to stop thinking especially in relation to productive work. On the subject of the creative child making problems for himself Torrance cites Barron's (1958) observation that the creative individual rejects the demands of his society's claim that all its members should adapt themselves to a norm for a given time and place.

Common to all these adjustment problems of the highly creative child and of central relevance is his psychological isolation and estrangement from peers, teachers and parents since his propensity to be non conforming independent and productive in his thinking create tensions between himself and others leading to the application of pressure tactics of one kind or another to bring him in line.

The highly creative child may find ways and means to remain both productive and socially acceptable, and this is where we come in to help him acquire those skills and strategies that will allow him to accomplish this; or he may repress his creativity, and while appearing to conform is probably having internal conflicts that will lead him to require remedial measures of counseling or therapy.

Repression of his creative needs may lead the highly creative child to become overly conforming obedient and dependent, with damaging consequences to his concept of self. It may also lead to serious learning disabilities and behavioral problems where in preferring to learn by authority he sacrifices his natural tendency to learn creatively by questioning, guessing exploring and experimentation with consequent loss of interest in and resistant to learning with development of awe of masterpieces and a spread of feelings of inadequacy from deficiency in one area of learning to other areas of learning where no deficiency exist, and where the highly creative child acquires aggressive behaviors in the classroom much of which can be traced to his inability to use creative and scientific thinking strategies to overcome his tensions often arising out of his reactions to a school curriculum that is unchallenging, repetitive, reproductive and boring, before they become problems that result in his misbehavior.

The more serious problem of prolonged enforced repression of the creative child's needs may lead to emotional problems and neurosis, and even psychosis (e.g.; Gowan and Bruch, 1971; Torrance, 1962; Watson, 1965). Neurosis, as you know, is a condition generated by acute and prolonged anxiety states and can be very much the case of continued repression of creative needs especially in the context of conflict situations. Neurosis hinders rather than facilitates the functioning of the creative process contrary to popular opinion. Kubie (1958) in his book *Neurotic Distortion of the Creative Process* suggests that many a creative man of the arts and sciences refuses therapy because he erroneously believes that his "creative zeal and spark" is dependent upon his neurosis; what is really essential is that the preconscious process functions freely to gather, assemble, compare and reshuffle ideas in the activity of creation.

Torrance (1962) writes of psychosis relative to maladjustment of the creative individual in a special sense. In psychosis resulting from the blocking of creative energies, thinking is often paralyzed and the imagination functions in a way that cannot distinguish between reality and irreality. The creative individual who has his productivity blocked may develop behavior traits similar to those of psychotics: "his reaction to reality may be very much like the behavior of the paraonoid personality. For example, a highly creative individual because of the very superiority of his thinking and production may be threatening to others. In actuality he may experience a great deal of persecution. His reaction of this reality may be very much like the behavior of the paranoid personality in some respects. Or in order to accomplish significant creative work, an individual may have to behave in ways which are judges as withdrawn or schizophrenic" (P. 136). These conditions no longer bespeak of the thin partitions that divide the two regions of genius and madness that Alexander Pope poeticized about—they become indistinguishable in psychosis. The distinctive feature of the mentally healthy creator as it were in his ability to cross over at will momentarily the boundary in the act of creation with controls to return from fantasy to reality.

Another problem of the highly creative child is to be found in circumstances of deprivation. The child who comes from poorer home environments are at a disadvantage: not only does he lack material things but also intellectual stimulation. Besides, he may be hindered as well from acquiring adequate verbal concepts and communication skills to handle the mental operations which are usually demanded on traditional measures of intelligence with consequent misinterpretation of the child's potential so that he is erroneously labelled as mentally retarded and treated as such. Many of the other problems already described (e.g. behavioral disorders, faulty concept of self, and learning disabilities) are also pertinent to the highly creative but socio-economically disadvantaged child.

ROLE OF THE PARENT*

As you know a person may be gifted in a number of different ways. You can find this out by talking to a psychologist who can by examining how your child has done on parts of a test tell you what his strong and weak abilities are. Sometimes he may have to use more than one test to find out this information which can be more important to know than just the child's I.Q. In this way you can find out for instance what abilities he tends to use more often than others, and which of them can be put to work for better performance. In this respect Guilford's model of the intellect as a center for processing different kinds of information has encouraged the production, for instance, of a series of books on developing the five intellectual processing capacities, namely, cognition, memory, convergent thinking, divergent thinking and evaluation (Meeker and Sexton, Nd.).

The best of the individual I.Q. tests are the *Stanford Binet* and the *Wechsler Scales of Intelligence for Children.* Of course there are group I.Q. tests, but it is preferable to have your child screened for I.Q. by one of the individual measures. However, it may not always be possible. If your child is screened by a group test and there is reason to doubt the findings check this out by arranging that your child be given either the Binet or Wechsler Scale.

However, obtaining your child's I.Q. is not enough. You should also see to it that your child is screened for creative thinking abilities as well. Guilford's *Creativity Tests for Children,* the *Torrance Tests of Creative Thinking,* and *Thinking Creatively with Sounds and Words* may be used for the purpose. The combined information so derived will help you get a clearer picture of how gifted your child is and in what areas.

While you may have to rely on the help of a psychologist to formally determine that your child is creatively gifted you can also screen your child using a measure which will not require any special training. One such instrument is a creativity checklist or inventory called *Something About Myself:* it is an instrument designed in a way that teachers and parents can use. Another companion instrument is *What Kind of Person Are You?* Both are published as the *Khatena-Torrance Creative Perception Inventory,* and are suitable for identifying children who are creatively gifted 12 years and up when children are required to write their own responses.

Something About Myself has also been successfully tried with children who were 10 and 11 years old as well but with adult help. If the measure is to be used with younger children, then an adult must observe the child and respond to the items of the inventory for the child. The instrument has not as yet been used with children below the age of 10 and may not be suitable for purposes of identifying very young creatively gifted children. Quite simply, administer the test according to the instructions given in the Directions Manual. You can then find out how creative he perceives himself to be by just a straight count of his positive responses: the higher the score obtained the more creative he is according to the scale. The measure also group the items into six creative

*This section has been abridged from Khatena (1978) with permission.

orientations, namely, Environmental Sensitivity, Initiative, Self Strength, Intellectually, Individuality and Artistry. A very highly creative child will tend to be high on all six creative orientations. But generally I have found that the child is low on Initiative, and to some extent below average on Artistry.

Once you have determined his scores on the total scale and the six creative orientations you will have identified not only how creative he is but his strengths and weaknesses on the scale. Your next step would be to plan experiences that will help encourage the use of those creative characteristics in which he is weak. There are also prepared published exercises on the development of many of the characteristics in the inventory that you may use as well. *New Directions in Creativity* (Renzulli, 1973), *Classroom Ideas for Encouraging Thinking and Feeling* (Williams, 1970, and *Structure of Intellect Abilities Workbook* on Divergent Thinking (Meeker and Sexton, Nd.), provide many useful exercises as well. Some of the exercises will have to be developed relative to the characteristics of the measure. With a bit of imagination and effort you can have a fine program going for your child at home and in the classroom. The important thing is that this puts you in the driver's seat, and you can go places with your children in developing the use of their creative qualities.

It is very important that you pay attention to your child's use of analogy and imagery, both of which are very closely related to the creative imagination at work. You can encourage your child to think in ways that break old habits of thought, to use the thinking process that will allow them to pull apart things organized in one way so that he may rearrange the parts in fresh and novel combinations, and to process information in many different and new combinations. You may plan experiences for him that call for the use of analogy and figures of speech all of which have been described, and with some exercises that you can use, modify and extend for your own needs.

I have found that children tend to use the direct analogy form most of all, and that they need practice in the use of personal analogy and fantasy analogy as well. The use of symbolic analogy is dependent on the child's intellectual maturity and can be delayed until the child is in high school. I have also found that children tend to use simple images rather than complex images when he is in the upper elementary grades, and that as he grows older he tends to use more complex images. One of the things you can do would be to assist him in learning how to add meaningful details to the simple images he produces.

You will find your gifted child generally a healthy person both in mind and body, able to get along rather well with others, and does well in school. However, if he is continually restricted in his development and learning you may find him becoming increasingly troublesome. You can help by freeing him from some of the restrictions that do not allow him to grow, and help him to achieve independence and be himself.

Restrictions cause tensions and conflicts, and over long periods of time may lead to the child's mental ill-health. You cannot really remove all the obstructions in his life but you can help him learn to cope with them. Teach him to recognize that there are many alternatives to the solution of a problem, that he may have to know as much as he can about a problem before he can begin to handle it, that he may need to think of many ideas that could be used to solve the problem and write them down, that he will have need to judge the best idea for the solution and he can do this by deciding what is required for a good solution—in short he needs to know about the creative problem solving process and taught to use it. In this respect, you will find the books

Creative Behavior Guidebook and *Creative Behavior Workbook* (Parnes, 1977) to be very useful. Thinking by analogy may also be helpful, and if your child understands how to use this mechanism he may find that solutions to problems come to him more easily.

There are many suggestions about what you can do to help your child overcome and prevent problems. Briefly, they tell you not to over emphasize what the child must do because of being a boy or a girl; to help him continue to be productive without being obnoxious about it; to help him understand why sometimes he tends to be separate from others; to reduce his anxieties by helping him deal with them; to learn to accept failure and use it in a way that will lead to success; and to approach learning by way of experimentation, and experimentation without the stress of constant supervision and evaluation.

Further, you may help him by being nuturant to and supportive of his attempts to create; by allowing him to work within a set of values he had some part in setting and so obtain his commitment to what he does; by taking care of his more basic needs of body, safety, love and esteem so that he can do the things that will lead to self-fulfillment; by helping him to understand and value himself and his ideas; by encouraging him to play about with his ideas and draw from his preconscious; by praising new formed ideas and encouraging their development; and by helping him to get along with others and to overcome the difficulty of finding friends who are also gifted.

There are periods in a child's life when he is most affected by stress and strains of growing up so that his creativity suffers. This has been found to be just at the time the child enters first grade, at the fourth grade level, entry in junior high school and high school. Not only demands put on him by the school, his peers and teachers, but also changes in school seem to affect him adversely. The worst of the slumps seems to take place at the fourth grade level, and this tends to happen when the child experiences developmental changes that bring about a shift in focus in his life, so that control of the environment through affectional relations of the parent of the opposite sex, which is central to his creativity at this time, shifts to control of the environment through increased understanding of it. At these times you can help him by reducing the tensions of change and restrictions, by establishing caring relations with him, by providing stimulating creative activities and conditions of learning, and by encouraging greater use of fantasy, analogy and the creative imagination. You may also show that you appreciate his use of creative abilities and productions, and reward him for his efforts.

You will note that there are times when your child will be more creative than others—a time at which a kind of welling up of some super energy takes place that transforms the everyday activities and happenings into something "rich and strange;" and there are other times when this dynamic play of forces do not occur. Be sensitive to these fluctuations in his life, supporting and approving of creative thoughts and deeds that do occur, and arranging for circumstances that will facilitiate similar creative occurrences during the low periods. You have it in your power to cause creativity to happen and flourish before your very eyes. Be the catalyst of the mystery and magic of existence, for in the creativity of your child may lie a magnificent future for all.

References

Barron, F. The psychology of the imagination. *Scientific American,* 1958, 199, 151–161.

Bledsoe, J. C. The gifted child in the family and the importance of self-esteem. Unpublished manuscript, University of Georgia, 1973.

Bledsoe, J. C., and Khatena, J. Factor analytic study of Something About Myself. *Psychological Reports,* 32, 1176–1178.

Gowan, J. C., and Bruch, C. B. *The academically talented student and guidance.* New York: Houghton Mifflin, 1971.

Khatena, J. Something About Myself: a brief screening device for identifying creatively gifted children and adults. *Gifted Child Quarterly,* 1971, 15, 262–266.

Khatena, J. Attitude patterns as providing validity evidence of Something About Myself. *Perceptual and Motor Skills,* 1972, 34, 563–564.

Khatena, Joe, *The Creatively Gifted Child: Suggestions For Parents and Teachers.* Vantage Press, 516 W. 34th St. NYC, 10001, $7, 1978.

Kubie, L. S. *Neurotic distortion of the creative process.* Lawrence, Kan.: University of Kansas Press, 1958.

Maslow, A. H. *Motivation and personality.* New York: Harper & Brothers, 1954.

Mackinnon, D. W. Personality correlates of creativity. In C. E. Bish (ed.) *Productive thinking in education,* Washington, D.C.: National Education Association, 1965, 159–171.

Meeker, N. M., and Sexton, K. *Structure of intellect workbooks.* Los Angeles, Ca.: Loyola-Marymount Education Department, N.D.

Meeker, Mary, 1976, *Advance Teaching Judgment, Planning And Decision Making.* SOI Institute, 214 Main St., El Segundo, Ca. 90245, 246 pp.

Parnes, S., Noller, Ruth, and Biondi, A. *Guide To Creative Action* (rev. ed.) 400 pp. $8.95; *Creative Actionbook* (rev. ed.) (workbook for above), 217 pp, $4.95, New York: Chas. Scribner's Sons. 1977.

Renzulli, J. S. *New directions in creativity.* Harper & Row, 1970.

Renzulli, J. 1977 *The Enrichment Triad Model.* The Creative Learning Press, 530 Silas Deane Hy., Wethersfield, Ct. 06109, $7.95.

Torrance, E. P. *Guiding creative talent.* Englewood Cliffs, N.J.: Prentice-Hall, 1962.

Torrance, E. P. *Creativity.* San Rafael, Calif.: Dimensions, 1969.

Watson, G. H. Emotional problems of gifted students. In W. Barbe (Ed.) *Psychology and education of the gifted.* New York: Appleton-Century-Crofts, 1965, 342–353.

Williams, F. E. *Classroom ideas for encouraging thinking and feeling.* Buffalo, N.Y.: D. O, K., 1970.

IX

IMAGERY AND THE RIGHT HEMISPHERE

30. INCUBATION, IMAGERY, AND CREATIVITY

J. C. Gowan

Abstract

Right-hemisphere imagery is the vehicle through which incubation produces creativity. Incubation involves any technique of relaxation which allows us to pay attention to the imagery which is continually going on in the right hemisphere. The key elements in this relaxation appear to be a) lowering sensory input and b) stopping internal verbal chatter. That such imagery is the precursor to creativity is the testimony of geniuses in both art and science. The function of the left hemisphere appears to be to prepare an alphanumeric matrix so that the image can be intellectually negotiated with others.

Right-hemisphere Imagery is the vehicle through which incubation produces creativity. In his famous paradigm of creative process, Graham Wallas (1926) identified four components: preparation, incubation, illumination, verification. By incubation, he meant any technique of relaxation of the conscious cognition (left-hemisphere function), such as, but not confined to, dreams, daydreams, fantasy, hypnosis, meditation, diversion, play, etc., which allows subliminal processes (right-hemisphere functions) to operate. He saw preparation (academic discipline), as the necessary, and incubation (relaxation), as the sufficient condition for creative insights to emerge.

We shall assume the definition of mental imagery implicit in this Journal,—namely, essentially nonverbal (in the Guilford Structure of intellect parlance—nonsymbolic) material occurring in consciousness not immediately preceded by perceptual intake. By creativity, we shall mean the production of material or relationships new to the culture. To open up the discussion, we follow our initial statement with further elaboration: Whereas most functions of the left hemisphere are concerned with convergent production as described by Guilford, functions of the right hemisphere are principally concerned with divergent production. These functions involve imagery through which incubation produces creativity.

The seat of this imagery appears to be in the Wernicke area of the right cerebral hemisphere (Jaynes, 1975, pp. 101–9). While it was once thought that special means were necessary to elicit this imagery, more recently it has appeared that the process, like the shining of the stars, goes on all the time but, during our waking hours under most circumstances, is overlaid by the more cognitive activity of the generally dominant left hemisphere. Cognitive activity involves the handling of incoming perceptual information and its processing into thought and decision via language, and the continual stream of internal discourse which accompanies consciousness. Remove both of these activities from left-hemisphere function through relaxation, meditation, hypnosis, fantasy,

Reprinted by permission from *Journal of Mental Imagery*, Vol. 2, 1978.

daydreaming, sensory deprivation or some similar state, and the imagery of the right hemisphere is at once brought into focus.

That the imagery occurs is an experiential fact which needs no further validation for most of us. The question: "Where does it come from?" leads us into the realm of philosophy. While we cannot speculate about this question for long, a short discussion may be useful. Here are a few possibilities:

a) all imagery is postperceptual, after-imagery, or a kind of eidetic imagery consequent on the sensorium;

b) since the right hemisphere "operates" (thinks) in terms of imagery, it is there all the time, only we are not usually attentive to it, since the left-hemisphere operation overrides;

c) imagery is some kind of psychic resonance, like a TV picture, which occurs when the right hemisphere is in tune with cosmic, interior or transpersonal sources;

d) images are expressions of archetypal material which is slowly being expressed into conscious awareness;

e) imagery is the first level of descent or "degradation" of cosmic consciousness from void to existence.

This hypothesis is not as wild as might be supposed. Wilber says (1977, p. 109) in regard to the theories of mathematician Spencer Brown in *Laws of Form:*

> Following upon this primary dualism there arises according to Brown several departures from the void, four of which he chooses to emphasize: void to form, form to indication, indication to truth, and truth to existence. Speaking of these general processes he states: "We left the central state of the form, proceding outwards and imagewise towards the peripheral condition of existence."

Later in quoting Benoit and Krishnamurti, Wilber (1977, p. 319) declares: Here Krishnamurti is agreeing completely with Benoit that the machinery of image production is inattention or as Benoit calls it, passive attention.

A more practical question than "Where does imagery come from?" is "Under what conditions does imagery occur?" It is now quite obvious that, while imagery occurs spontaneously under hypnosis, and in trance, dreams, hypnogogic and hypnopompic states, as well as in other natural and induced altered states of consciousness, it can be found also in the more normal states, such as, daydreaming, fantasy, meditation, creative spells, relaxation, sensory deprivation, and the like, where the ego and full memorability are present. The key elements in the situation appear to be a) lowering the sensory input and b) stopping the internal verbal chatter; both of these point to allaying the overriding function of the left hemisphere. From the above it appears that right-hemisphere imagery goes on all the time and that it is merely necessary to pay attention to it. Learning of how to do this is obviously a new educational challenge, if we are to educate both halves of the brain and hence stimulate creativity in young people.

The use of art and music education to stimulate right-hemisphere activity and hence improve creative function has been mentioned by a number of writers. Williams (1977) in an article on "Why Children Should Draw" points out that art stimulates a child's curiosity. He quotes Houston: "Verbal-linear-analytical intelligence is a small part of the intelligence spectrum. There is also visual-aesthetic-plastic (working with the hands) intelligence." This right-hemisphere intelligence is what, in an earlier day, Lowenfeld called "Haptic," and what Ferguson (1977) calls "thinking with pictures" which he believes to be an essential strand in the history of technology development, although it is presently neglected in scientific education.

Again to quote Williams:

> The differentiation of the brain into left and right hemispheres certainly plays a role in arts-centered learning. . . . A child without access to a stimulating arts program, according to Houston 'is being systematically cut off from most of the ways in which he can perceive the world. His brain is being systematically damaged. In many ways he is being de-educated.'

Williams then cites a number of elementary schools where an enriched arts program has improved general performance.

Jaynes (1976, pp. 364–9) devotes several pages to the importance of music and musical instruction in stimulating the right hemisphere. After citing a number of authorities and facts in support of the special relationship of music to the right hemisphere, and hypothesizing (on the basis of experiments on neonates) that "the brain is organized at birth to obey musical stimulation in the right hemisphere," he concludes that the research points "to the great significance of lullabies in development, perhaps influencing the child's later creativity."

If the function of incubation is to allay the activity of the left hemisphere so that right-hemisphere imagery can be consciously observed, how better can we learn about this process than through the testimony of geniuses? We shall see that, whereas the left hemisphere seems to act as a problem solver, the right seems to act as a radio receiver. Thus, when the static of the left hemisphere has been abated, some type of resonance phenomenon is set up, of which the first evidence is *vibrations*. Consider what the composer Brahms told Arthur Abell (Abell, 1964, pp. 19–21):

> I immediately feel vibrations which thrill my whole being. . . . In this exalted state I see clearly what is obscure in my ordinary moods, and I feel capable of drawing inspiration from above, as Beethoven did. . . . Those vibrations assume the form of distinct mental images. . . . Straightaway the ideas flow upon me . . . and not only do I see distinct themes, . . . but they are clothed in the right forms. . . . I have to be in a semi-trance condition to get such results— a condition when the conscious mind is in temporary abeyance, and the subconscious is in control.

Similar statements by Puccini and Wagner will be found in a discussion of the discrete steps in the creativity of musical composers (Gowan, 1976, pp. 378–86) from which is quoted:

> For most, it will be seen that the process of such high creativity consists of three phases: 1) the prelude ritual. . . . 2) the altered state of consciousness or creative spell, during which the creative idea is born, starting with vibrations, then mental images, then the flow of ideas which are finally clothed in form. This syndrome often proceeds with extreme and uncanny rapidity in what is always referred to as a trance, dream, revery, somnambulistic state, or similar altered condition, and 3) the postlude in which positive emotions about the experience suffuse the participant.

The casual reader might allow that such things go on in music and the arts but hardly in the world of science, where the logic of the left hemisphere should reign supreme. But curiously, it is here, in the area of scientific invention, that we find the strongest case for right-hemisphere imagery. Indeed, we may go further and assert that in the case of every historic scientific discovery and invention which is researched carefully enough, we find that it was imagery, either in dreams or in a waking state which produced the breakthrough. We have the testimony of men such as Archimedes, Newton, Faraday, Agassiz, Hilprecht, Poincare, Mendeleev, Kekule, Loewi, and others (Ghiselin, 1952; Gowan, 1974) that this is so. Perhaps the most authoritative recent statement on the subject is that of Prof. E. S. Ferguson in *Science* (1977), who says:

> Many features and qualities of the objects that a technologist thinks about cannot be reduced to unambiguous verbal descriptions; they are dealt with in his mind by a visual, nonverbal process. His mind's eye is a well developed organ that not only reviews the contents of his visual memory, but also forms such new or modified images as his thoughts require.
>
> It is nonverbal thinking, by and large, that has fixed the outlines and filled in the details of our material surroundings. . . . Pyramids, cathedrals, and rockets exist not because of geometry, theory of structures or thermodynamics, but because they were first a picture—literally a vision—in the minds of those who built them.
>
> Galton, speaking of "inventive mechanicians" observed that "they invent their machines as they walk and see them in height, breadth and depth as real objects, and they can also see them in action". How to cultivate this "visualizing faculty" without prejudice to the practice of abstract thought in words or symbols was, to Galton, one of the "many desiderata in the yet unformed science of education."
>
> Much of the creative thought of the designers of our technological world is nonverbal, not easily reducible to words. Its language is an object or a picture or a visual image in the mind.

The following anecdotes are excellent examples of this ability of mechanical geniuses to think in images:

Hunt and Draper (1964) describe an experience of the young Nicola Tesla quoting poetry to a friend:

> As he was walking toward the sunset quoting these words, the idea came like a flash of lightning and the solution to the problem of alternating current motors appeared before him as revelation. He stood as a man in a trance, trying to explain his vision to his friend. . . . The images which appeared before Tesla seemed as sharp and clear and as solid as metal or stone. The principle of the rotating magnetic field was clear to him. In that moment a world revolution in electrical science was born (p. 33).

Koestler (1964) cites the experience of the Dutch chemist Kekule who was trying to synthesize benzene:

> I turned my chair to the fire and dozed. Again the atoms were gamboling before my eyes. The smaller groups kept modestly in the background. My mental eye, rendered more acute by visions of this kind, could now distinguish larger structures, of manifold conformations, long rows sometimes more closely fitted together, all twining and twisting in snake-like motion. But look! What was that? One of the snakes had seized hold of its own tail and the form whirled mockingly before my eyes. As if by a flash of lightning I awoke (p. 118).

This imagery granted Kekule a glimpse into noncategorical reality, from which he wrote down the now-famous formula for the benzene ring. But the imagery equally applies to the DNA molecule, which lack of adequate preparation prevented Kekule from discovering.

The case for differentiation between right-hemisphere divergent production (creativity) and left-hemisphere convergent production (problem solving) can be strengthened by consideration of two rather cogent arguments.

A curious characteristic of creativity which appears to have escaped critical attention is that its variability in individuals far exceeds the variability of other traits and abilities. Wechsler (1974, p. 109), for example, has conclusively demonstrated that the interpersonal variability of such psychological and physiological measures as height, weight, cranial capacity, grip strength, blood pressure, respiration rate, reaction time, pitch, Snellen acuity, intelligence, mental age, and memory span has a limit of e/1, where e = 2.818, the basis of the natural logarithm system, and in most cases has a mean of 2.3 or less. Yet comparing the creative productions of a genius such as Einstein, Mozart, or Picasso with those of more ordinary mortals, one finds a ratio of 100/1 or over. Obviously the trait and factor theory of creativity cannot account for all of the variance.

The second argument notes that even the most intelligent person cannot be creative at will, and there are many bright people who are never creative. Mastery of a particular discipline is a necessary, but not a sufficient, condition for creative production. The sufficient condition, as we have said before, is incubation and the production of imagery, or at least the ability to allay left-hemisphere function enough to pay some conscious attention to it. Failure to acquire this ability is apparently what keeps some gifted persons from becoming creative, so in this sense, creativity can be taught.

The relationship of imagery to creativity is well recognized. Says Leuner (1977):

> Imagination and imagery, a visualization of mental contents, appear very closely related to visual fantasies and daydreaming. For the present purposes, it is unnecessary to examine the significance of these two elements in the creative process in detail; suffice it to say that in regard to creativity . . . visual imagery appears an early primitive form (p. 74).

Khatena (1978), in discussing creative imagination, remarks:

> Much of brain activity relative to the creative imagination has to do with imagery or the re-experiencing of images.
> My recent research on the creative imagination has led me to define the function of the imagination as the chemistry of mental processing where interactive intellectual and emotional forces participate in stimulating, energizing and propagating the creative act.

Khatena in this article and elsewhere (1975, 1977 a, b, c, 1978) has made exhaustive surveys of the function of imagery in creativity, and of the effects of educational techniques to stimulate such imagery and creativity. For other source books on such educational techniques, the reader is referred to Arieti (1976), Biondi and Parnes (1976), Feldhusen and Treffinger (1976), Gowan (1972), Gowan, Khatena, and Torrance (1978), Guilford (1977), Khatena (1977), Parnes, Noller, and Biondi (1977), Rothenberg and Hausman (1976), Stanley, George, and Solano (1977), and Torrance and Myers (1970).

Right-hemisphere function, imagery, and creativity were connected in research by Harnad, quoted by Krippner (1972) and others in which it was hypothesized that the direction in which a subject looks when confronted with a problem, indicates that it is the opposite side of the brain which is active. Left-movers were found to have more visual imagery and to score higher on a creativity test than right-movers. Earlier research in this area of a confirming nature, was done by Bakan (1971).

Elmer and Alice Green of the Menninger Clinic (1977) have also connected relaxation, hypnagogic imagery, and creativity. In describing a biofeedback technique to improve creativity, they say:

> Many described a kind of reverie or near-dream state in which intuitive ideas and solutions came to consciousness in the form of hypnagogic images. . . . Perhaps everybody is creative and merely needs training in order to increase the object evidence of it (p. 124).

They add:

> Is it not interesting that, on the one hand, many outstandingly creative people have reported their greatest insights . . . were associated with reverie and hypnapompic imagery,

and, on the other hand, the imagery and insights reported by college students in the theta training project involved changes in their personal lives. . . . These are also amenable to insight, intuition and creativity. It is in this sense that we say we are all creative (p. 149).

Webster defines "imagination" as "the act of process of imagining; the formation of mental images of objects not present to the senses, especially those never perceived in their entirety; hence mental synthesis of new ideas from their elements experienced separately."

Arieti (1976, p. 37) defines imagination as the ability of the awake mind to produce symbolic functions without effort. These include imagery, ideas, and sequences of words. Imagination is a "precursor of creativity," subsequent elaborations being necessary for it. It is imagery which "plays a crucial role in the process of creativity" (ibid:46), and is facilitated by "rest, solitude, darkness and meditation."

A somewhat different view is taken by Bachelard (1971, p. 1) who sees imagery as an absolute, a starting point of consciousness. He quotes Shelley (ibid., p. 13) "The imagination is capable of making us create what we see." He concludes. "The phenomenology of perception must stand aside for the phenomenology of the creative imagination." Later (ibid., p. 112) he suggests a method of incubation by the statement that "reverie is the mnemonics of the imagination."

Koestler (1964) devotes a chapter to the image which he sees as the basis of analogy. He quotes Kretschmer that:

> Creative products of the artistic imagination tend to emerge from a state of lessened consciousness and diminished attention to external stimuli. . . . The condition is one . . . providing an entirely passive experience of a visual character, divorced from space and time, and reason and will (p. 325).

The highest aspect of imaginative imagery occurs in the syntactic processing of verbalization in what we call creative states. (A clear example is Coleridge's composition of *Kubla Khan.*) This is a complex process and appears to involve first the production of images and then the substitution of words, music, or mathematics for the images. Consider some very authoritative testimony on this subject:

Coleridge (quoted by Ghiselin, 1952) speaking of himself in the third person says: All the images rose up before him like *things,* with a parallel production of the corresponding expressions, without any sensation of conscious effort (p. 85).

The creative geniuses are most eloquent in their imagery testimony. Says the great Einstein (Ghiselin, 1952, p. 43):

> Words or language do not seem to play any role in my mechanism of thought. The psychical entities which seem to serve as elements in thought are certain signs and more or less clear images.

Sometimes the image is a vision. Krippner (1972) reports:

> In 1869 D. I. Mendeleev went to bed exhausted after struggling to conceptualize a way to categorize the elements based on their atomic weights. He reported "I saw in a dream a table where all the elements fell into place as required. Awakening I immediately wrote it down on a piece of paper. Only in one place did a correction later seem necessary." In this manner, Mendeleev's Periodic Table of the Elements was created.

What genius does naturally by intuition, education can help the less able to learn by accretion, but the mechanics of the process must be understood, which is precisely the reason for this article.

We now possess enough facts and hunches regarding right-hemisphere functions to be able to put this knowledge to practical use. Admittedly in this article we have looked at the forest rather than the trees, brushing with broad strokes over a wide canvas. What has been said, for example, must be qualified as applying only to left-hemisphere dominance (right-handedness), and any sophisticated reader will once recognize other exceptions and singularities which later will have to be dealt with separately. But the broad pattern leading from incubation, through imagery to creativity is clear, and if we wish to produce a more creative tomorrow, we should act on it in education today. The civilization we save thereby may be our own.

CONCLUSIONS

Putting together elements discussed previously, as well as information presented elsewhere, (Gowan, 1967, 1972, 1974, 1975, 1976, 1977, 1978; Gowan, Khatena, and Torrance, 1978) we may summarize the metamorphosis characteristic of incubation in which nonverbal imagery plays a central part, as follows:

0) There has previously been intense left-hemisphere study and analysis of the problem/ situation, whose apparent function is to prepare a matrix of vocabulary and verbal description so that the ultimate creative solution can be "intellectually negotiated" and hence shared with society.

1) Through accidental or contrived means, the protagonist is placed in an environment which triggers emotion, where he is alone and undisturbed and, under ardent desire and fixed purpose, finds himself in the altered state of consciousness of right-hemisphere process in a creative spell, fantasy, dream, vision, revery (which are probably mere names for the uncanny feeling which goes with allaying left-hemisphere function).

2) With left-hemisphere function allayed, and right-hemisphere function active, some sort of resonance effect takes place often accompanied by somatic feelings of vibration; and all takes place in condensed time.

3) Out of the vibrations come images, which may be indistinct or virtual images which appear superimposed on the visual field. The images are not passive, but, partaking of the function of archetypes, have a certain generating and heuristic effect, in that they lead to discovery and action.

4) This process is accompanied by intense positive emotion of awe, joy, content, satisfaction, completion, somewhat similar to, but often greater and more sublime than sexual orgasm and remarkably like the "peak experience" described by Maslow. In obedience to the James-Lange theory this condition persists for a time after the experience.

5) In the case of all save artistic creativity, there now ensues intense left-hemisphere activity to notate, verbalize, describe, and operate this imagery into "intellectually negotiable" form, so that it can be "consensually validated" by others. This activity which is part of the Wallas "evaluation," may go on for a long time. It requires the precursor "preparatory," stage so that the matrix is ready to clothe the images in verbal or numerical form. While this element is termed "creative," it is probable that the true "Wallas Illumination" occurs with imagery. If the matrix has not been prepared, the right-hemisphere activity will merely evoke a pleasant emotion, and no lasting social creative product will emerge.

Incubation is the mental analog of physical gestation in which an ovum is developed into a baby. Incubation is the process of metamorphosis, and right-hemisphere imagery is the vehicle through which incubation produces creativity.

References

Abel, A. M. *Talks with the great composers*. Garmisch-Partenkirchen, Germany: G. E. Schroeder-Verlag, 1964.

Arieti, S. Creativity: *The magic synthesis*. New York: Basic Books, 1976.

Biondi, A., and Parnes, S. *Assessing creative growth* (vols 1 and 2). New York: Creative Synergetic Assn., 1976.

Bachelard, G. *The poetics of reverie*. Boston: Beacon Press, 1971.

Bakan, P. The eyes have it. *Psychology Today* 1971, 4, 64–67, 96

Feldhusen J., and Treffinger, D. *Teaching creative thinking and problem solving*. Dubuque, Ia. 52001, Wm. C. Brown Company Publishers Kendall/Hunt Publishing Company, 1976.

Ferguson, E. S. The mind's eye: Nonverbal thought in technology. *Science* August, 1977, 827–836.

Ghiselin, B. (ed.) *The creative process*. Berkeley: University of California Press, 1952.

Gowan, J. C., Demos, G. D., and Torrance, E. P. *Creativity: Its educational implications*. New York: Wiley & Sons, 1967.

Gowan, J. C. *Development of the creative individual*. San Diego, R. Knapp 1972.

Gowan, J. C. *Development of the psychedelic individual*. Buffalo: Creative Education Foundation, 1974.

Gowan, J. C. *Trance, art, and creativity*. Buffalo: Creative Education Foundation, 1975.

Gowan, J. C. The view from myopia, *Gifted Child Quarterly*, 1976, 20, 378–87.

Gowan, J. C. Some new thoughts on creativity, *Journal of Creative Behavior*, 1977, 11, 77–91.

Gowan, J. C. Editorial: Gifted Child Education in Utopia, *Gifted Child Quarterly*, 1978, 1, 1ff (a)

Gowan, J. C. The Role of Imagination in the Development of The Creative Individual, *Humanitas*, 1978, (in press), (b)

Gowan, J. C., Khatena, J., and Torrance, E. P. (Eds.) *Educating the ablest* (rev. ed.) Itasca, Ill.: F. E. Peacock, 1978 (in press).

Green, E. *Beyond biofeedback*. New York: Delcorte Press, 1977.

Guilford, J.P. *Way beyond the IQ*. Buffalo: Creative Education Fd., 1977.

Hunt, I., and Draper, W. W. *Lightning in his hand: The life story of Nicola Tesla Hawthorne*, CA: Omni Publications, 1964.

Khatena, J. Creative imagination imagery and analogy. *Gifted Child Quarterly*, 1975, 19, 2.

Khatena, J. Advances in research in creative imagination imagery. *Gifted Child Quarterly*.

Khatena, J. *The creatively gifted child*. New York Vantage Press, 1977. (c)

Khatena, J. Advances in research in creative imagination imagery *Gifted Child Quarterly*, 1977, 21, 4 (b).

Khatena, J. *The creatively gifted child*, New York: Vantage Press, 1977 (c).

Khatena, J. Creative imagination through imagery: Some recent research. *Humanitas*, 1978, 1, (in press).

Kosetler, A. *The act of creation*. New York: MacMillan, 1964.

Krippner, S. The creative person and nonordinary reality. *The Gifted Child Quarterly*, 1972, 16, 203–228.

Jaynes, J. *The origin of consciousness in the breakdown of the bicameral mind*. Boston: Houghton Mifflin Co. 1976.

Leuner, H. Guided affective imagery: An account of its development *Journal of Mental Imagery*, 1977,1, 73–92.

Parnes, S., Noller, R., and Biondi, A. *Guide to creative action* (rev. ed.). New York: Chas. Scribner's Sons, 1977.

Rothenberg, A., and Hausman C. R. (Eds.) *The creativity question*. Durham, N.C.: Duke University Press, 1976.

Stanley, J. C., George, W. C. and Solano, C. II. (Eds.) *The gifted and the creative: A fifty year perspective*. Baltimore MD.: The Johns Hopkins University Press, 1977.

Torrance, E. P., and Myers, R. E. *Creative learning and teaching* New York: Dodd & Mead Co., 1970.

Wallas, G. *The art of thought*. London: C. A. Watts, 1926.

Wechsler, D. *The collected papers of David Wechsler* New York: Academic Press, 1974.

Wilber, K. *The spectrum of consciousness*. Wheaton, Ill.: Theosophical Publishing House, 1977.

Williams, R. Why children should draw. *Saturday Review*, Sept. 3, 1977, 11–16.

31. THE NUTURE OF IMAGERY IN THE VISUAL AND PERFORMING ARTS

Joe Khatena

By visual arts we probably mean drawing, painting, sculptor, designing, and related productions of art forms that appeal to the eye; by performing arts we probably mean music, dance, oratory, drama and all other related forms of art that require performance. A person engaged in the production of such works of art has to possess certain talents that allow him to perceive the ordinary world with an "uncommon eye" that stores as images sensory impressions that go beyond the visual, auditory and kinesthetic, where sensory boundaries are crossed so that, for instance, what is heard is seen, and what is touched is visualized. To these may be added a sensitivity to rhythm and a depth for feeling that when energized by the creative imagination brings about a "magic synthesis" of the elements into an image that is precursor to a work of art.

CREATIVE IMAGINATION IMAGERY

Imagination has been defined in many ways. In Webster, we find imagination defined as "the act or process of imagining; the formation of mental images of objects not present to the senses, especially those never perceived in their entirety; hence mental synthesis of new ideas from their elements experienced separately." Imagination has also been defined as the mental capacity to produce or reproduce several symbolic functions while in a conscious state without deliberate effort to organize these functions (Arieti, 1976).

The magic and mystery of the imagination set in motion by creative energy have given articulation to the world, transforming reality to dreams, and dreams to reality. William Blake saw it as "some form of spiritual energy" in whose exercise we experience in some way the activity of God. Samuel T. Coleridge regarded the imagination as an ability of first importance, since human beings involved in creative activities simulate in some way the creative act of God. More recently C.M. Bowra (1950) astutely observed that the function of the imagination was a mysterious activity of the mind in the act of solving problems; for most of us "when we use our imagination are in the first place stirred by some alluring puzzle which calls for a solution, and in second place enabled by our own creations in the mind to see much that was before dark or unintelligible. I have defined the function of imagination as the chemistry of mental processing where interactive intellectual and emotive forces participate in stimulating, energizing, and propagating the creative act (Khatena, 1973).

Imagination as creative problem solving process was identified by Wallas (1926) as involving four distinct steps namely, *preparation* (investigation of the problem in all directions), *incubation* (not consciously thinking of the problem), *illumination* (the effortless appearance of happy ideas during a state of relaxation and rest, and *verification* (conscious effort to determine the validity of the solution according to some criteria or rules).

Reprinted by permission from *Gifted Child Quarterly*, Vol. 23, No. 4, 1979. Paper presented at the Expressive Therapies and Creative Education and the Gifted Education Program Conference at the University of Georgia, Athens, Georgia, March 29, 1979.

Recent theorizing by Vargiu (1977) describes imagination as activity of creative energy fields that are both mental and emotive. He likens their activity to the well-known behavior of a thin layer of iron particles arranged randomly in the presence of a magnet. As the intensity of the magnetic field increases with its approach to the iron particles, and the iron particles become magnetized by induction generating their own magnetic field, and on overcoming friction, they will move toward the formation of or transform themselves into a pattern with a suddenness and rapidity that is independent of the magnet that set them in motion. Mental evens, Varigu suggests, pass through the stages of preparation, frustration, incubation, illumination and elaboration; and the suddenness of illumination he explains as 'avalanche effect'. Prior to illumination, is the state of incubation, which he suggests is not a statically random ordering of mental elements by the dynamism involved by the creative energy field that in the initial part of the creative process passes through the stages of preparation, confusion, and frustration which lay the ground work for incubation and illumination.

Both Wallas and Vargiu see preparation, incubation, and illumination as essential steps in the creative process; however, Varigu's additional step of frustration occurring prior to incubation adds strength to Wallas' model since it is *that* energy which is needed to give focus and direction to the incubation process. The final step in the creative process identified as verification by Wallas is identified by Varigu as elaboration. Both see *incubation,* an irrational process related to pre-conscious activity, as important and conducive to imaging just prior to the illumination phase which occurs with a suddenness that Varigu explains as 'avalanche effect' (Khatena, 1978).

We can recognize that the function of creative imagination involves intellectual abilities as well as energy fields, that operate in various ways to lead to incubation, creative imagery, and illumination in the creative process. Drawing from Guilford, Wallas and Vargiu's writings it is possible to perceive abilities energized by magnetic field of forces that are both mental and emotive as central to creative functioning. Activity set in motion by imagination causes these forces to act and interact with each other and with intellectual abilities. This activity may be deliberate or ongoing without our full awareness; however, if a problem is presented for processing this activity, incubation is induced, often producing imagery that leads to illumination and problem solution.

Jaynes (1976) locates such imagery in the Wernicke are of the right cerebral hemisphere where it goes on all the time though overlaid most frequently with left brain or dominant hemisphere cognitive activity which Gowan (1978) has likened to the "static of a radio receiver; it is when this activity of the left hemisphere abates (and this can be brought about through relaxation, meditation, hypnosis, fantasy, day-dreaming, sensory deprivation or some similar state) that some type of resonance phenomena is set up, the first evidence of which is 'vibrations' followed by the occurrence of imagery.

Brahms (Abell, 1964) has attributed the source of 'vibrations' prior to musical composition to the 'awe-inspiring experience' with his Maker. He tells us that when he feels the urge to compose.

> . . . I begin by appealing directly to my Maker. . . . I immediately feel vibrations which thrill my whole being. . . . In this exalted state I see clearly what is obscure in my ordinary moods; than I feel capable of drawing inspiration from above as Beethoven did. . . .

He then describes that while he is in a semi-trance like state, these vibrations take the shape of distinct mental images that precipitate the flow of ideas to give birth to musical composition:

> . . . Those vibration assume the form of distinct mental images. . . . Straightaway the ideas flow in upon me, directly from God, and not only do I see distinct themes in the mind's eye, but they are clothed in the right forms, harmonies, and orchestration. Measure by measure the finished product is revealed to me when I am in those rare, inspired moods. . . .

In a recent analysis of the process of high creativity of musical composers, Gowan (1977) identifies three phases as follows:

1. the prelude ritual, which may be conscious or unconscious, ending often with an invocation;
2. the altered state of consciousness, or creative spell, during which the creative idea is born, starting with vibrations then mental images, then the flow of ideas which are finally clothed in form; this syndrome often proceeds with extreme and uncanny rapidity in what is always referred to as a trance, dream, revery, somnambulistic state, or similar altered condition; and
3. the postlude in which positive emotions about the experience suffuse the participant.

THE FUNCTION OF IMAGERY

In psychology an image is defined as a perception in the absence of an external stimulus irrespective of the sense modality in which it occurs. Rosemary Gordon (1972) tells us that when she speaks of 'an image' she speaks of:

> . . . the perception of forms, or colors, or sounds, or smells, or movements, or tastes in the absence of an actual external stimulus which could have caused such perception. This does not mean that such external stimuli did not present themselves in the past nor that the image is independent of such past experiences. But it does mean that at the time of the perception of the image no such stimulus is present. (P. 63)

An individual perceives the external world through his senses, and records these messages about the world in his brain as images later to be retrieved from storage in the absence of the original stimulus event. These images can be of photographic likeness without the mediation of emotive-motivational processes unique to each individual; but this is unlikely, and images can be expected to differ from one person to the next though the original stimulus events were the same. The image has the importance of giving coherence to a multitude of sensory input data about the world, it orders events, experiences, and relationships; it links the past and present and projects the future; it is the repository of experiences, needs, frustrations, and projects the uniqueness of individual personality; it provides information about the inner life or private world of the individual; and it is the key to man's creativity.

Gordon (1972) has examined at length this privacy and exclusiveness of the image world unique to each individual that musicians, artists, and film-makers assume with 'arrogant certainty' to be similar. That our image worlds are so different from one another is natural since a great many variables affect them, among which are dimensions of content, sense modality, flexibility-rigidity, divergency-convergency, autonomy-control, and active-passive. These dimensions are further affected by whether a person's imagery is predominantly reconstructive or constructive and inventive. She suggests that perhaps these are the distinguishing features of the artist or the creative versus the non artist or the critic. To these different dimensions of imagery may be included the world of the *synaesthetic* where "visual images evoked sounds and tastes, and tones mixed up with colors and touch sensations." Edgar Allan Poe in one of his poems "hears" the approach of darkness; in another Poe describes sensations that accompanies death as follows:

> . . . Night arrived; and with its shadows a heavy discomfort. It oppressed my limbs with the oppression of some dull weight, not unlike the distant reverberation of surf, but more continuous, which beginning with the first twilight, had grown in strength with the darkness. Suddenly lights were brought into the room . . . an issuing from the flame of each lamp there flowed unbrokenly into my ears a strain of melodious monotone.

Different artists need different kinds and combinations of imagery (e.g., the playwright, film-maker, and theatre directors need both visual and auditory images whereas the artist needs visual and the musician auditory images). These differences in imagery also vary for artists in different culture (e.g., a Chinese artist's sketches of London that looked more like China) or for artists living in different times (e.g., Shakespearian costumes mark Elizabethan England rather than the times the story assigns), and Gordon concludes that while the image world of an individual is personal and private it is open to influence and change. Arieti (1976) on the subject of art, the individual and society, perceives in the individual's dynamic relationship and creative exchange with society the magic synthesis that leads to invention, discovery, and eminence.

PERCEPTION IMAGERY AND ART

Arieti (1976) says that a person may paint what he sees (e.g., a tree, human being, an animal) in which case he relies on *perception,* or he may paint not by looking at but by remembering what he saw, in which case he resorts to his *imagery* (e.g., earliest expressions of art on caves were made by artists who relied on their own images, since the animals they portrayed were not in the caves). An artist who relies on imagery has to perceive the object before he can evoke it through imagery, and he can always check what he is doing through imagery by seeing the object in reality thereby re-experiencing the original perception (something that cave dwellers probably did in the course of their paintings).

Perception of an object of course if affected by thoughts feelings and past experiences, so that the inner representation of the outer object is not an exact replica. Arieti tells us that Cezanne did not wish to reproduce nature in mirror-like fashion as was conventionally done but to represent it. His art after a long period of realism opened the door to subjectivity, and following him, the subjective element in art grew in importance learning more toward the primary rather than secondary process. This meant a greater reliance on imagery and imagination than on perception and memory, thereby allowing a fuller and more profound expression of the human spirit. No longer is the artist bound by the dictates of the retina: he soars in the realms of fantasy propelled by the emotions and given to symbolize rather than to describe or narrate. In a more general sense, Man has found through art forms a way of breaking the seal that locks him fast to his inner world and through which he can communicate with least distortion the essential nature of the original message (Gordon, 1972).

Gowan (1975) sees art as the final product in the parataxic (i.e., experience of the numinuous received as images) totemization of the traumatic aspects of the numinous element: by art the individual finds external form for his fears, fantasy, and psychic tension constructively and in so doing achieves cartharsis while simultaneously producing objects of social value, beauty, and delight. The production of a masterpiece is explained by Gowan as:

> . . . the long journey from the collective unconscious (archetypes) to the personal unconscious (icons) through creativity to the personal preconscious, and finally to external collective display (art). (P. 227)

On the subject of art as image-magic, Gowan draws our attention to the parataxic mode which he says is characterized by the production of images which first served as the objective of magic elements (symbols) the origin of visual art, then as signs (as in icons or signs), and finally as pictures as in modern art. In creating images that find expression in some form of art, Man gains autonomy, purpose, and security. This "therapeutic magic finds expression in Picasso's reaction on seeing the first exhibition of African art in Paris:

> . . . Men had made those masks and other objects for a sacred purpose, a magic purpose, as a kind of mediation between themselves and the unknown hostile forces that surround them, in order to overcome their fear and horror by giving it a form and an image. At this moment I realized that this was what painting was all about. Painting isn't an aesthetic operation; it's a form of magic designed as a mediator between this strange, hostile world and us, a way of seizing power by giving form to our terrors as well as our desires. When I came to that realization, I knew I had found my way (Gilot, 1944).

ABILITIES AND THE VISUAL-PERFORMING ARTS

Intelligence has been recognized as having some relevance for the visual and performing arts. Generally, however, those individuals who show themselves as having extraordinary talent in the arts tend to be highly gifted intellectually though they may not necessarily show this to be the case on an IQ test.

Another aspect of importance to consider as it relates to the intellect is the symbolic system that is acquired and used by individuals in these special fields of talent. The symbolic system of verbal language is generally not the major system used for communication in the visual and performing arts. Musical notation provides the basis for communication of music (though some have attempted to substitute a number system for it, for instance, in the Far East and South East Asia). Nonverbal systems are the substitute for the verbal in the visual arts and dance unlike oratory and drama which are dependent on the verbal language system for communication, though dance, acting and oratory all make use of body language as well in performance.

Imagery (visual, auditory, and kinesthetic to mention three of several sense modality correlates as we have seen) is an important component of thinking and expression in the visual and performing arts. In the various theoretical models of intellect imagery lies in the nonverbal domain. Its role in art, music, dance, and acting is significant for imagery overcomes the barriers of intermediary symbolic systems to present to the individual visions that eventually find themselves expressed in one art form or another.

Common to all these art forms is creativity, a processing and an energizing agent that differs in degree for its operation depending upon the art form used. Guilford (1968) on the subject of creativity and the visual arts focuses attention on the importance of three divergent production abilities in the figural dimension of the structure of intellect, namely, fluency, flexibility, and elaboration. Communication of meaning in the visual arts is done in nonverbal ways and often involves these three divergent thinking abilities. *Fluency* in the figural information area is broken down into *ideational fluency* (or the ability to generalize many ideas), *analogy fluency* (or the ability to rapidly organize figural information as systems). Two kinds of abilities relate to shift in thinking from one class to another, with *'spontaneous flexibility'* indicating the shift in thinking without being told, and *'adaptive flexibility'* where shifts in thinking calls for different solutions to a single problem. *Elaboration,* he considers, as very important to art where early in a creative production a general schema, motif, or plan develops, psychologically a system to which details are added as the system becomes distinct.

Other abilities that also have important and relevance for creative artistic production are the ability to visualize changes in figural information (transformation ability outside the divergent production category), the ability to evaluate one's own total production of an art object, and ability in the behavioral category as this relates to the translation of semantic or behavioral information to figural information.

Lowenfeld and Brittain (1964) discussing the creative and mental growth of talented children related to art, identify five major characteristics. The first, is 'fluency of imagination and expression' where ideas spontaneously flow and imagery expands with the creative process like a chain reaction. The second, is a 'highly developed sensibility' toward movement, rhythm, content and organization that varies with the talented individual, where integration of thinking, feeling, and perceiving is experienced to a higher degree by the person. The third, is 'intuitive quality of imagination' where *imagery* important to the creative act is possessed to a high degree by the talented individual. The fourth, 'directness of expression' relates to the self-confidence expressed by the talented individual in the act of artistic creation. The fifth, is a 'high degree of self-identification' with the depicted experience that is exhibited by the gifted individual.

FACILITATING THE USE OF IMAGERY

In his discussion of the parataxic mode and the arts, the mode in which a person experiences the numinous received as images and finds an objective correlative in an art form, Gowan deals with art as image-magic, art as representation of the numinous, metaphysical art, and art and creativity. Something has already been said about the first two. On metaphysical art Gowan points out that while the parataxic mode is made a part of modern art since impressionism, the personal element has receded progressively in the works of the surrealists (who began the dismantling of personality as required in the knowledge-contact-ecstasies) and continued by the abstractionists, the geometric art, and the illusionists (in which there was further depersonalization corresponding to the higher knowledge-contact states).

The tendency to move away in abstract art from imagery to expression of pure imagination, the externalization of a purely inner process, fetches the comment by Arieti (1976) that art by its very nature of being visual cannot be imageless and shapeless, nor can it be exclusively symbolic for a work of art stands for artistic reality:

> . . . Abstract art would tend to escape from imagery and become pure imagination. But inasmuch as any visual art *must* be visual, the imagination cannot really escape. A compromise must be reached with the creation of an imagery that is unrelated or almost free from previous retinal experience. The work of art is an externalization of a purely inner process. . . .

. . . Abstract art is supposed to have no content, to be imageless and shapeless. But whatever is to be seen has *some* shape. No matter how much the abstract artist would unshape the world, he will do some shaping. . . . Art cannot be exclusively symbolic; that is, it cannot stand for something totally not present. The work of art itself *is* present: it stands for itself, as artistic reality. Like literature, it becomes 'a second reality'. Its potentiality is also its power to evoke in us an aesthetic response, an aesthetic pleasure. (P. 233–234)

Creativity in art Gowan points out is parataxic creativity or creativity with images in a nonverbal mode and because of this, investigating the psychology of artistic creativity is difficult. Nevertheless some studies have been done and which he has classified as theoretical, factor analytic, psychometric, and training.

A few representative studies cited by Gowan on training related to an examination of the effects of massed and spaced practice on artistic creativity, short-term sensory enrichment and creativity in art, levels of creative performance in the visual arts, group creative art activities and visual perceptual abilities in brain-injured children, ways to assist sixth graders to incorporate more original ideas into their art production in an effort to free them from responses similar to teacher's directions, and perceptual behavior of sixth graders in relation to their art. Of course mention must be made as well to a doctoral dissertation of Marvin Grossman (a student of Art Education at the University of Georgia) on the subject of developing aesthetic and creative visual abilities in kindergarten children through a structured developmental art program in which he developed and used the *Draw-a-Clown Test* (1969).

Studies on facilitation of imagery processes in the visual and performing arts have not been done. In attempting to discuss how we might nuture imagery in the arts, we will have to draw upon the findings of studies on imagery training in general (e.g., Khatena, 1978). Hence the suggestions that follow must be exploratory in nature.

APPROACHES TO ENCOURAGE USE IMAGINATION IMAGERY

In a recent paper (1978) Gowan had pointed out the importance of knowing theories of creativity and developmental stages generally and the function of the preconscious particularly. The source of much of our creativity lies with the preconscious, and by 'gentling the preconscious' (i.e., by learning to organize and control it so that the experience we have with it is not traumatic but can be symbolized and usefully employed) a vast storehouse of imagery for creative use becomes available. Approaches that relate to the use of imagination imagery include the use of creative thinking strategies, incubation, autonomous imaging, and multi-sense modalities.

(a) Approaches at stimulating and facilitating the use of the creative imagination to produce creative imagery have been described in terms of a number of creative thinking strategies, namely, breaking away from the obvious and commonplace, restructuring, synthesis, and analogy. These strategies can be taught for application in many areas of visual performing arts. For instance in *music,* a student who has learned these strategies may choose say the strategy of *restructuring,* take a piece of music he knows well, play or sing it several times, shut his eyes and image the tune, then image parts of it, rearrange these parts in different ways to come up with another tune, which can then be set to music or recorded on tape. As this related to *synthesis,* two tunes may be picked out, and following some warm-up, the tunes can be imaged, as wholes, then broken up in parts, and the parts rearranged to give one or even several different tunes. This may also be done visually with musical notation and can lead to fruitful musical composition. Such exploration can also be done with a variety of rhythms and instruments that express them. *Analogy* can also be a powerful tool for producing all kinds of images prior to composition and performance. Images in the several sense modalities can be recalled while in a relaxed state that can be used in themselves or in combination to produce all kinds of rhythmic and melodic effects that border on the original. If an assignment to a make-up artist required the production of a fantasy character (e.g., Caliban in Shakespeare's *Tempest*) imagery can be most effectively harnessed. Having entered into the experience of the play and the character that is to be made up, the artist should give himself to imaging the creative possibilities of making up this monstrosity. The make-up artist can facilitate this imaging by using several thinking strategies.

(b) Incubation can be tied up with imaging where instead of immediate closure in say musical composition or stage make-up activity imaging, a period of rest time or relaxation is allowed for simmering to take place that may lead to some very fine artistic expressions. The previous creative thinking strategies and the activities in music and stage make-up suggested could well serve as preparation for incubation towards illumination. This process if set to work often enough will facilitate some very fine productive imaging.

(c) Autonomy of imagery is related to creative mental functioning and should be encouraged. One way of doing this is by inducing a relaxed state for imagery to flow. Students can be guided to free themselves from external stimuli by shutting their eyes in a quiet atmosphere created for the purpose. They can then be encouraged to visualize in their mind's eye an event or experience that can lend itself to artistic expression. Early occurring images may be encouraged to take a life of their own. Single images may fall into simple patterns growing in complexity with practice that can give rise to artistic production or performance. For instance, a dancer who hears music can be encouraged to enter into the experience and image herself making various movements, relative to the music, combining movements imaged in different ways, finding analogues for movement in the rush of wind, in the sparkling flow of water, in the flight of a bird, and the like. The art of Escher offers an illustration of image autonomy as expressed in a work of art. The expanding motif of earlier images with its organic-geometric qualities under development and transformation to be metamorphosized into a rich work of art.

(d) Students should be encouraged to use all their senses in their interaction with the world. Their greatest strengths appear to lie with the use of the visual, auditory and tactile sense modalities singly or in combination. Some arrangement should be made for them to use their other senses in gaining command of the world while enhancing the use of the three senses they seem able at applying. Give exercise in the use of a sense and encourage creative imaging. An exercise suggested by Lee and Pulvino (1978) relates to 'cross sensory experience' where music is used. "Listening to music with your ears in a relaxed state. Then close your eyes and hear music with all your senses: feel music as a touch on your skin, brushing gently over you; see the music—maybe like heat waves, colors floating before you; and smell the music—like a flower, perfume, familiar home smells. This can enhance the imaging that is involved in the activities already suggested and may make available many more dimension sources than we are fully aware for producing the conditions that preface expression in one or another art form.

These are some of the approaches that may be found useful to facilitate the imagination and imagery activity essential to creative production in the visual and performing arts. They lie across a continuum of secondary process activity to primary process activity stimulated by procedures found to be related to the creative imagination. All that I can say is that it is a beginning in what can be done to energize the processes we know are involved in the arts. But for the inspiration, the fire, the thrill and trauma of experiencing the numinuous we have to look elsewhere. It may be that in activating the process involved in the creative act we may reverse the process so that the individual feels 'vibrations' and comes into contact with the source of power itself.

References

Abell, A. M. *Talks with great composers*. Garmisch-Partenkirchen, Germany: G. E. Schroeder—Verlag, 1964.

Arieti, S. *Creativity: The magic synthesis*. New York: Basic Books, 1976.

Bowra, C. M. *The romantic imagination*. London: Oxford University Press, 1950.

Gordon, R. A very private world. In Peter W. Sheehan (Ed.), *The function of imagery*. New York: Academic Press, 1972. Pp. 63–80.

Gowan, J. C. *Trance, art and creativity*. Buffalo, N.Y.: Creative Education Foundation, 1975.

Gowan, J. C. Creative inspiration in composers. *Journal of Creative Behavior*, 1977, 11(4), 249–255.

Gowan, J. C. The role of imagination in the development of the creative individual. *Humanitas*, 1978, 24(2), 197–208.

Grossman, M. J. Developing aesthetic and creative visual abilities in kindergarten children through a structured developmental art program. *Dissertation Abstracts International*, 1970, 30(8).

Guilford, J. P. Creativity in the visual arts. In J. P. Guilford, *Intelligence, creativity, and their educational implications*. San Diego, Ca.: Robert R. Knapp, 1968.

Jaynes, J. *The origin of consciousness in the breakdown of the bicameral mind*. Boston. Boston, Ma.: Houghton Mifflin, 1976.

Khatena, J. Imagination and the production of original verbal images. *Art Psychotherapy*, 1973, 1(¾), 193–200.

Khatena, J. Frontiers of creative imagination imagery. *Journal of Mental Imagery*, 1978, 2(1), 33–46.

Lowenfeld, V., and Brittain, W. L. *Creative and mental growth*. New York: Macmillan, 1964.

Vargiu, J. Creativity: The purposeful imagination. *Synthesis*, 1977, 3–4, 17–53.

Wallas, G. *The art of thought*. London: C. A. Watts, 1926.

32. ROLE OF HEMISPHERICITY IN PERFORMANCE ON SELECTED MEASURES OF CREATIVITY

E. Paul Torrance and Salah Mourad

There is now a great deal of discussion concerning the role of hemisphericity or style of processing information in creative behavior. Hemisphericity is defined briefly as the tendency for a person to rely more on one than the other cerebral hemisphere in processing information. The left cerebral hemisphere seems to be specialized for the logical, sequential processing of information and deals primarily with verbal, analytical, abstract, temporal, and digital materials (Bogen, 1969; Gassaniga, 1970; Ornstein, 1972). The right cerebral hemisphere processes information nonlinearly, wholistically, simultaneously dealing with a variety of variables and different kinds of information. It seems to be specialized for primarily nonverbal, concrete, spatial, analogic, emotional, and aesthetic materials.

There is some documentation to support the common notion that the right hemisphere is dominant in creative thinking (Krueger, 1976; Torrance and Reynolds, 1978). However, the accumulating evidence suggests that creative thinking or problem solving required both left and right cerebral hemisphere functions. For example, West (1976), after examining findings in neurophysiology, observations of renowned creative scientists, and the development of artificial intelligence, has concluded that major acts of genius require activity in both the intuitive right hemisphere of the brain and in the rational left hemisphere. Brandwein and Ornstein (1977) similarly concluded that the cultivation of creativity requires that both modes of processing information must be developed. They concluded further that the creative person must develop the ability to inhibit either mode when it is inappropriate to what is being done or to bring the two together in a complementary fashion. This is essentially in harmony with the contentions of Alex F. Osborn (1952), the originator of "brainstorming" and Creative Problem Solving methodologies. Osborn emphasized deferred judgment, maintaining that the mind could not effectively at the same time produce creative alternatives and judge them. Thus, Osborn's Creative Problem Solving model calls for alternating periods of left and right hemisphere processing.

In an attempt to explore this problem among healthy, normal adults superior in both intelligence and creativity, the present study examines the relationship of style of learning and thinking (hemisphericity) and scores on a rather large variety of contemporary tests of creativity.

METHOD

The subjects of the study were 28 graduate students, 6 men and 22 women, enrolled in the senior author's course in creative thinking. All of them had met the criteria for admission to graduate study and may therefore be assumed to be superior in intellect, having attained satisfactory scores on the *Graduate Record Examination Aptitude* test. On a variety of creativity tests administered during the course, the class usually attained scores averaging one to two standard deviations above the published norms for superior adult groups.

Reprinted by permission of the authors and *Gifted Child Quarterly*, Vol. 23, No. 1, 1979.

Instrument for Hemisphericity Classification

The instrument for classifying the subjects according to hemisphericity or style of processing information was Torrance, Reynolds, and Riegel's (1976) *Your Style of Learning and Thinking, Form A*. This is a 36-item self report, multiple choice questionnaire which classifies respondents according to right, left, and integrated styles of information processing. It was based on a thorough analysis of the research regarding the specialized cerebral functions of the right and left hemispheres. Each item presents the respondent with three choices—one a right hemisphere mode of processing information, one a left hemisphere mode, and the other an integrated way of processing information.

Fairly extensive norms, reliability data, and validity information have been accumulated and documented in journal articles (Torrance, Reynolds, Riegel, and Ball, 1977; Torrance and Reynolds, 1978) and the norms-technical manual (Torrance, Reynolds, Riegel, and Ball, 1978). The mean of the test-retest coefficients of correlation is about .85. Right hemisphere classification has been shown to be associated with the following variables: enrollment in courses in creative thinking, participation in the Creative Problem Solving Institute, enrollment in self-directed study programs, enrollment in courses in creative invention, scores on a test of all self-directed study readiness, giftedness in the visual and communication arts in the Georgia Governor's Honors Program, flexibility and originality scores on the verbal form of the *Torrance Tests of Creative Thinking*, Stein's *Physiognomic Cue Test*, the creativity personality style as assessed by the Khatena-Torrance *What Kind of Person Are You?* test, the creative resolution of problems involving collision conflicts, and originality scores on the *Sounds and Images* test.

Instruments for Assessing Creative Functioning

All subjects were administered the following tests of creative functioning:

1. *What Kind of Person Are You?* (Khatena and Torrance, 1976). This instrument provides a measure of the creative personality style and consists of 50 objectively scored, forced choice items. Factor scores derived from this instrument include: Acceptance of Authority, Self Confidence, Awareness of Others, and Disciplined Imagination. A considerable amount of reliability and validity evidence is summarized in the norms-technical manual (Khatena and Torrance, 1976).

2. *Something About Myself* (Khatena and Torrance, 1976). This is a 50-item checklist of creative achievements and behaviors. A wide variety of reliability and validity evidence has been accumulated and is summarized in the norms-technical manual. The following factor scores derived from this instrument are used in the present study: Environmental Sensitivity, Intuitiveness, Intellectuality, and Individuality.

3. *Stein's Physiognomic Cue Test* (Stein, 1975). This instrument consists of 32 line drawings, each provided with two descriptive alternatives. One alternative pertains to the drawing's form, shape, or structural characteristics. The other, the physiognomic alternative, attributes feeling, action, or some representational characteristic to the drawing. The test was developed as a measure of cognitive control and is thought to be associated with creativity. The norms-technical manual reports three empirical studies which support a moderate relationship between physiognomic alternative scores and indicators of creative behavior.

4. *Remote Associates Test* (Mednick and Mednick, 1967). This instrument was developed as a measure of ability to think creatively and has been used widely with graduate and professional students and with other groups of superior adults. The test is based on an "associative" interpretation of the creative thinking process. The test consists of 30 problems which require the subject to find a criteria-meeting mediating link to combine three words for mutually remote associate clusters. For example, the word linking "surprise, line, and birthday" is "party." The norms-technical manual summarized a variety of reliability and validity data. The reliability data seem quite adequate, coefficients ranging from .81 to .92. The validity findings are quite mixed. Scores on the test appear to predict certain kinds of creative behavior but appear to be unrelated to other kinds of creativity criteria.

5. *Sounds and Images* (Khatena and Torrance, 1973). This instrument provides a measure of originality and requires subjects to describe the images suggested by each of a series of four sounds. The sequence is presented three times. The reliability and validity of this measure has been documented in a variety of studies and summarized in the norms-technical manual (Khatena and Torrance, 1973) and appears to be reasonably satisfactory. Scoring was accomplished according to the published scoring guide.

6. *Onomatopoeia and Images* (Khatena and Torrance, 1973). This instrument is quite similar to *Sounds and Images*. It makes use of onomatopoeic words such as "bang," "ouch," and "whiz" rather than sounds. The sequence of words is presented four times. Reliability and validity data are summarized in the norms-technical manual (Khatena and Torrance, 1973) and appear to be reasonably satisfactory.

7. *Welsh Figure Preference Test* (Welsh, 1949). This instrument consists of 400 drawings and the subject is asked to rate each drawing as "Like" or "Dislike." Measures derived from this instrument, especially the Barron-Welsh Art Scale and the Revised Art Scale, have been widely used as measures of creativity. These scales differentiate the preferences of artists from the general population. The present study makes use of two recently developed scales, Origence and Intelligence (Welsh, 1975), and three of the older empirically developed scales which seem to be related theoretically to creative behavior, Conformity, Childlikeness, and Masculinity/Feminity (Welsh, 1959).

8. *Torrance Tests of Creative Thinking, Figural and Verbal Forms A* (Torrance, 1974). Each form of this instrument was designed to assess a somewhat different kind of creative thinking and all test tasks are open ended, permitting the subject to respond in terms of his own experiences whatever these may have been. The figural forms each consist of three test tasks: Picture Construction, Incomplete Figures, and Repeated Figures. The verbal forms consist of the following seven tasks: Ask Questions, Guess Causes, Guess Consequences, Product Improvement, Unusual Uses, Provocative Questions, and Just Suppose. Both forms are scored according to the published manuals for Fluency, Flexibility, and Originality. In addition, the figural form is scored for Elaboration and for a series of creativity indicators such as: unusual visual perspective, resistance to premature closure, abstractness of titles, humor, expression of emotion, colorfulness of imagery, and the like. A recently developed scoring system (Torrance and Ball, 1978) provides a procedure

for combining these indicators into a "Creativity Index." Over one thousand studies using these tests have been reported and a large number of them supply a great deal of validity and reliability data. Much of these data have been summarized in the norms-technical manual (Torrance, 1974).

Hemisphericity [*Style of Information Processing*] *Classification*

On the basis of their scores in *Your Style of Learning and Thinking* (SOLAT) (Torrance, Reynolds, Ball, and Riegel, 1978) the subjects were classified according to learning style into three categories: Right, Left, and Integrated. The following general rule was used in making these classifications: Respondents having standard scores of 120 (mean = 100 and standard deviation = 20) or higher on one of these three styles was placed in that particular category. Nine subjects were classified as having a Right hemisphere style of information processing; 5, as Left; and 14, as Integrated. Three other persons could not be assigned to either of these three categories and were not included in the study.

RESULTS

Table 1 reports the means and standard deviations of subjects in each of the three styles of information processing categories on each of the creativity measures. It will be noted that subjects in the Right category attained the highest scores on most of the measures. Subjects reporting a Left style of information processing had the highest scores on Acceptance of Authority, Self Confidence, Remote Associates Test, and Conformity. Those reporting an Integrated style scored somewhat higher than the other groups on Creative Personality and Awareness of Others.

To test the statistical significance of these observed differences analysis of variance and Duncan Multiple range tests were conducted. The results are reported in Table 2.

On the measure of Creative Personality derived from *What Kind of Person Are You?*, the differences are significant at the .001 level and the Duncan Multiple Range Test computed for the .05 level of confidence indicates that those reporting a Left style of information processing are significantly lower than those reporting Right and Integrated styles. On the measures of Acceptance of Authority and Self Confidence, the Lefts are significantly higher than both the Rights and the Integrateds. On Disciplined Imagination, however, the Lefts are significantly lower than the Rights and Integrateds. The Rights are significantly lower than the Integrateds on Awareness of Others.

On the overall measure of creative achievement and behavior derived from *Something About Myself*, the Lefts are significantly lower than both the Rights and the Integrateds. The Lefts are lower than the Rights on Environmental Sensitivity; the Rights are higher than the Integrateds on Intuitiveness; the Rights are higher than the Lefts on Intellectuality; and the Lefts are lower than both the Rights and Integrateds on Individuality.

Although the Rights tend to be higher than the other groups on Stein's *Physiognomic Cue Test*, the differences are not significant at the .05 level.

Although the Lefts tend to excel the other groups on the *Remote Associates Test*, none of the differences reach the .05 level of significance.

Table 1
Means and Standard Deviations of Selected Creativity Variables of Graduate Students with Right, Left, and Integrated Styles of Learning and Thinking

Creativity Measure	Right (N=9)		Left (N=5)		Integrated (N=14)	
	Mean	S.D.	Mean	S.D.	Mean	S.D.
Creative Personality (What Kind of Person Are You?)	37.6	5.1	23.2	8.7	38.1	3.6
Acceptance of Authority	0.6	0.7	3.6	1.7	0.4	0.5
Self Confidence	4.2	2.2	6.6	2.7	4.1	1.3
Awareness of Others	5.1	1.9	6.8	1.5	7.3	1.6
Disciplined Imagination	6.9	2.0	4.0	2.5	7.1	1.5
Creative Achievements (Something About Myself)	36.8	8.5	23.2	5.7	32.8	8.1
Environmental Sensitivity	6.8	1.4	4.8	1.1	6.0	1.7
Intuitiveness	2.8	2.2	2.0	0.7	1.4	1.2
Intellectuality	8.0	2.4	5.0	1.9	7.4	2.3
Individuality	4.7	1.1	1.8	1.1	4.0	1.8
Cue Test (Stein)	143.7	27.1	116.2	18.8	130.9	24.5
Romote Associates Test	17.1	3.5	21.8	4.4	30.0	4.4
Sounds and Images	42.8	4.7	31.0	3.3	37.9	5.5
Onomatopoeia and Images	127.2	22.2	90.4	20.1	106.8	24.6
Origence (Welsh)	57.6	20.2	44.4	27.1	47.0	17.5

Creativity Measure	Right		Left		Integrated	
	Mean	S.D.	Mean	S.D.	Mean	S.D.
Intellectance (Welsh)	33.4	8.7	28.6	8.2	31.4	4.4
Revised Art Scale (Welsh)	42.8	12.0	39.4	10.2	35.4	11.7
Conformity (Welsh)	22.4	5.1	29.2	5.3	22.4	4.1
Childlikeness (Welsh)	27.4	9.4	16.0	7.2	23.5	7.2
Masculinity/Femininity (Welsh)	29.6	6.6	23.6	4.3	27.8	5.6
TTCT Figural Fluency	22.0	9.0	21.6	5.3	18.7	8.1
TTCT Figural Originality	17.0	7.5	14.4	5.3	13.4	7.0
TTCT Figural Elaboration	70.0	15.6	26.0	12.5	43.5	13.1
TTCT Figural Creativity Index	185.6	17.1	145.2	20.2	157.4	19.6
TTCT Verbal Fluency	28.8	8.7	18.6	7.2	24.9	6.3
TTCT Verbal Flexibility	11.6	3.4	8.2	2.5	11.0	3.4
TTCT Verbal Originality	38.1	11.6	24.6	6.3	33.5	11.1

Table 2
Results of Analyses of Variance and Duncan Multiple Range Test Comparing Three Styles of Learning on Creativity Variables

Creativity Measure	F-Ratio	Level Signif.	Differences at .05 Duncan Mult. Range
Creative Personality (*What Kind of Person Are You?*)	14.47	.001	Left<Right/Integ.
Acceptance of Authority	27.74	.001	Left>Right/Integ.
Self Confidence	3.51	.05	Left>Right/Integ.
Awareness of Others	4.69	.02	Right<Integrated
Disciplined Imagination	5.54	.01	Left<Rigt/Integ.
Creative Achievements (*Something About Myself*)	4.81	.02	Left<Right/Integ.
Environmental Sensitivity	2.80	.08	Left<Right
Intuitiveness	2.36	.11	Right>Integrated
Intellectuality	2.92	.07	Right>Left
Individuality	6.01	.01	Left<Right/Integ.
Cue Test (Stein)	2.01	.15	-------------------------
Remote Associates Test	2.57	.10	-------------------------
Sounds and Images Originality	9.16	.001	Right>Left/Integ. Left<Right/Integ.
Onomatopoeia and Images	4.41	.02	Right>Left/Integ.
Origence (Welsh)	0.98	.39	-------------------------
Intellectance (Welsh)	0.85	.44	-------------------------
Revised Art Scale (Welsh)	1.15	.34	-------------------------
Conformity (Welsh)	3.17	.05	Left>Right/Integ.
Childlikeness (Welsh)	2.81	.08	Right>Left
Masculinity/Femininity (Welsh)	1.44	.26	-------------------------
TTCT Figural Fluency	0.54	.60	-------------------------
TTCT Originality	0.76	.48	-------------------------
TTCT Figural Elaboration	18.31	.001	Right>Left/Integ. Left<Integ./Right
TTCT Figural Creativity Index	9.12	.001	Right>Left/Integ.
TTCT Verbal Fluency	3.19	.05	Right>Left
TTCT Verbal Flexibility	1.84	.18	-------------------------
TTCT Verbal Originality	2.59	.09	Right>Left

On both *Sounds and Images* and *Onomatopoeia and Images,* The Rights are significantly higher than the other two groups. Also, the Lefts are significantly lower than the other two groups on *Sounds and Images.*

On the *Welsh Figure Preference Test,* there were no statistically significant differences for Origence, Intellectance, the Revised Art Scale, and Masculinity/Femininity. On Conformity, the Lefts were significantly higher than the other two groups and on Childlikeness the Rights were significantly higher than the Lefts.

On the *Torrance Tests of Creative Thinking,* Figural From A, the differences on Fluency and Originality were not statistically significant. However, on Elaboration the Rights were higher than the other two groups and the Lefts were lower than the other two groups. On the Creativity Index using the new creativity indicators, the Rights were higher than the other two groups.

On the Verbal Form A of the *Torrance Tests of Creative Thinking,* the Rights were higher than the Lefts on Fluency and Originality but not on Flexibility.

CONCLUSION

Using *Your Style of Learning and Thinking* to classify superior adults for hemisphericity and a variety of measures of creative thinking ability, creative personality, and creative behavior, it appears that both cerebral hemispheres are involved in creative behavior. However, the evidence produced by this study indicates rather clearly that persons classified as having a left hemisphere style of processing information attained lower scores than the other two groups on the measures of creative thinking ability and on the personality measures associated with creative behavior. On the measures of creative thinking ability, only on the *Remote Associates Test* did the Lefts tend to excel the other two groups and the overall differences were not statistically significant. On this measure, the scores of the lefts and Integrateds are almost identical; the Rights tended to have greatest difficulty in the kind of creative thinking involved in this test which deals with verbal materials and requires a great deal of evaluative, logical thinking. There seem to be no differences among the three cerebral hemisphere groups on the Cue Test, Origence, Intellectance, the Revised Art Scale, Masculinity/Femininity, Figural Fluency and Originality, and Verbal Flexibility.

Very few differences emerged between the Rights and the Integrateds. The Rights, however, did appear to be less aware of others and more intuitive and attained higher scores than the Integrateds on the originality scores of *Sounds and Images* and *Onamatopoeia and Images,* elaboration on the figural form of the *Torrance Tests of Creative Thinking* and on the Creativity Index of the figural form of the *Torrance Tests of Creative Thinking.* Thus, the extent to which hemisphericity affects creativity is likely to vary according to the nature of the task. However, superior adults having a style of information processing associated with right cerebral hemisphere functions and those having an integrated style of information processing appeared to be generally more effective than those with a left style and to have the motivations and personality characteristics usually associated with creative achievement.

SUMMARY

A sample of 28 superior adults were studied intensively to explore problems related to the role of hemisphericity in creative functioning. They were classified for hemisphericity on the basis of scores on Torrance, Reynolds, and Riegel's *Style of Learning and Thinking* test, a self report instrument. Nine were classified as Rights, 5 as Lefts, and 14 as Integrateds. The Rights excelled the Lefts on: the creative personality style as assessed by *What Kind of Person Are You?*, a lack of acceptance of authority, a lack of a feeling of certainty, disciplined imagination, creative achievements as assessed by *Something About Myself*, environmental sensitivity, intellectuality, individuality, lack of conformity, childlikeness, figural elaboration, figural Creativity Index, verbal fluency, and verbal originality. Although the evidence suggests that among superior adults both cerebral hemispheres are involved in creative thinking, a style of information processing characterized by the specialized functions of the right cerebral hemisphere or by both hemispheres functioning in a complementary manner seems to be most favorable generally. Similar intensive studies need to be conducted with other types of populations and with a greater variety of creativity tests.

References

Bogen, J. E. The other side of the brain: Parts I, II, and III. *Bulletin of the Los Angeles Neurological Society,* 1969, 34, 73–105, 135–162, 191–203.

Brandwein, P., and Ornstein, R. The duality of the mind. *Instructor,* 1977, 86(5), 54–58.

Gazzanigna, M. S. *The bisected brain.* New York: Appleton-Century-Crofts, 1970.

Khatena, J., and Torrance, E. P. *Norms-Technical manual: Thinking creatively with sounds and words.* Lexington, Mass.: Personnel Press/Ginn and Company, 1973.

Khatena, J., and Torrance. E. P. *Manual for Khatena-Torrance creative perception inventory.* Chicago: Stoelting Company, 1976.

Kruger, T. H. *Visual imagery in problem solving and scientific creativity.* Derby, Ct.: Seal Press, 1976.

Mednick, S. A., and Mednick, M. T. *Examiner's manual: Remote associates test, College and adult form 1 and 2.* New York: Houghton Mifflin Company, 1967.

Ornstein, R. E. *The psychology of consciousness.* San Francisco: W. H. Freeman, 1972.

Osborn, A. F. *Applied imagination.* New York: Charles Scribner's, 1953.

Stein, M. I. *Manual: Physiognomic cue test.* New York: Behavioral Publications, 1975.

Torrance, E. P. *Norms-technical manual: Torrance tests of creative thinking.* Lexington, Mass.: Personnel Press/Ginn and Company, 1974.

Torrance, E. P., and Ball, O. E. *Streamlined scoring and interpretation guide and norms manual for figural form A, TTCT.* Athens, Ga.: Georgia Studies of Creative Behavior, University of Georgia, 1978.

Torrance, E. P. and Reynolds, C. R. Images of the future of gifted adolescents: Effects of alienation and specialized cerebral functioning. GIFTED CHILD QUARTERLY, 1978, 22, 40–54.

Torrance, E. P., Reynolds, C. R., and Riegel, T. *Preliminary norms-technical manual for "Your Style of learning and thinking."* Athens, Ga.: Georgia Studies of Creative Behavior, University of Georgia, 1976.

Torrance, E. P. Reynolds, C R. Riegel, T., and Ball, O. E. Your style of learning and thinking, forms A and B. Preliminary norms abbreviated technical scores scoring keys, and selected references. GIFTED CHILD QUARTERLY, 1977, 21, 563–573.

Torrance, E. P., Reynolds, C. R. Riegel, T., and Ball. O. E. *Revised norms-technical manual: Your style of learning and thinking, Forms A and B.* Athens, Ga.: Georgia Studies of Creative Behavior, University of Georgia, 1978.

Welsh, G. S. *Research edition: Welsh figure preference test.* Palo Alto, Calif. : Consulting Psychologists Press, 1949.

Welsh, G. S. *Manual [research edition]: Welsh figure preference test.* Palo Alto, Calif.: Consulting Psychologists Press, 1959.

Welsh, G. S. *Creativity and intelligence: A personality approach.* Chapel Hill, N.C.: Institute for Research in Social Science, University of North Carolina, 1975.

West, S. A. Creativity, altered states of awareness, and artificial intelligence: *Journal of Altered States of Consciousness,* 1976, 2, 219–230.

33. THE ROLE OF THE RIGHT HEMISPHERE IN LEARNING AND CREATIVITY IMPLICATIONS FOR ENHANCING PROBLEM SOLVING ABILITY

Ron Rubenzer

Abstract

By generating empirically testable physiological models of cognition and affect, the understanding and facilitation of learning and problem solving can be advanced. A review of the representative research and theoretical literature on right hemisphere processes and psychophysiological models regarding the functional organization of the brain is presented. The major roles of the right hemisphere processing modes in language, learning, perception, creativity and affect are discussed. A psychophysiological model of problem solving is proposed.

The necessity for attempting to more fully understand, and thus perhaps more directly enhance learning and creativity has been considered by Guilford (1975) to be central to education, as indicated when he stated, "I have advocated, and I still do, that the student be taught about the nature of his own intellectual resources, so that he may gain more control over them" (p. 120).

A technique for investigating the nature of these "intellectual resources" which appears to circumvent some of the conventional biasing factors (subject fatigue, socioeconomic background, attitude, test reliability and validity (Anastasi, 1971) involved in paper and pencil testing through which most hypothetical models of intellectual functioning have been constructed, is the psychophysiological approach (psychophysiology is "the study of physiology in relation to the mind and its processes." Hinsie and Campbell, 1960, p. 610) The psychophysiological approach to the analysis of mental functioning is gaining great impetus (Brandwein and Ornstein, 1977; Brown, 1977; Gowan, 1975; Green et al., 1969;. Mulholland, 1971; Ornstein, 1978; Samples, 1975; Schwartz, 1976). Davidson and Krippner (1971) have coined the expression "the science of subjective experience" for the psychophysiological method of research. In describing this "science of subjective experience" they state:

> Through the use of converging operations (recurrent specific physiological patterns) we can obtain objective evidence for the existence of hypothetically constructed psychological states. That is, if we ask a subject what is going through his mind and we simultaneously obtain a variety of physiological measures, we can determine whether a specific physiological indicator correlates with the subject's verbal report. . . . Through the combined use of verbal reports and physiological measures, "subjective" states of consciousness can be studied with a scientific precision that was, until recently, unavailable. (p. 30)

One of the major psychophysiological approaches involves correlating the degree of left or right hemisphere involvement with reported cognitive and affective states.

This review of the empirical and theoretical literature regarding the cognitive and affective functions of the right hemisphere is a synthesis and interpretation of representative hemisphericity research (the study of the functional organization of the brain according to the left or right

Reprinted by permission from *Gifted Child Quarterly*, Vol. 23, No. 1, 1979.

hemisphere within the last 15 years. The hemisphericity research reviewed included medically intrusive[1] (commissurotomy—Gazzaniga, 1967; Sperry, 1974, lobotomy—Maksymczuk, 1973; hemispherectomy—Burkland and Smith, 1977; electroconvulsive therapy—Fromholt et al., 1973; and sodium amytal—Branch et al., 1964), medically nonintrusive (electroencephalography-Newton, 1975; lesion diagnosis—Luria, 1970) and non-medical non-intrusive (dichotic listening tasks—Kimura, 1967; visual field-Day, 1964; Olson, 1977; saccadic eye movement—Harnad, 1972; and laterality—Williams, 1976) studies. The studies reviewed included approximately 1,600 subjects and only those studies specifying the subject variables of age, handedness and sex were reviewed. Unless otherwise noted, the subjects were right-handed adults. (See reference note)

THE ANATOMICAL AND FUNCTIONAL CHARACTERISTICS OF THE RIGHT HEMISPHERE

The right hemisphere, sometimes referred to as the minor or nondominant hemisphere because of its lesser role in verbal functioning (Darvai and Smyk, 1972) was found by Geschwind (1970) in a neonatal study to be anatomically smaller than the dominant or left hemisphere.

Verbal processing. As more research on hemisphericity is being conducted, it is becoming evident that the right hemisphere is not totally silent. In fact, it has been discovered that the language function is somewhat more equally shared between the left and right hemispheres before the age of five (Lenneberg, 1967) and for left-handed (Goodglass and Quadfasel, 1954) and ambidextrous adults (Kupfermann, 1977). Furthermore, the results of studies demonstrate that the right hemisphere is capable of processing language if the discriminations are uncomplicated (e.g., a positive from a negative statement) (Butler and Glass, 1974) and sufficient time is allowed (Bogen and Gazzaniga, 1965; Gazzaniga and Hillyard, 1971; Nebes and Sperry, 1971; Weisenberg and McBride, 1935). It was found by Moscovitch, Scullion, and Christie in 1976, that the sufficient time for right hemispheric processing of "uncomplicated" verbal discriminations was 100 msec, or double the amount of time required for the left hemisphere to process the same information.

The analysis of voice intonation, an integral component of language, appears to be a function of the right hemisphere (Van Lanker, 1975). The primary verbal expressive mode of the right hemisphere is speculated to be metaphorical in nature (poetry, analogies) (Eccles, 1973; Ornstein, 1972; Samples, 1975); however, in general the verbally communicative ability of the right hemisphere is relatively limited.

Visual processing. The interpretation of complex visual patterns has been found by several researchers to be a predominantly right hemisphere function (Compton and Bradshaw, 1975; Goyvaerts, 1975; Moscovitch, Scullion and Christie, 1976; Schwartz, Davidson and Pugash, 1976). Further, the right hemisphere is much more adroit in the recognition and retention of facial features (Hecaen, 1973; Hillard, 1973; Muller, 1973), while the left hemisphere remembers the names that go with the faces. The retention of visual patterns, such as geometric designs and graphs is believed to also be in the dominion of the right hemisphere (Hines, et al., 1976; Smith, 1972; Vega and Parsons, 1969). It is also contended that the iconic presentation of information (e.g., graphic displays, diagrams, flow charts, etc.) greatly facilitates both the comprehension and

---

1. Medically intrusive research denotes direct alteration of the structure or function of the brain, whereas medical non-intrusive studies involve the measurement of the brain functions without neural tissue or function interference.

retention of information, and that this iconic memory is primarily a function of the right hemisphere (Taylor, 1978). Visuo-spatial perception and reasoning, which are posited to be right hemispheric operations (Benton, 1969; Hunter, 1976; Kinsbourne and Smith, 1974, Knox and Kimura, 1970; Milner, 1971; Warrington—Rabin, 1970), are the processing skills that are required in such tasks as architecture and sculpture.

Auditory processing. For most individuals, the perception and retention of complex nonverbal auditory patterns, such as music or morse code occur in the right hemisphere (Buffery, 1976; Dumas and Morgan, 1975; Entus, 1975; Faglioni, Springer and Vignolo, 1969; Kimura, 1973; Molfese, 1975; Olson, 1977; Schwartz, Davidson and Pugash, 1976). It should be noted, however, that Bever and Chiarello (1974) reported that experienced musicians analyze musical patterns via the left hemispheric processing mode, similar to the manner in which most individuals analyze speech patterns.

Proprioceptive processing. Awareness of body position, spatial orientation, and the perception of fine and gross motor activities all come within the realm of the right hemisphere (Brandwein and Ornstein, 1977; deRenzi and Nichelli, 1975). This kind of bodily awareness is the *sine qua non* of ballet and other types of dance, gymnastics, and most activities requiring synchronized bodily movements. Haptic or tactile perception is contended by Kimura (1973) to be a right hemispheric function, based on the observation that there is a pronounced preference for the left hand to be used in the reading of braille. This inference is based upon the principle of contralaterality of hemispheric processing. That is, when stimuli are received in the left visual, auditory or sensory field, it is assumed that these stimuli will be processed in the right (opposite) hemisphere (Lawson, 1975; Kimura, 1967; Williams, 1976.)

The Right Hemisphere in Education

The subjects that are speculated to be processed by the right hemisphere are art, music, and physical education (Samples, 1975). Geometry, which is primarily iconic (graphic) in its format has also been attributed to right hemispheric processing (Hunter, 1976).

Cognitive Styles of the Right Hemisphere

The cognitive styles which are considered characteristic or right hemispheric processing are those skills which are indispensable for generating solutions to problems for which there are no apparent answers. The predominant cognitive styles of the right hemisphere have been described as creative (Bogen and Gazzaniga, 1965; Harnad, 1972; Tart, 1972; Torrance, 1978) and divergent (Kinsbourne and Smith, 1974; Peronne and Pulvino, 1977; Samples, 1975; and Williams, 1976). Another characteristic of the right hemisphere is the capacity to simultaneously (but not sequentially) process several variables, or to deal with information analogically (Salk, 1973). The ability to obtain a global view or a "gestalt" of a situation or task also appears to be a primarily right hemisphere capacity (Diamond and Beaumont, 1974; Papcun, 1974). Intuitive reasoning has been attributed to the right hemisphere as well (Garrett, 1976; Rennels, 1976).

The right hemisphere, perhaps because of its capacity to process multiple stimuli simultaneously, has been described as being satisfied with "approximate knowledge" (Prince 1976), and is more diffuse and less clearly demarcated in its cognitive style than the left hemisphere (Semmes, Weinstein, Ghent and Teuber, 1960). The "Education of Relations" (May, 1977) or the ability to analogically perceive relationships among apparently unrelated concepts or stimuli (which could be considered to be tantamount to generalization ability) also appears to rely predominantly upon the right hemisphere processing mode.

Affective Concomitants of the Right Hemisphere

It is contended (Schwartz, 1975) that the right hemisphere plays a predominant role in the affective domain. Research indicates that the right hemisphere is generally involved in aesthetic judgment tasks, and when the stimuli being processed are perceived as aesthetically harmonious, the accompanying affective state is pleasurable and positive. Negative emotions are believed to be associated with the right hemisphere's processing of stimuli which are perceived as discordant or cacaphonous (Hadamard, 1945; Hebb, 1966).

CURRENT RESEARCH REGARDING THE PHYSIOLOGICAL CORRELATES OF COGNITIVE AND AFFECTIVE FUNCTIONING

The method of ascertaining the degree of hemispheric involvement in cognitive and affective tasks which is currently receiving unprecedented attention is electroencephalogram (EEG) pattern analysis (Brown, 1977; Green, Green and Walters, 1970; Ornstein, 1978). Basically, the EEG is the graphic record of the regular, spontaneous oscillations of the electrical activity of the brain (Hinsie and Campbell, 1960, p. 259). It has been asserted that EEG pattern analysis is the most accurate measure of neurological concomitants of mental activity because it is the total resultant of bioelectrical activity of the neurons (Darwai and Smyk, 1972). Furthermore, in the EEG pattern analysis of cognitive and affective functioning there is no alteration of neural tissue (as in commissurotomy, hemispherectomy and lobectomy research) or cognitive or affective states (as in electroconvulsive or sodium amytal studies). The principle concerns in EEG research are the correct placement of the electrodes on the subject's scalp and the accurate interpretation of the EEG.

The cognitive and affective functioning paradigms currently being developed as the result of EEG pattern analysis research appear to be accurately predictive, i.e., the cognitive affective states of subjects can be predicted at a much greater than chance level based solely on EEG pattern analysis (Brown, 1977; Green, Green and Walters, 1970; Kamiya, 1967, 1969; Luria, 1970; Ornstein, 1978).

Varying modes of cognitive and affective functioning appear to have characteristic and concomitant EEG patterns which can be divided into four basic frequency ranges (the frequency of the electrical activity of the brain is measured in cycles per second or hertz (Hz), delta, theta, alpha and beta. The reported cognitive and affective states which have been found to be associated with each of the four EEG frequency ranges are as follows:

Delta. The delta EEG wave pattern is characterized by regular slow frequency waves ranging from .5 to 3.0 cycles per second (Hz.) (Brown, 1977; Green, Green and Walters, 1970). The delta EEG pattern is recorded most often during the deeper stages of sleep, and is associated with the dream state (Brown, 1977; Green, Green and Walters, 1970).

Theta. The theta EEG wave pattern has a relatively faster frequency than the delta EEG pattern, generally occurring within the 3.5 to 7.5 Hz. frequency range. Theta is most often recorded during the semi-sleep state; that is, between dreaming and waking. It has been found that most individuals are in this theta state about 5% of the time (Green, Green and Walters, 1970). Evidence indicates that it is during this state between dreaming and waking, which is consistently characterized by the theta wave pattern, that insights or shifts in perspective (Budzynski, Stoyva and Adler, 1970; Brown, 1977; Gowan, 1974; Green, Green and Walters, 1979; McKellar and Simpson, 1954; Norman, 1977; Sittenfeld, 1972) and states of reverie occur (Green, Green and Walters, 1970). These "insight-reverie" states are considered to be essential components of creativity (Davidson and Krippner, 1971; Foulkes and Vogel, 1965; Luthe and Geissmann, 1963). Several studies of creative genius indicate that highly creative individuals experienced their most creative insights during states of dreamlike "reverie" whereby reality testing was temporarily suspended (Ghiselin, 1952; Gowan, 1972; Green, Green, and Walters, 1970). Green, Green and Walters (1970) have stated that "there are hundreds of anecdotes which show beyond doubt, that in some way, although not perfectly understood, reverie and creativity are associated" (p. 18). As previously indicated, it is estimated that only 5% of our time is spent in this "reverie state," as measured by the EEG record. Walkup (1956) has suggested that those individuals who have been considered truly creative, are those individuals who have learned how to consciously bring about these reverie or insight states. This insight-reverie mode has characteristics which reflect right hemisphere processing (Brandwein and Ornstein, 1977, May, 1977; Torrance, 1978).

Alpha. The alpha wave pattern is typified by EEG frequencies in the 8 to 13 Hz. range (Brown, 1977; Green, Green and Walters, 1970; Hinsie and Campbell, 1960). The cognitive styles which are associated with this alpha state have been described as receptive (Brown, 1977), problem finding (Deikman, 1971; Murphy, 1958), and involve narrowing of the perceptual field (Honorton, Davidson and Bindler, 1972; Lynch and Paskewitz, 1971). Illumination, insight or reverie experiences are also reported to occur during this state (Budzynski, 1971; Gowan, 1972; Green, Green and Walters, 1969, 1970; Kamiya, 1969; McKellar and Simpson, 1954; Norman, 1977). A state of "relaxed wakefulness" (Brown, 1977; Lindsley, 1960; Nowlis and Kamiya, 1970) is usually expressed by individuls who are in this state, as are feelings of psychological integration or physiological unity (Hellas and Gaier, 1970; Paskewitz, Lynch, Orne and Castello, 1970; Schwartz, 1976). This state of relaxed wakefulness appears to involve functions of both the right and left hemisphere, although the right hemisphere processes may be predominant.

Beta. The beta EEG pattern, which ranges from approximately 13.5 to 40 Hz. in frequency is generally accompanied by reports of externally focused attention (Deikman, 1971; Salamon and Post, 1965), and this increased external focus is evidenced by findings that reaction time to external stimuli is fastest in the beta state (Woodruff, 1975). This beta state has also been interpreted as being typified by increased problem-solving ability (Sheer, 1975). Deikman (1971) has stated that psychological manifestations of the beta state are "object based logic, heightened boundary perception, and dominance of formal characteristics over the sensory; (i.e., shapes and meanings have a preference over colors and textures)" (p. 59). These characteristics of the beta state are suggestive of what Deikman (1971) has coined the "action mode," which is evidenced by externally focused attention and goal orientation. The descriptions of the beta state correspond to left hemisphere functions almost exclusively (Gruzelier and Hammond, 1976; Kraft, 1976; Lawson, 1975; Maksymczuk, 1973).

An analysis of the EEG literature indicates that as the frequency range of the EEG pattern decreases from 40 Hz. to .5 Hz., cognitive and affective states acquire characteristics which are increasingly more descriptive of right hemisphere functioning. The degree of right hemisphere involvement also seems to be positively related to levels of relaxation as manifested by decreased muscle tension or other physiological parameters of relaxation.

THE ELICITATION OF VARIOUS COGNITIVE AND AFFECTIVE STATES

Recent findings in psychophysiological research suggest that not only can relationships between mental functioning and physiological states be established (as reflected by EEG patterns), but that these physiological states which are associated with certain types of cognitive-affective states can be consciously elicited (Green, Green and Walters, 1970; Kamiya, 1969; Schwartz, 1976). It has been empirically and consistently demonstrated that it is possible to consciously and predictably elicit certain physiological states (as measured by the EEG record) by selectively focusing on functions of the central nervous system (muscle relaxation, breathing) or particular thoughts. (Barber, 1971; Budzynski, Stoyva and Adler, 1970; Cacha, 1976; Dicara, 1970; Foulkes, 1965, Foulkes and Vogel, 1966; Green, Green and Walters, 1970; Hord, 1972; Jacobson, 1973; Honorton, Davidson and Bindler, 1972; Kamiya, 1969; Kimmell, 1967, Luthe Oand Geissman, 1963; Miller, 1969; Mulholland and Runnals, 1962; Nowlis and Kamiya, 1970; Paskewitz, Orne and Castello, 1970; Schwartz, Davidson and Pugash, 1976; Sheer, 1972; Sittenfeld, 1972).

The two predominant methods for facilitating desired physiological states (and thus fostering certain mental-emotional states) are Autogenic Training (Green, Green and Walters, 1977), and Progressive Relaxation (Jacobson, 1973). Both of these techniques require the subject to selectively attend to specific central nervous system functions (muscle relaxation) or particular thoughts (of warmth, sleepiness, aesthetically pleasing subjects). These techniques were originally utilized for elimination or mitigation of inappropriate anxiety symptoms (Kamiya, 1962, 1967, 1968); however, it has been found that deep relaxation is associated with what has been described in subjects' reports as creative or insight states (Brown, 1977). These relaxation techniques are in essence, an extension of gross and fine muscle pattern learning (learning a sport or learning to draw, etc.). It has been discovered that when subjects succeeded in producing the alpha EEG pattern, not only were the anxiety symptoms allayed, but the subjects reported shifts in cognitive styles and affective states. These states appeared to be closely related to insight states reported by creatively-productive individuals (Brown, 1977: Green, Green and Walters, 1977). The utilization of conscious elicitation of particular EEG patterns for the purpose of facilitating the cognitive and affective states associated with creativity is currently an area of active research (Green, Green and Walters, 1970; Honorton, Davidson and Bindler, 1972; Hord, Lubin and Johnson, 1975; Nowlis and Kamiya, 1970; Schwartz, Davidson and Pugash, 1976, Sittenfeld, 1972), and points to the possibility of assisting the individual in improving his/her own internal (cognitive-affective) environment and thus perhaps facilitating his/her own predisposition toward "creativity" states.

THE PSYCHOPHYSIOLOGICAL MODEL OF PROBLEM-SOLVING

In 1926, Graham Wallas proposed a 4-stage model of creativity inspired by the eminent German physicist Helmholtz's accounts of the subjective experiences he had encountered while realizing his greatest insights (Vernon, 1976). According to Wallas (1926), the creative thinking process consisted of four distinguishable, although overlapping stages. These four stages were:

(1) Preparation: the problem was investigated in all directions.

(2) Incubation: the individual was not consciously thinking about the problem.

(3) Illumination: the appearance of the "happy idea" together with the psychological events which, immediately preceded and accompanied the appearance of the happy idea.

(4) Verification: the individual then judges the worth of the solution or product (p. 80).

It is the opinion of this writer that there are both hemispheric and psychophysiological (EEG) correlates to Wallas' four stages of creative thinking which are incorporated in the "psychophysiological model of problem-solving." The theoretical bridge between Wallas' creativity model and the findings of psychophysiological research is provided by the theory of "action and receptive modes" proposed by Deikman (1971). The "action mode," is a state of cortical arousal (awareness) organized to manipulate the environment and acquire knowledge in order to change the environment. The focus of attention is external and the corresponding physiological indices of the "action mode" are the beta EEG pattern and increased baseline muscle tension. This "action mode" appears to correspond to Wallas' preparation and verification stages in which external focus and reality testing functions are required which are primarily left hemisphere functions. In contrast, the receptive mode is a state which facilitates the intake of the environment rather than the manipulation of the environment. The psychophysiological concomitants of the "receptive mode" are the alpha or theta EEG patterns and decreased muscle tension. Right hemisphere processes appear to be predominantly involved in the "receptive mode." It is hypothesized by Deikman (1971) that it is during this receptive state or when the person discontinues to focus consciously on a problem and directs his/her attention to other things, that solutions to problems manifest themselves as an "Aha!," "Eureka!" or "insight experience." This receptive mode could be interpreted as being analogous to Wallas' incubation and illumination stages where attention to the problem is defocused, and solutions or insights to problems spontaneously appear.

Training for Problem-Solving

A systematic approach to facilitating problem-solving skills could be designed as follows: First, mastery of an appropriate relaxation technique such as Progressive Relaxation (Jacobson, 1973) or Autogenic Training (Green, Green and Walters, 1977) would be achieved. (These relaxation techniques could be incorporated into physical education curricula). Once the individual demonstrated the ability to consistently elicit a particular state of relaxation as indicated by physiological measures (determined by the EEG pattern frequency (theta, alpha and beta states), the electromyogram (EMG), a graphic recording of skeletal muscle states associated with relaxation, or the Galvanic Skin Response (GSR), the measure of skin conductivity for minute electrical currents based on skin moisture related to varying states of relaxation (Brown, 1977), training for transfer to "real life" situations would be undertaken (Wolpe, 1969). According to the "psychophysiological model of problem solving," the following strategies would be employed according to the stages suggested by Wallas (1926):

The preparatory stage. In this stage, which corresponds to Deikman's (1971) "action mode," a general state of relaxation as indicated by a high alpha or low beta EEG pattern (10–12Hz.) would be brought about. It has been substantially concluded that there is a generally positive correlation between general problem-solving ability and measured (utilizing various physiological indices such as the EEG) or reported levels of relaxation (Bodi, 1970; Carlson, 1969; Frost, 1969; Harper, 1971; Mandler, 1952; Mann et al., 1968; Proger, 1969; Pulvina, 1972; Sarason, 1964.)

278

The incubation stage. This stage is similar to Deikman's (1971) "receptive stage." Attention would be focused inwardly, and a deeper state of relaxation would be attained. This deeper state of relaxation would be determined by the elicitation of the alpha (8.0–13.5 Hz.) EEG pattern. The individual would be instructed to produce as many solutions to the given problem without any evaluation as to their merit or practicality.

The illumination stage. The illumination stage also corresponds to Deikman's (1971) receptive mode, and would be characterized by a very deep state of relaxation reflected on the 3.5 - 7.5 Hz. theta EEG pattern. No conscious effort to focus on the problem would be attempted. Thoughts would be allowed to flow freely.

Verification. The individual would shift his/her focus of attention externally, and would again enter Deikman's "action mode." A normal state of alertness would be attained, which would be indicated by the high alpha or low beta (0–12 Hz.) EEG pattern. Evaluation of the products with respect to practicality and adherence to the initial goals of the problem-solving exercise would take place at this stage.

In essence, according to the psychophysiological model of problem-solving, it would be possible to more operationally define the cognitive and affective modes that would be most appropriate for the type of problem encountered. That is, if through psychophysiological research it were determined that particular physiological states (as indicated by the EEG or other physiological measures) were more conducive to the occurrence of a more creative or receptive mode, individuals could be taught how to replicate that psychophysiological state and thus produce the corresponding cognitive or affective state.

According to the proposed psychophysiological model of problem solving, it is hypothesized that appropriate shifts in the quality and focus of attention (from external to internal and vice-versa) could be consciously elicited through the mastery of systematic relaxation techniques. Consequently, it would be possible that the most advantageous cognitive or affective modes could be brought about apropos to the stage of problem-solving at hand. Furthermore, if the psychophysiological profiles of the most successful problem-solvers could be provided for replication by others, just as observable behavioral patterns of the most renowned musicians, artists and athletes have been emulated for centuries by aspiring novices, the psychophysiological patterns found to best facilitate problem-solving might be practiced just as a sonata is practiced to obtain mastery of the piano. This type of "practice" would involve what Wallas (1926) termed the "self-training of one's natural thought processes" (p. 79). If the creative or problem-solving process could be operationally defined according to quantifiable physiological parameters, perhaps this process could be utilized within the framework of creativity training models which are in use today e.g., "brainstorming" (Osborn, 1963; Parnes and Harding, 1962), "the Mindspring Theory" (Prince, 1976), to greatly increase the chances of generating solutions to heretofore unresolved problems.

SUMMARY

Despite the fact that information about the functional organization of the cerebral hemispheres has been collected for over a century (Eccles, 1973), the advent of non-intrusive, psychophysiological methods of investigation (EEG, dichotic listening tasks, visual field and saccadic eye movement observation) has greatly accelerated the understanding of the "bifunctional brain"

(Ornstein, 1978). A review of representative studies and theoretical literature on hemispheric functioning suggests that the following functions are localized in the right hemisphere: For left-handed adults and children approximately five years of age or under, language processing is more equally divided between the right and left hemispheres. The right hemisphere is more involved than the left hemisphere with the interpretation and retention or complex non-verbal visual and auditory patterns such as the recognition of facial features or recall of melodic patterns. The right hemisphere is predominant in processing the "artistic subjects" (music, art, dance, and physical education), and is theorized to be most adroit at processing tasks that require simultaneous and divergent cognitive styles. The right hemisphere appears to be relatively more involved with affective responses than the left hemisphere. Emotional responses which result from aesthetic evaluation or perceptions are hypothesized to be products of the right hemisphere.

Although the brain is "bifunctional," as substantiated by research on left and right hemispheric information processing styles and capacities, the most productive and creative intellectual functioning is theorized to occur when there is cooperation between hemispheres. In fact, early (before six or seven years of age) and excessive emphasis on the development of processing skills of either the right or left hemisphere to the neglect of the other can possibly lead to permanent cognitive (Passow, 1964; Rennels, 1976; Yakovlev, 1967) or affective (Crinella, Beck and Robinson, 1971) deficits. It has been found that educational experiences that were specifically designed to enhance right hemispheric processing (problem-solving skills) also improved performance on tasks considered to involve left hemispheric functions (verbal tasks) (Noller and Parnes, 1972; Samples, 1975). The results of EEG studies suggest that performance on tasks calling upon primarily left hemispheric (verbal) processing is improved when the right hemisphere is drawn into play (Kraft, 1976; Norman, 1977). Furthermore, it has been suggested that creative geniuses are most adroit at utilizing both the left and the right hemispheric processing modes (Ghiselin, 1952; Gilchrist, 1970; Kraft, 1976; Norman, 1977).

Through the use of the electroencephalogram (EEG) (the graphic recording of the measurement of the electrical potential associated with brain activity) (Hinsie and Campbell, 1960), some of the physiological correlates of cognitive and affective functioning are being identified. Through the "science of subjective experience" (Davidson and Krippner, 1971) these findings concerning physiological correlates of mental activity are being utilized to establish "information processing models" which are amenable to empirical investigation. Reciprocal relationships between physiological and mental modes have been incorporated into what Green, Green and Walters (1970) have termed "the psychophysiological principle." In the "psychophysiological principle" it is posited that certain physiological measures vary predictably as a function of particular cognitive and affective modes. Most importantly, those particular cognitive and affective modes can be elicited by producing the physiological state associated with those cognitive and affective states through systematic relaxation training techniques such as Autogenic Training (Green, Green and Walters, 1977) or Progressive Relaxation (Jacobson, 1973).

The results or research findings on hemispheric and psychophysiological correlates of information processing have been presented herein with Wallas, (1926) four-stage theory of creativity in order to develop the "psychophysiological model of problem-solving." In this proposed model, the physiological indices which appear to be closely associated with Wallas' four stages of creativity (preparation, incubation, illumination, verification) are presented in terms of empirically quantifiable physiological measures (EEG patterns). Therefore, the possibility of an operationally defined sequence for problem-solving is posited as an outcome of the proposed model. It is further hypothesized that via systematic relaxation training techniques, conscious elicitation of the various physiological states associated with each of the problem-solving stages can be attained, and more effective problem-solving can be made possible. It is also suggested that this proposed "psycho-physiological model of problem-solving," could be adapted to existing creativity training models, such as "brainstorming" (Parnes and Harding, 1962) to ascertain physiological aspects of these training models, and thus perhaps more operationally define and increase the replicability of successful creativity training and problem-solving strategies.

Through the psychophysiological approach to learning and problem-solving more precise learning and problem-solving paradigms could be constructed. This greater precision in developing learning and problem-solving paradigms could be accomplished because the influence of subject variables such as test anxiety, attitudes and cultural background of the subject, etc., would be either mitigated or more accurately accounted for as the result of a more direct measure of these influences.

Psychophysiological profiles of the most effective learners or problem-solvers could be provided for replication by other individuals just as the observable performances of outstanding musicians or athletes are studied and practiced by apprentices. Thus, the development of outstanding problem-solvers could be nurtured with the hope of increasing the chances of creative genius.

Reference Note

Contact the author for the complete review of the representative hemisphericity literature, which contains details on the studies reviewed and conclusions regarding the functional organization of both hemispheres.

514 West 122nd Street, #501
New York, New York 10027

References

*Anastasi, Ann *Psychological Testing. [3rd Ed.] London: The Macmillan Co., 1968*

*Barber, T. X., et al. (Eds.) *Biofeedback and self-control.* Chicago: Aldine, 1971.

Basser, L. S. Hemiplegia of early onset and the faculty of speech with special reference to the effects of hemispherectomy. *Brain, 85,* 427–460.

*Benton, A. L. Disorders of spatial orientation. In P. J. Vinken and G. W. Bruyn (Eds.), *Handbook of clinical neurology,* (Vol. 3), Amsterdam: North Holland Publishing Company, 1969.

*Bever, T. J., and Chiarello, R. J. Cerebral dominance in musicians and nonmusicians. *Science,* 1974, *183,* 537–539.

*Bodi, Elizabeth M. The effect of human relations training upon the academic achievement of pre and early adolescent children. *Dissertation Abstracts International,* 1979, *30,* (4–A), 1340.

*Bogen, J. E. and Gazzaniga, M. S. Cerebral commissurotomy in man: Minor hemisphere dominance for certain visuospatial function. *Journal of Neurosurgery,* 1965, *23,* 394–399.

Branch, C. et al. Intracarotid sodium amytal for the lateralization of cerebral speech dominance. *J. Neurosur. 21:*399–465, 1965.

*indicates those references used in the article "The Role of the Right Hemisphere in Learning and Creativity: Implications for Enhancing Problem Solving Ability."

*Brandwein, P., and Ornstein, R. The duality of the mind. *Instructor,* January, 1977, pp. 54–58.

Brazier, Mary A. B. *The electrical activity of the nervous system.* Baltimore: The William & Wilkins Company, 1968.

Brown, B. B. *Stress and the Art of Biofeedback.* New York: Harper & Row, 1977

Brown, J. W. The neural organization of language: Aphasia and lateralization. *Brain and Language,* October, 1976, *3*(4), 482–494.

*Budzynski, T. H. Some applications of biofeedback produced twilight states. Paper presented at the 1971 American Psychological Association Convention, Washington, D.C.

*Budzynski, T. H., Stoyva, J. M., and Adler, G. S. the use of feedback-induced muscle relaxation in tension headache: A controlled-outcome study. Annual Meeting of the American Psychological Association, Miami Beach, Florida September 3–8, 1970(b).

*Buffery, A. W. H. Sex differences in the neuropsychological development of verbal and spatial skills. In D. J. Bakker and R. M. Knights (Eds.) *The neuropshychology of learning disorders.* Baltimore: University Park Press, 1976, pp. 187–205.

Burklund, C. W. Cerebral hemisphere function in the human: fact versus tradition. In W. L. Smith (Ed.) *Drugs, development and cerebral function.* Springfield, Illinois: Charles C. Thomas, 1972, pp. 8–36.

*Burkland, C. W. and Smith, A. Language and the cerebral hemispheres. *Neurology,* July, 1977, *27,* 627–633.

*Butler, S. R., and Glass, A. Asymmetrics in the electroencephalogram associated with cerebral dominance. *Electroencephalography and Clinical Neurophysiology,* 1974, *36,* 481–491.

Cabral, R., and Scott, D. F. The degree of alpha asymmetry and its relation to handedness in neuropsychiatric referrals. *Acta Neurologica Scandinavica,* May, 1975, *51* (5), 380–384.

*Cacha, B. Figural creativity, personality and peer nominations of pre-adolescents, *The Gifted Child Quarterly,* 1976, *XX*(2), 187–195.

Calearo, C., Verbal tests of central audition, *Audiology,* 1975, *14*(4), 300–311.

Callaway, E., and Harris, P. R. Coupling between cortical potentials from different areas. *Sciences,* 1974, *183,* 873–875.

*Carlson, J. Levels of cognitive functioning as related to anxiety. *Journal of Experimental Education,* 1969, *37*(4), 17–20.

Chadwick, J., and Mann, W. N. *The medical works of Hippocrates.* Oxford: Blackwell, 1950.

Cherlow, D. G., and Serafetinides, E. A. Speech and memory abilities in psychomotor epileptics. *Cortex,* March, 1976, *12* (1), 21–26.

*Compton, A., and Bradshaw, J. L. Differential hemispheric mediation of nonverbal visual stimuli. *Journal of Experimental Psychology: Human Perception and Performance,* August, 1975, *104*(1),(3), 246–252.

Crinella, T. M., Beck, F. W., and Robinson, J. W. Unilateral dominance is not related to neuropsychological integrity. *Child Development,* December 1971, *42,* (6), pp. 2033–54.

Curry, F. W. A comparison of the performances of a right hemispherectomized subject and 25 normals on 4 dichotic listening tasks, *Cortex,* 1968, *4,* 144–153.

*Darvai, B., and Smyk, K. Interhemisphere asymmetry in electroencephalographic alpharhythm and the problem of cerebral hemisphere dominance. *Voprosy Psykhologii,* May, 1972, *18*(3), 149–154.

*Davidson, R., and Krippner, S. Biofeedback research: The data and their implications. *Biofeedback and Self-Control,* 1971, p. 23–34.

*Day, M. E. An eye-movement phenomenon relating to attention, thought, and anxiety. *Perceptual and Motor Skills,* 1964, *19,* 443–446.

Debono, E. *The use of lateral thinking.* Toronto: Holt Publishing Co., 1971.

*Deikman, R. Bimodal consciousness. *Biofeedback and Self Control,* 1971, 58–73. d'Elia, G., Lorentzson, S., Raotman, H., and Widepalm, K. *Comparison of unilateral dominant and non-dominant ECT on verbal and nonverbal memory. Acta Psychiatrica Scandinavia.* February, 1976, *53*(2), 85–94.

*deRenzi, E., and Nichelli, P. Verbal and non-verbal short-term memory impairment following hemispheric damage. *Cortex,* December, 1975, *11*(4), 341–354.

*DiCara, L. Learning in the autonomic nervous system. *Scientific American,* January, 1970.

*Dimond, S. J., and Beaumont, J. G. Experimental studies of hemisphere function in normal and brain-damaged individuals. In S. J. Dimond and J. G. Beaumont (Eds.), *Hemisphere functions of the human brain.* London: Elek Science, 1974.

Dimond, S., Farrmington, L., Johnson, P. Differing emotional responses from right and left hemispheres. *Nature,* 1976, 261, 690–692.

Doyle, J. C., Ornstein, R., and Galin, D. Lateral specialization of cognitive mode: II. EEG frequency analysis. *Psychophysiology,* 1974,*11,* 567–568.

*Dumas, R., and Morgan, A. EEG asymmetry as a function of occupation, task, and task difficulty. *Neuropsychologica,* April, 1975, *13,* (2), 219–228.

*Eccles, J. C. *The understanding of the brain.* New York: McGraw-Hill Books, 1973.

*Entus, A. K. Hemispheric asymmetry in processing of dichotically presented speech and nonspeech sounds by infants. Meeting of the Society for Research in Child Development, 1975, (Abstract).

Epinas, J. Neurophysiological aspects of laterality. *Revue de Neuropsychiatrie Infantile et d'Hygiene Mentale de l'Enfance,* January, 1975, *23,* (1), 5–11.

*Faglioni, P., Spinnler, H., and Vignolo, L. A. Contrasting behavior of right and left hemisphere-damaged patients on a discriminative and semantic task of auditory recognition. *Cortex.* 1969, *5,* 366–389.

Fleminger, J. J., and Bunce, L. Investigation of cerebral dominance in "left-handers" and "right-handers"— using unilateral electroconvulsive therapy. *Journal of Neurology, Neurosurgery and Psychiatry,* June, 1975, *38*(6), 541–545.

*Foulkee, D., and Vogel, G. Mental activity at sleep onset. *Journal of Abnormal Psychology,* 1965, *70,* 231–243.

*Foulkes, D. *The psychology of sleep.* New York: Scribners, 1966.

*Fromholt, P., Christensen, A. L. and Stromgren, L. The effects of unilateral and bilateral electroconvulsive therapy on memory. *Acta Psychiatrica Scandinavica,* 1973, *49*(4), 466–478.

*Frost, B. Uzudies of anxiety and educational achievement. *Revista Interamericana de Psicologia,* 1969, 3(2), 83–91.

*Garrett, S. V. Putting our whole brain to use: A fresh look at the creative process. *Journal of Creative Behavior,* 1976, *10* (4), 239–249.

*Gazzaniga, M. S. The split brain in man. *Scientific American,* 1967, *217* (2), 24–29.

*Gazzaniga, M. S., and Hillyard, S. A. Language and speech capacity of the right hemisphere. *Neuropsychologia,* 1971, *9,* 273–280.

*Geschwind, N. Language and the brain. *Readings from Scientific American: Recent Progress in Perception.* San Francisco: W. H. Freeman & Company, 1970.

Getzels, J. W., and Jackson, P. W., *Creativity and intelligence.* New York: John Wiley & Sons, Inc., 1962.

Ghiselin, B. (ed.). *The Creative Process.* New York: New American Library, 1952.

Gilchrist, M., and Taft, R. Creative attitudes and creative productivity: A comparison of two aspects of creativity among students. *Journal of Educational Psychology,* April, 1970, *62* 136–143.

*Goodglass, H., and Quadfasel, F. A. Language laterality in left-handed aphasics. *Brain, 1954. LXVII,* 521–548.

*Gowan, J. C. Trance, art and creativity. *Journal of Creative Behavior,* 1975 *9,* 1–11.

*Gowan, J. C. *The development of the creative individual.* San Diego: Robert Knapp, 1972.

Goyvaerts, Monique Recent advances in language acquisition. *Communication and Cognition.* 1975, *8* (1), 45–67.

Green, E., Green, A., and Walters, D. *Outline of Verbal Procedure Used in Developing Voluntary Control of Internal States in Autogenic Feedback Training.* Topeka, Kansas Research Department, The Menninger Foundation, 1977.

*Green, E. E., Green, A. M., and Walters, E. D. Voluntary control of internal states: psychological and physiological. *Journal of Transpersonal Psychology,* 1970, *2,* 1–26.

Green, E. E., Walters, E. D., Green, A. M., and Murphy, G. Feedback technique for deep relaxation. *Psychophysiology,* 1969, *6,* 371–377.

*Gruzelier, J., and Hammond, N. Schizophrenia: A dominant hemisphere temorallimbic disorder? *Research Communications in Psychology, Psychiatry and Behavior,* 1976, *1,* 33–72.

Guertin, W. H., Ladd, E. E., Frank, G. H., Rabin, A. I., and Hiester, D. S. Research with the Wechsler Intelligence Scales for adults, 1960–1965. *Psychological Bulletin.* 1966, *66,* 385–509.

Guilford, J. P. Varieties of creative giftedness: Their measurement and development. *The Gifted Child Quarterly,* 1975. *XIX.* (2).

Guilford, J. P. *Intelligence, creativity and their educational implications.* San Diego, California: Knapp, 1968.

Hac, P. M. Short-term memory in patients with left (dominant) frontal lobe lesions. *Psychologia: An International Journal of Psychology in the Orient,* December 1974, *17* (4), 186–192.

*Hadamard, J. *The Psychology of invention in the mathematical field.* Princeton: Princeton University Press, 1945.

*Harnad, S. R. Creativity, lateral saccades and the nondominant hemisphere. *Perceptual and Motor Skills,* 1972, *34,* 653–654.

Harper, F. B. Specific anxiety theory and Mandler-Sarason Test Anxiety questionnaire. *Educational and Psychological Measurement,* Autumn–winter 1971, *31.*

Harris, L. J. Functional specialization of the cerebral hemispheres in infants and children: New experimental and clinical evidence. Paper presented at the Biennia Meeting of the Society for Research in Child Development, Denver, Colorado, April 13, 1975.

Hart, J. T. Autocontrol of EEG alpha. Paper presented at the Seventh Annual Meeting of the Society for Psychophysiological Research, San Diego, October 10–22, 1967.

Hassett, J., and Schwartz, G. E. Relationships between heart rate and occipital alpha: A biofeedback approach. Psychophysiology, 1975, *12,* 228 (Abstract).

*Hebb, D. O. *A textbook of psychology.* Philadelphia: Saunders, 1966.

*Hecaen, H. Functional hemispheric asymmetry and behavior. *Social Science Information.* December 1973, *12* (6), 7–23.

*Hellas, M., and Gaier, E. L. Identification of creativity: the individual. *Psychological Bulletin,* 1970, *73,* (1), 55–73.

*Hellige, J. B., and Cox, P. J. Effects of concurrent verbal memory on recognition of stimuli from the left and right visual fields. *Journal of Experimental Psychology: Human Perception and Performance,* May 1976, *2* (2), 210–221.

*Hillyard, R. D. Hemispheric laterality effects on a facial recognition task in normal subjects. Cortex. September 1973, *9*(3), 246–258.

*Hines, D., Sutker, L. W., and Satz, P. A. Recall of letters from the left and right visual half-fields under unilateral and bilateral presentation. *Perceptual and Motor Skills,* 1976, *42* (2), 531–539.

*Hinsie, L. E., and Campbell, R. J. *Psychiatric Dictionary,* New York: Oxford University Press, 1960.

*Honorton, C., Davidson, R. J., and Bindler, P. Shifts in subjective state associated with feedback-augmented EEG alpha. *Biofeedback and Self-Control,* 1972.

*Hord, D. J., Naitch, P., Johnson, L. C., and Tracy, M. L. Intra-hemispheric phase relationships during self-regulated alpha activity. *Biofeedback and Self-Control,* 1972.

*Hord, D. J., Tracy, M. L., Lubin, A., and Johnson, L. C. Effect of self-enhanced EEG alpha on performance and mood after two nights of sleep loss. *Psychophysiology 12* (5), 1975, 585–590.

Humphrey, M. E., and Zangwill, O. L. Cessation of dreaming after brain injury. *Journal of Neurolog. Neurosurg. Psychiat.,* 1951, *14,* 322–325.

*Hunter, M. Right-brained kids in left-brained schools. *Today's Education,* November–December 1976, 45–48.

Jackson, J. Right cerebral lesion of aphasia. *Medical Times Gazette,* 1866, (2), 210.

Jacobson, E. Electrophysiology of mental activities. *American Journal of Psychology,* October 1932, *44,* 677–694.

*Jacobson, E. *Teaching and learning new methods for old arts.* U.S. National Foundation for Progressive Relaxation, 1973.

Janes, J. *The origin of consciousness in the breakdown of the bicameral mind.* Boston: Houghton-Mifflin Co., 1976.

Johnson, D. M. *Systematic introduction to the psychology of thinking.* New York Harper, 1972.

Johnson, G. L. An experimental study of the effects of three modes of test administration on the reading achievement of fifth graders grouped according to test anxiety. *Dissertation Abstracts International,* 1969, *30* (9–A), 3789–3790.

Kamiya, J. Conditioned discrimination of the EEG alpha rhythm in humans. Paper presented at the Meeting of the Western Psychological Association, San Francisco, April 1962.

*Kamiya, J. EEG operant conditioning and the study of states of consciousness. In D. X. Freedman, Laboratory studies of altered psychological states, Symposium at the American Psychological Association, Washington, D.C. September 4, 1967.

*Kamiya, J. Operant control of the EEG alpha rhythm and some of its reported effects on consciousness. In C. T. Tart (Ed.) *Altered states of consciousness,* New York: John Wiley & Sons, 1969.

Kasamatsu, A., and Hirai, T. Science of zazen. *Psychologia,* 1963, *6,* 89–91.

Khatena, J. Educating the gifted child: Challenge and response in the U.S.A. *Gifted Child Quarterly,* 1976, *XX,* (1), 76–90.

Kimmel, H. D. Instrumental conditioning of automatically mediated behavior. *Psychological Bulletin,* 1967, *67,* 335–345.

*Kimura, D. Functional asymmetry of the human brain in dichotic listening. *Cortex,* 1967, *3,* 163–178.

*Kimura, D. The asymmetry of the human brain. In *Recent Progress in Perception,* March, 1973, 246–254.

*Kinsbourne, M., and Smith, W. L. Hemispheric disconnection and cerebral function. Springfield, Illinois: Charles C. Thomas, 1974.

*Knox, C., and Kimura, D. Cerebral processing of nonverbal sounds in boys and girls. *Neuropsychologia,* 1970, *8,* 227–237.

*Kraft, R. H. An EEG study: Hemispheric brain functioning of six to eight year-old children during Piagetian and curriculum tasks with variation in presentation mode. Ph.D. Dissertation, the Ohio State University, 1976.

Kupfermann, I. *The Neural Sciences* (Lecture Syllabus). New York. College of Physicians and Surgeons, Columbia University 1977 pp. 463–467.

Laski, M. *Ecstasy,* Bloomington Indiana: Indiana University Press, 1962.

*Lawson, A. E., and Wollman, W. T. *Hemispheric dominance, conservation reasoning and the dominant eye.* National Science Foundation, Washington D.C., November, 1975.

*Lenneberg, E. *Biological foundations of language.* New York: Wiley, 1967.

Levy, J. Possible basis for evolution of lateral specialization of the human brain. *Nature,* 1969, *224,* 615–651.

*Lindsley, D. B. Attention, consciousness, sleep and wakefulness. In J. Field (Ed.) *Handbook of physiology, Section I: Neurophysiology,* Vol. III, Washington D.C.: American Physiological Society, 1960.

*Luria, A. R. The functional organization of the brain. *Readings from Scientific American: Recent progress in perception.* San Francisco: W. H. Freeman & Co., 1970.

*Luthe, W., Jus, A., and Geissman, P. Autogenic state and autogenic shift: psychophysiologic and neurophysiologic aspects. *Acta Psychother.,* 1963, *11,* 1–13.

*Lynch, J. J., and Paskewitz, D. A. On the mechanisms of the feedback control of human brain wave activity. *Journal of Nervous and Mental Disease,* 1971.

Mackinnon, D. Creativity and transliminal experience. Unpublished paper given at the American Psychological Association Convention in Los Angeles, California, 1964.

*Maksymczuk, A. Disorders in remembering the structure of serial material with individuals following a unilateral temporal lobectomy. *Studia Psychologiczne,* 1973, *12,* 127–165.

Mandler, G., and Sarason, S. A study of anxiety and learning. *Journal of Abnormal and Social Psychology,* 1952, *47,* 166–173.

Mann, L., Taylor, R., and Barton, R. Test anxiety and defensiveness against admission of text anxiety induced by frequent testing. *Psychologival Reports,* 1968, *23,* 1283–86.

Maslow, A. H. *Towards a psychology of being.* Princeton: D. Van Nostrand, 1962.

*May, R. Freedom, determinism and the future. *Psychology,* April, 1977, 6–9. McFie, J., and Piercy, M. F. Intellectual impairment with localized cerebral lesions. *Brain.* 1952, *75,* 292–311.

McGuineess, D., and Pribram, K. Male, female perceptual differences: What they imply. *Brain/Mind Bulletin,* February, 1978, p. 3.

McKee, G., Humphrey, B., and McAdam, D. W. Scaled lateralization of alpha activity during linguistic and musical tasks. *Psychophysiology,* 1973, *10,* 441–443.

*McKellar, P., and Simpson, L. Between wakefulness and sleep. *British Journal of Psychology*, 1954, *45*, 266–276.

Miller, N. E. Learning of visceral and glandular responses. *Science*, 1969a. *163* 434–445.

*Milner, B. Interhemispheric differences and psychological processes. *British Medical Bulletin*, 1971, *27*, 272–277.

Milner, B. Psychological defects produced by temporal lobe excision. *Res. Publ. Assn. Nerv. Ment. Dis.*, 1958, *36*, 244–257.

*Molfese, D. L., Freeman, R. B. Jr., and Palermo, D.S. The ontogeny of brain lateralization for speech and nonspeech stimuli. *Brain and Language*, 1975, *2*, 356–368.

Morgan, A. H., McDonald P. J., and MacDonald, H. Differences in bilateral alpha activity as a function of experimental task, with a note on lateral eye movements and hypnotizability. *Neuropsychologia*, 1971, *9*, 459–469.

*Moscovitch, M., Scullion, D., and Christie, D. Early versus late stages of processing and their relation to functional hemispheric asymmetries in face recognition. *Journal of Experimental Psychology: Human Perception and Performance*, August, 1976, *2*(3), 401–416.

*Mulholland, T. B. Can you really turn on with alpha? Paper presented at a meeting of the Massachusetts Psychological Association, Boston College, May 7, 1977.

Mulholland, T. B., and Runnals, S. A stimulus-brain feedback system for evaluation of alertness. *Journal of Psychology*, 1962a, *54*, 69–83.

*Muller, E. On the objectivization of the symptom impaired facial recognition: An experimental psychological study of psychiatric-neurological groups of patients. *Zeitschrift fur Klinische Psychologie*, 1973, *2*(2), 126–144.

*Murphy, G. *Human potentialities*. New York: Basic Books, 1958.

Nebes, R. D. Hemispheric specialization in commissurotomized man. *Psychological Bulletin*, January, 1974, *81*, (1).

*Nebes, R. D., and Sperry, R. W. Hemispheric deconnection syndrom with cerebral birth injury in the dominant arm area. *Neuropsychologia*, 1971, *9*, 247–259.

*Newton, M. A. A neuro-psychological investigation into dyslexia. Paper presented at the International Federation of Learning Disabilities (Second International Scientific Conference, Brussels, Belgium, January 3–7, 1975.

Noller, R. B., and Parnes, S. J. The creative studies project, part one—the development. *The Journal of Creative Behavior*. 1972, *6*, (1), 11–22.

*Norman D. EEG patterns and reported insight states. *Brain/Mind Bulletin*, Spring, 1977, *2*(13).

*Nowlis, D. P., and Kamiya, J. The control of electroencephalographic alpha rhythms through auditory feedback and associated mental activities. *Psychophysiology*, 1970, *6*, (4), 476–484.

*Olson, M. B. Visual field usage as an indicator of right or left hemispheric information processing in gifted students. *Gifted Child Quarterly*, 1977, *XXI* (1), 116–120.

*Ornstein, R. E. *The psychology of consciousness*. New York: N. H. Freeman & Co., 1972.

Ornstein, R. The split and the whole brain. In *Nature*, May, 1978, p. 76–83.

*Osborn, A. F. *Applied imagination*. New York: Scribner's, 1963.

*Papcun, G. Is the left hemisphere specialized for speech, language and/or something else. *Journal of the Acoustical Society of America*, 55, (2) February, 1974.

*Parnes S. J., and Harding, H. F. Do you really understand brainstorming? In S. J. Parnes and H. F. Harding (Eds.), *A sourcebook for creative thinking*. New York: Scribner's, 1962, 283–290.

*Paskewitz, D., Lynch, J. J., Orne, M. T., and Castello, J. The feedback control of alpha activity: Conditioning or disinhibition. *Psychophysiology*, 1970, *6*, 637–638.

Passow, A. H. The nature and needs of the disadvantaged. In P. Witty (Ed.) *The sixty-sixth yearbook of the National Society for the Study of Education*. Chicago: University of Chicago Press, 1967, 1–39.

Penfield, W., and Roberts, L. *Speech and brain mechanisms*. Princeton: Princeton University Press, 1959.

*Perrone, P., and Pulvino, C. J. New directions in the guidance of the gifted and talented. *Gifted Child Quarterly*, 1977, XXI, (3), 326–335.

Pincus J., and Tucker, G. *Organic brain syndromes.* Oxford: University Press, Inc., 1974.

*Prince, G. M. The mindspring theory: A new development from synectics research. *The Journal of Creative Behavior,* 1976, *9,* 159–87.

*Proger, B. B. The relationship between four testing programs and resultant achievement and test anxiety levels of high and low previous achievement on 6th grade arithmetic studies. *Dissertation Abstracts International, 1969, 28*(11-A), 3880.

Pulvino, C. J., and Hansen, J. C. Relevance of needs and "Press" to anxiety, alienation and G.P.A. *Journal of Experimental Education,* 1972, *40,* (3).

Rather, L. J. *Mind and body in eighteenth-century medicine: A study based on Jerome Gaub's De regimine mentis.* Berkeley: University of California Press, 1965.

*Rennels, M. R. Cerebral symmetry: An urgent concern for education. *Phie Delta Kappan, 57,* (7), March, 1976, 471–472.

*Salamon, I., and Post, J. Alpha blocking and schizophrenia. *Archives of General Psychiatry,* 1965, *13,* 367–74.

*Salk, J. *The survival of the wisest.* New York: Harper & Row, 1973.

*Samples, R. Educating for both sides of the human mind. *The Science Teacher, 1975. 42,* (1), 21–23.

*Sarason, S., Hill, K., and Zimbardo, J. A longitudinal study of the relation of test anxiety to performance on intelligence and achievement tests. *Monographs of the Society for Research in Child Development,* 1964, *29*(7 whole No. 98).

Scheffler, I. In praise of the cognitive emotions. Paper presented at annual Meeting of the American Psychiatric Association. Brooklyn College: Brooklyn, New York, 1976.

Schultz, J., and Luthe, W. *Autogenic training: A psychophysiologic approach in psychotherapy.* New York: Grune & Stratton, Inc., 1959.

*Schwartz, G. E. Biofeedback, self-regulation, and the patterning of physiological processes. *American Scientist,* 1975, *63,* 314–324.

*Schwartz, G. E., Davidson, R. J., and Pugash, E. Voluntary control of patterns of EEG parietal asymmetry: cognitive concomitants. *Psychophysiology,* November, 1976, *13,* (6), 498–504.

*Semmes, J., Weinstein, S., Ghent, L., and Teuber, H. L. *Somatosensory changes after penetrating brain wounds in man.* Cambridge, Massachusetts: Harvard University Press, 1960.

Shankweiler, D. Effects of temporal-lobe damage on perception of dichotically presented melodies. *Journal of Comparative and Physiological Psychology,* 1966, *62,* 115–119.

Sheer, D. E. Electrophysiological correlates of memory consolidation. In A. Ungar (Ed.) *Molecular mechanisms in memory and learning.* New York: Plenum Press, 1970. p. 177.

*Sheer, D. E., Neurobiology of memory storage processes. Winter Conference on Brain Research, Vail, Colorado, 1972.

*Sheer, D. E. Biofeedback training of 40 Hz EEG and behavior. In N. Bruch and L. Altschuler (Eds.) *Behavior and brain electrical activity.* Plenum Publishing Corp. 1975.

*Sittenfeld, P. The control of the EEG theta rhythm. *Biofeedback and Self-Control,* 1972.

*Smith, A. Dominant and nondominant hemispherectomy. In W. L. Smith (Ed.) *Drugs, development and cerebral function.* Springfield, Illinois: Charles, C. Thomas, 1972.

*Sperry, R. W. Messages from the laboratory. *Engineering and Science,* January, 1974.

Springer, S. P., and Eisenson, J. Hemispheric specialization for speech in language-disordered children. *Neuropsychologia,* 1977, *15,* 287–294.

Stoyva, J. M., and Kamiya, J. Electrophysiological studies of dreaming as the prototype of a new strategy in the study of consciousness. *Psychological Review,* 1968, *75,* 192–205.

Tannenbaum, A. J. Meta learning. Presented at seminar—Nature and Needs of the Gifted, Teachers College, Columbia University, October, 1977.

*Tart, C. T. *Altered states of consciousness.* Garden City, New York: Doubleday, 1972.

Taylor, R. Computers and hemispheric functioning. Presented at Seminar, Teachers College, Columbia University, New York, New York, February, 1978.

Thurstone, L. L. Implications of factor analysis. *American Psychologist,* 1948, *3,* 402–428.

Torrance, E. P. *Guiding creative talent.* Englewood Cliffs, New Jersey: Prentice-Hall, 1962.

*Torrance, E. P., and Reynolds, C. R. Images of the future of gifted adolescents: Effects of alienation and specialized cerebral function. *The Gifted Child Quarterly,* 1978, *XXII.* (1), 40–54.

Torrance, E. P., Reynolds, C. R., Riegel, T., and Ball, O. Your style of learning: An r/l test. *The Gifted Child Quarterly,* 1977, *XXI,* (4), 563–585.

*Van Lanker, D. Heterogeneity in language and speech: neurolinguistic studies. *Working Papers in Phocstics,* April, 1975, 29.

*Vega, A. J., and Parsons, O. A. Relationship between sensory-motor deficits and WAIS verbal and performance scores in unilateral brain damage. *Cortex,* 1969, 5.

*Vernon, P. E. *Creativity.* New York: Penguin Books, 1976.

*Walkup, L. E. Creativity in science through visualization. *Perceptual Motor Skills,* 1965, *21.* 34–41.

Wallach, M. A., and Kogan, N. *Modes of thinking in your children.* New York: Holt Rinehart & Winston, 1965.

Wallas, G. *The Art of Thought.* Jonathan Cape, 1926, pp. 79–96.

*Warrington, E. K., and Rabin, P. Perceptual matching in patients with cerebral lesions, *Neuropsychologia,* 1970, 8, 475–487.

*Weisenberg, T., and McBride, K. E. Aphasia: a clinical and psychological study. New York: Commonwealth Fund, 1935.

Williams, B. B. The relationship between lateral dominance and divergent cognitive thought. Paper presented at the Annual Meeting of the Eastern Psychological Association, New York, New York, April 22–24, 1976.

Willis, A. and Grossman, D. *Medical Neurobiology,* St. Louis. The C. V. Mosby Co. 1973 pp. 334–366.

*Wolpe, J. W. *The practice of behavior therapy.* New York: Pergamon Press, 1969.

Wood, C. C. Goff, W. R., and Day, R. S. Auditory evoked potentials during speech perception. *Science,* 1971, *173,* 1248–1251.

*Woodruff, D. S. Relationships among EEG alpha frequency, reaction time, and age: A biofeedback study. *Psychophysiology,* 1975, *12*(6), 673–689.

Yakovlev, P. I., and Lecours, A. R. The myelogenetic cycles of regional maturation of the brain. In A. Minkowski (Ed.) *Regional development of the brain in early life.* Philadelphia: Davis, 1967, 3–78.

Zaidel, D., and Sperry, R. W. Performance on the Raven's colored progressive matrices by subjects with cerebral commissurotomy. *Cortex,* 1973, *9,* 33–39.

Zangwill, O. L. Speech and the minor hemisphere. *Acta Neurologica Psychiat. Belgica.* 1961, *67,* 1013–1020.

Zellinger, R. Removal of left cerebral hemisphere. *Arch. Neurology Psychiatry,* 1935, 34, 1055–1064.

X

SUMMARY

34. CREATIVE INSPIRATION IN COMPOSERS

John Curtis Gowan

What is the difference between talent and genius? This question vexes any of us interested in the condition and promise of the artist. Talent and discipline are obviously necessary conditions, but of what consists the extra sufficiency which culminates in great creations? This question is most germane to those of us who deal with gifted children, for even without our ministrations they will grow up into gifted adults. And what we hope for them is that they shall also be creative.

There is a charming anecdote about the great George Gershwin and his second and junior, Oscar Levant. On one of their frequent tours, Oscar, as usual, got the upper berth on the train. Leaning down one night he queried George: "Why is it that I always get the upper?" To which George replied: "That's the difference between talent and genius."

In earlier days psychologists used to define genius as very high mental ability, or high talent. But even a cursory study of history will show that some very highly gifted persons were far from geniuses in the sense of producing lasting creations, and some much more moderately talented individuals were, in fact, geniuses.

It is here suggested that genius is not merely very high mental ability, but that it is literally "possession by genii." (The *New Standard Dictionary* defines an ancient meaning of "genius" as "a benevolent attendant spirit," such as the daemon of Socrates.) In terms of modern psychology, a genius in this definition would be a person of talent who is psychologically open to creative inspiration from some preconscious or transpersonal source.

When the sculptor Vigeland was commissioned to do a statue of the great Norwegian mathematician, Abel, he boldly discarded conventions of the past, and posed Abel naked upheld by two gigantic forms. Stang (1965) describes Vigeland's concept.

> The two wingless figures which carry Abel on his flight were termed genii by Vigeland. This vague concept, these genii, occurs constantly in Vigeland's work—only occasionally in the finished work, more frequently in the studies in the round, and repeatedly in the drawings. As a rule these genii are symbols of poetic inspiration, sometimes of germination and growth, and occasionally of ideas themselves.

When Michaelangelo did the Sistine Chapel he painted both the major and minor prophets. They can be told apart because, thought there are cherubim at the ears of all, only the major prophets are *listening*. Here, exactly stated, is the difference between genius and talent. In a more religious day, the composer Puccini says the same thing (Abell, 1964):

> It is the same with a composer. He must acquire by laborious study and application the technical mastery of his craft, but he will never write anything of lasting value unless he has Divine aid

Reprinted by permission from *The Journal of Creative Behavior*, Vol. 11, No. 4, 1977.

also. There is a vast amount of good music paper wasted by composers who don't know this great truth. . . . Dante, Raphael, Stradivarius all drew on the same Omnipotent power. . . . Inspiration is an awakening, a quickening of all man's faculties, and it is manifested in all high artistic achiements. . . .

While it is obvious that talent and training are required for artistic or, indeed, any kind of creative product, it is also important to distinguish between those products which are creative only for the artist, and those which have universal and timeless appeal. The dichotomy here merely represents two ends of a continuum, but it seems to us that inchoate or subconscious mental processes in ordinary creativity may be somewhat better defined in the extreme cases. It was also felt that the actual details of the metamorphosis might be clearer in the case of musical genius than any other kind. We therefore sought to find out how several of the world's greatest composers described the process of creation in their own words. We are looking at the process of inspiration and any commonalities. Since most of these nineteenth century composers were orthodox Christians, we must expect that their words will be clothed in religious forms.

Here is what Brahms says (Abell, 1964):

To realize that we are one with the Creator as Beethoven did is a wonderful and awe-inspiring experience. Very few human beings ever come into that realization, and that is why there are so few great composers or creative geniuses. . . . I always contemplate all this before commencing to compose. This is the first step. When I feel the urge I begin by appealing directly to my Maker. . . . I immediately feel vibrations which thrill my whole being. . . . In this exalted state I see clearly what is obscure in my ordinary moods; then I feel capable of drawing inspiration from above as Beethoven did. . . . Those vibrations assume the form of distinct mental images. . . . Straightaway the ideas flow in upon me, directly from God, and not only do I see distinct themes in the mind's eye, but they are clothed in the right forms, harmonies, and orchestration. Measure by measure the finished product is revealed to me when I am in those rare, inspired moods. . . . I have to be in a semi-trance condition to get such results—a condition when the conscious mind is in temporary abeyance, and the subconscious is in control, for it is through the subconscious mind, which is a part of Omnipotence that the inspiration comes.

R. Strauss in talking about two operas, *Elektra and Rosenkavalier* (Abell, 1964), has this to say, comparing the two:

While the ideas were flowing in upon me—the entire musical, measure by measure, it seemed to me that I was dictated to by two wholly different Omnipotent Entities. . . . I was definitely conscious of being aided by more than an earthly Power, and it was responsive to my determined suggestions. A firm belief in this Power must precede the ability to draw on it purposefully and intelligently. . . . I know I can appropriate it to some extent. . . . I can tell you from my own experience that an ardent desire and fixed purpose combined with intense resolve brings results. Determined concentrated thought is a tremendous force, and this Divine Power is responsive to it. I am convinced that this is a law, and it holds good in any line of human endeavor.

The great Puccini has much the same story to tell (Abell, 1964):

The great secret of all creative geniuses is that they possess the power to appropriate the beauty, the wealth, the grandeur, and the sublimity within their own souls, which are a part of Omnipotence, and to communicate those riches to others. The conscious purposeful appropriation of one's own soul-forces is the supreme secret. . . . I first grasp the full power of the Ego within me. Then I feel the burning desire and intense resolve to create something worthwhile. This desire, this longing, implies in itself the knowledge that I can reach my goal. Then I make a fervent demand for and from the Power that created me. This demand or prayer must be coupled with full expectation that this higher aid will be granted me. This perfect faith opens the way for vibration to pass from the dynamo which the soulcenter is, into my consciousness, and the inspired ideas are born. . . . The music of this opera (*Madame Butterfly)* was dictated to me by God; I was merely instrumental in putting it on paper and communicating it to the public. . . .

And here is the composer Humperdinck, quoting his friend, the even greater composer, Richard Wagner (Abell, 1964):

I am convinced that there are universal currents of Divine Thought vibrating the ether everywhere and that anyone who can feel these vibrations is inspired provided he is conscious of the process and possesses the knowledge and skill to present them. . . . I have very definite impressions while in the trance-like condition which is the prerequisite of all true creative effort. I feel that I am one with this vibrating Force, that it is omniscient, and that I can draw upon it to an extent that is limited only by my own capacity to do so. . . . One supreme fact which I have discovered is that it is not will-power but fantasy-imagination that creates. . . . Imagination is the creative force . . . imagination creates the reality.

Now we hear from none other than Mozart who says in a letter to a friend (quoted in Vernon, 1970):

All this fires my soul and, provided I am not disturbed, my subject enlarges itself, becomes methodized and defined, and the whole, though it be long, stands almost complete and finished in my mind, so that I can survey it, like a fine picture or a beautiful statue, at a glance. Nor do I hear in my imagination the parts *successively,* I hear them, as it were, all at once. What a delight this is I cannot tell! All this inventing, this producing, takes place in a pleasing, lively dream.

And finally, Tschaikowsky, from another letter (quoted in Vernon, 1970):

Generally speaking, the germ of a future composition comes suddenly and unexpectedly. . . . It takes root with extraordinary force and rapidity, shoots up through the earth, puts forth branches and leaves, and finally blossoms. I cannot define the creative process in any other way than by this simile. . . . It would be vain to try to put into words the immeasurable sense of bliss which comes over me directly [when] a new idea awakens in me and begins to assume a definite form. I forget everything and behave like a madman; everything within me starts pulsing and quivering; hardly have I begun the sketch, ere one thought follows another. In the midst of this magic process, it frequently happens that sone external interruption awakes me from my somnambulistic state . . . dreadful indeed are such interruptions . . . they break the thread of inspiration. . . .

Table 1 indicates some of the many commonalities in these remarkable testimonies. For most, it will be seen that the process of such high creativity consists of three phases: (1) the prelude ritual, which may be conscious or unconscious, ending often with an invocation; (2) the altered state of consciousness, or creative spell, during which the creative idea is born, starting with vibrations, then mental images, then the flow of ideas which are finally clothed in form. This syndrome often proceeds with extreme and uncanny rapidity in what is always referred to as a trance, dream, revery, somnambulistic state, or similar altered condition; and (3) the postlude in which positive emotions about the experience suffuse the participant. Both Brahms and Puccini enjoined on Arthur Abell a wait of a half century before this testimony could be published, so sacred and private did they feel this revelation to be.

TABLE 1
Discrete steps in creativity of musical composers.

Description of the Composer	Brahms	Strauss	Puccini	Wagner	Mozart	Ts'ky
1. environment triggers emotion					X	
2. alone and undisturbed	X	X	X	X	X	X
3. determined, concentrated thought		X				
4. belief in transpersonal, omniscient Power	X	X	X	X	X	
5. feel at one with Power	X			X		
6. ardent desire, fixed purpose	X	X	X			
7. invocation, demand, request			X			
8. full expectation of results			X			
9. creative spell begins (conscious semi-trance)	X		X	X		X
10. conscious of, at one with vibrations	X		X	X		X
11. mental images come fast	X					X
12. ideas flow instantaneously	X	X			X	X
13. they are clothed in form	X				X	
14. need to get down immediately	X		X			X
15. creative spell fades away	X	X	X	X	X	X
16. it was sacred, private experience	X	X	X			
17. It was dictated by higher power	X	X	X			
18. power is responsive to man	X	X	X			

Let us analyze the initial effect experienced in the altered state of consciousness. It is *vibrations* (the very word is used by Brahms, Puccini and Wagner, while Tschaikowsky speaks of "pulsing and quivering"). For anyone familiar with physics, vibrations immediately suggest a resonance effect. (We all know how through sympathetic vibrations, that a depressed silent piano key will begin to sound when that exact pitch is played on another nearby instrument.) "Being in tune with the Infinite" may be more than a mere religious figure of speech of yesteryear. For the nearest modern physical model is that of a radio receiver, which, when tuned to the exact wavelength of the sending station, can amplify and recover sound made miles away. Resonance effects are also playing an important part in the development of recent particle physics, so it is clear that these statements of creative composers have guided us to an important behavioral science principle completely congruent with physical science models.

Let us now examine the function of very high intelligence in furthering this creative afflatus. The following are some speculations which need to be verified by future research:

1) High intelligence may be necessary for the energy and amplification necessary to receive the signal at all—this would correspond to the power aspects of a radio receiver.

2) High intelligence may be necessary for the ability to translate the vibrations into images and then to musical notation. This would correspond to the high fidelity aspects of the receiver.

3) High intelligence may be necessary for the intuitive leaps by which creative geniuses reach fully formed conclusions.

4) High intelligence is necessary for storing the memory bank with the words, notes, and numbers which can be actuated by the flash of inspiration.

It is also noteworthy that not all of the steps occurred in any one of the accounts. We do not know whether they were not remembered, taken unconsciously, or skipped over in a burst of intuition. We are dealing here with testimony which is very hard to elicit, about a very unusual state found in very few people, when things were happening very rapidly. It is remarkable, under these circumstances, that there is as much inter-witness-reliability as we find, and this fact tends to confirm both the validity of the process, and the importance of the syndrome for those present and future artists who may wish to graduate from talent to genius.

References

Abell, A. M. *Talks with the great composers*. Garmisch-Partenkirchen, Germany: G. E. Schroeder-Verlag, 1964.

Stang, R. *Gustave Vigeland: the sculptor and his works*. Oslo: Johan Grunat Tanum Forlag, 1965.

Vernon, P. E. (ed.). *Creativity*. Middlesex, England: Penguin Books, 1970.

35. SOCIODRAMA AS A CREATIVE PROBLEM-SOLVING APPROACH TO STUDYING THE FUTURE

E. Paul Torrance

The term "futuring" is being heard more often as people recognize the importance of studying the future and as we develop skills for doing so. A new profession of futurists—people working in such fields as forecasting, policy research, futuristics, etc.—has been developing. Futurists stress future alternatives, opening up possibilities, imagining "unimaginable worlds," and fitting us all into them. They do not wish to ignore the past or to manipulate the future, but try to keep us from letting the future take us too much by surprise and show us that choices being made today influence what will happen tomorrow.

The idea of futures studies in schools was advocated in the 1930's and 1940's but the idea failed to catch on then. Now the need for futures studies is more obvious and we also know more about the abilities, skills, and methods required in such studies. Almost all of the programs that have been developed for teaching creative thinking and creative problem-solving have emphasized these abilities and skills. A variety of ways for teaching children to study the future have been suggested; however, fundamental to all of these methods is the ability to solve problems creatively. Children who have learned and can practice creative problem-solving skills will be able to solve future problems. They will be better prepared to cope with situations where basic information has changed, as it were, overnight.

FUTURISM IN CHILDREN'S SOCIODRAMATIC PLAY

Young preschool children are studying the future when they engage in spontaneous socio-dramatic play or role playing. Two- and three-year-olds derive a great deal of satisfaction from playing mother and father and other adult family roles. However, two or three years later these same children seem to take these roles for granted and, though they still make use of them, it is not with the same excitement. The child's social world is expanding and so is his concept of the future.

Since sociodramatic play is such a natural way of exploring and studying the future, the procedures suggested here seem very natural. The child entering kindergarten or first grade already has the intellectual skills for engaging in this kind of study. By adding to it the discipline of creative problem-solving, it should become increasingly productive as the child develops and matures. It should also be a useful technique with adults.

SOCIODRAMA AS A CREATIVE PROBLEM-SOLVING PROCESS

In *Creative Learning and Teaching* (Torrance and Myers, 1970) I described sociodrama as a creative problem-solving process. Sociodrama at its best is a group creative problem-solving process, and the problem-solving process in sociodrama can be as deliberate and as disciplined as

Reprinted by permission from *The Journal of Creative Behavior*, Vol. 9, No. 3, 1975.

any other creative problem-solving approach. The general principles of sociodrama have been formulated by Moreno (1946) and have been refined by Moreno himself (1952), Moreno and Moreno (1969), Haas (1948), Hansen (1948), Klein (1956), and others.

Sociodrama can be conducted in the ordinary classroom or in practically any other physical setting, if the director or teacher can create the proper atmosphere. Some children and adults find it easier to identify with a role if they are furnished with a single, simple stage prop, such as a cap, helmet, shoe, coat, or even superman gear. The director must be imaginative in transforming an ordinary desk and chair into a ship or a jet aircraft or whatever the occasion calls for.

The objective of sociodrama is to examine a group or social problem by dramatic methods. In the case of futuristic sociodrama, the problem focus is a problem or conflict which is expected to arise out of some trend or predicted future development. Multiple solutions may be proposed, tested, and evaluated sociodramatically. As new insights or breakthroughs in thinking occur, these too can be practiced and evaluated. The planning, selling, and implementing stages of problem-solving can also be practiced and tested. The production techniques and their power to induce different states of consciousness facilitate creative breakthroughs and increase the chances that creative solutions will be produced.

A number of things can be done to produce readiness for sociodrama. Perhaps the most important thing is to set aside one or more periods prior to the sociodrama for a free and open discussion of the problem to be studied. Efforts should be made to generate as much spontaneity as possible in these discussions. This is a part of the process of becoming aware of puzzling situations, gaps in information, conflicts, dilemmas, and the like. The problem selected for sociodramatic solution should be one that the group members have identified as important to all or most of them.

Although not necessary, the use of music, lights, and decorations can do much to set the right mood for a sociodrama.

The steps in the problem-solving process in sociodrama are quite similar to those formulated by Osborn (1963) and Parnes (1967) for creative problem-solving.

Step 1: Defining the Problem. The director, leader, or teacher should explain to the group that they are going to participate in an unrehearsed skit to try to find some ways of solving some problem of concern to all of them. It is a good idea to begin by asking a series of questions to help define the problem and establish the conflict situation. At this point, the director accepts all responses to get facts, to broaden understanding of the problem, and to word the problem more effectively, and asks other questions to stimulate or provoke further thinking about the real problem or conflict. This produces what Parnes (1967) refers to as "the fuzzy problem" or "the mess" and leads to the establishment of the conflict situation (statement of the problem).

Step 2: Establishing a Situation (Conflict). Culling from the responses, the teacher or director describes a conflict situation in objective and understandable terms. No indication is given as to the direction that the resolution should take. As in creative problem-solving, judgment is deferred. The conflict situation is analogous to problem definition in the creative problem-solving model.

Step 3: Casting Characters (Protagonists). Participation in roles should be voluntary. The director, however, must be alert in observing the audience for the emergence of new roles and giving encouragement to the timid person who really wants to participate and is saying so by means of body language. Rarely should roles be assigned in advance. Several members of the group may play a particular role, each trying a different approach.

Step 4: Briefing and Warming Up of Actors and Observers. It is usually a good idea to give the actors a few minutes to plan the setting and to agree upon a direction. While the actors are out of the room, the director should warm up the observers to the possible alternatives. Members of the audience may be asked to try to identify with one or the other of the protagonists or to observe them from a particular point of view. When the actors return to the room, they can be asked to describe the setting and establish more fully their role identities. A brief but relaxed procedure, it warms up both the audience and the actors.

Step 5: Acting Out the Situation. Acting out the situation may be a matter of seconds or it may last for 10 or 20 minutes. As a teacher or leader gains experience as a sociodrama director, he will be able to use a variety of production techniques for digging deeper into the problem, increasing the number and originality of the alternatives, getting thinking out of a "rut," and getting group members to make bigger mental leaps in finding better solutions. The director should watch for areas of conflict among group members, but not giving clues or hints concerning the desired outcome. If the acting breaks down because a participant becomes speechless, the director may encourage the actor by saying, "Now, what would he do?" or turning to another actor and saying, "What happens now?" If this does not work, it may be necessary or desirable to "cut" the action. The use of the double technique may also be used to cope with such a crisis.

Step 6: Cutting the Action. The action should be stopped or "cut" whenever the actors fall hopelessly out of role, or block seriously and are unable to continue; whenever the episode comes to a conclusion; or whenever the director sees the opportunity to stimulate thinking to a higher level of creativity by using a different episode. A description of some of these production techniques will be given later.

Step 7: Discussing and Analyzing the Situation, the Behavior and the Ideas Produced. There are many approaches for discussing and analyzing what happens in a sociodrama. Applying the creative problem-solving model, it would seem desirable to formulate some criteria to use in discussing and evaluating alternatives produced by the actors and audience. In any case, this should be a rather controlled or guided type of discussion wherein the director tries to help the group redefine the problem and/or see the various possible solutions indicated by the action.

Step 8: Making Plans for Further Testing and/or Implementing Ideas for New Behavior. There are a variety of practices concerning planning for further testing and/or implementation of ideas generated for new and improved behavior resulting from the sociodrama. If there is time or if there are to be subsequent sessions, the new ideas can be tested in a new sociodrama. Or, plans may be related to applications outside of the sociodrama sessions. This step is analogous to the selling, planning, and implementing stage in creative problem-solving. For some time, role playing has been a widely used technique for preparing people to sell and/or implement new solutions. What happens in Step 8 of sociodrama is quite similar to what has happened through this particular use of role playing.

As Stein (1974) indicates, most discussions about role playing, psychodrama, and sociodrama as techniques for stimulating creativity discuss potential usefulness for hypothesis formation. Usefulness at the hypothesis making (solution finding) stage is obvious, because playing a role permits a person to go beyond himself and shed some of the inhibitions that stifle the production of alternative solutions. Playing a role gives a person a kind of license to think, say, and do things he would not otherwise do. In my experience I have found that the sociodramatic format can facilitate all other stages of the creative problem-solving process as well. Children who have internalized and practiced the creative problem-solving process move spontaneously into such stages as developing criteria, evaluation of alternatives, and implementing solutions when engaged in sociodrama.

DIFFERENT STATES OF CONSCIOUSNESS

There is considerable evidence to indicate that the production of breakthrough ideas usually occurs during states of consciousness other than the ordinary, fully rational state. Gordon (1961), for example, has maintained that "in the creative process the emotional component is more important than the intellectual, the irrational more important than the intellectual, the irrational more important than the rational."

He states further that these emotional, irrational elements can and must be understood in order to increase the probability of success in a problem-solving situation. He explains that these ideas must be subjected to logical, rational tests once they have been produced but that this is not the way breakthrough ideas occur.

The term "arational" rather than "irrational" would probably be more appropriate. Some psychologists would attribute the phenomena to a difference in the way the brain processes information. Ornstein (1972) and others explain much of what happens in terms of the differential functions of the right and left hemispheres of the brain. The left hemisphere processes information by means of the ordinary mode of consciousness—the analytical, logical, sequential way of thinking that most of us have learned to take for granted. The right hemisphere of the brain, it appears, operates in a very different way—another way of perceiving reality, of processing information. Rather than processing information linearly and sequentially, it processes information globally, non-linearly. It does not deal very much with words but rather with spatial form, movement, and experience. It processes information more diffusedly and its responsibilities demand a ready integration of many inputs simultaneously. Its functioning is more holistic and relational. There are some indications that this functioning can be facilitated through states of consciousness other than ordinary awareness. Such states of consciousness as heightened awareness, rapture, regression, meditation, reverie, and expanded awareness would appear to be especially facilitative.

It is my hypothesis that sociodrama can facilitate the induction of these states of consciousness, if the sociodramatic director employs those production techniques that encourage the above states of consciousness. In the section that follows, I shall identify and describe briefly some of the production techniques that would seem best to facilitate the induction of these states of consciousness and thus the production of breakthrough ideas that could not be produced by logical reasoning.

SOCIODRAMATIC PRODUCTION TECHNIQUES

A variety of production techniques have been developed by Moreno (1946, 1969) and his associates. Some of them seem much better than others for engendering different states of consciousness and facilitating the production of creative ideas. I shall identify and describe briefly some of these along with a few that my students and I have invented.

Direct Presentation Technique (Moreno and Moreno, 1969). Group members are asked to act out some problem situation, new situation, conflict situation, or the like related to the statement of and/or solution of the problem under study. In using sociodrama to study the future, problem situations will usually be anticipated future problems of concern to group members.

The following are good sources of such problems:

The Futurist and many other materials published by World Future Society, 4916 St. Elmo Avenue (Bethesda), Washington, D.C. 20014.

Footnotes to the Future published by Futuremics, Inc., 2850 Connecticut Avenue, N.W., Washington, D.C. 20008.

Futureport published by Future Forum, 12 Shattuck Street, P.O. Box 1169, Nashua, N.H. 03060.

Futuribles (cards containing 288 possible futures) published by Cokesbury Press, P.O. Box 840, Nashville, Tenn. 37202.

Future Planning Games Series published by Greenhaven Press, Box 831, Anoka, Minn. 55303.

While the direct presentation production technique can usually be counted upon to produce increased alertness and even expanded awareness at times, it is not as likely to induce other states of consciousness as some of the other production techniques. At times, however, actors become so caught up in the sociodrama that they seem to lose ordinary awareness, at least for a time, and new insights burst forth.

Soliloquy Technique. In the soliloquy, the actors share with the audience their normally hidden and suppressed feelings and thoughts. The actor (protagonist) turns to one side and expresses his feelings in a voice different from that used in the dialogue. One type of soliloquy may take place immediately after the enactment of a conflict situation. The protagonist may be walking home, driving, riding a bus, trying to study, or just engaging in reverie. On the three-level stage, the actor performs on the lower, larger level. In another type of soliloquy, the portrayal of hidden, unverbalized feelings and thoughts are portrayed by side dialogues parallel with other thoughts and actions. It permits the actors to share experiences which they feared to bring to expression or failed to perceive in the direct presentation.

This production technique frequently evokes original ideas which later stand the test of logic. The states of consciousness most likely to be induced are reverie, internal scanning, fragmentation, and regression. In the terminology of creative problem-solving, incubation is likely to occur both among the actors and the audience. The time out for soliloquy, though brief, gives a chance for the incubation process to operate and new ideas may burst forth and then be applied immediately in the ongoing dramatization.

Double Technique (Toeman, 1948: Moreno and Moreno, 1969). In this production technique, one of the actors in a conflict situation is supplied with a double who is place side by side with the actor and interacts with the actor as "himself." The double tries to develop an identity with the actor in conflict. By bringing out the actor's "other self," the double helps the actor achieve a new and higher level of creative functioning. The Actor-Double situation is usually set up following the use of a Direct Presentation after the actor has withdrawn from the conflict. He imagines himself alone in the woods, walking along the street or in a park, or sitting at home. This production technique may also be used following the Soliloquy technique to speed up or facilitate the production of alternative solutions.

The whole idea of Double Technique (Toeman, 1948) is rooted in ideas concerning creativity in altered states of consciousness. The idea appears in the mythology of many different cultures. Many highly creative people have reported having doubles. The famous French author, de Maupassant, reported that his double would come into his room and dictate his work to him. In executing the Double Technique, the protagonist and the double are on the stage together and the double acts as the protagonist's invisible "I," the alter ego with whom he talks at times but who exists only within himself. This invisible double in sociodrama is projected into space, embodied by a real person and experienced as outside of the protagonist. The double may try to stir the protagonist to reach deeper levels of expanded consciousness. He reaches for those images which a person would reveal when talking to himself in privacy. It is a shared task. In one sense, it is dyadic brainstorming at a very intense level. The protagonist may experience many kinds of resistance. The double makes use of this resistance to suggest even more diverse ideas or solutions and to work through to deeper and more expanded states of consciousness.

Any one of several states of consciousness may emerge. The most likely include: expanded consciousness, internal scanning, stored memories, reverie, suggestibility, regression, and rapture.

In using sociodrama as a deliberate method of solving problems creatively, the sociodramatic director may instruct the double and the protagonist to engage in dyadic brainstorming for alternative solutions. At times, it may even be useful to have someone record the alternatives produced. At the end of the dyadic brainstorming, the audience can be given an opportunity to add alternatives that did not occur on the stage.

Multiple Double Technique (Moreno and Moreno, 1969). This is a variation of the "standard" double technique and is especially useful for bringing different points of view to bear on a conflict situation and provides a good vehicle for group brainstorming. The actor in the conflict situation is on stage with two or more doubles of himself. Each portrays another part of the actor (different moods, different psychological perspectives, etc.).

This production technique is especially effective when turned into a group brainstorming session, involving from three to six people. The traditional rules of brainstorming may be applied or they may be relaxed. If brainstorming rules (Osborn, 1963) are relaxed and negative criticism occurs, one of the doubles can talk back in a way that is not possible in ordinary brainstorming. This may heighten the conflict and lead to a kind of arousal which will produce breakthrough ideas. After such a brainstorming session, additional ideas may be obtained from members of the audience who were identifying with one of the actors.

Identifying Double and Contrary Double Technique (Pankratz and Buchan, 1965). This technique is a variation of the Multiple Double Technique. The protagonist is given an identifying double and a contrary double to represent the "good" and "bad" parts of his thoughts. These two doubles are encouraged by the director to influence the protagonist. The doubles may be quite forceful with their lies, promises, and distortions. The protagonist is encouraged to evaluate carefully both sides of the issue or conflict.

Mirror Technique (Moreno and Moreno, 1969). In this production technique, another actor represents the original actor in the conflict situation, copying his behavior patterns and showing him "as in a mirror" how other people experience him. This technique may help the audience and actors become aware of emotional blocks to conflict resolution.

In sociodrama, I have found the Mirror Technique less frequently useful than in psychodrama. However, I have found that an effective variation of the Mirror Technique can be produced in sociodrama when the protagonist leaves a conflict situation involving two or more alter egos. The alter egos can then mimic, as frequently occurs in real life, the behavior of the protagonist. This variation of the Mirror Technique makes it clear to the group that more of the same kind of behavior will only make matters worse and that the problem situation should be restructured and the problem redefined. Once this happens, the group is ready to produce and test solutions quite different from the ones being used.

The Mirror Technique may be used in sociodrama when the protagonist cannot represent his role. The mirror may be exaggerated, employing techniques of deliberate distortion in order to arouse the protagonist or a member of the audience to correct what he feels is not the accurate enactment and interpretation of the role. In sociodrama, the audience may become the protagonist and react to two or more mirror presentations of some human drama relevant to the central conflict.

Role Reversal Technique (Moreno and Moreno, 1969). In this particular technique, two actors in the conflict situations exchange roles—a mother becomes the child and the child becomes the mother; a teacher becomes a pupil and a pupil becomes a teacher, etc. Distortion of the "other" may be brought to the surface, explored, and corrected in action, and new solutions may emerge. In sociodrama, representatives of different social roles should reverse roles. For example, a black person should play a white person's role and vice versa.

Moreno and Moreno (1969) considered role reversal the direct route to the co-conscious and the co-unconscious. Many workers have reported that through role reversal they can get to preconscious thinking within a single one-hour session. By reversing roles one actor tries to identify with another. Experience has shown that persons who are intimately acquainted reverse roles more easily than those who are separated by a wide psychological, ethnic, or cultural distance. In sociodrama, however, there are values to be derived from errors in identification due to this distance and misunderstandings can at times be reduced.

Future Projection Technique (Yablonsky, 1974). In using sociodrama to study the future, this production technique is of course, quite basic. In it, the actors show how they think the conflict will "shape up" in the future. An intense, effective warm-up is highly essential and the known particulars and specifics of the situation should be given. Generally this will involve dyadic brainstorming between the director and the protagonist. However, the audience may also help construct the future situation, pooling their already acquired information about the future. Daydreaming, expanded awareness, internal scanning, and stored memories are the major states of consciousness likely to be tapped by this production technique.

Auxiliary World Technique. The entire future world of the protagonist is structured through a series of acts or episodes as he envisions them. Each of these acts should portray some part of the protagonist's future world that is likely to influence the behavior of members of the group and have consequences for the resolution of the conflict situation. Basically, this production technique facilitates daydreaming, internal scanning, and expanded awareness.

Magic Shop Technique (Moreno, 1946). The Magic Shop Technique is useful in providing groups with insights into their real goals and desires in life. In studying the future, it provides a natural vehicle for testing out and evaluating new alternative life styles. The group or a representative of the group is confronted by the proprietor of the Magic Shop, who may be either an auxiliary ego or the director. In this confrontation, the proprietor offers the group anything that they may want in the future, such as the end of racial discrimination, elimination of pollution, increased intelligence or creativity, a particular style of life, and the like. The proprietor demands as payment something that the group may also value, such as leisure, a high standard of living, etc. This places the group in a dilemma and usually brings about immediate introspection or internal scanning. The result of this confrontation is an acceptance or rejection of the "bargain" or, as occurs in many cases, the inability of the customer to make a decision. To push thinking further, such techniques as Soliloquy, Double, Multiple Double etc., may be used to facilitate meditation, daydreaming, and expanded awareness.

High Chair and Empty Chair Techniques (Lippitt, 1958). These production techniques are especially useful with groups lacking in self confidence about their futures. In the Empty Chair Technique, the protagonist acts out problems by imagining his enemy seated in an empty chair on the stage, and he interacts with the "phantom" being (common enemy), even to the extent of reversing roles and, in the phantom role, intereacts with the imaginary other person in the role of the one who is absent.

In the High Chair Technique, either an ordinary chair is placed on a box so that when the protagonist sits on it he is higher than anyone else seated, or he stands on a chair so that he stands higher than anyone else on the stage. This is a useful technique for helping a protagonist acquire a feeling of power needed to deal effectively with enemies or strange future situations. The group can then brainstorm analogues to the high chair which will give equivalent advantages.

Dream/Fantasy Technique (Z. T. Moreno, 1959). This production technique allows a group to enact its dreams and hopes and test and change them. Or it may put its delusions and fantasies about the future to a test. This technique is good for encouraging "freewheeling" and "wild ideas" which, once they are produced, can be tamed or modified.

Therapeutic Community Technique (Moreno and Moreno, 1969). This production technique projects a community in which disputes, conflicts, etc., between individuals and groups are settled under the rules of therapy instead of the rules of the law. In a difficult, depressing situation when few constructive solutions have been produced, the use of this technique is useful for ending the session on a "high, hopeful note."

Sociodramatic—Dance Technique (Fine, Daly, and Fine, 1962). In this production technique participants sit in a circle and listen to music. They become warmed up at their own pace. It can be combined with other production techniques such as double ego, multiple role playing, etc. It is a non-verbal approach that is useful for emotional expression, or learning new behavior. It is facilitative of a variety of states of consciousness (expanded awareness, reverie, regression, etc.).

"Silent" Auxiliary Ego Technique (Smith, 1950). In this production technique, the actors communicate by gesture rather than speech and activities are suggested in the same manner. States of consciousness such as heightened alertness and expanded awareness should be encouraged.

Magic Net Technique (Torrance, 1970: Torrance and Myers, 1970). This is especially useful for warm-up purposes in heightening anticipation and expectations. About five volunteers are given the "Magic Net" (pieces of nylon net in various colors). Having created an atmosphere of "magic," these volunteers imagine that they have been transported into some future and are asked to name their future roles. The director then gives the group a future problem and the audience is asked to make up a story to solve the problem, using the characters that have been transformed by the magic net. The storyteller (problem-solver) is also supplied with a magic net, distinctly different from those of the role players. As the storyteller relates the story, the actors mime the action. This technique is especially useful with disadvantaged children, some emotionally disturbed children, and mentally retarded children.

REALITY LEVEL SOCIODRAMA

An entire classroom, school, or other learning situation may be turned into a sociodrama stage through Reality Level Sociodrama. Perhaps the most commonly practiced Reality Level Sociodrama has been the application of the Role Reversal technique to real life situations. In the home, the father and the mother may reverse roles or one of the children may exchange roles with one of the parents. In the school, the teacher may take the role of a student and the student may take the role of the teacher. Reality Level Sociodrama may be more inclusive, however, and involve an entire class in establishing a community or some other social group faced with a future problem. A very powerful description of Reality Level Sociodrama is found in *A Class Divided* by Peters (1971). For one week the teacher treated as inferior all children with brown eyes and as superior children with blue eyes. Later, the direction of the prejudice was reversed and the brown eyed children became the favored group and the blue eyed ones became the disfavored group. Such real-life experiments could be made more powerful by injecting the creative problem-solving process to understand the problems involved, define them, search for solutions, evaluate alternatives, and to test the best alternatives.

References

Blatner, H. A. *Acting-in: practical applications in psychodramatic methods.* NYC: Springer, 1973.
Feinberg, H. The ego building technique. *Group Psychotherapy,* 1959, *12,* 230–235.
Fine R., Daly, D., and Fine, L. Psychodance, an experiment in psychotherapy and training. *Group Psychotherapy,* 1962, 15, 2–3–223.
Frields, G. *Sociodramatic play: a framework for a developmental preschool program.* Dubuque, IA: Kendall/Hunt Publishing Company, 1974.
Gordon, W. J. J. *Synectics.* NYC: Harper & Row, 1961.
Greenberg, I. A. (ed.). *Psychodrama: theory and therapy.* NYC: Behavioral Publications, 1974.
Haas, R. B. The school sociatrist. *Sociatry,* 1948, *2,* 283–321.
Hansen, B. Sociodrama: A methodology for democratic action. *Sociatry,* 1948, *2,* 347–363.
Klein, A. F. *Role playing in leadership training and group problem solving.* NYC: Association Press, 1956.
Lippitt, Rosemary. The auxiliary chair technique. *Group Psychotherapy,* 1958, *11,* 8–23.
Maier, N. R. F., Solem, A. R., and Maier, A. A. *Supervision and executive development: a manual for role playing.* NYC: Wiley, 1956.
Moreno, J. L. *Psychodrama. First Volume.* Beacon, NY: Beacon House, 1946.
Moreno, J. L. Psychodramatic production techniques. *Group Psychotherapy,* 1952, *4,* 243–273.
Moreno, J. L., and Moreno, Z. T. *Psychodrama. Third Volume.* NYC: Beacon House, 1969.
Moreno, Z. T. A survey of psychodramatic techniques. *Group psychotherapy,* 1959, *12,* 5–14.
Ornstein, R. E. *The psychology of consciousness.* San Francisco: W. H. Freeman, 1972.
Osborn, A. F. *Applied imagination.* 3rd ed. NYC: Scribner, 1963.
Pankratz, L. D. and Buchan, G. Exploring psychodramatic techniques with defective delinquents. *Group Psychotherapy,* 1965, *18,* 136–141.

Parnes, S. J. *Creative behavior guidebook*. NYC: Scribner, 1967.

Parrish, M. M. Psychodrama: Description of application and review of techniques. *Group Psychotherapy,* 1953, *6,* 63–89.

Peters, M. R. *A class divided*. Garden City, NY: Doubleday, 1971.

Shaftel, F. R. and Shaftel, G. *Role playing for special values*. Englewood Cliffs, NJ: Prentice-Hall, 1967.

Smith, M. R. The "silent" auxiliary-ego technique in rehabilitating deteriorated mental patients. *Group Psychotherapy,* 1950, *3,* 92–100.

Stein, M. I. *Stimulating creativity*. Vol. 1. NYC: Academic Press, 1974.

Toeman, Z. The "double situation" in psychodrama. *Sociatry,* 1948, *1,* 436–446.

Torrance, E. P. *Encouraging creativity in the classroom*. Dubuque, IA: Wm. C. Brown Company Publishers, 1970.

Torrance, E. P., and Myers, R. E., *Creative learning and teaching*. NYC: Dodd, Mead, 1970.

Yablonsky, L. Future-projection technique. In Greenberg, I. A., ed., *Psychodrama: theory and therapy*. NYC: Behavioral Publications, 1974.

Yablonsky, L. Psychodrama lives! *Human Behavior,* 1975, *4*(2), 25–29.

36. CREATIVITY, GENERAL SYSTEMS AND THE GIFTED

Joe Khatena

Over the past few years many of us have discussed the topic of the "gifted" in a number of different ways, and several of us have attempted to describe and appraise what we considered advances in thought on the gifted, even suggesting that certain things could be done or changes made in our education system to properly adjust to them (e.g. Gowan, 1977; Khatena, 1976; Mirman, 1971; Torrance, 1974). In an effort to classify what he called "research milestones", Gowan identified four in the area of intelligence and its identification, three in the area of curriculum, and two in the areas of development, and two in creativity, the last four areas of which he suggests need pursuing. For the pursuit to be productive he indicates that a shift be made from *surface symptoms* to underlying basic concepts, i.e.:

(1) from the misleading stereotyped concept of intelligence as unidimensional to intelligence as multidimensional best expressed in terms of the Structure of Intellect;

(2) from gifted child to creative individual, since we should redefine giftedness as the potential to become verbally creative, and talented as the potential to become creative in other ways (such as in the performing arts);

(3) from chronological growth to development stages (continuous versus discontinuous); and

(4) from acceleration, enrichment, and grouping to a qualitatively differentiated curriculum that has the capacity to induce creative performance based on stimulation of structure of intellect factors at appropriate developmental levels.

These observations bring to mind that we are really dealing with a highly complex construct when we use the term "gifted" and hence have to approach handling it in ways that will allow its complexity to be evident. There is no doubt in my mind that regarding intelligence as consisting of many abilities defined possibly by the Structure of Intellect is not enough; we need to recognize that "ability" is one dimension of the multi-modal construct, to which needs to be added "energy" (derived from emotive-motivational fields of forces); for ability needs to be energized before it can become active and operative I am also convinced that the conceptual model of developmental stages, especially as it relates to the periods of an individual's life when verbal and nonverbal creativity can be most effectively activated, holds significant implications for our gifted. Further, that any attempt at educational facilitation has to bear in mind the abilities potential of the individual has attained.

Attempts that have been made over the past 25 years to realize these and related issues, especially as they impinge upon the gifted, have included the designing of theoretical constructs, models or plans. Such approaches will stand the best chance of success since they aim at coherence and higher levels of organization that must give meaning and fruitful direction to what is advocated or done at the unit levels. Examples of such structures or systems can be seen in Guilford's SOI

Reprinted by permission from *Gifted Child Quarterly,* Vol. 23, No. 4, 1979. Presidential Address at the Silver Anniversary Annual Convention of the National Association for Gifted Children in Houston, Texas, on November 2, 1978.

304

model, Gowan's periodic table, Williams model for implementing cognitive affective behaviors in the classroom, Renzulli's enrichment triad, and the like.

Recently, the search for models and plans have been intensified, and attempts have been made to discover constructs that would allow for conceptions of greater order and generalizability. Seeing of principles in patterns for the derivation of even higher levels of order have attracted no small attention and have given rise to some extremely valuable contributions recently to thought. Theoretical speculation rooted to and deriving insights from such disciplines as biology, physics, chemistry, mathematics and psychology have produced a way of thought that has been called General Systems. It prompted Derald Langham originator of the Genesea model to preface his version of General Systems with the following questions:

> "If you had a magic key that would fit all makes of truth, would you use it? If it revealed principles and made them available to you, would you use them? If it unveiled answers to your problems, would you be happy?"

Besides this interest in General Systems is the fresh focus given to development as occurring in discrete stages rather than in continuous fashion, and its emergent properties that have found significant linkage with General Systems. Yet another viable interest that has become noticeable of late is "imagery" especially as it relates to creative imagination, incubation and right brain activity, which may be linked with development stage theory and processes, and as a sub system of General Systems. These may provide some new perspectives in thought on the gifted and suggest some fresh approaches to enhance their creativity.

GENERAL SYSTEMS

1. Elizabeathen World Picture

A number of recent scholars have as some before them strived to find explanation for the way things are in the universe, to discover the design of life, to explore the relationship of order and disorder. Tillyard (1956) on writing about Shakespeare's history plays saw the need to understand the world as seen from the Elizabeathen eye, and sketched the system of thought and belief that governed their behavior, which he called the Elizabeathen World Picture (Tillyard, 1958). We learn from this system that order which prevails in heaven is duplicated on earth—the king corresponds to the sun, so that disorder in the heavens breeds disorder on earth; that everything was connected in a chain-of-being from the lowest forms of life through Man to the highest archangels with *degree* as a key concept—what Tillyard calls the vertical dimension of the world picture. This world picture was also organized horizontally to consist of a number of planes arranged one below another in order of dignity but connected by an immense net of correspondences. The different planes were the divine and angelic, the universe or macrocosm, the commonwealth or body politic Man or microcosm, and the lower creation. What took place in one plane affected other planes. The notion derived from the early Greek philosophers that creation was an act of music and that the created universe was itself in a state of music, or one perpetual dance implying degree in motion, appealed to the poetically and mystically minded, and had its place in this system of thought as well. This is one kind of general system having evolved from religion, philosphy, politics, and generally from the way of life of a people; other general systems similarly derived are epistomology, ethology, cybernetics and so on.

2. General Systems Approach

In the past few years drawing from the advances in scientific and mathematical thought, Stuart Dodd, Derald Langham, George Land, John Gowan and several others have each attempted to find general principles to explain existence and behavior. Interacting with one another by mail, visits and meetings such as the 1974 and 1975 ones held at the Creative Problem Solving Institutes in Buffalo, New York, they attempted not only to convince one another of the significance of their systems but also to attempt to find a system of systems. As Gowan and Dodd observe (1977), "because General Systems theory is about generalities and not specifics it is difficult to explain." However, George Land tells us that the "idea of General Systems is not complication but just the opposite—simplification i.e., to discover the fundamental laws of Nature that apply in theory and practice to everything. Relevant to our discussion are George Land's Transformation Theory and John Gowan's Developmental Stage Theory.

3. Land's Transformation Theory

Land (1972) prefaces a discussion of his model with several highly relevant observations about systems as follows:

(a) In a system it is important to differentiate between the parts of the system from the whole system and to see their relationship to each other as well.

(b) Things move from states of disorder to states of order, and from these states of order to disorder prior to attaining higher states of order.

(c) The scientific method encourages partialistic thinking through analysis to a solution—solving always creates new problems because the part effects the whole.

(d) Systems may be seen as subsystems of larger systems.

(e) A whole system may be identified by its organization, by its boundary that sets it apart from its environment (where it takes in things from and puts things out into its environment), and by its synergetic character (since a mature system is more than the sum of its parts).

(f) The self-regulation of a system must have more than negative or positive feedback; it must have feedforward or shared regulation such that new information derived from its environment provides the system continuously for proper connection and adaptation to its changing environment.

Then comes the key concept of his theoretical model—"growth"—which he defines as "the process by which things become connected with each other and operate at higher levels of organization and complexity," and which guides all systems and subsystems.

The following citation summarizes and extends these basic concepts to include his transformation model (Land & Kenneally, 1977):

"A general system starts with a very high degree of polarity—that is, on the one hand great disorder and, on the other, great order."
"At this initial stage connections are made between order and disorder by dominance and absorption—control. Initial order grows at the expense of the disorder. If successful, a pattern of order—an identity—is discovered and the system passes into its second stage, that is the

306

pattern is copied with few changes and either produces or connects to likenesses. The relationships in this stage, rather than those of control or being controlled, now change to those of *influence and being influenced.* Rapid growth is possible since there is a pattern to follow. Inevitably the second stage of growth will use up its environment, i.e., run out of materials that fit easily into the initial and modified patterns. When this happens, the third stage of growth is reached in which the growing thing is forced to accommodate differences in the environment to continue growing. It is at this point that it becomes very sensitive and responsive to its environment and its *relationships shift from the influence type of those of mutual sharing,* simply because that is what works."

"Once a system has absorbed all the differences it can within its environment, and because they are shared, the differences become new sameness and the organism finds a new identity. It must begin to relate to a new and broader environment—a new disorder—and the process starts all over again at a higher level. (Pp. 19–20)

Here we have in essence Land's three distinctly different forms of growth. The first three stages he labels as *accretive, replicative,* and *mutualistic* respectively, and the fourth which represents a transition to a new and higher level of development he names *transformation.*

On the relationship of General Systems and the creative process, Land suggests four different kinds of creativity and techniques that relate directly to his four stages of growth:

(a) The most primitive level of creativity simply produces enlargement of an idea or concept (accretive)—a change in scale creating a supermarket from a grocery store. This has been identified by Guilford and Torrance as the ability to elaborate.

(b) The next level of creativity make modifications in the form of the pattern but not its basic function (replicative)—modification that could lead to the improvement of something, making it lighter and stronger, more efficient and so on. This is similar to Osborn's use of categories to induce shifts in creative thinking which Torrance for instance has called flexibility.

(c) The next higher level of creativity relates to making of high level combinations, analogies, and metaphors (mutualistic).

(d) The fourth level relates to transformation where invention or the recombination of the old concept at a higher level of relationship to the environment occurs and involves destructuring and reintegration.

These four stages of creativity are most clearly illustrated in the following example (Land & Keneally, 1977):

"If we look at the process of a child putting together a Tinker Toy, first we see exploration to discover a pattern—a simple box for example. Level two follows by adding other boxes, modified to accommodate different shapes and sizes. At the third stage all the pieces that can be easily made into boxes have been exhausted and the child begins to make rearrangements in order that the odd pieces that didn't fit well at first can now become a part of the whole. This mutual stage of combining differences not only produces a new looking whole, *but uses up the Tinker Toy.*
This is where we run into the level-four problem—and opportunity. If this whole structure is now to join with other things in the room where the child is playing—the child must *take an entirely new viewpoint* toward his creation. In a sense the beauty and perfection of the whole he created must be dismembered to accommodate its joining with other things in his environment."(P.23)

Regarding method or technique, Land suggests specific creative techniques at particular levels of product development. Relevant to the replicative level he suggests one of the steps in the Osborn-Parnes brainstorming technique—quantity breeds quality—where a wide range of alternatives is necessary to produce new combinations that can fit a new and evolving environment. For the third level or mutualistic stage, where we have to innovate, metaphor, analogical and morphological techniques that force combination of ideas seemingly quite different from each other and where appropriateness is critical are recommended.

4. Gowan's Developmental Stage Theory

John Gowan's (1972, 1974, 1975) contribution to General Systems comes in the form of developmental stage theory. Like Land he perceives "growth" as an essential phenomenon of his system but prefers to regard it as "development"; making a distinction between the two he says that "development is to growth as quality is to quantity—the apple enlarges but it also ripens."

Gowan (1977) observes that although Land's evolutionary process approach and his individual development process approach are diverse they obey the same laws of nature. Interaction between Gowan and Land a couple of years ago at CPSI in Buffalo, NY, to find common ground for the two systems, led to some creative sights for bonding of their models whose implications are yet to be worked out. However, it led Gowan to reiterate that "the developmental cycle is discontinuous and not continuous as previously believed."

Gowan's system pivots on the development of the creative individual and so concerns itself with those stages of development optimal to creative interactions of the inner and outer worlds of the individual, Land's third or mutualistic stage in his general systems interpretation of the creative process.

Freud, Erickson and Piaget have all subscribed to the concept of developmental stages, though each had used different names to describe the stages. Gowan suggests that Freud's five affective developmental stages fit rather neatly the chronological divisions of Piaget's cognitive stages, and to Freud's final stage of development Erickson has added four more stages. A simplification of Gowan's periodic table of developmental stages can be found in my book *The Creatively Gifted Child: Suggestions for Parents and Teachers* (Khatena, 1978a) as follows:
An individual goes through three stages of development, namely, Latency, Identity, and Creativity at each of three levels of growth, namely, Infant, Youth and Adult.

(a) The Latency Period (Stages 1, 4, and 7)

For the infant (0–1), this is the period when he gets to know the things around him, to experience the thing character of the world. As a youth (7–12) he begins to know things for their size, shape, form, and color and what one makes out of them. As an adult (26–40) he is concerned with others who are important to him such as children, their productions, art creations, and other "mental children."

Common to the infant, youth, and adult is his immersion in the world of senses. Things get done, changes occur, no self-consciousness is felt, very little time is left to assess feelings or to be concerned with the questions of "Who am I?" Accomplishments strengthen and prepare the person to search for his identity.

(b) Identity (Stages 2, 5 and 8)

The infant, youth, and adult are concerned here with questions like "Who am I? Why do I exist? How am I in relation to others? What happens to me when I die? Will I be saved?" During these times the person searches within himself for answers, withdraws rather than returns, defies authority rather than obeys it, and "marches to the music of a different drum." At each stage, he tries to come to terms with himself: as an infant he searches for his identity, as a youth he redefines it in terms of the meaning of his life and death in the cosmos.

Others find it difficult to live with an individual passing through these stages—the infant with his negativism, and adolescent with his idealism, demand for independence and rebellion against authority both by his attitudes and actions. During this time of turning into himself and away from the world it is easy for him to believe that no one understands him, often spending too much time in self-examination, forgetting the real world outside himself leading to moodiness resulting from the discrepancy between what he wants to be and what he finds he can be and do.

(c) Creativity (Stages 3, 6 and 9)

During stages 3 and 6, which deal with love, the person passes from love of self through love of parent of the opposite sex to generalized love of people of both sexes and to love of one person of the opposite sex. Stage 9 may very well exist where love is for all mankind given in the way of Buddha and Christ (Agape-Love).

Gowan sees *love* as required for creation both physically and mentally. That is why stages 3 and 6 are important: creativity first develops during stage 3 when a person gains control of his environment through affectional relations with the parent of the opposite sex such that "boys" who are affectionately close to their mothers and "girls" who are unusually close to their fathers, during 4 to 7 years, tend to become more creative than others of similar ability. It is during this period that warm affection given by the opposite sex parent freely enlarges the bridge between the fantasy life and real world of the child.

Again in stage 6, adolescent creativity is normally enhanced through the inspiration of loving and being loved by a person of the opposite sex; however, in some cases of adolescent love, consummation involving physical relations tends to reduce the high energy potential aroused but when delayed or partly prevented from being used, great art, music and literature result.

Love in our lives is seen as *central to creativity* so that if we want to be creative we should put more love into our lives. Although the developmental process of stages 3 and 6 naturally emphasize creativity, it is not completely absent at the other stages of development. Love and creativity may enter into our lives environmentally at any time and the degree to which love is abundant is the degree to which creativity is likely to be present. However, a good start in stage 3 is expected to give the best assurance that creativity will occur again in stage 6. Gowan says:

> "One becomes creative as a by-product of the beloved. One strives to please, and in pleasing the loved one, pulls out of the *preconscious* that one hardly knew was there. Or alternatively, because one's mental health is improved, one finds the preconscious teeming with treasure to share with the beloved, and these goodies often bubble forth without conscious effort (1971, pp. 162–163)."

The term preconscious originated with Freud who divided the mental life of the psyche of a person into unconscious, preconscious and conscious. This is very simply explained by Sullivan (1953, p. 161) as the "bad-me," "not-me," "good-me," or the unconscious, refers to that part of our mental life that stores ideas and drives that cause too much pain, anxiety or guilt to us if we are conscious or aware of them; and we do this to defend the self (ego) by pushing them aside (repression) and in other ways. Of course these ideas and drives remain active in our unconscious and without our awareness are the cause of some of our behaviors. Sometimes we notice them when our defenses are relaxed as in dreams, in slips of the tongue, or when we are under the influence of alcohol or drugs. "Good-me" is that part of our mental life of which we are aware which can be called the "conscious positive self-concept." "Not-me" is the part of our mental life where frightening and uncanny experiences occur like those we meet in dreams and nightmares. It is the preconscious or "not-me" area of our mental life that is the source of much of our creativity (Gowan, 1974, p. 81).

In one analogy he compared the preconscious to an enlarged fluid container through whose permeable membrane creative ideas leak into consciousness (1974, p. 83).

Gowan also tells us that the preconscious is the *source* of man's creativity especially if it is strengthened, protected and enlarged through regular use and through increased mental health. At first the creative person makes use of his preconscious intuitively, when leaks occur through the permeable membrane, as it were by osmosis, and manifests itself in works of art of one kind or another. At a higher level of creativity (*psychedelia* or state of mind expansion that takes place naturally and not with the help of drugs), the barriers that separate the preconscious from the unconscious and conscious are thought of as doors that swing open to let in, as it were, the resources of the preconscious for cognitive processing. If the preconscious becomes open in this way to a person then he becomes creative (1974, p. 83).

Where stage 6 in the periodic table stresses creative forces at work, it is an intuitive kind of creativity that prepares a person for psychedelic creativity of stage 7 when the resources of the preconscious become available not so much by chance but almost at will.

Gowan asks us to observe an important happening in nature and human life which he relates to a transformation of *energy* that takes place from one level of development to the next higher level of development. This he calls *periodicity,* which "occurs when the same pattern of events is seen to run through higher development as has been contained in a corresponding pattern from a lower sequence."

Two of his concepts with essential implications for the gifted are "escalation" and "dysplasia" (Gowan, 1974). By analogy he defines "escalation" as the jump from one riser to the next on a staircase, consisting of five interrelated aspects: discontinuity, succession, emergence (the debut of new powers), differentiation, and integration. "Dysplasia", he explains, occurs when one aspect of the psyche (e.g., affective) continues to escalate, although another aspect (e.g., cognitive) becomes arrested at a given stage—a condition which produces block or *anomie* and eventual neurosis,

"Transformation" in Land's model is little different from Gowan's "periodicity": both preface the entry into the next higher level of "growth" or "development." In both the models the highest level of creative process that prepares for transformation involves the functioning of analogical and metaphorical brain activity, and the tapping of the preconscious, what some at the present would refer to now as right brain functioning, or the functioning of the creative imagination and its imagery correlates.

CREATIVE IMAGINATION AND IMAGERY

In recent years Gowan (1978ab) and I (e.g., Khatena, 1977ab, 1978bc) have written about the creative imagination and imagery and tried to discuss some of the major advances that have been made in thought and research on the subject. The relevance of imagery and the creative imagination to education have been reiterated by both of us.

(a) Imagination and Creativity

Poets have been inclined to regard imagination as some force outside the human being that is responsible for creative experiences and works. This force that sets in motion their creative acts have often been referred as the "muses". Blake describes imagination as "spiritual energy" in whose exercise we experience in some way the activity of God. It has also been called by Coleridge "an ability of prime importance" since the human being in his creative activity simulates the creative act of God. Wordsworth refers to imagination as another name for "absolute power," identifying it with clearest insight," "amplitude of mind," and "Reason in her most exalted mood."

Imagination as an action of mind to produce new ideas and insights, to generate new hypotheses, and to be involved in the act of problem solving have been explained to us, for instance, by Gerard (Ghiselin, 1952), or Bowra (1950) who adds that:

". . . when we use our imagination we are first stirred by some alluring puzzle which calls for a solution, and then by our own creations in the mind we are able to see much that was before dark or unintelligible."

Coleridge considers imagination as seminal rather than equivalent to preception and differentiates it as *primary* imagination and *secondary* imagination. "*Primary imagination* is the first and continuing activity of the mind by which the mind knows itself to be, as coexistent with the phenomenal universe that is known, that the *secondary imagination* is the expression of all these higher mental powers operative on a conscious level, the ultimate exercise of which is sure and undeniable faith in God."

John Eccles (1958) sees creative imagination as brain activity. For a brain to exhibit creative imagination it must have a sufficient number of neurons with a wealth of synaptic connections that have the sensitivity to increase their function with usage so that they may form and maintain a wealth of memory patterns or engrams. Such a brain must also have a unique for unresting activity that combine and recombine these patterns in continually novel ways for the creative to occur. (Land's mutualistic stage; Gowan's stages 6 and 7)

Research over the past few years has attempted to explain different modes of mental functioning in terms of the left and right hemispheres of the brain (e.g., DeBono, 1971; Olson, 1977; Samples, 1975; Sperry, 1974), such that "although each hemisphere shares the potential for many functions, and both sides participate in most activities, in a normal person the two hemispheres tend to specialize." (Ornstein, 1972). Whereas the left brain specializes in the handling of incoming perceptual information, processing it into logical-analytical thought and decision via language in a continual stream of internal disclose that accompanies consciousness, the right brain specializes in the handling of divergent thinking operations, intuition, insight, invention, metaphor, analogy and the production of creative imagination imagery. Jaynes (1976) locates such imagery in the Wernicke area of the right cerebral hemisphere where it goes on all the time though overlaid most

311

frequently with left brain or dominant hemisphere cognitive activity which Gowan (1978ab) has likened to the "static" of a radio receiver.

Imagination as it relates to the creative process has been described by Vargiu (1977) as activity of creative energy fields that are both mental and emotive, such that mental elements have properties that respond to the influence of the creative field and to one another with a tendency for them to be organized by the emotional energy field into configurations that correspond to its own energy patterns. It is the interaction between these two energy fields that cause feeling charged images to be formed in the mind.

Wallas (1926) identifies four steps in the creative process, namely, preparation, incubation, illumination, and verification, whereas Vargiu (1977) identifies five steps, namely, preparation, frustration, incubation, illumination, and elaboration. Both see preparation, incubation and illumination as essential steps in the creative process; however Varigius' additional step of frustration occurring prior to incubation adds strength to Wallas' model since it is *that* energy which is needed to give focus and direct to the incubation process. The final step in the creative process identified as verification by Wallas is identified by Vargiu as elaboration. Both see *incubation,* an irrational process related to preconscious activity as important and conducive to imaging just prior to the illumination phase which occurs with a suddeness that Vargiu explains as "avalanche effect."

We can recognize that the function of creative imagination involves intellectual abilities as well as energy fields, that operate in various ways to lead to incubation, creative imagery, and illumination in the creative process. Drawing from Guilford, Wallas and Vargiu's writings it is possible to perceive abilities energized by magnetic field of corces that are both mental and emotive as central to creative functioning. Activity set in motion by imagination causes these forces to act and interact with each other and with intellectual abilities. This activity may be deliberate or ongoing without our full awareness; however, if a problem is presented for processing this activity, incubation is induced, often producing imagery that leads to illumination and problem solution.

(b) Imagination and Imagery

John Eccles (1958) speculates that much brain activity has to do with imagery or re-experiencing images and their language correlates. *Artistic creation* of a simple or lyrical kind results from the evocation by association of images that are beautiful, subtle, harmoniously blended and expressed in some language—verbal, musical or pictorial. Image making of a different order leads to illumination that gives a new understanding and insight, and relative to *science* it may be the formulation of a new hypothesis that transcends the older hypothesis.

Creative imagery provides the artist or poet with the central idea for a picture or poem (Richardson, 1969). For instance, Coleridge describes his experience of images prior to the composition of *Kubla Khan* and refers to them as "things" that rose before him. Brahms describes his creativity prior to musical composition as felt vibrations, that thrilled his being and exalted his state, that assumed the form of distinct mental images: at once God derived ideas flowed into him to be seen as distinct themes, clothed in the right forms, harmonies and orchestration (Abell, 1964).

In Science, Darwin's theory of evolution or Kekule's experience of imagery just prior to and contingent on illumination led to the clue for the structure of the carbon ring that became the foundation of organic chemistry (Koestler, 1964). Einstein tells us that images not words or

312

language served him as elements of thought. The principle of the rotating magnetic field appeared to Tesla as images that were as sharp, clear and solid as metal or stone: the illumination revolutionized electrical science (Ghiselin, 1952).

Imagination imagery may be said to be the province of Land's mutualistic stage and Gowan's creativity-psychedelic stages that relate to high levels of psychological functioning. It is at these stages that high level combination and connections are made by analogy and metaphor, and at which time the preconscious is tapped. Transformations occur when movement takes place from a lower level of order moves to a higher level of order via the process of destructuring.

ENCOURAGING THE GIFTED TO PRODUCE CREATIVE IMAGERY

What has systems, creative imagination (incubation—imagery—illumination) to do with facilitating the gifted to be more creative? We know that gifted children must not only be bright but also productive. Like most students in school the gifted are taught and encouraged to use left brain functions more often than right brain functions. In the past twenty years or so many have advocated the use of creative or divergent thinking and creative problem solving in the classrooms (e.g., Guilford, 1967; Meeker, Sexton and Richardson, 1970; Parnes, 1967; Renzulli, 1973; Taylor, 1978; Torrance and Myers, 1970; Williams, 1971), and these have taken a number of different forms. These and related techniques were discussed in a comprehensive paper by Torrance entitled "Can We Teach Children to Think Creatively" a few years ago. The reactions have been very favorable, and today if we were to visit schoolrooms around the country we will find at least some emphasis placed on encouraging children to be creative using one or another of the many techniques available. Recently, Renzulli's Enrichment Triad Model" (1978) has gained notice and is being used in some classrooms and a number of state or Federal funded projects on the gifted.

To all these valuable attempts at more challenging education and encouragement of creativity that would educate what Lee and Pulvino (1978) call "the forgotten half" must be added some of the thrusts that have been made on stimulating the creative imagination to produce imagery, a process that some of the foremost creative people in the arts and science describe as the percursor to illumination and discovery.

(a) Stimulating Imagination Imagery

In several papers (e.g., Khatena, 1977b; 1978bc) and a recent book (Khatena, 1978a) approaches at stimulating and facilitating the use of the creative imagination to produce creative imagery have been described, and these have been by way of a number of creative thinking strategies, namely, breaking away from the obvious and commonplace, restructuring, synthesis, and analogy. Details of these steps relative to using both verbal and figural experiences can be found in the *Creatively Gifted Child: Suggestions for Parents and Teachers* (Khatena, 1978a). These strategies can be taught to gifted children and varied experiences in their use can be provided. When the students have adequate preparation these approaches can be integrated with curriculum materials used in everyday classroom activities. Take for instance, analogy and its metaphorical thinking correlates can be used with daily classroom writing (in composition, story-play-verse writing) and speaking activities. After sensitizing gifted children with certain information and background to a subject follow this with some written work. Later screen one or two representative accounts for *factual* as distinct from metaphorical representation of the information.

313

This could be followed up by some work-up activities in the use of metaphorical language which then can find application in the factual account. A fine interplay between composition and analysis will help. Examples of composition where rich use of imagery and metaphor is evident can serve as strong stimuli, and if handled properly, as inspiration to creative writing. Spoken dialogue—conversation can likewise be handled with assistance of a tape recorder in a dynamic way to encourage the use of rich exciting imagery. At a later stage, when gifted children should become aware of this potentiality which when in use taps the preconscious, Harry Stack Sullivan's "not-me," the Aladdin Cave according to Gowan (1972), the richest source of imagery. Problem-solving that includes the use of incubation and not limited to a cognitive approach to solution finding can be very powerful. More often than nought problems are presented to students with demand for immediate solutions. This is not always to be recommended as frequently the most common answers are found. Arrange to provide problems or use problems that sometimes occur spontaneously in the classroom during say one session and regard this as preliminary and preparatory work. Ask for solutions if you like only to make students aware that these group of solutions are some possible ones. Do not effect closure. Tell them you would like them to mull over what they had done. Let this simmer in their minds for a while—maybe for a day or two (sometimes this can even be done within a single period once the students acquire the knack). There is need for fermentation and growth to take place beyond the conscious awareness of the individual with the expectation that after such a brain activity over a period of time illumination may take place. Have the student expect to think in images that can occur when the time is right at the point of solution and possible discovery. Coleridge seems to have allowed his exercise with metrical devices and reading of Purchases' Pilgrimage to incubate and in a relaxed state following the intake of opium, images appeared before him having an autonomy of their own and presenting themselves in a thematic connectedness that produced one of the most beautiful, and many would think, one of the most complete poems in English Literature.

(c) Autonomy of Imagery

Autonomy of imagery is related to creative metal functioning and should be encouraged. One way of doing this is by inducing a relaxed state for imagery to flow. Children can be guided to free themselves from external stimuli by shutting their eyes in a quiet atmosphere created for the purpose. They can then be encouraged to visualize in their mind's eye an event like going to visit a favorite aunt or uncle where at certain point the event is left open-ended and images can flow beyond direct control. This can be done with a scene that is familiar, a quarrel with a friend and the implications, leading on to building castles in the air type situations. This imaging should follow a brief period of the rest each time. Other relaxation exercises have been suggested by Lee and Pulvino (1978) for tapping the preconscious.

(f) Sense Modalities and Imagery

Children should be encouraged to use all their senses in their interaction with the world. Their greatest strengths lie with the use of the visual, auditory and tactile sense modalities singly or in combination. Some arrangement should be made for them to use their other senses in gaining command of the world while enhancing the use of three senses they seem able at applying. Give exercise in the use of the sense and encourage creative imaging. An exercise suggested by Lee and Pulvino relate to "cross sensory experience" where music is used. Listening to music with your ears (relaxed state). Then close eyes and hear music with all senses. Feel music as a touch on your skin, brushing gently over you; see the music—might be like heat waves, colors floating before you; and smell the music—like flower, perfume, familiar home smells.

These are only a few suggestions that may be tried with gifted children and adolescents. Some important advances in thought have taken place over the past few years on creative imagination imagery, and the linkage of this with general systems is of great significance. It is important that we keep alert to these advances as they offer valuable clues to us to educate productive and contributing gifted individuals. As John Gowan so insightfully and succinctly writes in my book for parents and teachers:

> . . . Suppose we were to cultivate and domesticate creatvity—to reward it in our homes and schools; to develop it to the fullest—we would see a renaissance the like of which would make Periclean Athens, the golden age of Rome, the *Renaissance* in Italy and all the rest seem sterile."

References

Abell, A. M. *Talks with great composers.* Garmisch-Partenkirchen, Germany: G. E. Schroeder—Verlag, 1964.

Debono, E. *The use of lateral thinking.* Toronto: Holt, 1971.

Eccles, J. C. The physiology of imagination (1958). In Readings from *Scientific American,* 1972, Pp. 31–40.

Ghiselin, B. (Ed.). *The creative process.* New York: New American Library, 1952.

Gowan, J. C. The development of the creative individual. Gifted Child Quarterly, 1971, 15(3), 156–174.

Gowan, J. C. *The development of the creative individual.* San Diego, Ca.: Robert R. Knapp, 1972.

Gowan, J. C. *The development of the psychedelic individual.* Buffalo, N.Y.: Creative Education Foundation, 1974.

Gowan, J. C. *Trance, art and creativity.* Buffalo, N.Y.: Creative Education Foundation, 1975.

Gowan, J. C. Creativity and gifted child movement. *Journal of Creative Behavior,* 1978, 12(1), 1–13.(a)

Gowan, J. C. The role of imagination in the development of the creative individual. *Humanitas,* 1978 24(2), 197–208. (b)

Gowan, J. C. Incubation, imagery and creativity. *Journal of Mental Imagery,* 1978, 2(2), 23–32.(c)

Gowan, J. C., and Dodd, S. C. General systems: A creative search for synthesis. *Journal of Creative Behavior,* 1977, 11(1), 47–52.

Gulford, J. P. *The nature of human intelligence.* New York: McGraw-Hill, 1967.

Jaynes, J. *The origin of consciousness in the breakdown of the bicameral mind.* Boston, Ma.: Houghton Mifflin, 1976.

Khatena, J. Advances in research on creative imagination imagery. *Gifted Child Quarterly,* 1977, 21(4), 433–439. (a)

Khatena, J. Creative imagination and what we can do to stimulate it. *Gifted Child Quarterly,* 1977, 21(1), 84–96. (b)

Khatena, J. *The creatively gifted child: Suggestions for parents and teachers.* New York: Vantage Press, 1978. (a)

Khatena, J. Creative imagination through imagery: Some recent research. *Humanitas,* 1978, 14(1), 227–242. (b)

Khatena, J. Frontiers of creative imagination imagery. *Journal of Mental Imagery,* 1978, 2(1), 33–46. (c)

Koestler, A. *The act of creation.* New York: Macmillan, 1964.

Land, G. T. L *Grow or die.* New York: Random House, 1972.

Land, G. T. L., and Kenneally, C. Creativity, reality, and general systems: A personal viewpoint, *Journal of Creative Behavior,* 1977, 11(1), 12–35.

Lee J. L., and Pulvino, C. J. *Educating the forgotten half: Structured activities for learning.* Dubuque, Ia.: Kendall/Hunt Publishing Company, 1978.

Meeker, M. N., Sexton, K., and Richardson, M. O. *SOI abilities workbooks*. Los Angeles, Ca.: Loyola-Marymount University, 1970.

Mirman, N. Education of the gifted in the 70's. *Gifted Child Quarterly,* 1971. 15(1), 217–224.

Olson, M. Right or left hemisphere processing in the gifted. *Gifted Child Quarterly,* 1977, 21(1), 116–121.

Ornstein, R. *The psychology of consciousness*. New York: Freeman, 1972.

Parnes, S. J. Creative behavior guidebook. New York: Charles Scribner's, 1967.

Renzulli, J. S. *New directions in creativity*. New York: Harper & Row, 1973.

Renzulli, J. S. Developing defensible programs for the gifted and talented. *Journal of Creative Behavior,* 1978, 12(1), 21–29.

Richardson, A. *Mental imagery*. New York: Springer, 1969.

Samples, R. W. Learning with the whole brain. *Human Behavior,* February, 1975, 17–23.

Sperry, R. W. Messages from the laboratory. *Engineering and Science,* January, 1974.

Taylor, C. W. How many types of giftedness can your program tolerate? *Journal of Creative Behavior,* 1978, 12(1), 39–51.

Tillyard, E. M. W. *Shakespeare's history plays*. London: Chatto & Windus, 1956.

Tillyard, E. M. W. *The Elizabethan world picture*. London: Chatto & Windus, 1958.

Torrance, E. P. Retooling education for creative talent: How goes it? *Gifted Child Quarterly, 1974,* 18(4), 233–238.

Torrance, E. P., and Myers, R. E. *Creative learning and teaching*. New York: Dodd Mead, 1970.

Vargiu, J. Creativity: The purposeful imagination. *Synthesis,* 1977, 3–4, 17–53.

Wallas, G. *The art of thought*. London: C. A. Watts, 1926.

Williams, F. E. *Total creativity program for elementary school teachers*. Englewood Cliffs, N. J.: Educational Technology Publications, 1971.

37. THE SOCIETY WHICH MAXIMIZES CREATIVITY

John Curtis Gowan
Meredith Olson

If we give any credence to the genetic theory of intelligence, it follows that individuals of high ability must be born in a fairly random fashion as regards time and place. Yet scholarly analysis (Arieti, 1976) supports casual observation that productive geniuses are clustered into "golden ages" of which Periclean Athens, the Renaissance, and the Federalist Fathers are but a few examples. Clearly there is a social and cultural influence operating between potential genius (defined in terms of high intelligence) and actualized genius (defined in terms of high creativity). From this very simple argument two immensely important conclusions follow:

1. since the number of actualized geniuses is but a fraction of potential geniuses, we are left with the clear possibility of increasing the former several fold;
2. since cultural influences do make the difference, a study of those influences, resulting in the ability and will to duplicate them in educational intervention would result in a super-Renaissance, created permanently by design and not intermittently by accident.

Having now glimpsed the importance of this issue, let us turn at once to a survey of what has been done about it. The conscientious reader will find perhaps the best introduction to the subject in chapters thirteen and fourteen of Arieti (1976) which are devoted to the effects of societal culture on creativity. Arieti starts with the tantalizing question of why productive geniuses are clustered into golden ages. He quotes the research of the first modern investigator, Kroeber (1944), as follows:

> More individuals born with the endowment of genius have been inhibited by the cultural situations into which they were born than have been developed by other cultural situations.

Kroeber set the stage for future researchers by cataloging the occurrence throughout history of geniuses in various disciplines such as science, mathematics, music, literature, etc. He did not advance an explanation of why the clustering occurred.

Gray (1958, 1961, 1966) continued Kroeber's work, compiling creativity levels for Western culture, and advancing an epicycle theory in explanation. This theory views history as composed of an economic, a social, and a political cycle. Each goes through four different stages at different rates: the formative, the developed, the florescent, and the degenerate. Clusters of cultural creativity occur when the florescent and developed stages of several cycles coincide. Then by an analysis of history, Gray showed that favorable economic, social, and political factors promote creativity.

An analysis of the work of these pioneers led Arieti (1976) to conclude that "the potentiality for genius is much more frequent than the occurrence" with implications similar to those stated at the beginning of the article. He called the society which promotes creativity the "creativogenic society." Arieti then discussed nine conditions for the creativogenic society. They are:

1. availability of cultural and physical means;
2. openness to cultural stimuli;

Reprinted from *Journal of Creative Behavior*, Vol. 13, No. 3, 1979.

3. stress on becoming and not just on being;
4. free, non-discrimatory access to cultural media for all;
5. decrease in oppression or exclusion;
6. exposure to different, contrasting cultural stimuli;
7. tolerance for diverging views;
8. interaction of significant persons;
9. promotion of rewards and incentives.

He stressed that while these were the necessary conditions, the sufficient condition was the creative person himself.

One of the earliest writers on the relationships between civilizations and creativity was the British historian, Arnold Toynbee, in his monumental *A Study of History* (1947). Briefly, Toynbee's thesis was that civilizations arose because of the innovative response of a creative minority to the challenge of the environment. This successful solution is *imitated* by the mass in what Toynbee calls *mimesis:*

> . . . in societies in process of civilization, mimesis is directed towards creative personalities who command a following because they are pioneers. In such a society "the cake of custom" is broken . . . and society is in dynamic motion along a course of change and growth.

But success begets other challenges whose nature shifts:

> Growth means that the growing personality or civilization tends to become its own environment, and its own challenger, and its own field of action. In other words, the criterion of growth is progress towards self-determination. . . .

In addition, those who have been the successful innovators of the past, tend to disqualify themselves for successful innovation in the future. Toynbee (1947) calls this the "mimesis of creativity," and says of it:

> . . . if it is true that the successful creator in one chapter finds his very success a severe handicap in endeavoring to resume the creative role in the next chapter, so that the chances are always against "the favorite" and in favor of the "the dark horse"—then it is plain that we have here run to earth a very potent cause of the breakdown of civilizations.

The mimesis has three parts: idolization of an ephemeral self, of an ephemeral institution, and of a ephemeral technique, any one of which is enough to transform the creative minority into a dominant minority which rules by oppression. Toynbee's model, therefore, is one where a breakdown and disintegration of civilization is to be expected, and the latter half of his opus is devoted to this decline and its symptoms.

In addition to this rather gloomy assessment of society, Toynbee (1947) is equally lugubrious with regard to the fate of the creative individual. He first defines such an individual as follows:

> The new specific character of these rare and superhuman souls that break the vicious circle of primitive human social life and resume the work of creation may be described as personality. It is through the inward development of personality that human beings are able to perform these creative acts in the outward field of action that cause the growth of . . . societies.

Toynbee (1947) then quotes Bergson who equates the creative genius with the mystic in saying:

The mystic's direction is the very direction of the *elan* of life. It is that *elan* itself, communicated
. . . to privileged human beings whose desire it is thereafter to set the imprint of it upon the
whole of mankind.

But, there are grave difficulties in the way. As Toynbee continues:

The social situation presents a dilemma. If the creative genius fails to bring . about in his milieu
the mutation which he has achieved for himself, his creativeness will be fatal to him. . . . On
the other hand if our genius does succeed . . . he thereby makes life intolerable for men and
women of common clay unless they can succeed in adapting . . . to the new social milieu
imposed on them. . . .

The mimesis of the common man can hence never be more than a partial ritual. As Toynbee sadly
concludes:

All acts of social creation are the work either of individual creators, or at most, creative
minorities; at each successive advance, the great majority of the members of society are left
behind. . . . The superior personalities, geniuses, mystics, or superman—call them what you
will—are never more than a leaven in the lump of ordinary humanity.

Writing from the point of view of Psychosynthesis, Varigu (1977) presents a view of creativity as an energy field, which uses the behavior of iron filings in a magnetic field as a homologue.
As the magnetic field is increased, the filings, heretofore arranged randomly will "become magnetized by induction . . . that is they generate their own field." As soon as the field has reached
sufficient strength to overcome friction, the transformation will take place with extreme rapidity.
The instantaneous and holistic qualities of creative illumination in the individual are due to a
similar "avalanche effect" according to Varigu. While he does not apply the theory to society as
a whole, it is easy to see that the same considerations would be effective. Unfortunately, while
such a theory explains the effect, it does not offer specific rationales on input which would hasten
or augment it.

Another writer with similar ideas on creativity is Land (1972). His concepts of accretive,
replicative, and mutualistic growth, especially when compared with those of the senior writer,
(Gowan and Dodd, 1977), indicate a cyclic appearance and return of creativity during the mutualistic phase. Again, however, the theory does not offer specifics in regard to the social and
personal inputs required to continue the cycle, although some broad implications are suggested.

While neither completely deterministic nor pessimistic, the theories connecting creativity
and culture in this introductory section do not provide much of a logical rationale for hope or
improvement in the future. The forces which control the efflorescence of creativity in civilization
appear to be cyclic or intermittent, or otherwise beyond the control of mankind. For a more
optimistic view of the situation, which suggests that positive action may be more effective and
permanent, we turn to important recent research of D. K. Simonton.

In his Harvard doctoral dissertation, Simonton (1974) posed the crucial question of why
creative geniuses appear in some periods of history but not in others.[1] His results suggested that
various cultural events such as education, role-model availability, wars, civil disturbances, and
political instability had a critical impact on the development of creative potential in the young
nonartistic genius during his formative period. A factor analysis of a sample of over 5000 creative
individuals ranging for 700 B.C. to 1900 A.D. (as developed by Kroeber, 1944) was conducted
after dividing the subjects into fifteen categories: physical science, biological science, miscellaneous

[1]For the ideas in this section consult Simonton, 1975, 1976 (a,b,c,d), and 1978.

science, philosophy, religion, miscellaneous philosophy, poetic literature, prose literature, miscellaneous literature, painting, sculpture, architecture, miscellaneous art, musical composition, and miscellaneous music. While there were five factors found, two of them appeared most important:

a) a "discursive communication" factor (Langer, 1942), consisting of science, philosophy, poetry, and prose—a verbal factor;
b) a "presentational form" factor (Langer, 1942) consisting mainly of painting, sculpture, and architecture—a nonverbal factor.

Simonton found that the frequency in society of first factor creatives was much affected by the presence of untoward cultural events such as lack of education and role-model availability, wars, etc., during their adolescence, whereas the second factor group did not. This finding would agree with the hypothesis that right-hemisphere (nonverbal) creativity is easier to express than verbal creativity which must be mediated through the left hemisphere after being developed in the right. A stable environment is evidently necessary here.

For further insights, we quote Simonton (1978) directly:

In a series of recent investigations I have attempted to discern the consequences of this distinction. One of the most significant findings is that developmental period influences are far more important than productive period influences. In other words, the development of creative potential is often critically affected by external events, whereas creative productivity is virtually immune from such influences.

Nonetheless, when we survey the relationship between external events and creative development, a diversified list of influences has been found. The following seven are probably the most important:

1. *Formal education.* In a multivariate analysis of the 301 eminent geniuses studied by Cox (1926), I found that achieved eminence is partly a function of the amount of formal education (Simonton, 1976a). Significantly, the precise form of this function depends on whether eminence was achieved as a creator (scientist, philosopher, writer, artist, or musician) or as a leader (soldier, statesman, revolutionary, or religious leader). For creators, eminence is a curvilinear inverted—U function of formal education. Thus formal education tends to increase creativity up to a certain point, after which it has a negative effect. Clearly some formal education greatly aids the development of creative potential, but excessive amounts may inhibit creative development by enforcing an overcommitment to traditional perspectives. This finding fits nicely with some previous research on creative development in contemporary children (e.g., Torrance, 1962). Curiously, for leadership the functional relation between eminence and formal education is strictly negative: The ultimate achievement of politicians, soldiers, and religious leaders is inhibited by the kind of training offered by colleges and universities.

2. *Role-model availability.* Recent studies have shown that the number of eminent creators in one generation is largely a function of the number of eminent creators in the previous generation (Simonton, 1974, 1975). In other words, the more creative individuals available for emulation when a genius is in his or her developmental period, the greater the increase in creative potential. Subsequent research has indicated that the availability of role models increases creativity largely through a single intervening variable, namely, creative precociousness. The greater the number of adult creators around for possible imitation, the sooner the youthful genius begins producing

320

creative works. This creative precociousness then leads to enhanced creative productivity and creative longevity, which in turn raise the eventual level of achieved eminence.

3. *Zeitgeist*. In one study I attempted to determine the relationship between the fame of a given thinker and the prevailing zeitgeist (Simonton, 1976e). Is it the case that the major minds in the history of ideas tend to be ahead of their time? Or is it the case that the major figures in intellectual history tend to be highly analysis of 2,012 famous thinkers in Western history revealed a surprising result: The answer to both of these questions is "no"! Rather than epitomize the prevailing beliefs and mores of their generation, and rather than be precursors of the subsequent generation's zeitgeist, the most eminent philosophers tend to be *behind* their times. Unlike the lesser thinker, the major thinker seems to be most influenced by the zeitgeist which dominated the intellectual scene during his or her developmental period. What seems to be happening is that the most famous thinkers are synthesizers who take the accomplishments of the preceding generation and consolidate them into a single, unified philosophical system.

4. *Political fragmentation*. In a pioneer cross-historical investigation, Naroll et al. (1971) tried to discover what political and economic circumstances are most favorable to creativity in four civilizations. The one variable found to have a consistent effect was political fragmentation, or the number of independent states into which a civilization is divided in any given century. Unfortunately, Naroll et al. used rather large time-wise units, and therefore, they could not determine whether political fragmentation acts on creative productivity or on creative development. Nonetheless, I have argued that political fragmentation indicates a large amount of cultural diversity and that cultural diversity tends to nurture the development of creativity (Simonton, 1974, 1975). Such cultural diversity tends to encourage the capacity for divergent thinking, remote association, breadth of perspective, and related cognitive attributes required for a fully-developed creative potential.

5. *War*. The ideology of the mature thinker is also influenced by the occurrence of warfare during the stage of creative development. In fact, the impact of war on the youthful genius is virtually the opposite from that of political fragmentation. Thinkers whose early years were characterized by constant warfare tend to be *less* likely to advocate empiricism, skepticism, materialism, temporalism, nominalism, singularism, and the ethics of happiness (Simonton, 1976f). Thus while political fragmentation tends to encourage the development of a mind open to experience, change, individualism, and material welfare, war tends to discourage such intellectual qualities.

6. *Civil disturbances*. Yet a third political variable tends to affect the ideology of the adult creator by influencing the course of creative development. Thinkers whose youth was surrounded by popular revolts, rebellions, and revolutions tend to adopt highly polarized philosophical positions as adults (Simonton, 1976f). Even though civil disturbances thus polarize the forthcoming generation in quite contrary directions, the intriguing fact remains that such political events have a truly potent effect on creative development. The exposure to political conflict seems to instill the need to take extreme stances on philosophical issues as well. Given this finding, it is perhaps not surprising that civil disorder also encourages general creative development, as one empirical study has shown (Simonton, 1975c). That is, eminent creators in Western history tend to be most likely

to grow up in times of revolts, rebellions, and revolutions, especially those directed against large empire states. Such disturbances seem to heighten cultural diversity in a given civilization (Simonton, 1975; Simonton, 1976c).

7. *Political instability*. So far we have not mentioned any political events which might hinder the development of creative potential in the youthful genius. But imagine, if you will, a political milieu where violent conflict among the ruling elite is the natural order of things, where a coup d'etat by some military figure is commonplace, where political assassinations are the norm, or where strife among rival claimants to the throne is chronic. Such political instability might well prove detrimental to the development of creative potential. And two recent studies have actually shown that political instability, while having no appreciable impact on creative productivity, does damage the prospects for creativity in the forthcoming generation.

It must be stressed that research on the sociocultural context of creative development is a relatively recent enterprise. So future research may add many more influences, including economic and demographic factors. Still, the evidence gathered to date allows us to conclude that sociocultural conditions play a significant part in the development of creative potential in the youthful genius. The following three sociopsychological processes are especially central to creative development:

1. The potential genius must have access to numerous role models very early in life. Without such models, the genius may have a lower probability of being precocious, and such precociousness is apparently essential to creative productivity and longevity in adulthood.
2. Exposure to cultural diversity also seems to nourish the precocious youth. Thus, on the one hand, political fragmentation and civil disturbances tend to increase creative potential by injecting an awareness of diverse perspectives, whereas excessive formal education can harm creative potential by placing too much emphasis on a restricted range of solutions to creative problems.
3. The young genius adapts to the political environment by generating a set of philosophical beliefs. Should the genius grow up to become a thinker, these intellectual adaptations will influence his or her philosophical leanings. Even more importantly, certain political events may produce an ideological disposition which proves antithetical to adulthood creativity. This latter possibility may be illustrated by the manner in which political instability inhibits creative development by producing a fatalistic *Weltanschauung* in the would-be genius.

To summarize, the Golden Ages of history may have given the young genius the necessary role models, the cultural diversity, and the philosophical commitment essential to the development of creative potential. This potential was then merely actualized in adulthood without much hinderance or help from external events.

Turning now from a sociological to a psychological model, the theories of the second author, Olson, will be presented. Quite briefly, these views argue the equivalence of three complementary dichotomous pairs: right vs. left cerebral hemisphere stimulation, empiricism (visual observation) vs. analysis (logical thought), and creativity growth vs. creativity decline in a civilization.

Beneath the rise of every civilization it is possible to detect a wave of empirical thought. In each case, man may be seen as developing the ability to focus his concentration on events in the natural world around him and to verbalize a logical analysis of these events. Empiricism and analysis: these are the hallmarks of civilization on the rise.

Our task in examining the creative development of mankind is to delineate educational attitudes which occur in repeating long-range patterns, and are therefore hard to detect. In the last decade a proliferation of factual detail concerning right and left hemispheric functions now enables us to piece together a new conceptualization controlling the fate of civilizations. We will argue that all civilizations rise on a crest of empirical zeal balanced by analysis commensurate with their philosophical sophistication. It appears that when empiricism falls from public concern civilizations deteriorate. Empiricism and analysis encoded in right and left hemispheric function organize our understanding of civilization.

Tribal man observed nature well enough to achieve domestication of plants and animals. Although much of his analysis of these events revolved around magical rituals, Booz and Malanofski (Boaz, 1938) suggest that this should not imply a lack of logic. Rather this demonstrates an attempt to impose one's will on nature. They suggest that magic is an important step in increasing the range of human consciousness and confidence, and focuses attention on cause and effect, empiricism, and analysis.

The great Egyptian civilization must have been infused with careful observation of reality to have achieved the engineering sophistication exhibited by obelisks and pyramids. The Ebers and Smith papyrus (Sarton, 1959) indicates close-attention to empirical observation of physiology and the course of disease. Sarton's extensive documentation demonstrates the thesis that Egyptian civilization flourished during a time of empirical observation coupled with discourse, analysis, and recording of these ideas.

The Ionian Greeks represent the beginning of another major civilization. Homer and Hesiod demonstrated considerable knowledge of navigation which may have come in part from the oral tradition of the Phoenicians. They understood solstices, equinoxes, and the monthly lunar period. Schools of thought grew up on the Ionian coast exemplifying the first major attempt to use reason as a tool to explain nature. Obviously much empirical data was recognized as the basis for consideration of ideas, Empedocles of Agrigentum (Sarton, 1959) set out to demonstrate the existence of air in the fifth century B.C. by placing a bottle upside down in water and reflecting on why the water did not run into it. Although Alemeon of Croton postulated the interaction of the soul with the body, he was enough of an empiricist to be the first Greek to perform dissections. Hippocrates argued against philosophical speculation and advocated careful observation of symptoms in order better to predict the outcome of disease. In general, however, thinkers were becoming more concerned with analysis than with observation.

Anaxagoras was one of the later Ionian philosophers who exemplified the increasing concern with the validity of considering the "ultimate truth." Mainland Greece was attracted to early Ionian thought but shifted the emphasis from nature to man. With this shift came the beginning of the end of Greek civilization.

Socrates felt it was possible to discover truth by debate. He helped give birth to the analysis of logic and in doing so turned the thoughts of his culture from empiricism to metaphysical constructs which effectively placed a lid on empirical investigation. Plato and Aristotle carried on empirical and logical activities but the trend of developing thought was increasingly away from belief in observation and toward the unknowable metaphysical essence of things (Sarton, 1959). The intellectual development that occurred during the Greek civilization is an agreement with the assertion that civilizations rise at a time when the educational environment stimulates both empiricism and analysis.

Islam and the Saracenic civilization also rose to its height at the time when it was making its greatest achievements in sciences such as astronomy, mathematics, physics, and chemistry. Although they admired Aristotle, (Thompson, 1937) they were not bound by his metaphysics. They developed algebra, trigonometry, optics, and their attempts to transmute gold led to discoveries of borax, carbonate of soda, alum, bichloride of mercury, nitrate of silver, saltpeter, nitric acid, and sulfuric acid. A medical school and a whole series of astronomical works were established at Jundishapur (Sarton, 1959) including giant sundials and triangles to view the stars and record their directions with great accuracy.

A great effort was directed at empirical verification and correction of Greek translations. Avicenna discovered the contageous nature of tuberculosis and carefully described other diseases beyond the scope of Greek translations. The idea that disease could spread through contamination of water was the result of careful observation. When the translations were completed, empiricism declined. A growing belief in the predestination of all things turned intellectual energy to armchair speculation and social concerns, thus speeding the demise of this civilization as a world power.

The period labeled as the Dark Ages of Western society may be characterized by a lack of interest in cognitive processing and a focus on small scale interpersonal socialization. The first inkling of renewed empirical activity in Europe came not from educational institutions but from stone masons who became intoxicated with the power of observation. Each structure was grander than the last until the medieval cathedral arose (Bronowski, 1973).

Intellectualism grew from technological empiricism as Ferguson (1977) has pointed out. As trade picked up in Europe, men began to play with little mechanical toys and to look at the world again. Maps were drawn in Flemish schools by Artclius and Mercator (Singer, 1959), while Alexander of Neccam and Petrus Peregrinis discussed the attributes of the lodestone (Singer, et al. 1957). Singer also cites William Gilbert as conducting experiments in chemistry and electricity. He discusses that a revival of interest in astronomy by Nicholas of Cusa, George Purbach, Regiomontanius, and Copernicus directed thoughts to observations as a source of knowledge. Tycho Brahe epitomized this empirical zeal by spending his life collecting astronomical data accurate to within less than half a minute of arc (Arons, 1965).

Empirical activity thus became valued again as the context against which to verbalize. Johannes Kepler exemplifies this great awakening. A convinced Copernican in his belief in simple, uniform, circular motion, Kepler, after years of work, threw out his preconvictions when he found that his data showed definite elliptical planetary paths (Arons, 1965). Kepler ushered in modern science and educational theory when he bowed to the supreme arbiter of physical theory—not logic, rhetoric, or the metaphysical good—but the stark evidence of precise and quantitative empirical observation.

Empiricism and analysis are the salient features of intellectualization in our Western culture. Technological advances and the identifiable uniqueness of Western culture can be traced to this counterpoint. There appears to be strong correlation between our emphasis on empiricism and the development of Western society. Western societal advance begins simultaneously with empirical awakening and its development correlates with greater numbers participating in empirical activities and subsequent analysis. Low or slow spots in Western societal development correlate with slow times of empirical activity. When empirical cathedral building was ended by a return to philosophical speculation of the metaphysical good, the budding Western civilization declined.

Social ferment and religious zeal do not show this correlation: if anything they have a slight negative relationship. What is the future graphical profile of Western society? We have every reason to believe that it will parallel the curve of empirical activity found in Western culture.

This historical analysis has profound implications both for philosophy and for educational theory. Can the "truth preserving" desires of the classical philosophers be expected to provide the dominant organizer for advancing society? Empiricism establishes concepts that are neither absolutely true nor final. Empiricism, by its very nature, continually subjects its concepts to tests, and corrects and embellishes them according to new and more precise experience. Even the absolute existence of self may be called into question by the Piagetian concept of developing logical awareness and by the verbal and nonverbal logical activities present in the human mind revealed by recent split brain surgery. The world speaks to us through our senses. It is only after this has occurred that analysis is possible.

The implications of this analysis are crucial for the development of educational theory and pedagogical technique. We are interested in the development of logical abilities in society. Piagetian logical tasks (Fogelman, 1970) ask students to look at objects and make verbal analysis of them: empiricism and analysis. Neurological analysis affirms the idea that observation of objects is controlled by the left brain. Recent work (Olson, 1977) indicates that a surprising variability exists in the predicted hemispheric use. It would appear that only those individuals who have achieved formal logical abilities process printed school work as predicted by neurology. There appears to be a strong correlation between scientific insight and hemispheric processing (Olson, 1977). We suggest that the opportunity for empiricism coupled with logical analysis should play a more important role in the educational philosophy of our country. The very existence of schools implies that cognitive processing is learnable. It is time for our pedagogy to address those critical experiences which must take place in the life of a child in order to preserve the growth and development of society.

Most civilizations of the past have had rather short histories of dominance—a few centuries at most. Thus a study of history indicates that no one should be too surprised if our own civilization fades soon. Yet our point of view leads us to believe that there is something special and worth saving in our culture—something truly unique: it has demonstrated the ability to provide a far greater number of individuals with the desire, capacity, and freedom for inquiry and analysis than any other. While at first glance the goal of a democratic society may appear to be the education of an enlightened electorate, in actuality a democracy is only as functional as is each individual member of that society. Self-actualized innovative individuals with full reasoning capacities must form the creative minority of such a constituency. If indeed this presence is the key to greatness, then our attention should turn to educational experiences which conserve that trend to empiricism, experimentation, and creative thought.

We must recognize that social relevancy and human rights are not goals that can be taught, except in superficial terms. Once we all feel that it would be lovely if everyone knew how to think inspiring thoughts, we are stopped. All conflicting conceptions of curricula must, in the last analysis, come to terms with the neurological process of information processing unique to the human mind. Bilateral processing appears to be a key to all curricular conceptualizations. It is the long wave undergirding the shorter social concerns. Without recognition of the long wave our view is analogous to a choppy sea that tosses boats to and fro without placing any on the shore. When the long waves are detected they may be ridden to place the human race squarely on the shore of human development no matter how much surface tossing has occurred.

Admittedly this paper has raised more questions than it has answered, but if the well-being of civilizations depends on the maximization of creative persons within it and if that frequency can be increased by a better balance of empirical observation and rational thought, and if this stable symbiosis can in turn be achieved by more early right hemisphere logical stimulation which produces a coordinated right/left hemisphere operation in the brain, then it is possible to safeguard the continuance of a permanent Renaissance by this educational technique of increasing the percent of creative adults in the culture. Certainly we can strengthen right-hemisphere processes by stimulating them more in the classroom and laboratory.

Besides knowing the psychological and educational processes noted above which must be part of the education of the individual, we have also learned of the social processes which must be simultaneously at work in the culture. We have seen the need for role models, cultural diversity, political fragmentation, and philosophical commitment in the milieu of the developing genius. The combination and continuance of these conditions is well within the control of a modern pluralistic culture: thus we now possess both the knowledge and capability to produce a permanent super-Renaissance.

When we look at History from the point of view of the theories and research noted herein, several issues become obvious:

"Golden ages" of history appear to be produced by an unusual clustering of creative geniuses.

The forces which produce this clustering appear to act by accident, and without conscious societal manipulation.

As this article makes clear, we are beginning to understand the dynamics of these forces, which is the first step in their control and conscious production.

As the implications of these dynamics for society and education become clearer and more specific, it is logical to expect that some society will gain enough control of the situation, to maximize consciously a continuing clustering of creative geniuses which will produce a permanent and much enhanced Renaissance.

The minute one society sets out to accomplish this goal, all other societies must do so or else become obsolete.

Hence, the immediate furtherance of these researches, implications, and goals is imperative for any society which aspires to survive, and particularly so for a free society. The society we save, thereby, will be our own.

References

Arieti, S. *Creativity: the magic synthesis*. NYC: Basic Books, 1976.

Arons, A. B. *Development of concepts of physics*. Boston: Addison-Wesley, 1965.

Beals, R. L. and Hoijer, H. *An introduction to anthropology*. NYC: Macmillan, 1953.

Boaz, F. *The mind of primitive man*. NYC: Macmillan, 1938.

Bronowski, J. *The ascent of man*. Boston/Toronto: Little, Brown, 1973.

Burns, E. M. and Ralph, P. L. *World civilization*. NYC: Norton, 19 .

Cox, C. *The early mental traits of 300 geniuses*. Stanford, CA: Stanford University Press, 1926.

Fegelman, K. R. *Piagetian tasks for the primary school*. Windsor, England: The NEFR Publishing Co., 1970.

Ferguson, E. S. The mind's eye: nonverbal thought in technology. *Science,* 1977, *August 26, 197: 827–36*

Gowan, J. C. and Dodd, S. General systems: a creative search for synthesis. *Journal of Creative Behavior,* 1977, *11 (1),* 47–52.

Gray, C. E. A measurement of creativity in western civilization. *American Antropologist,* 1966, *68,* 1384–1417; 1961, *63,* 1014–37; 1958, *63,* 1014–37.

Khatena, J. Advances in research in creative imagination imagery. *Gifted Child Quarterly,* 1977, *21 (4),* 437.

Krober, A. *Configurations of cultural growth.* Berkeley: University of California Press, 1944.

Land, G. L. *Grow or die.* NYC: Random House, 1972.

Langer, S. *Philosophy in a new key.* NYC: Scribners, 1942.

Naroll, R., Creativity: a cross-historical pilot survey. *Journal of Cross-Cultural Psychology,* 1971, *2,* 181–188.

Olson, M. Right or left hemisphere processing in the gifted. *Gifted Child Quarterly,* 1977, *21(1),* 116–121.

Piaget, J. *The construction of reality in the child.* NYC: Balantine Books, 1954.

Sarton, G. *A history of science.* Cambridge: Harvard University Press, 1959.

Singer, C. *A short history of scientific ideas.* NYC/London: Oxford University Press, 1959.

Singer, H., Hall, and Williams, (eds.). *A history of technology.* Vol. III. NYC/London: Oxford University Press, 1957.

Simonton, D. K. The eminent genius in history: the critical role of creative development. *Gifted Child Quarterly,* 1978, *22,* 187–195.

Simonton, D. K. Biographical determinants of achieved eminence: a multivariate approach to the Cox data. *Journal of Personality and Social Psychology,* 1976, *33,* 218–226. (a)

Simonton, D. K. The casual relation between war and scientific discovery: an exploratory cross-national analysis. *Journal of Cross-Cultural Psychology,* 1976, *7,* 133–144. (b)

Simonton, D. K. Ideological diversity and creativity: a re-evaluation of a hypothesis. *Social Behavior and Personality,* 1976, *4,* 203–207. (c)

Simonton, D. K. Interdisciplinary and military determinants of scientific productivity: a cross-lagged correlation analysis. *Journal of Vocational Behavior,* 1976, *9,* 53–62. (d)

Simonton, D. K. Philosophical eminence, beliefs, and zeitgeist: an individual-generational analysis. *Journal of Personality and Social Psychology,* 1976, *34* 630–640. (e)

Simonton, D. K. The socio-political context of philosophical beliefs. *Social Forces,* 1976, *54,* 513–523. (f)

Simonton, D. K. Sociocultural context of individual creativity: a transhistorical time-series analysis. *Journal of Personality and Social Psychology,* 1975, *32,* 1119–1133.

Simonton, D. K. The social psychology of creativity: an archival data analysis. Unpublished doctoral dissertation, Harvard University, 1974.

Thompson, J. W. and Johnson, E. *An introduction to medieval Europe.* NYC: Norton, 1937.

Torrance, E. P. *Guiding creative talent.* Englewood Cliffs, NY: Prentice-Hall, 1962.

Toynbee, A. *A study of history.* London: Oxford University Press, 1947.

Varigu, J. Creativity. *Synthesis,* 1977, *3 (4),* 17–55.